UNIFYING
INDIVIDUAL AND
FAMILY THERAPIES

DAVID M. ALLEN

UNIFYING
INDIVIDUAL AND
FAMILY THERAPIES

Jossey-Bass Publishers

San Francisco • London • 1988

UNIFYING INDIVIDUAL AND FAMILY THERAPIES
by David M. Allen

Copyright © 1988 by: Jossey-Bass Inc., Publishers
350 Sansome Street
San Francisco, California 94104
&
Jossey-Bass Limited
28 Banner Street
London EC1Y 8QE

Library of Congress Cataloging-in-Publication Data

Allen, David M., date.
   Unifying individual and family therapies / David M. Allen. — 1st
ed.
   p. cm. — (The Jossey-Bass social and behavioral science
series)
   Bibliography: p.
   Includes index.
   ISBN 1-55542-078-8 (alk. paper)
   1. Psychotherapy. 2. Family psychotherapy. 3. Individuation.
4. Self. I. Title. II. Series.
   [DNLM: 1. Family. 2. Family Therapy. 3. Individuation.
4. Psychotherapy. WM 420 A4247u]
RC480.5.A45 1988
616.89′14—dc19
DNLM/DLC
for Library of Congress   87-46328
                                                              CIP

Manufactured in the United States of America

The paper in this book meets the guidelines for
permanence and durability of the Committee on
Production Guidelines for Book Longevity of the
Council on Library Resources.

JACKET DESIGN BY WILLI BAUM

FIRST EDITION

Code 8750

THE JOSSEY-BASS

SOCIAL AND BEHAVIORAL SCIENCE SERIES

CONTENTS

Preface   xi

The Author   xvii

**Part One: Linking Individuals, Families,
and Cultural Systems**

1. Relationship Between Self and System   1

2. Emergence of the Self from the System   28

3. Sacrifice of the Self   67

4. Dysfunctional Interactions in Families   110

5. Personality Disorders in a Systems Context   177

Part Two: A Unified Approach to Psychotherapy

6. Systemic Change Through Individual Therapy   215

7. Involving the Patient   242

8. Framing the Problem   256

9.   Coaching and Role Playing   298

10. Special Problems and Termination   331

     Conclusion: The Duality of Self and System   353

     References   357

     Index   361

PREFACE

The field of psychotherapy is being rocked by a major theoretical schism—a schism even more serious than the ongoing
rifts among the various psychodynamic schools and between the
psychodynamic and behavioral schools. Individually oriented
psychological theories and therapies are being attacked by therapists who have backgrounds in family therapy and systems theory. These therapists, such as Jay Haley, Murray Bowen, and
Salvador Minuchin, believe that human behavior cannot be
understood by observing individuals in isolation. They conceptualize individual behavior as a small part of a larger whole—the
family system, a multibodied organism that is far greater than
the sum of its constituents. The family system is thought to be
ruled by mechanisms designed to maintain smooth functioning.
Dysfunctional homeostatic mechanisms and other systemic family processes are thought to be responsible for dysfunctional behavior exhibited by any member of the system. Family members
are seen as being controlled by these forces through cybernetic
feedback loops; individual behavior is thought to be almost entirely a reaction to the needs of the larger group.

On the other side of this theoretical schism are the individually oriented theorists and therapists, who continue to insist that the individual is not a powerless pawn of a larger group,
but has a unique self with complex individual motivation and an
independent psychic apparatus. The various individually oriented
schools disagree about the nature of the self and how it develops, but they agree that human beings are entities unto them-

selves. Behavior that appears to be self-destructive or dysfunctional is usually attributed to some sort of impairment or defect in the individual's self or psychic apparatus, or to a physiological abnormality. Psychodynamic theorists consider the views of systems therapists to underestimate the uniqueness and independence of the individual.

On the infrequent occasions when the leaders of both schools get together to exchange views—such as in December 1985 during the Evolution of Psychotherapy Conference in Phoenix, Arizona—they often seem to address completely different subjects. Nonetheless, they share the same object of interest—human behavior and impaired functioning. The community of mental health providers has an intense need to reconcile these two widely disparate points of view, so that individual psychotherapists can become more effective in inducing patients to change their behavior in a timely fashion. Although several recently published books have attempted this reconciliation, most new books seem to merely attach concepts from individually oriented therapy to family therapy or vice versa. One exception to this is the work of Murray Bowen (1978), which provides an integrated conceptual model.

Unifying Individual and Family Therapies is an effort to expand on Bowen's model in order to provide a true synthesis, a unified view of self and system, which can be employed in a highly utilitarian fashion to help people change. This volume includes a practical and detailed explanation of a method of psychotherapy that is based on this model. The method I describe is designed primarily for, and is most effective with, young to early middle-aged adults who are not psychotic but who have a history of self-destructive behavior, family discord, or chronic affective symptomatology. As I explain in Chapter Six, a different approach becomes necessary when a child or adolescent is the identified patient within the family.

In this volume, I advocate that the individual self, the family system, and the larger cultural system are all part of a duality: the self evolves from the system, separating and individuating from it, in a way that parallels the proliferation and differentiation of species described by evolutionary biologists.

Individuals are gradually released from their enmeshment in the family system as they develop individually and as the larger cultural system evolves over history. The concept of separation/individuation—which is central to many theories of individual development—is expanded in this volume to encompass the notion of this separation of the self from the family system over time. Problems associated with the evolution of individuality are seen as the cause of self-destructive behavior.

I have written *Unifying Individual and Family Therapies* primarily for professional mental health providers: psychiatrists, psychologists, social workers, family and marriage counselors, and other psychotherapists. I hope to provide readers with a fresh perspective on their patients, one that will be useful in solving the vexing clinical problem of helping patients to stop self-destructive behavior. Although this book assumes some degree of familiarity with ideas from a wide variety of schools of psychological thought, students in the mental health field may also find it helpful.

Overview of the Contents

In Part One of this volume, I examine the nature of the self/system duality, its evolution over time, and the causes of various forms of self-destructive behavior. In Chapter One, I begin by rejecting the notion that self-destructive behavior in neurologically intact individuals stems from a defect in the individual. I show how this idea is not only present in individually oriented psychotherapies but in family systems therapies as well. Then, I go on to discuss the usefulness of an intrapsychic conflict model, which involves a conflict not between the parts of a divided self, but between the needs of a holistic self and the needs of a larger human collective. The remainder of Chapter One is dedicated to the development of ideas concerning the nature of the interface between the self and those larger systems.

Chapter Two takes a closer look at the separation and individuation of the self from the family system or human collective, and I show how this process has changed throughout history as human culture has evolved. I demonstrate how the conflicting predispositions of biological systems toward species survival and species evolution are expressed by both the family system and the individual. At the systems level, the development of homeostatic mechanisms ensures the continuation of the family and, therefore, the species through time. At the individual level, the organism values the smooth operation of the family more than his or her idiosyncratic concerns. I also explore what happens when people attempt to allow their own individual needs to take precedence over systemic needs.

In Chapter Three, I examine the various mechanisms individuals develop to sacrifice their own natural predispositions when the good of the family collective seems to demand it. I show how this sacrifice is destructive not only to the individual but also, eventually, to the family system. I investigate the concept of the persona or false self in the context of the family system. Then I go on to examine traditional and nontraditional ways in which psychotherapists can unmask the individual's true self.

Chapter Four details the nature and causes of disturbances in the homeostasis of a family system that induce self-destructive behavior. I demonstrate how systems attempt to adapt to evolutionary changes in the ambient culture and how the failure to adapt results in the phenomenon called *cultural lag*. I propose a model that shows how the development of a maladaptive personality trait can appear to restore family homeostasis in such a situation and why the appearance of a whole cluster of maladaptive traits may sometimes become necessary. I show how siblings and spouses interrelate when such traits occur. Finally, I provide two detailed case examples of maladaptive family role functioning.

Using the model constructed in Chapter Four, I explain several well-known personality disorders in Chapter Five. I examine the cultural and family systems contexts of four dysfunctional types: the hysteric, the borderline, the narcissist, and the "defective."

Part Two of this book addresses a method of psychotherapy based on the perspective presented in Part One. In Chapter Six, I demonstrate that individual psychotherapy can be the preferred treatment for adults whose problems involve their entire family and I explain how the therapist can encourage individuals to accurately describe the inner workings of their family system. The goals of therapy are to help individuals give up destructive behavior patterns *and* help the entire family solve evolutionary problems. I explain a perspective on transference that is useful for achieving this aim.

In Chapter Seven, I present an overview of an eight-stage method for working with individuals in psychotherapy and detail the first stage: involving the patient in therapy.

Chapter Eight describes stages two through five: eliciting the patient's problem, establishing the patient's altruistic motivation, showing how the patient's behavior backfires, and offering an alternate solution to the family's problem. Several case examples are presented for each stage of therapy.

Chapter Nine is devoted to stages six and seven: exploring the difficulties clients can face in implementing the alternate solution and teaching them through role playing how to overcome these difficulties. The alternate solution involves sending clients back to their families of origin to effectively metacommunicate about the family problems, even when the family collective does everything in its power to stop them. The therapist teaches clients how to be empathetic toward family members who provoke their anger, how to reduce their emotional reactivity, and how to respect the potency and integrity of all of their family members.

In Chapter Ten, I examine some miscellaneous difficulties and resistances to the alternate solution—such as triangulation, existential resistances, power struggles with the therapist, and the influence of deceased family members—and describe ways to deal with them. I also look at the final stage of therapy: termination.

Acknowledgments

I am indebted to Michael Braver, a colleague and friend, who introduced me to family systems thinking and inspired many of the ideas expressed in this volume. I have appreciated the assistance of Rose Kreitzberg, who helped me to write with clarity and provided reactions from someone outside the field of psychotherapy. Finally, I would like to acknowledge an intellectual debt to all those authors who have attempted to piece together the puzzle of self-destructive behavior, in particular Murray Bowen.

Burbank, California   David M. Allen
January 1988

THE AUTHOR

David M. Allen is a board-certified psychiatrist in private practice in Burbank, California, and an associate clinical professor of psychiatry at the Loma Linda University School of Medicine. He received his B.A. degree (1970) from the University of California, Los Angeles, in bacteriology, his M.D. degree (1974) at the University of California, San Francisco, and his psychiatric training (completed in 1977) at the Los Angeles County-University of Southern California Medical Center.

UNIFYING
INDIVIDUAL AND
FAMILY THERAPIES

RELATIONSHIP
BETWEEN SELF
AND SYSTEM

What makes people behave as they do? Their actions appear, at least on the surface, to be purposeful. Subjectively, we feel that we do things with the intention of accomplishing some goal. Perhaps this is an illusion and all human behavior is instinctual; perhaps the whole notion of "will" is a fiction. Perhaps we are all preprogrammed and predetermined, pawns of unseen forces that control our destinies to some ultimate, unknowable end or to some mystical, religious purpose. Perhaps, as some systems theorists have suggested, we are pawns of our family systems, trapped by mysteriously prefabricated rules of systemic functioning that are completely out of the range of our control. Can it be that individuals lack the ability to independently process information from the environment with at least partial objectivity, in order to creatively devise behaviors that can be directed toward an end that they feel to be valuable or important?

Asking individuals why they feel moved to engage in one or another behavior often elicits an answer that is clearly superficial, evasive, or downright untruthful. Even more frustrating, people often answer when challenged that they do not have the slightest idea what is motivating their actions but that they nonetheless feel impelled to carry them out.

The most confusing of all aspects of human motivation is the widespread occurrence of self-destructive acts that are engaged in repetitively and compulsively. Individuals seem doomed, like Sisyphus, to repeat over and over again actions that bring upon themselves nothing but misery. A woman whose previous husbands frequently beat her senseless marries yet another abusive spouse each time she gets up the nerve to leave the last one. A business executive frays his own nerves and alienates his family with his workaholism. A victim of bullies remains passive even when he has the opportunity to defend himself. Nations spend millions on armaments while their populations starve. What can behavioral scientists make of the so-called repetition compulsion, when direct questioning of the repeater leads to unsatisfactory answers? Should they conclude that many human beings are irrational or crazy? Are some of us lemmings in disguise? Can there be faulty central nervous system functioning where there is no obvious anatomical or physiological abnormality?

The psychological theories currently used to explain maladaptive behavior and the therapists who subscribe to them fall into two general categories: those who look at what is wrong with the individual exhibiting the behavior and those who look at what is wrong with the social system of which he or she is a part. Those therapists who fall into the first group tend to work with individuals; those in the latter group tend to work with families. Recently, efforts have been made to reconcile these diametrically opposite points of view (Bowen, 1978; Slipp, 1984; Wachtel and Wachtel, 1986). This volume is dedicated to that end. I believe in the existence of a self that is separate from yet an integral part of a variety of social systems. My goal is to be able to understand and treat self-destructive behavior.

This chapter will look at the nature of the relationship between the self and the social system. The social system will at times be referred to by a term with more political connotations, the *collective*. Before getting to that, I would first like to address a problem that I feel is common to almost all of the theories of psychopathology currently in vogue.

Are Troubled People Defective?

One of the most frequent explanations for the repetition compulsion, and one that unfortunately has rather disturbing implications for the possibility of behavioral change with or without treatment, involves the non sequitur "they always do, therefore they must," or, inversely, "they never do, therefore they cannot": individuals behave in the same illogical, destructive way over and over again simply because, for various reasons, they lack the ability to do otherwise. One may argue that these explanations are logical in that they are inductive, rather than deductive, conclusions; that is, they are conclusions of fact rather than reasoning, based on repeated observations. If these ideas are inductively correct, then few or no exceptions to them should exist. I will show that, in fact, many exceptions exist in cases of compulsive behavioral dysfunction.

Faulty reasoning based on these non sequiturs is most obvious in discussions of compulsive or addictive behavior but is rampant throughout psychoanalysis and systems theory in general. The borderline personality, for instance, is frequently observed by clinicians reacting to people as if they were all good or all bad, with tragic consequences for the borderline's interpersonal relationships. The conclusion the analyst draws is that the borderline, who rigidly engages in this behavior known as splitting, is incapable of forming an integrated image of any person. In systems theory, individuals in a family are seen conforming to the same rules of intrafamilial communication no matter how unproductive the results. The conclusion the systems theorist draws is that people are incapable of bucking the mechanisms that run the family system. Therapists involved in a chemical dependency treatment program observe that the alcoholic cannot stop drinking after the first glass. They conclude that the alcoholic is incapable of controlling the urge to drink.

In individually oriented theoretical constructs, the non sequitur is hidden in discussions of ego "deficits" or stunted ego "development." The idea that psychological abilities "develop" almost independently of the childhood maturation of central nervous system anatomy and physiology, or that psychological abilities can "fixate" or even "regress" to levels seen in normal children, is practically a given in much of psychological research. If toddlers cannot delay gratification, an adult who cannot delay gratification must not have matured psychologically after the age of five. As we shall see when I discuss the example of alcoholism, this confusion of behavior with ability does not hold up under close scrutiny.

The developmental view of human behavior leads to the idea that the patient exhibiting dysfunctional conduct has somehow become innately defective, an idea that is insidiously pernicious. A therapist is left with the impression that he or she must either be able to reparent the child from the ground up or be content with damage control, rather than behavioral change, as the goal of therapy. If a patient in therapy does not get better, the therapist can rationalize that the treatment failure was due to the patient's being too "disturbed"—that is, too defective—rather than to the limitations of the individual therapist, the theory being used, or humankind's present state of knowledge on how to treat difficult patients. If therapists instead view their own shortcomings as evidence that they are innately defective, they may choose to believe that treatment failures are due to a countertransference difficulty in every instance.

An even more pessimistic version of the "people-as-innately-defective" type of reasoning is used by organic psychiatrists, who believe that many maladaptive behavior patterns are caused entirely by miswiring of the central nervous system or neuroendocrine disorders of one sort or another. Endless research is done on the physiology of people suffering from the various categories of psychiatric disturbance. Levels of metabolites of neurotransmitters in experimental and control groups are compared; minor nonspecific electroencephalographic changes are catalogued; differences in glucose metabolism in different parts of the brain are mapped by new scanning devices. Twin and adoption studies are performed to prove the existence of a genetic component to psychological disorders. Many differences between diagnostic groups in these biological parameters do in fact approach or even reach statistical significance. A drug that might correct the assumed physiological abnormality that "causes," say, compulsive hand washing is the ultimate goal.

Unfortunately, drugs that do correct any differences that are found ultimately do not reverse dysfunctional behavior in a significant number of subjects, nor do they do so consistently for the subjects that do seem to improve.

This is not to say that pathophysiological processes do not affect human behavior at all, or that a pathophysiological process cannot be the main cause of a behavioral or cognitive disorder. The obvious example of the latter is Alzheimer's disease. No one to my knowledge has had the nerve to argue that senility is caused by impaired childhood psychological development, poor mothering, or dysfunctional family rules. Extremely convincing evidence also exists, both from physiological studies and from the startling response to medications, that major affective disorders such as bipolar disease are the result of pathological shifts in brain chemistry in genetically susceptible individuals, most likely initiated by psychologically stressful situations. Despite claims to the contrary, the majority of scientists agree that twin and adoption studies do demonstrate a significant genetic component to schizophrenia. No one seriously doubts that psychological stress can produce real anatomical changes, such as peptic ulcers and myocardial infarctions.

Clearly, both emotional, physiological factors and pathophysiological factors contribute to the development of psychosomatic disease. Minuchin, Rosman, and Baker (1978), in a beautifully designed experiment, demonstrated that free fatty acid levels in juvenile diabetics change under very specific types of family stress and that the dynamics of families with uncontrolled diabetics differ significantly from those of families with controlled diabetics. The results of this study show that if family dynamics change, and the diabetic child is therefore less subjected to certain forms of stress, the effects of any physiological defect that does exist will be less severe. Schizophrenia may turn out to be an analogous psychosomatic type of disease process, which would explain the presence of both organic and psychological/family disturbances present in those suffering from this disease.

The "people-as-defective" type of explanation reaches its height in the discussions of that most intractable of mental disorders, alcoholism. Alcoholics are often seen as *both* psychologically and physiologically defective. At this point, I will dissect some instances of this fallacy in explanations of alcoholic behavior. Alcoholics, it is said, have a disease that renders them simply incapable of controlling their drinking. Not only that, but if they are vicious, passive-aggressive, or obnoxious while or after they are inebriated, this behavior is due solely to the effects of the alcohol and is completely beyond their control. In no way is the alcoholic's behavior of this type an act of will. This view, while clinically useful to some extent, is nonetheless patently absurd. Now, I would agree that alcoholism is a disease if one defines disease as any process, behavioral or physiological, that is destructive to the organism. If, on the other hand, one defines disease as a developmental or pathophysiological defect, then the full-blown syndrome of alcoholism is decidedly not a disease.

What does it mean to say that alcoholics cannot control the urge to drink and that they cannot control their behavior after they start? Of course, it is quite true that all of us will engage in behaviors while intoxicated that are uncharacteristic of our normal actions. This results to a certain extent from the fact that alcohol is a tranquilizer and that some conduct that would normally make us too anxious to enact can be performed in the absence of that anxiety. One might argue that a tranquilizer effect enhances our behavioral control, rather than diminishes it, in this specific sense. Alcohol can also be a depressant and affect behavior that way, and it certainly diminishes coordination.

Now, having said all that, are alcoholics really incapable of controlling their behavior, in terms of both the urge to take the first drink and the behavior afterward? I submit that they are not. If they were, the lack of ability would have to be due either to the abnormal physiological strength of their urges, caused by some abnormality in neural control mechanisms, or to the weakness—that is, defectiveness—of their egos in resisting those urges. Allow me to address the matter of urges. Urges are an entirely subjective experience. It is impossible to know whether an urge in one person is stronger or weaker than an urge in another person. In spite of this, human beings do belong, each and every one, to the same species, and therefore have many characteristics in common. This is true even when comparing pathophysiological processes to physiological processes. It is reasonable to assume, although admittedly by no means provable, that all human beings are subject at one time or another to very strong urges. The urges may have different objects —some people have a stronger predilection for food, others for sex, others for sensory stimulation, and so forth—but it is a safe bet that the strongest urges in one person are probably just as intense as the strongest urges in someone else. Yet somehow people usually do manage to control these strong urges when to give in to them would cause problems.

But no matter. Certainly alcoholics have other urges besides the urge to drink, so perhaps we must assume that since these other urges are often resisted, the drinking urge must be far stronger than all the rest—stronger than the sex drive, stronger than the wish for happiness, stronger even than the drive for self-survival in those alcoholics who are willing to continue drinking even when they are dying from cirrhosis of the liver. In the latter case, the urge to drink must be stronger than the urge to avoid excruciating pain from esophageal varices and other complications of liver disease. I must confess that it is difficult for me to believe that the urge to feel what the alcoholic feels while under the influence is *that* strong, but as I said, how can we really know how irresistible the alcoholic's urge to drink is?

One thing that can be said is that even the worst alcoholic who ever lived did not drink in every instance where alcohol was available. Alcoholics about to drink a first sip from an open container while driving a vehicle will in most instances put the bottle down if they notice a police car behind them. Most, unless they are more than usually self-destructive, will do this even if they are already intoxicated. If their urge to drink were irresistible, or for that matter if their egos were too "weak" to resist the urge, then they would go ahead and imbibe anyway. Beyond a shadow of a doubt, every alcoholic is at least capable of resisting the urge to drink given *some* contingency, even while inebriated. If you do not believe that, ask yourself how many drunks would continue to drink, assuming that they were not overtly suicidal at the time, if they believed that someone pointing a gun at their heads would shoot them the moment they picked up the glass.

At this point, logicians reading this might accuse me of engaging in a logical fallacy. I am picking extreme cases of contingencies wherein alcoholics might be able to control themselves and offering them as evidence that they can do so. The traditional argument is not that alcoholics can never resist the urge to drink but that either the urge is relatively irresistible or that their egos are somewhat defective, so that in *most instances* alcoholics will be unable to control their drinking. Am I setting up a straw man?

I think not. First, I would question why alcoholics might be able to resist the urge to drink in order to avoid certain undesirable consequences but not in order to avoid others that are equally or even more self-destructive. They might avoid drinking on the job to avoid getting fired, for instance, yet not avoid drinking at home despite the fact that they are causing their beloved children to despise them. Second, if alcoholics are subject to a disease that renders them incapable of controlling drinking, how do we explain the fact that after a brief rehabilitation program in which alcoholics give themselves over completely to the teachings of Alcoholics Anonymous, they are suddenly able, at least for a time, to control their drinking? Oh, we can say that they are never really cured and could go back to drinking at any time, but nonetheless, they are controlling their drinking for the time being. It is highly doubtful that in the course of a month, an alcohol treatment program could have reparented them from the ground up. No curative physiological change has occurred in their neurocontrol centers in that period of time—detoxification and a month of forced abstinence by themselves do not stop an alcoholic from drinking. The only real change that has occurred during the month is in what the alcoholics say about what they believe about themselves. The only difference after the program is a cognitive one. What has become of the alleged defect?

As another example of a questionable defect, in this case

a purported developmental one, consider the behavior known as "splitting." The developmentally oriented, ego psychology approach to this phenomenon posits that persons diagnosed as having a borderline personality disorder are incapable of integrating positive and negative traits simultaneously in their view of self or others. They either completely idealize or completely devalue—or so it seems. But is the borderline truly incapable of seeing good and bad in the same person at the same time, or does this apparent inability manifest itself only at certain times and in certain situations? I submit that the incapacity is extremely selective. The borderline behaves as if people were either gods or piles of manure only in certain types of emotionally meaningful relationships. In particular, a therapist will get an extremely biased view of the borderline precisely because the borderline behaves in this manner most outrageously when relating to doctors, as well as to parents, authority figures, and lovers. Borderlines will exhibit much less of this behavior with some friends, less still with remote acquaintances, and least of all with strangers in situations where no one they know is watching. I have personally heard, on many occasions, borderlines in moments of candor listing the good and bad points of even the closest of family members, yet soon thereafter refusing to acknowledge that the family member is anything but either a villain or a hero.

Yet another variation of the "they do, therefore they must" or "they do not, therefore they cannot" fallacy involves the ability of individuals to think for themselves. A widespread belief exists that since people often behave in a mindless manner, they therefore have no minds. A return to the subject of chemical dependency will yield many instances of the presence of this fallacy in explanations of human motivation. Two blatant examples are seen in explanations that consider the role of peer pressure in the genesis of drug abuse. We have all seen the thesis advanced that peer pressure is the primary cause of drug use among adolescents, but the notion that peers have no effect at all has also been bandied about.

Undoubtedly, many teens have experimented with drugs in order to gain acceptance by a specific clique, but is peer pressure really enough to cause adolescents to abandon their own sense about what is good for them and what is not? Is it really enough to cause them to begin to use drugs in a self-destructive manner? For generations, mothers have been ridiculed for answering their children's cries of "everybody's doing it" with statements such as "if everybody jumped off a bridge, would you join them?" Nonetheless, there is considerable validity to the implications of this question. The fact is clear that peers strongly pressure other peers to engage in a wide variety of behaviors. Some of these behaviors are performed, while some most decidedly are not. Additionally, it is also a misstatement of fact that "everybody's doing it." Of course, everybody is not doing it. In fact, even kids who enjoy a great deal of peer acceptance and popularity are not doing it. With which peer group the child chooses to associate is a matter of choice, not accident.

On the opposite side of the coin, "family modeling" is frequently proposed as the major determining factor in causing behavior, in this case drug or alcohol use. For example, in an otherwise excellent monograph entitled *Co-Alcoholic and Para-Alcoholic,* Jael Greenleaf (1981) proposes that when a family consistently models certain behaviors, such as lying to make oneself look better, then a child has simply no basis on which to believe that any alternate moral system might be preferable, even after he or she grows up. What makes this assertion—and variations of it are widely advanced by psychodynamic and systems theoreticians—the opposite of the "peer pressure" explanation is that it suggests that peers, not to mention print media and television, have no effect whatsoever. While the peer pressure explanation systematically overemphasizes peer pressure, the family modeling explanation systematically underestimates it. It portrays individuals as mindless robots that cannot see the ill effects that are generated by their family's moral code, that cannot know that their neighbors do not all subscribe to it, and that, having seen others behave differently, are incapable of questioning the family values to the point where they might look for a book that describes still other alternatives.

In systems theory, the variation of the family modeling/ mindlessness explanation that is often encountered, although less so recently, is the view that individuals are helpless pawns of the family system of which they are members. The family is treated like an organism unto itself, with the individual functioning with no more independence than a cell in a multicellular animal. No individual behavior is thought to be truly self-motivated. Anything anyone ever does is entirely a response to something somewhere else in the family. The perception that one is acting for individual purposes is a hallucination.

This view, I believe, ignores two important facts. First, individual responses to the system are determined by individual perceptions, which are unique. We have no direct contact with the outer environment but encounter it only indirectly, through our senses. The information from the senses is then filtered through our central nervous systems, which are characterized by millions of separate nerve cells with enumerable connections, and which are formed by a genetic code unique to each individual. Our only knowledge of what the world is really like is the mental model of the world that we construct within our brains. Because we are separate in time and space, we each have different information coming through our senses, and therefore our intrapsychic representations of the world we live in are all different. Moreover, we each have relationships with different people who are parts of different systems or subsystems and who influence our perceptions. No two family members are parts of identical collectives. Second, if we are capable only of responding to our current environment, and not capable of transcending it, how then does one explain creativity and innovation? How can we take information and reprocess it to form brand-new ideas? Why are we not still hunter-gatherers living in caves?

The existence of human motivation that is divorced from the needs of the functioning of larger human systems is, nonetheless, a difficult thing to prove. The vast majority of human behavior seems to be determined by the functioning of the system. However, if psychoanalysis has proved one thing, it is that there is more to human behavior than meets the eye. All schools of individually oriented psychotherapy are designed to unmask hidden aspects of human motivation. When one exam-

ines the individual with a discerning eye, motivation that super-
sedes the functioning of the system becomes readily apparent.
I am not minimizing the importance of social and ecological
contexts in determining behavior—far from it. I believe that
they are by far the most important determinants. Even so, people do have separate, individual selves with independently functioning minds, despite appearances to the contrary.

Psychoanalysis recently seems to have changed from a
theory of maladaptive behavior based on the notion of "intrapsychic conflict" into object relations theory, which is basically
a model built on the idea of human defectiveness. In order to
further set the stage for a discussion of the nature of the relationship between the self and the system, I would like to address the following question.

Are Troubled People in Conflict?

When Freud first began to subject the individual to psychological dissection, he also began to view the psychological
functioning of human beings as being split into different com-
partments. Rather than envisioning human consciousness as a
unified whole, he thought that it was divided topographically
and structurally. The concept of psychic agencies, although
originally meant to be a vehicle for making generalizations
about the various functions of the human brain, became reified
over time to the point where these agencies were discussed by
psychoanalysts as if they actually existed as concrete entities. A
person's impulses, conscience, and integrative functions were
thought to come from different places. Some psychic processes
were thought to be accessible to conscious thought and some of
them to be inaccessible. The various agencies were seen as almost invariably at war with one another. Even fantasies were
anointed with independent existence; analysts spoke of intro-
jected and projected ideas as if they were pieces of consciousness that could be split off from the individual and sent through
the air like guided missiles, piercing into the brains of others and
incorporated into them much in the way that alien viral DNA
can be incorporated into a chromosome.

Freud's ideas about psychic agencies probably stemmed from the simple fact that people often seem to have conflicts over how to behave. They experience impulses that appear to spring from normal physiological functioning, but they do not always feel themselves free to do what comes naturally. The needs of civilization, as well as the needs of the individuals themselves, demand that certain activities be restricted to certain times and certain places and that other activities not be performed at all. Society would not be able to function if, for instance, individuals had sexual intercourse with whomever they pleased and whenever they felt in the mood. The needs of the larger group, the collective, must in the vast majority of instances take precedence over the desires of individuals. Otherwise, the human species could not survive and prosper.

The impulses of an individual and the needs of the collective more often than not conflict. Not only that, but the acting out of these "id" impulses may also be detrimental to the individual's own safety. People who have an impulse to strike someone else must usually refrain from doing so, for their own good as well as the good of the person they would like to hit. Freud views self-destructive behavior as stemming from a conflict between two powerful agencies, the id and the superego, with the ego mediating. When one or the other of these agencies is too strong or too weak for whatever reason, the functioning of the individual within his or her environment becomes impaired. The concept of psychic agencies is a powerful metaphor for explaining human behavior, but it is problematic. First, the idea of overly weak or overly strong psychic agencies flirts dangerously with the defectiveness model of dysfunctional behavior and has indeed led to the concept of impaired psychic development inherent in much of today's analytically oriented psychological theories. Second, there is no physiological evidence that sexual and aggressive impulses can be so clearly divided from impulses to conform to societal expectations. Human consciousness appears to many of us to be an indivisible whole. Fritz Perls (1973) was one of the first to challenge Freud's idea of intrapsychic agencies and to view the human self holistically, as it had been viewed previously to Freud.

The confusion about whether the human self or human consciousness is a holistic entity or can be divided into constituents seems to me to result partially from metaphorical language. Therapists have frequently been heard to make statements to their patients such as "a part of you hates your mother" or "a part of you wants to punish yourself." In everyday conversations, nontherapists as well make this kind of remark. A more accurate way to state these ideas would be to say that the whole person is ambivalent about these activities. Indecision and mixed feelings relate to pro and cons, things others do that we find appealing and things they do that we find appalling, and so forth. They do not relate to internal fragments of self fighting with one another. The self has activities and characteristics, not components. Being green is not a "part" of being chlorophyll, it is a characteristic of being chlorophyll. Likewise, a cognition, or an action, or a perception, or a desire, is not a "part" of the self, it is a characteristic of the self. Different stimuli affect the self differently at different times. This does not mean that different components of the self are in command at different times; it means that the self is a complex entity capable of a wide variety of responses.

In my view, the idea that a conflict between the needs of the collective and the wishes of individuals can create dysfunctional behavior is a good one. However, one need not invoke the concept of psychic agencies in order to construct a useful model for self-destructive behavior. One can look at the problems created for a holistic self by the various desires of that self and the consequences of those desires.

Fritz Perls (1973) not only attacked the idea of a split consciousness but also challenged the concept that individuals exist apart from their environmental field. He discussed dysfunctional behavior in terms of a disturbance in the "contact boundary" between individuals and their environment. "No individual," he wrote, "is self-sufficient; the individual can exist only in an environmental field. The individual is inevitably, at every moment, a part of some field. His behavior is a function of the total field, which includes both him and his environment. The nature of the relationship between him and his environment determines the human being's behavior. If the relationship is mutually satisfactory, the individual's behavior is what we call normal. If the relationship is one of conflict, the individual's behavior is described as abnormal. The environment does not create the individual, nor does the individual create the environment. Each is what it is, each has its own particular character, because of the relationship to the other and the whole" (p. 16). Perls believed that if individuals impinge too heavily on the environment, they become criminals; if they allow the environment to impinge too heavily on them, they become neurotics. He added, "the imbalance arises when, simultaneously, the individual and the group experience different needs, and when the individual is incapable of distinguishing which one is dominant" (p. 28). The group could be the family, the state, or any combination of persons in a functional relationship.

Unfortunately, Perls's Gestalt psychotherapy, in both theory and practice, fails to maintain its emphasis on the total field—the system. It has a tendency to focus alternately on either the individual or the rest of the environment, rather than on the big picture. The boundary disturbance is seen as resulting primarily from the *individual's* inability to find the proper balance between the self and the rest of the world. One way that this inability is supposedly rectified in therapy is by the therapist encouraging patients to ventilate feelings so that they might rid themselves of "unfinished business." The business is most usually the patient's unexpressed anger toward those family members who have impinged too heavily upon him or her. Although the therapist does not intend for it to do so, the latter maneuver often has the effect of motivating individuals to shift the entire blame for psychological problems from themselves onto everyone but themselves. They can then become people who are long on righteous indignation but short on tact, sensitivity, and empathy.

Systems and communications theorists are more successful at maintaining the emphasis on the total field. Their ideas shift the focus of blame for emotional difficulties entirely away from any one individual—parent or child—and onto the entire group or system. Groups are defined in much the same way as

Perls defined them but with primary emphasis on the extended family. The culprit responsible for emotional disturbance is thought to be a malfunctioning family process or rule. The group is seen as a system of interconnected individuals or parts. Interactions among group members and between the group and the external environment are governed by mutually regulated cybernetic feedback loops. This internal regulation is designed to maintain group functioning within a constant, effective range, called a steady state. The mechanism whereby the steady state is maintained is called "family homeostasis," named after a phenomenon seen in physiology. The steady state may change and evolve to meet new environmental contingencies. When asked why and how the steady state originally came into being, some systems therapists claim lack of interest. It might have developed along any number of pathways, they say, and the present functioning is determined exclusively by the system's current parameters. Why worry about etiology? To understand any current dysfunction, the problems created by the steady state in the here and now are all that need be considered.

While the systems view is accurate descriptively and powerful therapeutically, it leaves much to be desired as a complete explanation of human behavior. It views the individual as "a part of a larger whole rather than as a whole in itself. The behavior of the part is explained in terms of its relationship with other parts and its function for the whole" (Schultz, 1984, p. 56). As mentioned, this view strongly implies that the behavior of an individual is entirely reactive. Self-generated individual initiative and individualistic desire would either not exist or be astonishingly unimportant. The individual would have hardly any self to call its own. I have already expressed my reservations about that idea.

The existence of a self that is distinguishable from the family and that is a center of initiative, and mechanisms through which such a self might interact with larger human systems, have been discussed by several authors. In the next section, I will look at some of those ideas from a new perspective, in order to present my view of the nature of the relationship between the self and other human systems. The section is not meant to be a thorough review or critique of the theories of the various authors.

Concepts of Self–System Interaction

Murray Bowen: The Variability of Differentiation. Bowen addresses the problem of the self versus the system by conceptualizing a relationship between the two. This relationship is characterized by a variable degree of differentiation or fusion between self and system. The idea that the relationship between the self and larger human systems is a variable rather than a constant will be a key concept throughout this volume. Bowen sees persons as varying in the extent of their enmeshment in or individuation from the family organism; that is, some people are more controlled by systemic considerations than others. "The greater the degree of undifferentiation (no self), the greater the emotional fusion into a common self with others (undifferentiated ego mass)" (Bowen, 1978, p. 472). He envisions a scale, called the "differentiation of self scale," that roughly quantifies how far the individual or self has separated itself from the system whence it came. He believes that a person's position on the scale is relatively static throughout life. The wide shift in functional levels of self seen in an individual in the course of a lifetime is explained through the concepts of "basic," or "solid," self and "pseudo-self":

> The solid self is made up of clearly defined beliefs, convictions, opinions, and life principles. Each is incorporated into self, from one's own life experience, after careful intellectual reasoning and weighing the alternative and accepting responsibility for his own choice. . . . The pseudo-self is acquired under emotional pressure and it can be changed by emotional pressure. It is made up of random and discrepant beliefs and principles, acquired because they were required, or it is the right things to believe and do, or to enhance the self image in the social anagram. The solid self is incorporated into self

in contrast to the pseudo-self which is appended to
self. The pseudo-self is a "pretend" self. It was ac-
quired to conform to the environment, or to fight
it, and it pretends to be in harmony with all kinds
of discrepant groups, beliefs, and social institutions
[p. 365].

Bowen believes that when individuals marry, they generally choose someone with a level of differentiation of basic self
similar to their own. In poorly differentiated individuals, the
desire for fusion with the spouse is great. Because of the inherent instability of this fused state, however, one or the other
member of the couple will usually assume a dominant position
and appear to be the "stronger." The "strength" of the dominant individual, because it is a response to the needs of the
spousal system rather than something that the individual ini-
tiates on his or her own, would be pseudo-self rather than solid
self.

The problem with the differentiation of self scale is that
it once again presumes that persons lower on the scale are suffering from some sort of defect that renders them incapable of
either becoming aware of or acting on the knowledge of their
own unique separateness. If one neurologically intact, fully developed adult can understand this and act on it, how is it that
another cannot? Bowen himself believes that the level of "basic
self" can be changed by merely coaching individuals to relate
differently to their families. If this be so, how "basic" can the
self that Bowen observes really be? As I shall discuss later, it seems
to me more likely that what Bowen considers to be basic self
can often be merely a more entrenched form of pseudo-self.
Bowen's statement that the solid self is "incorporated into self"
is instructive in this regard. That presumes some sort of greater
self into which the basic self can be incorporated.

Heinz Kohut: Differentiation and Development. Kohut
(1971, 1977), a maverick psychoanalyst, discusses a concept of
a self that, after birth, initially interacts in an enmeshed fashion
with significant others in the environment. He, like Bowen, feels

that the degree of enmeshment of self and others is a variable. However, he speaks of a loosening of the fusion *over time* through the process of physical and psychological development. Throughout childhood, a separate, integrated sense of self *emerges* in the individual. This occurs physically through the maturation of the central nervous system and psychologically through a mechanism that he calls "mirroring." I believe that some of his conceptions share much in common with the systems view despite their being couched in psychoanalytical terms. For example, his concept of the "self-object" is quite similar to the concept of an enmeshed dyadic system. A self-object is defined as another person, usually the mother, with whom an infant feels as one. "The small child . . . invests other people with narcissistic cathexis, and thus experiences them narcissistically, i.e., as self-objects. The expected control over such (self-object) others is then closer to the concept of the control which a grownup expects to have over his own body and mind than to the concept of the control which he expects to have over others" (Kohut, 1971, pp. 26–27). "The newborn infant cannot have a reflective awareness of himself" (Kohut, 1977, p. 99) because the apparatus of the central nervous system has not matured.

Kohut defines "self" as "a unit, cohesive in space and enduring in time, which is a center of initiative and a recipient of impressions." Its outward manifestations include ambitions and ideals. The self of the newborn is a self *in statu nascendi* ("in the state of being born"), a virtual self, "corresponding in reverse to that geometric point in infinity where two parallel lines meet." The self then *emerges* by way of the interactions between the budding self and the self-objects. "In countless repetitions, the self-objects empathically respond to certain potentialities of the child (aspects of the grandiose self he exhibits, aspects of the idealized image he admires, different innate talents he employs to mediate creatively between ambitions and ideals), but not to others. The *nuclear* self, in particular, is not formed via conscious encouragement and praise and via conscious discouragement and rebuke, but by the deeply anchored responsiveness of the self-objects, which, in the last analysis, is a function of the self-objects' own nuclear selves" (1977, pp. 99–101). The "deeply anchored responsiveness" is what is encompassed by the term "mirroring."

Kohut believes that if the parents are not capable of appropriate mirroring, because of the immaturity of their own nuclear selves, the individual's estimation of the stability and potency of his or her own self suffers. The unmirrored self suffers an "ill-defined yet intense and pervasive anxiety that accompanies a patient's dawning awareness that his self is disintegrating (severe fragmentation, serious loss of initiative, profound drop in self-esteem, sense of utter meaninglessness)" (1977, p. 103). The idea that the self can fragment is consistent with the traditional psychoanalytical view that human consciousness is not an indivisible whole, as Perls believed, but a composite. However, it contradicts Kohut's own definition of the self as a "unit cohesive in space and enduring in time." Kohut discusses fragmentation but never indicates into what he believes the self might fragment. What he does discuss is the effect of defective mirroring on an individual's regulation of her or his self-esteem and sense of purpose in life. These are cognitions. Cognitions are activities of the self, not fragments of it.

If the lack of appropriate mirroring affects only the cognitions of the self and does not result in the fragmentation or destruction of the self, then it would seem to me that mirroring is not necessary for the development of the self per se. Mirroring is a form of consensual validation. A mirrored activity or idea might seem more comfortable to children who are highly dependent upon their parents than one that is not mirrored, since at least one of the parents has agreed that it is valid. Mirroring would be very important for determining one's level of comfort with oneself, not for differentiating the self.

This view has, to my mind, implications that are profoundly different from those of the model of self proposed by Bowen. The self of the adult neurotic, rather than being seen as undifferentiated, could be seen as differentiated but *afraid* of differentiation. Fully grown human beings would always have attributes and cognitions that are completely unique to them and that are therefore different from those of all other members of their families. If such attributes were *expressed,* however, trouble might ensue. If they had never been mirrored, they might not seem real, since they had never been consensually validated. The sense of integrity of the self would become unstable, and the individual would then suffer a type of anxiety that has been frequently described by existential therapists.

Because of this anxiety, the self could then be understood as wishing to return to the more comfortable and familiar fused state, where self-generated, anxiety-producing ideas and activities do not exist. If the self had already differentiated, however, a return to the fused state would be an impossibility. The self might then attempt to pretend that it had not differentiated, in order to regain its equilibrium. A self that feigns fusion could very well be what Bowen is describing when he discusses the idea of a pseudo-self and also seems to be what Kohut is describing by the term *nuclear* self, despite the connotation of that word. The true self might attempt to limit the way in which it *expresses* its ambitions and ideals. It would act in ways that make it appear *as if* it were still enmeshed. My views regarding the nature and causes of existential anxiety will be an important component of the point of view advanced in these writings.

Carl Jung: The Nature of Individuation. Jung views the self as an archetype; that is, one of many primordial, instinctual patterns or schemata that characterize human ideation. Archetypes, along with instincts, designate "innate and purposeful modes of behavior and of experience" (De Laszlo, 1959, p. xxii). The archetype of self is an archetype of wholeness, "of the psyche in the totality of its conscious plus its unconscious components. This totality Jung has designated as the 'self.' The self by definition comprises the full scope of a personality from its most individual traits to its most generic attitudes and experiences, actual as well as potential. Hence, it transcends the existing personality" (p. xxii).

Jung sees the self as an entity that is definite, unique, and complete unto itself but that is also, simultaneously, indefinite and at one with the universe (or the system, as we are discussing it here). "Not only is the self indefinite but—paradoxically enough—it also includes the quality of definiteness and even that of uniqueness . . . the absolute individuality of the soul, which combines uniqueness with eternity and the individual with the universe. . . . The self is a union of opposites *par excellence.* . . . The self . . . is absolutely paradoxical in that it represents in every respect thesis and antithesis, and at the same time synthesis" (De Laszlo, 1959, p. 450). While these ideas may seem theological and internally contradictory, the idea that something could simultaneously exist in two different states is hardly unheard of in science. To steal an oft-used analogy from physics, light has been conceptualized as both a wave and a particle, depending on one's reference point.

Jung, like Kohut, speaks of a process by which the self emerges. He, along with later psychoanalysts, called the process "individuation." The idea of a process of separation and individuation of the self from some sort of collective entity—the objects relations theorists postulate a symbiotic relationship with the mother—has indeed become a mainstay of all psychoanalytical theory. Unlike Jung, most analysts think of the process as existing entirely within the mind of the individual, rather than between self and system. Certain of Jung's ideas regarding individuation have unique characteristics that, while rather mystical, will be useful in formulating a viable concept of the nature of the link between self and system and coming to an understanding of the separation-individuation process.

In *The Relations Between the Ego and the Unconscious,* Jung discussed his conception of the process of individuation. "Individuation means becoming a single, homogeneous being, and, insofar as 'individuality' embraces our innermost, last, and incomparable uniqueness, it also implies becoming one's own self" (De Laszlo, 1959, p. 143). He speaks of "self-realization," the process of ridding oneself of "alienations of the self, ways of divesting the self of its reality in favor of an external role or in favor of an imagined meaning. In the former case the self retires into the background and gives place to social recognition; in the latter, to the autosuggestive meaning of primordial images. In both cases the collective has the upper hand" (p. 143).

What Jung seems to be saying here is that the true nature of the self can be pushed into the background, sacrificing the "peculiarities of its nature" to the needs of the collective. The "collective" could easily refer not only to humanity as a whole but also to a family or a cultural system. Individuation, then, is the reversal of the process by which the true nature of the self is hidden by collectivist trappings.

Jung mentions two different ways that the self is "alienated" or hidden by collectivist considerations. One of these types, the "external role," is called the "persona" in Jungian terminology. Jung is quite down to earth in his discussions of the persona. The term *persona* comes originally from the Latin word for the mask used by actors to signify the role that they played. We all have certain functions to perform in our family and in our society, and we all have to fulfill these functions at times when our wish might be to do otherwise. The persona refers to the acting job that we all must execute in order to discharge the various duties necessitated by our trades and by our families. Jung points out that we are all familiar with this idea. In our language, we often speak of the many ways in which we "put on official airs" or "play a social role."

Oftentimes the persona is a cover-up of our true feelings and inclinations, a cover-up performed in order to react to the needs of the various systems of which we are a part. In this sense, it is a concept that shares much in common with the concept of the "pseudo-self." The degree to which we must retain our persona for the sake of the group when our self-interest is adversely affected could be thought of as corresponding to how reactive to or enmeshed in the system or collective we are.

The second type of alienation of the self can scarcely be described without resorting to spiritual or religious imagery and so might be considered to be outside of the realm of science and objectivism. Jung suggests that the self is a manifestation of and crystallizes out from something he refers to as the "collective unconscious." He presupposes the existence of a kind of cosmic oneness of psychic contents of all individuals that is parallel to the cosmic oneness of the universe itself described in Taoist, Buddhist, Hindu (Capra, 1975), and even Jewish mysticism. In all fairness to Jung, however, the idea of some sort of unified underlying principle of existence from which spring forth a multitude of individual forms is inherent in the "scientific" fields of astrophysics and evolutionary biology and is even seen in the arena of political science. Physicists and astronomers have found striking evidence that the contents of the universe are hurtling away from one another at enormous speeds and have postulated that all of the energy of the universe—indeed, the universe itself—was originally a single, infinitesimal, infinitely dense, and timeless point. The contents of the universe exploded in the "big bang" and then coalesced into stars, planets, nebulae, galaxies, and a host of other structures, which are gradually dispersing into finer and finer conglomerates spaced at ever-increasing distances. In biology, the evolutionary proliferation of increasingly differentiated life forms is thought to have sprung from the single DNA molecule. In the political arena, increasingly individualistic ideologies have evolved from—and continue to compete with—more collectivist ideologies.

The "scientific" concept that is closest to Jung's concept of the collective unconscious is "instinct." Certain patterns of behavior seen in members of the animal kingdom are unlearned and innate, wired, as it were, into their nervous systems. These patterns are identical in all members of a given species. The idea that conceptual ideation may be formed in the human mind in genetically predetermined, instinctive patterns that are shared in an undifferentiated form by all Homo sapiens is not all that mysterious. So-called primary process thinking, seen in children and in dreams and in the religious ideas of primitives, makes use of several schemata, such as symbol formation, that follow the same rules across the board in everyone. When Jung speaks of falling prey to the "autosuggestive meaning of primordial images," he is discussing a reversion to the idiosyncratic or autistic primary process thought patterns that are characteristic of schizophrenia.

Individuation, then, is the process of coming into our own, of freeing ourselves from the prison of instinctual thought patterns and role functioning, of being able to express our own special and singular qualities. Jung differentiates between individuation and individualism. "Individualism means deliberately stressing and giving prominence to some supposed peculiarity, rather than to collective considerations and obligations. But individuation means precisely the better and more complete fulfillment of the collective qualities of the human being. . . . The idiosyncracy of an individual is not to be understood as any strangeness in his substance or in his components, but rather as a unique combination, or gradual differentiation, of factions and faculties which in themselves are universal. Every human face has a nose, two eyes, etc., but these universal factors are variable . . . individuation . . . is a process by which a man becomes the definite unique being he in fact is" (De Laszlo, 1959, p. 144).

I left out one sentence in the above quotation so that I might conclude my discussion of Jung by placing stress on an extremely important point. Jung said, "adequate consideration of the peculiarity of the individual is more conducive to better social achievement than when the peculiarity is neglected or suppressed." In other words, collective entities such as the family system or the culture may in fact be better served when their constituents express the true nature of their individual selves than when this nature is hidden or sacrificed for the supposed good of the group. I will henceforth refer to this principle as the "altruistic paradox," a recurrent theme throughout this work.

A Word on Introjects. Some of the confusion and controversy regarding the nature and development of the self stems from the question of whether the self is an innate entity, latent or inherent in the individual human organism, that more or less develops on its own timetable regardless of the input of the environment—or can the self be irreversibly molded and changed by an environment that is in fact necessary for its normal maturation? Many analytical formulations take the latter view; the self is thought to be both altered and enlarged by the input of the environment, with its normal development dependent upon the proper input. Mental processes that come directly from the parents, such as concepts, ideals, ambitions, and even preferences, supposedly become incorporated into the self of the child, or into the psychic agency of the superego that is a part of the self of the child, as "introjects." Introjects are seen as being injected into an individual in a rather passive process, control of which is for the most part outside of the sphere of individual initiative. Although the blame for psychological illness in a child would seem to fall on the parents because of their own defective output—such as sexual conflicts, harsh toilet training practices, improper mirroring, and so forth—in therapy the analyst concentrates on fixing the damage done to the individual after the fact by focusing on the introjects that are seen as now being entirely within the patient's psyche.

Perls (1973) envisions the relationship of the development and growth of the self to the input of the environment as a more active process. Growth of the individual self occurs through the assimilation of "concepts, facts, standards of behavior, morality, and ethical, esthetic or political values" (p. 33) from the environment. However, he draws a distinction between "assimilation," which leads to enhancement of the self, and "introjection," which does no such thing. Personal growth through assimilation is a process analogous to bodily growth through the digestion of food. Input from the outside is destructured, digested, and then reconstituted in a form that is part and parcel of the organism and fits with its innate inclinations: "What we have really assimilated from the environment becomes ours, to do with as we please. We can retain it, or give it back in its new form, its distillation through us" (p. 32).

An introject, in contradistinction, is analogous to food that is swallowed whole and sits uncomfortably in the stomach. It is ingested but not digested. It is ideas that are accepted "whole hog and uncritically, on someone else's say-so, or because they are fashionable or safe or traditional or unfashionable or dangerous or revolutionary" (p. 33). An introject is really a characteristic that is appended to the self, rather than something that is incorporated into the self: "what we accept indiscriminately . . . is a foreign body. . . . It is not a part of us, even though it may look as if it is. It is a part of the environment." Perls's use of the phrase "it may look as if it is" is noteworthy. It is highly consistent, once again, with the concept of the pseudo-self, a phony act performed because of its effects on others within the system of which the self is part: "Introjection, then, is the neurotic mechanism whereby we incorporate into ourselves standards, attitudes, ways of acting and thinking, which are not truly ours. . . . When the introjector says, 'I think,' he usually means, 'they think' " (pp. 34–35).

To draw out the analogy of food digestion still further, it is undoubtedly true that some environmental inputs are totally indigestible to any given individual. Trying to personalize certain thoughts, feelings, and preferences would be a complete impossibility, like a person attempting to digest grass as does a cow. A father who forces his son to become a concert violinist when the true self of the son is inclined to be a forest ranger would be an example of that. No matter how hard the son tried to assimilate the father's wishes, they simply would not fit. A self can be likened to a template into which certain ideas can be molded to fit and certain others can never fit. Being a concert violinist for the son in my example would forever remain an introject, and self-realization would not take place.

We have now seen that the relationship between the self and the collective is not a constant but a variable. A true self that is completely distinguishable from the family system of which it is a part *emerges* as the individual develops through time in the process referred to as "separation-individuation." In the next chapter, I will take a much closer look at this process and how it relates to the functioning of the family system.

2

EMERGENCE
OF THE SELF
FROM THE SYSTEM

Biologists have long observed that the survival of an individual creature always seems to take a backseat to the survival of the species. In most of nature, once reproduction and propagation of the race have occurred, the individual becomes expendable. Most of the time, it dies, apparently of no further biological usefulness. The appearance of a species whose members' lives extend far past the time of reproductive ability—the human being—was a relatively recent development in evolution. Even with Homo sapiens, life expectancy for most was not much in excess of the end of reproductive ability until the advent of medical technology, with its life-extending ability. Survival of the species, however, is not the most driving of all forces in biology, despite its power.

Of even more primary importance than the survival of the species is a second biological propensity, the tendency of organisms to evolve. Species may come and species may go, but evolution continues unabated. The force of evolution, whatever its source, appears to be toward increased complexity and differentiation of the individual, so that a species higher up on the evolutionary ladder is different from one lower down in two important respects. First, the more complex, higher-order species is more capable, overall, of processing information from the environment and using the information to manipulate the environment. Second, there is more variance among individuals within the higher-order species.

In a sense, evolution is a process of separation-individuation, as we go from undifferentiated organic molecules to cellular organization, then to primitive organisms, and finally to more and more complex organisms. At each level, the various entities are more and more different and individualized from each other as well as from the entities below them on the evolutionary ladder. Additionally, as we climb this ladder, each entity becomes less and less dependent on the surrounding milieu to survive and, in a sense, more divorced and differentiated from the environment. A primitive cell was hardly distinguishable at all from the surrounding primordial ooze and its inorganic contents. Its only claim to fame was its ability to replicate exact copies of itself. Later, as various creatures came into being, each life form was suited only for the particular environment from which and in which it evolved. Change the milieu, and it would perish like the dinosaurs. Homo sapiens, the current pinnacle of evolution, has the ability to change the environment to suit itself, rather than the other way around. While it remains ultimately connected to the ecosystem, the links are far less impressive.

Survival of the species and the separation-individuation aspect of evolution will be relevant for our understanding of two of the main concerns of this book: the relationship between the self and the collective and the causes of self-destructive behavior. I will advance the thesis that the two biological propensities are expressed in the individual human being as a strong desire to protect the survival and evolutionary interests of his or her family system, even if it means the complete sacrifice of the individual. These propensities appear to be innate and instinctual. I would like to begin our discussion of how these biological givens affect human behavior by examining how they are seemingly reflected in the "evolution" of the human individual, its development. Later on we shall see that biological evolution is also reflected in the evolution of human culture. From there we will examine how all these related phenomena interact.

Evolution and Human Development

Embryologists long ago noted that "ontogeny recapitulates phylogeny." This means that fetal development goes through stages that appear quite similar to the stages of the evolution of the species. In a very early stage of development, the fetus looks not unlike an embryonic fish, the earliest vertebrate on the evolutionary chain that eventually reaches humanity. A bit later, it looks like a polliwog. Amphibians were the next link in the chain. Embryonic development, however, does not supply the only parallel between evolution and human development. Such a parallel to evolution can also be drawn with the human baby after birth.

Psychological theorists have long focused on a separation-individuation aspect of human development. After the umbilical cord is cut, human babies are distinct biological entities yet in a sense remain interconnected with the mother and the rest of the immediate social system to a far greater degree than they will be later in their development. The discussion of the concept of interconnectedness by psychological theorists often becomes esoteric and confusing, so I would like to clarify this idea before returning to the subject of the similarities between individual human development and evolution. Human infants are thought to experience themselves as almost one with the universe when they are first born. They are then thought to normally form an attachment to the primary caretaker, who is described in object relations parlance as the primary "object." Babies are then felt to experience themselves as one with the "object"; this is referred to as a "self-object." In my opinion, use of terms such as *self-object* represents a confusing reification, as it leads away from the idea of an interdependent dyadic system and more to a conception of a concrete entity.

The baby is a separate, finite individual from birth, but, as systems theorists have shown, it is also part of a system. It is part of a dyadic system with its mother and is also a part of a larger family system, an even larger cultural system, and a still larger ecosystem. The degree of connectedness to the system is reflected by the experience of the individual but is not entirely synonymous with experience. Adults often experience themselves as less a part of their social system than they actually are. The experience of the baby is in reality quite unknown. The inferences made by the object relations theorists from observed behavior of infants may have some validity, but they must of necessity remain even more highly speculative than most psychological theories. Babies communicate with the people in the environment in very sophisticated ways, but ways not complex enough to let us know how separate they feel or the content of their fantasies.

In describing the interconnectedness of human systems, subsystems, and the individual, I prefer to use a term used extensively by Minuchin and Fishman (1981). The term is *holon*. A holon is a subsystem that has properties distinct from the individuals that it comprises, as well as properties distinct from the larger systems than contain it. In other words, it is any grouping of interdependent individuals; it is more than the sum of its parts, and it is different in some ways from all other possible groupings. From a set theory perspective, a holon is a set that is not entirely defined by its constituents but that would not exist if its specific constituents were changed. In psychological theory, a holon can consist of an individual, any combination of individuals within a nuclear family, the nuclear family itself, the extended family, the community, the ethnic group, or the human race.

A holon is more than just a particular grouping of separate individuals sharing something in common, just as an organ is more than just an aggregate of cells and an animal is more than just an aggregate of organ systems. At each level, the holon has *functional* properties that go above and beyond the functional properties of the constituents. That is, the group takes action and produces effects that the individuals comprising the group are not inclined to do or are incapable of doing by themselves. This is true even though the functional properties of a larger body are entirely dependent upon the properties of the individuals constituting the group. Each holon acts as if it were an entity in and by itself. Moreover, the individual's functioning takes on properties of the larger holon in certain situations. As Minuchin states, we "know that the football player on a team, or the oboist in a quintette, somehow take on the excellencies of these more-than-human units. We experience the impulse that makes a stadium crowd of thirty thousand rise and yell in unison. And in therapeutic terms, any clinician can provide vignettes of the workings of the multibodied animal known as the family" (Minuchin and Fishman, 1981, p. 12).

The degree of interconnectedness, or interdependency, of individual constituents of the holon is one of the functional properties of the holon that distinguish it from those constituents. The degree of interconnectedness can be defined by two parameters. The first is the level of potential ability of the individual to manipulate the environment without the assistance of the system. The second is the level of development of the self of the individual. *Self* in this sense shall be used as it was defined in the last chapter. The meaning of interconnectedness will become clearer as we discuss how its level changes over time.

The degree of interconnectedness between the individual and the family holon diminishes as the child passes through its developmental stages. This process, called separation-individuation, is similar in many respects to the separation and individuation of species in the process of evolution. Though human beings always remain part of the system and are always affected strongly by it, the connection diminishes over time in two important respects. First, people become less and less dependent on those around them to take care of basic needs. As babies become toddlers, they learn to get around by themselves to go after more of the things they want and need with less and less assistance from family members. As they go to school and have more experiences, they learn things about the world that enable them to be more self-reliant. From having been passive recipients of all that the environment has to dish out, they gradually become beings who can manipulate the environment and dish back. This process is parallel to the way species evolved from being passively dependent on their milieu to being able to tailor the milieu to their own needs.

Second, as development proceeds, the child gradually becomes more of a unique individual, with thoughts, preferences, and emotions that are unduplicated by any other single human being. Just as no two individuals have identical fingerprints or perfectly identical faces, no two selves are exactly alike. The development of this mental-emotional fingerprint, if you will, parallels the individuation forces in evolution that we have previously discussed. Just as more highly evolved species show more individual variation, the more highly developed human beings become, the more they show a pattern of traits that is different from that of any other fellow creature. These traits stem both from innate tendencies and from assimilation from the environment in the manner described by Perls.

This process of separation-individuation occurs in a series of steps that psychologists refer to as developmental stages. Different aspects of the self develop at different times, but the basic thrust of development is to loosen the ties between individuals and the system of which they are a part. In order to illustrate the point, I will focus on two processes: the stages of intellectual development and the development of the self.

Piaget showed that normal intelligence does not come into being in its highest adult form at the moment of birth but evolves from a primitive, "sensory-motor" type of concrete, representational thinking in a series of steps (Ginsburg and Opper, 1969). The child is thought to first learn to think in terms of concrete images, then later to develop the ability to think symbolically through the use of words, and still later to become able to think in terms of more abstract concepts. The higher the intelligence of individual children, the faster this series of developmental steps proceeds and the greater is their ability to understand more highly complex abstractions at each step. However, unless actual brain damage or abnormality exists, all children will go through these stages irrespective of how far they may eventually be able to go. These developmental states parallel the evolution of the ability of life forms to manipulate the environment and therefore to gain some measure of independence from it. Abstract reasoning and the ability to use thought to partly substitute for actual trial-and-error behavior in problem solving give highly evolved creatures a definite boost in this regard.

Another interesting property of intellectual development is that it does not progress smoothly. Each stage proceeds without much obvious improvement for a time, and then suddenly a new stage, with all of its more complex abilities, appears in a sort of quantum leap. Once the leap is made, the new stage quickly settles in and becomes part of the way the child sees reality. The child reverts to the old ways of thinking only rarely. In my opinion, once the ability to use higher intellectual mechanisms appears, it is never lost, again unless some actual brain injury occurs. As we shall see, children may act as if one or another ability has been lost in an effort to appear less intelligent than they truly are. However, though they may never express the ability, I believe that it is still present.

The fact that intellectual development occurs in stages, as does the development of the self, may seem to some readers to be evidence that individual evolution is different from biological evolution in at least this one important respect. Does not evolution occur by the process of natural selection, and do not the forces of natural selection operate continuously and not episodically? Paleontologists no longer believe that natural selection accounts entirely for the process of evolution, and current thinking holds that evolution may in fact occur in a series of cataclysmic lurches. This is referred to by biologists as the theory of "punctuated equilibria," an idea strongly supported by fossil evidence. Evolution is most likely not a smooth process after all.

One other important aspect of intellectual development deserves comment. I believe that the input of the family system, while able to enhance or retard the *expression* of intellectual development, is powerless to stop it or to speed it up past a certain point, despite the fact that the individual is strongly enmeshed in the family system. For example, up to a certain age, which varies from child to child but which is in the same ballpark for all of them, a child cannot understand that the shape of a container has no bearing on the amount of liquid in it. Past the magic age, each child realizes that these two features are independent. The understanding of the "conservation" concept is an all-or-none phenomenon. Children either understand it or they do not. In terms of the point I am making here, all neurologically intact children exhibit this phenomenon. Every one of them develops an understanding of the concept after a point in time, and every one of them lacks it before that point. Furthermore, the conservation concept cannot be taught before that point is reached. Though an adult may explain the concept over and over again, the preconservation child will not understand.

Likewise, many other intellectual schemata develop in a similar manner. Inductively, it would appear that they all do. I realize that these experiments show only that the process cannot be sped up past a certain point by the environment and prove nothing regarding whether the environment can stop it from occurring. The intellectual functions discussed here, in their pure form, are unlikely to be subjects of attempts at destruction by a family system, because a reason for them to be a matter of distress is hard to imagine. Nonetheless, the fact that development proceeds in all individuals, regardless of the family system whence they came, does at least suggest that it is a progression that will occur regardless of the system. My belief that this is the case also stems from my experience in therapy. Often, patients will act in daily life as if they are unable to understand a relatively simple concept and will continue to make the same mistake over and over. If the therapist assumes that, in spite of the behavior, they do in actuality understand the basis of the error, and looks patiently for evidence of such understanding, vindication invariably follows.

All of the ideas that I have discussed concerning intellectual development also apply, in my opinion, to the development of the self. The self also develops in a series of stages that parallel the separation-individuation aspect of species evolution and that do not occur smoothly. The outward expression of self-development can be affected by the family system, but the self always goes through the stages regardless of the input of the family system. A higher level of separation-individuation will be reached at each stage, just as surely as the baby must inevitably lose its placental connection to the mother at the time of birth. That latter idea may be particularly difficult for many readers to accept, given the emphasis in current psychological theorizing on the concepts of regression and fixation as being reflective of the state of development of the individual. In my view, those current ideas about development represent a confusion between the development of the self as a unique, less interconnected entity and the development of personality, as described by Freud, Erikson, and others. Personality, as defined by these pioneers, can be viewed as a hybrid or mix between the person's true self and, to use Jung's term, a persona.

The self of the individual starts out as a virtual prisoner of biological needs. The newborn's thoughts, preferences, and emotions are consumed by the search for the attainment of nourishment, comfort, and the formation of a bond with a primary caretaker. When they are not engaged in activities related to these needs, human babies do little but sleep and appear to be unconcerned with everything else. Babies behave pretty much the same way no matter who they are; individual behavioral variation occurs in the level of the baby's arousal, spontaneous activity, and rate of subsequent development but in precious little else.

A second stage occurs when infants discover aspects of the outside world that are not directly related to their physical well-being. They suddenly become aware of the infinite variety of physical objects surrounding them and become interested in more than just what these objects provide for them. They are fascinated with shape, consistency, and movement. The desire to investigate objects prods them to make attempts at locomotion and spurs physical development. This desire is strong. When babies wish to have an object, they strive for it; if deprived of it, they go into a rage. I have always found the way that therapists often interpret the apparent inability of many fully formed adult human beings to identify what their preferences really are a bit curious when seen against the backdrop of the strong desires of the infant. How could it be that babies who are so sure of what they want become adults who are at a loss about it?

Surely the inability stems not from the lack of development or true disappearance of individuality but from its suppression.

Babies at this stage of development show a great deal more variation from their cohorts than do babies at the earlier stage. Different objects will hold more interest for one child than for another. Each will have a different pattern of fears. The nature and frequency of their temper tantrums vary widely. Nonetheless, behavior and cognition among babies at this stage show more similarities than differences when compared to various children at any later stage. With each subsequent progression, the similarity-difference ratio continues to diminish.

The attainment of autonomy, the ability to do things for oneself and the freedom to make at least some choices on one's own, supplants in the next stage the shape and texture of the physical world as the focus of the child's cognitions, preferences, and emotions. A major concern during this stage of self development is the improvement of muscular functioning and locomotion. The necessity of these abilities for the attainment of autonomy hardly merits further elaboration. The relationship between muscle control and autonomy is widely reflected in English colloquial expressions. We speak of standing on one's own two feet, having one's legs cut out from underneath, tripping oneself up, and walking the straight and narrow. Another concern of children at this stage is personal potency, a matter that I have touched upon previously. Their rallying cry is "I want to do it *myself!*" When children become able to do something that they previously could not, such as using a spoon correctly, they are as pleased and as proud as can be. A child at this age delights in being able to contribute to the family. If Daddy is fixing a door in the house and asks Mommy for a screwdriver, his son will serve as the messenger with a big smile on his face. He may even beg to do chores that shortly he will eschew as a fate worse than death.

Anyone who has children has observed the charge that toddlers get out of mastering some new function so that they can perform on their own. No one seems to doubt that all children do this. Yet, for some reason, many therapists are quick to assume that overly dependent adult patients have completely lost this pride in self-reliance and actually enjoy acting in a regressive manner and constantly being babied. Again, it seems far more plausible to me that people never lose the desire to be autonomous, no matter how they seem to behave. As we shall see, the person's desire to express autonomy and the conscious sense of that autonomy that is a reflection of that desire are extremely vulnerable to the input of the family system.

At the early toddler stage of development, concerns about relationships with other people center more around the child's needs for human contact and mirroring and less around the actual value of the others as people in their own right. In the next stage of development, later in toddlerhood and beyond, the child's self is taken with a new concern, that of learning an expanded repertoire of behaviors that affect the people in the environment, rather than the inanimate objects. Though awareness that other people are separate and have an existence apart from the child's has already been present for some time, the understanding of that concept has previously been vague and of little concern or consideration. With the new stage, the child becomes interested in similarities and differences between people, the advantages of cooperative ventures, and gender role models. In the days before the women's movement, for instance, the child learned that daddies go off to work and mommies stay home and do housework and that girls play with dolls and boys do not. Children can become quite upset if people suddenly engage in activities that violate their expectations in this regard.

A child at this age continues to require mirroring and nurturance, and if they are not present, there develops an emptiness that has devastating consequences for the personality, as we shall see. Nonetheless, children's differentiation from the surrounding milieu continues to progress. Their interest in other people and their desire to understand what interpersonal relationships entail, and what their own place in the world is, flower unabatedly. Until a later stage, the understanding to which they come will depend largely on what the system shows them. However, they do experience new cognitions, emotions, and preferences, regardless of what their family is doing.

As children go on to later stages, they continue to learn

more and more about people, as well as more about how to be autonomous and about the shape and texture of the physical world. The objects of their cognitions, desires, and emotions may go through a great deal of change, but they remain within a certain range. The range of concerns enlarges as the process of separation and individuation goes on to each successive stage. In discussions of personality development, the next period is referred to by Freudians as the "latency" period. The idea that something is latent during this period may reflect, rather than the state of the libido, the fact that no new stages of self-development occur until the threshold of adolescence. During the latency years, the range of concerns of the child's self shows no new periods of expansion. It is not that new interests do not develop, but only that the way the child sees her or his relationship with the world remains constant. The level of the child's individuation from the system shows little advancement.

During this time, the true self demonstrates a relative lack of awareness of a reality outside that defined by the family and the people of whom the family approves. Preadolescent children generally accept their family's views and explanations regarding reality as gospel, with little or no propensity to question and develop their own view. Latency-age children are capable of understanding abstractly that some people see things differently from the way that their family does, just as teenagers are able to understand abstractly that they will eventually grow old and die. Such understanding just does not appear to be particularly relevant. It is a matter of little immediacy. Early in this period, children will often ask a lot of "why" questions and not appear to be satisfied with the answers; they do not think that the parents' answers are incorrect, just that there may be more to it. The child will accept much that goes on in the family system at face value, almost as a matter of definition. As an example, I can recall from my own experience being incredulous when a playmate informed me that he had two grandmothers. I had only one, since my father's mother had died before I was born, so I naturally assumed that everyone else did also. I was fully aware that everyone had a mother, but my father had never discussed his, and no one in the family had really explained what the relationship of a grandmother to a child was. The matter just had never arisen.

The view of reality that we are discussing here, which the child seems unable to seriously question, does not exactly correspond to what the system presents on a verbal level. Often, a parent will tell children a bold-faced lie, and they will not have the slightest bit of trouble seeing right through it, even though they have no world view of their own. An example of this is a lie told to a daughter about a death in the family. Fearing the child to be too young to understand, the parents may tell her that the deceased has moved away. The child will see the grief on everyone's face and perhaps overhear whispering about funeral arrangements and will easily be able to question what she has been told and conclude the truth. What she will not question, however, is what she has learned about such matters as how a family handles death and when it is permissible to lie. If she is presented with contradictory information on these matters, what follows is not questioning but confusion and apathy.

The world view of latency-age children is that of their own system, which includes the values of both the parents and the community at large. If there is a major clash between the values of the community and those of the family or a group of families, children may find themselves outcasts in their school, and the parents may be pressured to teach the more acceptable values. This pressure often borders on violence—and at times spills over the border. A subculture may choose to provide its own schools, as the Catholics have done, or the community may enforce some sort of segregation so that the schools can be slightly different from one another. If this sort of separating-out process does not occur, children will experience an unnerving level of cognitive dissonance that may alienate them from peers or perhaps their families. From which of the two they become alienated will be determined by the characteristics of the family system.

The transition to the next stage begins around the time of earliest adolescence and represents perhaps the most traumatic change of all in the level of connectedness between the individual and the family system. Many people view the various forms of rebelliousness that characterize this period as the means by which children tear themselves away from the family and form lives of their own as adults. While this may be true, I prefer a slightly different concept of the rebelliousness. I see it as one method of coping with a tearing-away process that occurs no matter how much the individual would rather it did not. Adolescents start to become aware, and indeed can not help but notice, that they and their families no longer see eye to eye on many matters of importance. Whereas disagreement had previously occurred over what the child should or should not be allowed to do, the adolescent now finds disagreement with the parents about what the world is really like. He or she may suddenly discover that legitimate questions exist about the parents' view on religion, politics, or the work ethic. The individual's true self has come into its own, with perceptions, emotions, and preferences unduplicated by anyone, no matter how close. The vehemence of the family in insisting that the adolescent see things its way instead of her or his own will determine the particular way that the adolescent copes with the change, but it cannot prevent the change from occurring.

The process of learning about oneself results in periods of search and exploration and periods of looking for some sort of external validation or mirroring. An individual has a need to know that difference or idiosyncrasy is not synonymous with insanity, and it is reassuring to know that one is not the only person in the world to see something in a certain way. During the periods of search for validation, teenagers band together with others of similar propensities to form cliques. These cliques often viciously exclude those who are different. This may seem at first glance to be similar to the process of exclusion during the latency period that I have described, but the clannishness of adolescence stems more from the individual than from the family system, although the latter certainly is not devoid of significant input.

The development and the separation-individuation of the self do not cease with the end of the adolescence–early twenties period. After this stage, the individual is a fully formed adult, but the process of growth has not yet reached its final major transition. I am referring to what has come to be known as the "midlife crisis," primarily described by popular writers such as Sheehy (1974). This crisis is an existential crisis in the true sense of the word, in which awareness of separateness becomes an awareness of the true nature of aloneness. Individuals become painfully cognizant that they are free and cannot be otherwise, that they are finite and surrounded by an unbridgeable gulf, and that they really are going to die in a future that no longer seems distant. The uniqueness, specialness, and unattached nature of the individual self begin to reach their full flowering, at least to the extent possible in this lifetime as we know it, much like a crystal that has just completely precipitated out of a solution.

During the midlife period and beyond, the suppression of self becomes a far more difficult affair. The sense of being embedded in a system, which previously protected us from a sense of isolation and the need for which provided the driving force for self-suppression, suddenly crumbles in front of us. The sense of disconnectedness and isolation brings with it a far more profound awareness of death than ever before experienced, which can be utterly terrifying. When one is merely a part of a great system, one is protected from a sense of one's mortality by the comfortable sense of belonging to something that will be ongoing despite the death of any individual component. A grandparent may die, but seldom the family, more rarely the community, and more rarely still the culture of which one is a part. After midlife, however, comes the realization that one is distinct from this system and will therefore come to a finite conclusion, at least as far as we know, even as the system continues onward.

The process of separation and individuation of the individual has, surprisingly, undergone an evolutionary change throughout the course of human history. This is the subject of the next section.

The Evolution of Human Culture

In his landmark book *Escape from Freedom,* Erich Fromm ([1941] 1969) noted the similarities between the emergence of the individual as a free, separate, and potent being and the evolution of human culture, which seems to advance in ways that allow human beings to emerge even further in that direction. In Europe and in some of its colonies, for example, culture has evolved from primitive tribes whose functions were limited to hunting, gathering, socialization, and reproduction, to the early city-states of Greece and Rome, to feudalism, to the Renaissance and the Reformation, to the democratic and capitalistic ideals of the American and French Revolutions, to the Industrial Revolution and the refinement of the concept of division of labor, and finally to the present technological society, with its explosion of subcultures revolving around highly specified vocational and leisure-time pursuits and its emancipation from governmental constraints on individual expression. At each level, human beings have become less dependent on the environment and more able to express their uniqueness, in a process highly analogous to the separation and individuation of both species and the individual.

A good way to understand the relationship of cultural evolution to the individuation of members of a culture is to think in terms of the phenomenon of interconnectedness discussed in the last section. A culture that evolves to a new level allows a loosening of the bonds of the individual to all larger holons (the family system, the ecosystem, and so on) at *each stage* of individual development. This is especially true of the stages from latency onward. Young adults in feudal society, for instance, were more similar in their level of differentiation from their society to modern latency-age individuals than to modern young adults.

The process of cultural evolution is not a smooth one, nor does it proceed at the same rate everywhere in the world. Different societies can be at very different stages at the same point in history. As civilizations rise and fall, the level of interconnectedness between individuals and the collective can ebb and flow. The level of individuation may decline remarkably, as it did when the Roman Empire collapsed, and may remain low for long periods of time. Cultures will always show some signs of both collectivism and individuation; the balance will vary. This can sometimes lead to rather curious mixtures of individualistic and collectivist traits in a given society, such as one can see in modern-day Japan. My point is that over the centuries, and all over the world, the balance has, overall, steadily shifted toward individuation. In the rest of this section, I will briefly mention several landmarks in individuation that have occurred in certain cultures at certain points in history.

In the primitive tribes of early humans, individuals felt as if they were one with nature, both animate and inanimate. This is clearly reflected in early religion, where the heavenly bodies, flowers, trees, and the soil itself were seen as spirits, not entirely unlike the spirit that was thought to inhabit the human body. Humans were dependent on the environment and reacted to it with little understanding. They felt themselves to be as much a part of the scenery as a rock or a river, and they were completely at the mercy of the elements. In describing this, one could say that people exhibited a relative lack of differentiation from the environment. The sense of the term *differentiation* in this description is precisely the same as in my discussions of species and individual evolution.

So, too, early humans showed little individuation in the sense I have used it in those discussions. In the daily fight for survival, there was little time for the pursuit of individual aims, and any one member of the tribe was, for the most part, interchangeable with any other member. Primitive hunter-gatherers banded together for the safety of all, but little division of labor occurred outside of the different functions of males and females, necessitated by the physical limitations and childbearing function of the latter. Whatever functions existed outside of the daily search for food were shared by all; specialization was unheard of. More advanced tribes would show somewhat more specialization, although it was still minimal. A tribe might have a leader and a medicine man, but that was about it. The needs of the tribe as a whole always took precedence over the needs of any one member. If the tribe had to pull up stakes and move to ensure its survival, and a member was too old or too sick to make the journey, he or she was left to die. No other choice existed, and it is doubtful whether anyone complained about it. People were more than willing to sacrifice themselves for the needs of the tribe; to do otherwise was unthinkable. This tendency carried over through time as the willingness of citizens of more advanced civilizations to "die for their country," an idea that was not widely or seriously questioned until as recently as the 1960s.

With the advent of agriculture and primitive tools, people began to have time to devote to matters other than the search for food, and the ties that bound them to their milieu were loosened considerably. They no longer had to battle the environment for daily survival; it was partially under their control. Housing, more elaborate clothing, furniture, and many other items came into use, and it soon became apparent that these things could be produced more efficiently by some than by others. People began to trade, bartering items that they had in excess for items that they lacked. Cities began to develop along with primitive manufacturing. Since enough food for all could be produced by only a segment of the population, and since some individuals were more talented than others at certain skills, being a jack-of-all-trades was no longer quite so important. Individuals became more specialized. A social order was established, with authority no longer equally shared but parceled out to the most powerful and the most able. Individual differences began to be of some consequence, although far less than today.

Specialization developed gradually. Early civilizations such as those of Egypt and Greece were rather homogeneous societies. In ancient Egypt, the necessity of controlling and exploiting the Nile River, which was ultimately the only source of subsistence in an otherwise hostile desert ecosystem, spurred the development of technology. A degree of hierarchy developed in Egyptian society because of the complexity of such tasks as monitoring the flood cycles of the river. A priestly class arose to administer the production and distribution of agricultural products. The leader of the country, the pharaoh, was thought of more as a god than a human being; all of the citizens of the country belonged to him. Individual lives meant almost nothing.

The caste system developed further in classical Greece,

with its citizens and slaves. The city-state replaced the tribe as the primary embodiment of the collective for the Greeks, and the relationship of the individual to the city-state was of crucial importance to them. However, the individual citizen could for the first time achieve a degree of specialness that would set him or her apart somewhat from the masses (Braver, 1983). The Greeks recognized unusual civic or military contributions to the city-state as marks of distinction. Any other claim to individuality, nonetheless, was considered to be arrogance and a challenge to the gods. A claim to uniqueness was a claim to be as worthy as a god. While such challenges may have been covertly admired by many Greeks, the common perception was that they inevitably resulted in tragedy. The myth of Icarus, who fell to his death because he flew too near to the sun, may have been a metaphor for this perception. In the Roman Empire, the homogeneity of society began to dissolve further. A more far-reaching division of labor developed. The needs of an empire that extended for hundreds and hundreds of miles and that contained an assortment of peoples with different needs and different cultures necessitated the development of a wide variety of trades and skills.

After the empire collapsed, the Middle Ages came. Life for most citizens in northern Europe and England in the early Middle Ages revolved around the manor. The manor house was a large building with one room in which the lord of the manor and all of his serfs resided. The lord of the manor provided food, shelter, and protection for the serfs. The manor was like an extended family. This happy state of affairs was altered when a climatic change led to colder temperatures in much of Europe. This change led to the invention of the chimney (Burke, 1978, pp. 155–161), which allowed buildings with more than one room to be heated, as the fireplace was no longer confined to the center of the building. The resulting architectural changes in the manor house had two dramatic effects on individuation. The first was the separation of the classes. As Burke (1978, p. 161) points out, "the ties between [the classes] that had been expressed in the act of sleeping together at a common fire each night were broken. The tightly knit, agriculturally based feudal world had gone up the chimney." Second, separate rooms allowed individuals a degree of privacy that had previously been unavailable and not a matter of much concern. People could sleep apart from the collective, they could keep secrets from each other more easily, and sex became part of a more personal relationship that was based on romantic love. Individual differences were somewhat freer to develop.

Fromm ([1941] 1969) discusses the level of individuation and freedom in the evolving feudal system of the Later Middle Ages and how this changed with the Renaissance. During medieval times, artisans were organized into guilds with rigid rules, which to a major degree blocked competition among the members of the profession. Such organization worked to the benefit of all, but it was a detriment to the forces of individuation. A class system with a pecking order developed, with boundaries that were, for the most part, impermeable. People not only were fixed at one level socially but seldom wandered geographically. While the various roles in society differed from each other significantly, variation among members in the same position was limited. Leisure time was in short supply, and societal rules dictated the exact manner in which one should engage in one's occupation. Consequently, opportunities for the expression of individual differences were nearly nonexistent. Fromm neatly describes this level of individuality: "A person was identical to his role in society; he was a peasant, an artisan, a knight, and not an individual who happened to have this or that occupation. The social order was perceived as a natural order, and being a definite part of it gave a feeling of security and of belonging." He goes on to state that "awareness of one's individual self, of others, and of the world as separate entities, had not yet fully developed" (pp. 58–59).

This description has much in common with the description that I have given of the state of the individuation of the self in the latency period of human development. Latency-age children accept the way their family has presented the world to them as the way the world naturally is, just as the member of feudal society viewed the social order as the natural order. Neither has an idiosyncratic viewpoint. Both the preadolescent and the guild member gain a sense of security and belonging as they accept their position in the family system/society, and neither has a great tendency to question the validity of the norms of their respective systems. Even the labeling of the early feudal period as the *Dark Ages* connotes an idea of lack of progression that bears more than a passing resemblance to one of the connotations of *latency*.

If the Middle Ages were the latency period of cultural development, then surely the Renaissance was its adolescence. Fromm calls it the beginning of modern individualism. He describes the rise of capital, individual economic initiative, and competition and the concomitant destruction of the feudal social structure. Self-expression through art and philosophy, initiative and ambition, came into its own. For the first time, individuals saw themselves as potentially separate from the social order. Just as adolescence is a period filled with turbulence, the changes of the Renaissance were accompanied by growing pains that were most severe. Even those who championed the emerging individualism of the period were careful to phrase their ideas in religious terms, which have collectivist connotations. Competition gave rise to ruthlessness, greed, and despotism; the destruction of the medieval social structure gave rise to new feelings of insecurity and isolation and, above all, anxiety. Large segments of the population attempted to stop or slow the new changes, leading to the emergence of that most peculiar creature, the political reactionary, who has been with us ever since.

The Reformation was an expression of the same forces of cultural evolution as the Renaissance, but for a different segment of society in different areas of Europe. It gave expression to the individual's wish to be free of the authority of the Catholic Church but at the same time offered an answer to the loneliness and anxiety that accompanied this new feeling of freedom. Martin Luther offered a religious view that was, in effect, a partial renunciation of individuation. As Fromm describes it, Luther's view of the relationship of human to God, the embodiment of the collective, was one of complete submission and self-humiliation. "If you completely submit, if you accept your own individual insignificance, then the all-powerful God may be willing to love you and save you. If you get rid of your individual self with all its shortcomings and doubts by utmost self-effacement, you free yourself from the feeling of your own nothingness and can participate in God's glory" (Fromm, [1941] 1969, p. 100).

My description of this historical period is necessarily skeletal, and I leave it to the interested reader to read Fromm's scholarly treatment of the subject in its entirety. I would now like to go on to touch briefly on what I feel was a landmark of separation-individuation in cultural evolution: the American Revolution and, later, the French Revolution. In the former, for the first time in history, a land broke decisively from its mother country (and I use the term *mother* because of all of its connotations) and established a government that was dedicated to the proposition that all men are created equal (later conceived to include women), with a constitutional guarantee of the inalienable right to life, liberty, and the pursuit of happiness. Of course, the American government has had a less than perfect record on these ideals. In some respects, such as the institution of slavery and the decimation of Native Americans, the record has been abysmal. However, for these ideals to be even considered was a startling historical development. The pursuit of happiness, for heaven's sake! If ever there were an individualistic concept, the idea of personal happiness is that. What a far cry from the times when the individual was expendable. Individual human life and individual needs were considered important to a degree hitherto unthinkable.

To be sure, limits on personal initiative for the sake of the common good were and are required more and more, but they have been placed more in the spirit of equal opportunity and cooperation than of collectivism. Individuals are economically interdependent; individual initiative must have some limitations for society to survive. However, the rise of individualism is not at all inconsistent with this interdependency. As people become increasingly specialized in their work, economic interdependency actually increases. We have come to a stage where people are more than ever before affected by events that transpire in remote corners of the world. In the United States, antimonopoly and labor laws prevented power from being concentrated in too few hands. This actually furthered the cause of individualism, because it allowed a greater number of people a chance at financial success.

The individualistic philosophy of American culture allowed for the first time anywhere a pluralistic culture, where immigrants with significant differences in religion, life-style, race, and even language could live with relative tolerance, if not total harmony. One might wish to rebut the idea that this has occurred to a noteworthy degree by pointing to the numerous examples of racial and religious strife in United States history, but one need only think of the examples of modern-day Lebanon, Northern Ireland, or even Quebec to understand how remarkable and unique a place the United States is in this regard.

The emphasis on the rights and mental state of the individual as opposed to the collective or the state is clearly a development that has not yet taken hold in much of the world. Throughout the globe, countries and sects remain that wish to recover or retain the sense of security and belonging that is often lost when a culture first evolves in the direction of which I am speaking. New freedom brings with it a new sense of uncertainty and doubt and of personal responsibility that may be frightening. People fear this freedom and run from it. Reactionary cults and cultures attempt to protect their adherents from these unpleasantries by abolishing the new individuality as much as possible and returning to a more communal and collectivist life-style. Examples that come to mind are the Amish in Pennsylvania, Hassidic Jews in Israel, and Shia fundamentalists in Iran. In all these cultures, emphasis on sacrificing personal gratification and ambition for the collective, or its embodiment in some sort of religious ideal, is paramount. These groups demand sameness in dress, manner, and philosophy, with the most extreme consequences for deviation. When a son of a Hassidic family, for instance, decides to flout tradition, his parents may begin to sit "shiva," a process usually reserved for the mourning of the dead. The child will be thought of from that point on as having died, and the family will have nothing more to do with him. The Amish have a similar process. The elders of the community can rule that members who are out of line be shunned and no longer allowed to sit and eat with their own families. In Moslem fundamentalist societies, the consequences are even more severe, with death a not uncommon punishment.

Each of these cultures exhibits a rabid puritanism when it comes to sex. The enforcement of gender role stereotypy and control of the sexual drive is a very important means of controlling individualistic self-expression. The development of methods by which sexuality can be divorced from its procreative function, with the resulting ability of human beings to do much as they please in this regard, allowed for a level of differentiation that was unnerving to those unaccustomed to such freedom. Even in the United States, freedom of sexual expression and the blurring and expansion of gender role models were slow in developing and are still greatly frowned upon in some quarters.

The ideology that has been put into practice in the Soviet Union and China is, to my mind, also a reactionary ideology, according to the criteria I am here discussing. Even though the situation there has been changing as elsewhere, sameness of dress, personal sacrifice for the good of the motherland, uniformity in art, fanatical puritanism, and conformity of political thought are all highly valued. Political dissidence is equated with insanity, and dissidents are imprisoned in psychiatric hospitals. The equation by the Soviets of disagreement with mental illness is really quite rational given a collectivist perspective; being differentiated enough to have an idiosyncratic viewpoint would make no sense. The idea that today's Communism is reactionary may seem amusing in light of the fact that Communists see themselves as the leading opponents of reactionary philosophies and social systems. Marxist theoreticians even argue for the historical inevitability of communism. However, given the trends of cultural and individual evolution, if anything is inevitable, then it is that communism will not progress in the manner predicted by the Marxists. Once individuals gain a taste of seeing themselves as separate from the social order and as of unique importance, they cannot unlearn what they have come to know. They may fear the freedom that accompanies this knowledge and pretend that all is as it was before, but like children who suddenly understand the concept of conservation, they see the world through new eyes. They have bitten into the apple, and, like Adam, they know that they must leave paradise. One reason that revolutions in the Third World today tend toward Marxism may be that the emerging nature of the societies in those countries is still relatively collectivist. These peoples have not had sufficient time, as have the Europeans and Americans, to adjust to the forces of individuation inherent in the industrial democracies.

Accompanying the advent of democratic ideals was the Industrial Revolution. New machines and manufacturing methods changed the way occupations and professions were structured. With the idea of the assembly line, people began to spend their time in very specialized ways, and the number of these ways began to grow. These developments continued into the next major stage in the development of individuation in its cultural context, the explosion of knowledge and technology. Because manufacturing and other human endeavors could now produce a vast, ever increasing number of goods and services, occupations were forced to become more specialized, and their number grew almost exponentially. Not only that, but the amount of knowledge in the various technical fields became so extensive that it took longer and longer for even specialists to learn, necessitating that they spend less time broadening their horizons by learning about areas outside of their immediate concerns. No two people came to have an identical formal education.

In the leisure realm as well, an abundance of new lifestyles created by both technology and the expansion of leisure time allowed for a wide variance among people, consistent with the evolutionary trend toward individuation of which I speak. We are now at the point where practically no two individuals show an identical pattern of interests and occupational pursuits. In his book *Future Shock,* Toffler (1970) refers to this idea as an explosion of subcultures and details the stresses involved in having too many choices. A sense of isolation often accompanies this newfound uniqueness. Being different from everyone else is a lonely position in which to find oneself. The sense of isolation has been increased by the global trend toward the concentration of large populations in the cities. In places such as New York and Los Angeles, it is possible to mingle with literally thousands of people at a shopping center or a sporting event without ever seeing one familiar face. Because of this sense of isolation, people have developed a tendency to band with others with at least one obsession in common and form groups completely organized around the activity. Not surprisingly, the sense of cohesion with others that results from belonging to such a group can at times discourage individuality. Members often start to expect extensive participation by all and resent those among their club who dabble in too many other hobbies.

Another point made by Toffler, which in fact is the central thesis of his book, is also central to the understanding of the relationship between cultural evolution, individual evolution, and the creation of psychopathology. "Future shock" refers to the difficulty that people have adjusting to rapid changes in their environment. Toffler points out that the rate of change and the transience of different ways of being have increased dramatically. So too, the rate of development of the separation-individuation process in human culture has accelerated. In a sense, this speeding up of the process of change is analogous to the way that the sense of time shrinks for the self as it reaches successive developmental stages. The difficulty that people experience in making rapid changes leads to the phenomenon that sociologists have labeled "cultural lag." A complete discussion of how this creates psychopathology will be the subject of a later chapter. In the following section, I address the question of how the biological propensity to be concerned with the survival of the species expresses itself at both the family systems and individual levels and then discuss what happens if an individual attempts to ignore this propensity.

The Survival of the System

Family systems theorists have long been fascinated with the concept of family "homeostasis." This term was borrowed from physiology, where an organism shows an inbred tendency to correct any deviation from a baseline steady state in the concentration of such body chemicals as hormones or electrolytes. A family is viewed by these theorists as a system that has an integrity all its own and that operates in a consistent and only slowly changing, sometimes inefficient manner. The manner in which the system operates is determined by a set of rules that specify how individual parts of the system are to contribute to the functioning of the whole. The reason why the machine chooses any particular overall function is often not addressed in detail by systems theorists, although the survival and continuation of the system through time are implicitly viewed as paramount goals. Some systems theorists do briefly discuss the idea that the family system may serve as a holon of a larger cultural system. If the survival and continuation through time of the culture and, by implication, the species are viewed as the purpose of the machine, then their view is not much different from the one advanced here, although I would add evolutionary considerations to the survival ones. In any event, the family system has been described as being governed by a strong need for homeostasis.

Human systems are believed to have developed mechanisms that oppose changes that might destroy the integrity of the system. This idea came from observation of families in therapy, where getting them to make changes in the rules by which they operate is an extremely difficult undertaking, just as getting an individual to make major changes in behavior is always a challenge. Since human systems, assuming their existence as defined, are composed of biological entities, the idea that they might function in a manner parallel to physiology is not entirely surprising.

If it be true that human systems dampen deviation in the functioning of the system so that change is difficult—and clinical experience gives us every reason to believe this to be the case —then we are again struck by the parallels between human systems and biological "motivation." In this case, the resistance to change can be seen as motivation toward a steady state, which presumably has survival value just as does a physiological steady state. Individual members of a system would be less likely to survive if they were to operate totally independently and unpredictably than if they all worked smoothly together for the good of all. The tendency of a family toward homeostasis is the mechanism by which the biological tendency to protect the survival of the species is expressed at the family level.

The reader may have noticed that the biological propensity of human systems toward a steady state appears to run directly counter to another biological propensity I have greatly stressed. I have mentioned repeatedly an innate biological tendency toward evolution. If family systems are governed by biological principles, then it is reasonable to consider the hypothesis that they too have a tendency to evolve. This is a particularly reasonable hypothesis in light of what we have seen regarding the evolution of human culture. Evolution is anything but a steady state. Evolution is change. The tendency toward family system homeostasis seems to put this biological propensity in direct confrontation with another one.

Systems thinking does allow for evolutionary changes in the organization of a family, although most theorists believe that the change must be caused at least in part by factors that operate outside of the system. Indeed, therapy would not be possible if this were not the case. Therapists function as such an outside factor if they can avoid being incorporated to too great a degree by the family system in treatment and thereby promote change in a system that would not occur in their absence. Likewise, the evolution of species is often prompted by input from "outside the system," such as major climatic changes over geological time, selecting for organisms that are better equipped to survive in the new milieu, or a mutation in a gene caused by random background radiation. Because of outside factors, evolution is possible even in the presence of homeostatic mechanisms. However, the presence of homeostatic mechanisms can clash with the tendency of biological systems to evolve. This is a major factor in the interaction between individual, family, and cultural evolution, as we shall see. For the moment, let us return to a consideration of the question raised at the beginning of this section.

Many systems theorists believe that individual behavior

can be understood by considering its function within the family system. Some of them go on to presume that individual behavior is completely determined by the way the system operates. Family systems therapists argue convincingly from clinical evidence that people always follow the dictates of their family system. They demonstrate how, in cases where individual behavior seems to be at variance with or independent of the family system, the behavior actually continues to exert a stabilizing influence on that system. This is true even if communication apparently no longer exists between the individual and the family. Nonetheless, if individuals do in fact always follow the dictates of their family systems, this does not prove that individual motivation apart from the system does not exist, nor does it prove that human beings must follow the dictates of the larger holon. What the observations of the family systems therapists do suggest is that systemic motivation seems invariably to *take precedence* over any individual concerns. If indeed the concerns of the system are survival and evolution, as I believe them to be, then the thinking of the systems theorist is consistent with my thesis that the individual organism has a strong desire to protect the survival and evolutionary interests of the family system. The tendency of the individual to wish to maintain homeostasis in the family is the mechanism by which the biological propensity to protect the survival of the species is expressed at the individual level. In sum, the major concerns of family systems and individuals parallel one of the major propensities of biological systems, survival of the species, through homeostatic and perhaps other mechanisms. This concern is something that motivates individuals in a most central manner.

The family system attempts to survive through the maintenance of homeostasis, but it also attempts to adapt to cultural changes. The individual gives priority to helping the family achieve this end as well. The biological propensity to be concerned with evolution also is expressed at the individual and family system levels, as we shall see. In the next section, however, I would like to answer the following question: What happens if individuals ignore their propensity to be concerned with the survival of the species? More specifically, what happens to individuals who ignore family homeostasis in order to express their individuation at a level that disturbs it?

Mirroring and Groundlessness

At the end of the section on human development, I discussed the experience of the so-called midlife crisis, when individuals can develop a new and far-reaching awareness of their ultimate disconnectedness and can come to terms with it to a far greater degree than they could earlier in the life cycle. Existential psychotherapists such as Yalom (1980) have referred to the experience of disconnectedness as the sense of existential isolation. Yalom's descriptions of this sense are eloquent. He speaks of a sense of loneliness that is independent of the presence or absence of other people. It includes a sense of being exposed to and surrounded by nothingness, as if the rest of the world had melted away and a person became all there is. A person comes to an awareness that, ultimately, all other people and, indeed, all things that are not "self" are strangers, and that one can experience them only temporarily and incompletely. The awareness of isolation brings with it an awareness of freedom. One begins to realize for the first time that one truly is responsible for one's own life. Yalom describes it thus: "Responsibility implies authorship; to be aware of one's authorship means to forsake the belief that there is another who creates and guards one" (p. 357).

One other aspect of existential isolation will be important in our understanding of the individual who attempts prematurely to individuate from the system. Yalom refers to it as "defamiliarization," or groundlessness. In the normal course of everyday life, we feel at home in the world; we feel connected. Everything in the world about us—objects, people, roles, values, ideals, symbols, institutions, and even the sense of who we are in relationship to the rest of the world—seems comfortable, familiar, and meaningful. This meaning is reassuring and provides a sense of belonging, for while it is to some extent personal, it more primarily collective. We share much of our sense of meaning with others in the particular systems in which we operate.

The more close and immediate the system, the more meaning is shared. Our world view will have the most in common with that of our family, somewhat less in common with that of our ethnic group or community, somewhat less still with that of our nation, and so on. This sharing of meaning gives us a sense that our view of things has a reality independent of our own existence and a sense of mooring, of walking on solid ground. The concept of collectively shared meaning is quite similar to Jung's concept of the "archetype."

Every so often, however, one gets a disturbing feeling that all is not well, that the outward appearance of the world disguises the fact that its meaning and purpose are not at all clear. This strange feeling is the sense of groundlessness. To again quote Yalom, we gain a terrifying sense that "everything could be otherwise than it is; that everything we consider fixed, precious, good can suddenly vanish; that there is no solid ground; that we are 'not at home' here or there or anywhere in the world" (p. 361). Life begins to seem absurd and pointless, utterly devoid of significant meaning. Pushing on with one's goals begins to seem like an exercise in futility; what's the use? All that one holds to be important takes on a cast of silliness and, ultimately, unreality. The sense of unreality brings with it something that is even more unnerving, if that be possible, than the sense of meaninglessness: doubt. If everything one holds to be gospel is not at all real, then perhaps what I think I know I do not know. And maybe it is just me. Maybe I am wrong, but everyone else is right. Maybe what I feel is invalid; maybe I am a nothing.

The relationship between doubt and autonomy described by Erikson (1963) is no accident. A sense of being valid and right is an absolute necessity for the sense of personal potency that leads to autonomy. One must have some confidence in one's goals in order to push forward sufficiently to reach them on one's own; one must feel that one's perceptions are real and that one's power is real. If one doubts one's reality, one feels hopeless and helpless, for any mastery one achieves becomes nothing more than an illusion, a false perception.

Where and how do we gain a sense of reality? I have

touched on this question earlier. In order to feel right and valid, children require some sense of consensual validation from the adults that surround them. They come into this world with no understanding of how it operates and are totally dependent on those around them to help them learn. Their selves have not yet developed to a point where they are assured enough to confirm by and for themselves the ideas about the world that they have formed; they are equipped neither intellectually nor emotionally. They need "mirroring" (Kohut, 1971). The selectivity of the parents' mirroring responses will for the most part be determined by what they themselves feel is valid, which in turn is determined by what their parents mirrored for them. Of course, a mother is usually at the stage in her own development where she knows that reality is not entirely identical to what her parents saw as reality. She may be comfortable expressing all or part of her own world view as distinct from that of her family of origin, or she may not. Which of these two states applies will also have been determined by the mirroring she received from her parents—as an adolescent.

When children reach adolescence and begin to reformulate their conceptions of the world, the individuation itself may or may not be mirrored by the family system. If it is not, the adolescent will have little or no consensual validation for holding views separate from those expressed by the family. Some mirroring may be provided by the child's extended family or by peers. Such mirroring, while meaningful, is at the present stage of cultural evolution not nearly as powerful as mirroring from the parents. The parents do not have to agree with the adolescent in order to offer consensual validation. What they must offer is mirroring of the idea that people can disagree and that both views are real, regardless of their ultimate truth. Validation of this idea can be quite selective; two views on one subject may both be seen as valid, but two different views on another subject may not. Once again I must add that individuation will take place regardless of whether it has been mirrored. What is missing if the mirroring does not occur is a sense of reality. If a person expresses individuation and it is not mirrored over time, an existential crisis results. She or he begins to experience groundlessness and meets face to face with existential isolation many years before having developed a capacity to cope with it.

The degree to which individuation is accepted by the family holon, and on which subjects, will be determined by how far that individuation can proceed before it causes other important family members to feel groundless themselves. If the individuated behavior of a family member leads to existential anxiety in the rest of the family, family homeostasis becomes threatened. The limits on behavior within the family system provided by this process take on the appearance of family rules of conduct. These rules appear to be "enforced" by the behavior of the whole family, but it is each individual self that decides to follow them. Often family members are unaware of the way that their behavior is being interpreted by other family members, although they are almost always aware of what the others will do as an immediate response.

What transpires when a family member breaks the "rules"? If a family member begins to express a world view in a manner that would upset the family homeostasis, the anxiety level of the entire family system begins to rise, signaling the offending member to back off. Increased systemic tension may be signaled in a number of ways but is ordinarily signaled by increased anxiety or depression in one or both of the parents or in the parents' relationship. They are the leaders of the system. Family members are exceedingly sensitive to the level of existential anxiety of the leaders of the family system. This kind of parental anxiety is not synonymous with increased parental agitation. Agitation can be due to existential anxiety, but it can also be due to anger or irritation. Anger is not necessarily a signal for the offending member to back off; it can even be a signal for the family member to push on, for reasons that will become clear later.

When offending family members get a signal that they have violated a taboo, they will ordinarily back off very quickly. They love and care about their parents and hate to see the parents or the parental relationship become unstable. They will become particularly alarmed if their self-expression begins to unmask significant covert parental discord. If the repressed conflict were big enough and were suddenly brought to the fore, the parental union and therefore the integrity of the family system would be at risk. Such a development is, of course, a major threat to family homeostasis. Another threat to the integrity of the system would occur if one parent became so disturbed as to become incapacitated. Since individuals value the survival of the system more than any idiosyncratic concern, they will be induced to commit acts of self-sacrifice.

They may attempt to keep to themselves the offending perception, preference, or emotion. If that does not work for one reason or another, they will attempt to repress it. If this still does not work, the individual will attempt to divert the wrath of the parents on to him- or herself, so that the parents will channel their anger toward the offending child, not toward their own selves or each other. Because of the biological propensity to be concerned with the survival of the species, individuals will do anything to avoid increasing the level of systemic tension in the family to a point where family homeostasis is threatened. They wish fervently to preserve the family system and to avoid the sense of groundlessness that would result from its destruction. However, the act of self-sacrifice will eventually backfire.

What happens if our offending individualist misses the signal from the family to back off and pushes forward with the expression of his or her alarming and homeostasis-threatening selfhood? When this occurs, the level of systemic tension rises, and the family will take more active steps to restore the status quo. They will begin to disqualify whatever thought, emotion, or preference is disturbing the system. A disqualification goes much further than mere disapproval; it involves the mirroring function. The family not only will refrain from mirroring or any other form of consensual validation, they will do the opposite. They will communicate to the errant family member that he or she is invalid, irrational, selfish, uncaring, stupid, and wrong, wrong, wrong. They will let it be known directly or indirectly that the offending view does not count for anything to anybody at any time or in any way.

This can be accomplished by verbal put-downs or, in

more disturbed families, by manipulations that disqualify in ways both subtle and confusing. These manipulations generally take the form of communicating to transgressors that they have not even been heard or that they have been misinterpreted. Watzlawick, Beavin, and Jackson (1967) described it thus: "disqualifications cover a wide range of communicational phenomena, such as self-contradictions, inconsistencies, subject switches, tangentializations, incomplete sentences, misunderstandings, obscure style or mannerisms of speech, the literal interpretation of metaphor and the metaphorical interpretation of literal remarks, etc." (p. 76). The effect of direct or indirect disqualification on people who are subject to it can be immediate and dramatic. Individuators quickly begin to feel cast adrift by their system, on their own, naked in the universe. Their convictions lose their firm footing in reality, and each begins to experience his or her entire selfhood as resting on shifting sands. While this experience can be described as a sense of being annihilated or becoming fragmented, it is actually the sense of groundlessness and existential isolation I have described previously.

I had occasion to be a passive observer of such an occurrence in a natural, nontherapy setting. The subject of the family disqualification, Laura, was attempting to confront her sister Janis about the sister's estrangement. Janis had refused to have anything to do with Laura, while maintaining that this had nothing to do with Laura personally. Attempts by Laura to get closer were met with rebuff and occasionally open hostility. Our subject wanted to express directly to Janis how much she was hurt by all this and to see whether the problem that was creating the hard feelings could be identified and then solved. The only opportunities for such a confrontation, if it were going to be face to face and not over the telephone, were during family get-togethers, which occurred only on birthdays and holidays. Since Janis refused to get together with Laura alone or outside of this setting, the confrontation had to occur in the presence of their mother, who was always present on these occasions.

As Laura was anxious to get the confrontation over with, she wasted little time in bringing up the problem, giving the confrontation an abrupt quality that made it more likely to fail. Janis immediately seized on this abruptness and used it to try to derail the potential discussion of the family dynamics to which the confrontation would surely lead. "You know, you're really something! You just won't let go of this. The minute you see me you start in on me. Just lay off, will ya!"

Laura quickly became defensive and started arguing that it was Janis who continued to make the issue by refusing to discuss it. Laura also became hostile and began to attack her sister in retaliation for what appeared to be an infuriating personal slur. She implied that perhaps the whole problem existed because Janis was mentally ill. "Maybe you should go into therapy to find out why you act this way!"

At this point, the mother jumped into the discussion on the side of Janis in a process that I refer to as clustering. The mother said that the subject was completely out of line. It was her birthday, and it was therefore not the right time or the right place to have a big family fight. (Of course, it was never the right time or the right place.) Laura immediately fell into shocked silence, unable to press forward with the confrontation. An attempt at a discussion of the family problem, referred to by communications theorists as "metacommunication," had stalled.

Laura was later asked why she had given up so quickly once the mother entered the discussion. "I suddenly felt like a nothing" was the reply. She was unable to describe this sense of being a "nothing" more fully, but it was clear that she felt as if her ideas were invalid and did not count for anything. She experienced a sensation of annihilation because the rug was pulled out from underneath her sense of personal potency; her ideas and perceptions were seen by her family system as off base and off-center. No consensual validation for her opinions was available to her; she was cut off from the universe with ideas that the rest of the universe told her belonged to her and her alone. How can one maintain one's rightness if one is out of step with the major component of one's world?

A patient described a similar experience prior to entering a major depression with psychotic features. "I felt my identity disintegrate. My career was in jeopardy. Little flags of doubt about what I was doing led to a depression. I felt like a zero." A patient who was experimenting with behaviors that had not been mirrored by her family, as well as stopping behaviors that were held necessary by her family, described a feeling that she was "neither fish nor fowl." Other statements made by patients that indicate existential groundlessness include the following: "I felt as if I were on a different plane from everyone." "I felt I was overstepping my bounds." "I felt disconnected." "There was a barrier between me and everyone else." Patients may complain of feeling "amorphous" or "undefined and void."

The difference between "intellectual" and "emotional" insight, described by therapists who use an insight approach, can best be understood through the use of the concept of existential groundlessness. Patients often seem to have great understanding of their own emotional processes that they cannot seem to utilize for purposes of changing their maladaptive behavior. This sort of insight seems to be different from that which can be used for the purpose of change. The difference in the two types of insight is not a cognitive one at all but can be explained by the difference between understanding that induces existential anxiety and understanding that does not.

The refusal to mirror an expressed aspect of the self of one of its members is one way in which a family can induce a sense of groundlessness in that member. A second way that this type of anxiety can be induced is perhaps even more important in discussing psychopathology. In many cases, parents have an apparent need for a child to behave in a way that does not follow the natural inclinations of the self of the child. This occurs most commonly when parents have suppressed an aspect of themselves in order to maintain homeostasis in their family of origin. If the child acts out the suppressed aspect, the parents gain vicarious satisfaction of the suppressed impulses. They thereby gain some relief from the urge to express the forbidden aspect, and their persona or act is stabilized. The anxiety level of the parents and the whole system decreases, at least temporarily.

In this sort of situation, children gain mirroring and con-

sensual validation if they put on an act and receive none if they
do not. They experience groundlessness if they do not accept
the job of maintaining family homeostasis in this way and are in
a sense rewarded for suppressing themselves in order to play a
role. The mirroring they have received is faulty, because it is an
act that is being mirrored and not true self, but the groundlessness that results from the absence of mirroring is highly distressing nonetheless. I will be discussing examples of this shortly.
One additional point I would like to make here is that the parent does not literally make the child put on the act; the parent
may, in fact, not really like it at all. The child puts on the act
voluntarily in order to follow her or his propensity to be concerned with family homeostasis and avoid existential groundlessness. The conceptualization of this process in the manner I
have outlined is a slightly different way of understanding what
analysts refer to as "projective identification."

Just how important consensual validation really is was
demonstrated in the famous studies by Asch (1951, 1952,
1956), although his intent was to demonstrate the power of
group pressure to induce conformity of judgment. In these experiments, he ingeniously hired a naive subject to participate in
an experiment in which groups of people were asked to make
judgments regarding which of three lines was equal in length to a
reference line. The task itself was obvious and unsubtle; the
lines differed in lengths by from a quarter of an inch to an inch
and three-quarters. Seven to nine men were placed in a group;
each member of the group was asked in turn and in the presence of the rest to make the required judgment. Unbeknownst
to the naive subject, all the other participants in the experiment
were shills of the experimenter. The shills were all instructed to
give, unanimously, an incorrect response on some of the trials.
The groups were arranged so that the subject was one of the last
participants to perform the test, so that he would be in direct
opposition to the other participants if he chose the correct answer. In the first experiments, an astonishing 37 percent gave an
answer that conformed to the majority opinion. In interviews
following the trials, none of the subjects reported being unconcerned with the majority position, and most questioned their

own judgment, not that of the others. Most of the subjects who did not conform also added that they experienced a longing to be in line with the rest of the group.

In extrapolating these results to what might occur in a family system, two points must be kept in mind. First, the line judgment task is straightforward, with right and wrong answers that are unambiguous and obvious, with no room for nuances of interpretation. Second, the naive subject did not know the shills, and presumably they were of no emotional relevance or importance to him. If it were possible to design an experiment in which the task was open to many possible interpretations and the majority were important family members, I would predict with confidence that the percentage giving a conforming answer would be far greater, and the individualist would experience a lot more distress than just a sense of longing!

In sum, the answer to the question posed at the beginning of this section is that the result of ignoring the homeostatic needs of the family system is the experience of groundlessness. The distress of groundlessness seems to be something that is described only by intellectuals such as existential philosophers but is actually quite widespread. It is not often explicitly described precisely because people go to whatever means necessary to avoid it. It is seldom experienced for long periods of time. The common psychotherapeutic fallacy that, because compulsive behavior is done invariably, therefore the person is incapable of ceasing it has its roots in the fact that groundlessness is just about the most unpleasant sensation one can experience. Compulsive behavior is a tenacious form of role playing that, if stopped, exposes the individual to the unmirrored, groundless state that I have described. Therefore, the compulsive refuses to stop it in all situations and appears to be incapable of stopping. The groundlessness sensation, if experienced full force, is far more unpleasant than almost any physical or emotional torture, and if one has to be tortured in order to avoid it, then choosing torture is a rational alternative.

This brings us to the subject of self-sacrifice, the subject of the next chapter.

3

SACRIFICE

OF THE SELF

Under certain cultural or societal conditions, individuals will attempt to consistently and invariably act and think in ways that run counter to the natural inclinations of their true selves. They will do so in order to pretend to be something that seems to decrease the overall level of existential anxiety felt by other members of the family system. They will literally sacrifice themselves in order to restore the homeostatic functioning of the family collective. In this chapter, I will describe in detail the nature of self-sacrifice and discuss the mechanisms by which the true self is hidden. I will also show how self-sacrifice damages not only the person making the sacrifice but also the individuals within the system for whom the sacrifice is made. I refer to this phenomenon as the altruistic paradox.

The Altruistic Paradox

One of the central points of this volume is that self-destructive behavior can best be understood by viewing it as a form of sacrifice for the seeming good of others, rather than as something that is done for the benefit of the self. The altruistic paradox posits that self-sacrifice is the major cause of all dysfunctional behavior and thus is a highly significant component of many other forms of human misery. People engaged in self-sacrifice will invariably wind up doing severe damage not only to themselves but also to those people whom they are trying to help (Rand, 1961). The son who attempts to become a violinist so that he might follow the dreams of his father when his true nature would direct his career aspirations elsewhere not only damages his own prospects for self-realization but will eventually damage his father as well. In attempting to make his father feel better, he will be hard pressed to avoid, ultimately, making him feel worse. At the same time, the son's sacrifice will, in the long run, increase the overall level of anxiety and distress in his entire family system.

   Before explaining the seemingly noncommonsensical proposition that attempting to help others through self-sacrifice harms the person for whom the sacrifice is made, I must first clarify what I mean by the term *self-sacrifice.* An understanding of what is meant by self-sacrifice is essential in order to prevent conclusions being drawn from the paradox that are not only erroneous but extremely destructive. What the altruistic paradox does *not* say is that the act of giving to others per se, even at one's own expense, produces human suffering. The altruistic paradox does not justify a "me first, to hell with everyone else" attitude. It is not a justification for social Darwinism or fascism. Strangely enough, the altruistic paradox is precisely what leads to such attitudes. Sacrifice of the self, as I use the term, is what leads to the cruelty of humans to their fellow humans. This is the essence of the paradox; this is what makes it paradoxical.

   If self-sacrifice is not the same as giving to others at one's own expense, what then is the difference? What I mean by self-sacrifice corresponds to the first type of Jung's "alienations" of the self. It is the *consistent* camouflaging of characteristics of one's own basic nature in order to fill a role in one's family or culture that seems to make the rest of the family or cultural system more comfortable. Self-sacrifice is the attempt to change oneself like a chameleon, so that one appears to be what significant others seem to require in order to maintain their own equilibria. It is the process of developing a pseudo, false, or pretend self.

This formulation raises a question of definition that requires further elaboration. Does an act of self-sacrifice take place each and every time we ignore our own propensities in order to please other people or serve the needs of the collective? The answer to this question is an emphatic no. In fact, cooperation with and concern for others frequently enhance the functioning of our true selves. Self-sacrifice is not synonymous with the temporary suppression of the self. We all have certain collective obligations and considerations with which to concern ourselves that are entirely right and valid. In order to fulfill these, we must temporarily avoid paying attention to our natural inclinations, and not just on infrequent occasions. A construction worker cannot leave those who have hired him in the lurch because he feels like dropping everything and taking a nap; a physician cannot stop surgery in the middle of an operation because she develops a sudden urge to listen to Beethoven. The completion of necessary tasks often involves temporary inattention to our inner callings. Civilization and our very survival, let alone the predictability of our world, would be severely compromised if everyone behaved exactly according to her or his every whim at any given moment. The act of suppressing our desires in order to meet social responsibilities does not necessarily constitute self-sacrifice and is not the major factor in the development of human behavioral dysfunction to which I have alluded.

Often our true selves will temporarily wish to act against our own natural inclinations and desires, and even go without something we really might like, in situations where this activity is neither expected nor absolutely necessary for civilization or survival. We might wish to do this in order to please someone we care about, right what we perceive to be a social wrong, or better the lot of others. This kind of activity may or may not be an example of damaging self-sacrifice, depending upon whether in doing it we are attempting not only to ignore but to eradicate our own natural inclinations and pretending to be something we are not. We can give to others at our own expense without going as far as that, so such giving does not in itself represent self-sacrifice.

Suppression of characteristics of self becomes unhealthy self-sacrifice, damaging to self and others, when a person attempts to suppress them in a more global fashion. Self-sacrifice involves the complete eradication of thought, preference, and emotion, in addition to the absolute and permanent suppression of a particular behavior. When individuals do this, not only do they often behave in ways that contradict their natural tendencies, they always try to appear to *want* to behave this way, whether they truly do or not. Acting this way in order to decrease the anxiety of someone else is something that goes way beyond giving at one's own expense and is the behavior to which the altruistic paradox applies. I would now like to add one further point to the discussion of the definition of self-sacrifice, one that is important in understanding much of what follows in this book, by an analysis of its opposite. Let us take a closer look at self-expression.

The experience of a thought or emotional state is not the same thing as the behavior that occurs in response to it. This statement may appear to be obvious, but the confusion between experience and behavior is widespread and pervasive. Many patients in therapy often unnecessarily fear anger because they tell themselves that anger is, in a sense, synonymous with yelling, counterattacking loved ones and in the process hurting their feelings, or even becoming physically violent. In actuality, when people are angry, there is a large variety of behavioral options among which they can choose. For instance, without attempting to eradicate the existence of the angry feelings, one can choose to do nothing. This is a very difficult option, to be sure, because anger leads to a rather unpleasant state of physiological arousal that almost seems to demand some sort of physical action. Nonetheless, it is possible to remain quiet and to direct one's behavior toward lessening the physiological arousal rather than the anger. One might hit a punching bag, for example.

A second option, the one thought by many to be the only one, is acting out the anger. Acting out refers to a nonverbal or sometimes verbal communication made by the angry person toward the person to whom the anger is directed. This communication can take a number of forms, all of which are subsumed under the rubrics, used by assertiveness trainers, of "aggressive" and "passive-aggressive" behavior—violence, verbal abuse, covert revenge, abandonment, and so forth (Alberti and Emmons, 1974). A third option, clearly superior to the others, corresponds to the "assertive" category of behavior described in assertiveness training. This consists of an attempt by the angry person to engage in a productive verbal exchange with the object of the anger. The goal is expressing the involved feelings in such a way that the offender will understand the problem without feeling unduly besmirched. If this is done well, the offender will often then modify the anger-provoking behavior in such a way that mutual satisfaction can result.

In short, once an emotion or thought occurs, it can be expressed in a number of ways that do not involve self-suppression, only one of which is "acting out." Self-sacrifice occurs when individuals attempt to avoid any and all forms of expression of certain aspects or characteristics of themselves. As one might infer from the above discussion of self-expression, the task of not expressing oneself is fraught with extreme difficulty. Many psychological theorists believe that true characteristics of the self press for behavioral expression of some sort. The proposition of the existence of a "drive" toward the true self that causes the individual to experience a strong urge to express it, however, does not provide us with an accurate and complete description of what is taking place.

The problem is that *any* behavior is a form of self-expression, and it is impossible not to behave. Pretending to think thoughts one does not believe or feel emotions one is not experiencing is behavior. More problematic still, any attempt to express oneself that represents an effort at concealing the true nature of the self automatically uses the true nature of the self as a referent. In other words, the concealing behavior is directed toward that which is being concealed. Therefore, the true nature of the self is part and parcel of all behavior. All behavior, no matter how well the concealment is performed, contains an expression of the true self. It is literally impossible for anyone to be other than himself or herself. Since it is also impossible not to behave, this also means that it is impossible for the true self not to express itself. One does not have a "drive" to be one-self or to express oneself. One *is* oneself, and one cannot help but express it.

No matter how people feel about their thoughts, the fact remains that they think them. Nevertheless, people often have a strong desire to hide the true nature of the self. When an aspect of the self is to be kept hidden, the individual is forced to use extreme devices to effect the charade. These devices are similar to the psychoanalytical concept of defense mechanisms. Primary among the defense mechanisms described in psychoanalysis is repression, or relegating an offending impulse (or, as I am arguing, any undesirable aspect of the true self) to the "unconscious." In simple terms, people forget the aspect of themselves and claim either that it does not exist or that they are unable to bring it to mind. They deny that it was ever even there. Analysts often seem to refer to the "unconscious" as if it were a place or a thing to which offending aspects of self are sent. Cognitive therapists lean more toward viewing it as a matter of selective inattention, with the inattention itself being ignored. A better understanding of the unconscious can be had through a metaphor that I call the "actor's paradox."

In every way, pretending to be, feel, and think other than the way one truly does is comparable to an actor playing a role. The most popular method for teaching acting in widespread use today is "method acting." An actress attending acting school has to learn to suppress her real self, as much as possible, in order to play the role of the character she is portraying in a convincing manner. She must trick the audience into believing that she really *is* the character she is portraying, even if her out-of-character face is already familiar from other contexts. Individuals who are not in the acting profession but who are nevertheless attempting to trick the rest of a family into believing that they are or are not a certain way must likewise be extremely convincing, or they will defeat their purpose. In method acting, an actor is taught that the way to be most convincing is to imagine that he has truly *become* the character. In order to do so, the actor must convince himself that, as this character, he is really experiencing the emotions and events that are going on in the script. This is a paradox because the actor continues to know that he is himself, not the character.

Analogously, in order to convince the rest of the family system, self-sacrificers must act as if they truly believe that they and their roles are one and the same. They too must convince themselves that they really are experiencing the emotions or preferences that they are pretending to experience. At some level, of course, they know they are putting on an act. They certainly will not tell you this. If they are at all convincing, they will not in the least appear to be acting. This idea adds a new perspective to the reason behind why a psychological theorist is making a logical error whenever he or she assumes that just because a person never seems to engage in a behavior, that person is incapable of doing so. One can never know for sure whether the apparent inability is an act. Until we discover a way to read minds that can also reveal ideas currently not under the attention of the subject, this limitation will always remain.

Acting terminology is widespread throughout the literature of several forms of psychotherapy, used in ways that are entirely consistent with the sense of the actor's paradox. Transactional analysts speak of a "script," which is defined as a life plan given to individuals by their families to play out for the rest of their lives (Steiner, 1971). As previously mentioned, Jung speaks of the "persona" as a mask that individuals put on or a role that they play out in order to fulfill a collective obligation. Behavioral and Gestalt therapists use "role playing" as a therapeutic tool, and "psychodrama" (Moreno, 1985) is another commonly seen treatment modality. The act that is played can be likened to several concepts used by psychotherapists: "character armor," "as-if personality," and "false self."

Now that I have described what I do and do not mean by self-sacrifice, I am in a better position to discuss the altruistic paradox. How can it be that an act performed in order to help decrease the anxiety of others invariably damages them? In what way does it harm them? The myriad of forms that this harm can take will be clarified in later chapters, but so that the reader can attain an initial understanding, allow me at this point to develop a worst-case scenario. Let us imagine a man who believes that service to others is the be-all and end-all of human existence. Suppose he believes that taking anything, no matter how trivial, from anybody for selfish purposes is not only mean spirited but evil and sinful as well. Since we are all by nature at least minimally gratified by creature comforts, and since the acquisition of many of the creature comforts we enjoy invariably involves at least some partaking of the productions and capabilities of other people, a man who wishes to completely dedicate himself to living according to the above proposition must of necessity engage in a good deal of self-sacrifice. Even the thought of a selfish desire, let alone behaving in any way that might be considered to be parasitic in any conceivable fashion, would be abhorrent to such a man, both because of his beliefs about such thoughts and because it might interfere with his altruistic behavior.

This imaginary man undoubtedly goes around telling everyone, possibly because he is not all that convinced himself, that giving to others is life's most rewarding experience. He is, in fact, usually correct when he makes this assertion. However, he also believes that it is sinful to take for himself anything that anyone else might offer. He is, in effect, *depriving everyone else of the one activity that he himself identifies as life's greatest reward!* He allows no one else the pleasure of giving to him, thereby reserving entirely for himself the right to engage in the activity he lauds. In addition to becoming, paradoxically, selfish in this respect, our fantasy altruist harms others in yet another way. He makes them feel guilty. His holier-than-thou attitude makes others feel guilty that they are unable to be as altruistic as he is.

One major effect of many acts of self-sacrifice is damage to the sense of personal potency in the person for whom the sacrifice is made. The other person is often treated as someone who cannot tolerate anxiety, who cannot fend for herself or himself, who is too weak to take being exposed to uncomfortable situations, or who is cruel enough to prefer to make others suppress themselves. People's sense of their own effectiveness and inner worth is diminished by most acts of self-sacrifice made on their behalf by another family member.

By modifying my worst-case scenario, I would now like to show how damage occurs through altruistic self-sacrifice at the family systems level. Instead of a person who tries to give to everyone, let us now imagine a married couple who believe that it is the duty of parents to give everything they can to their children and accept nothing in return. These parents attempt to anticipate and, immediately if not sooner, fill their child's every need, no matter how insignificant. They are willing to buy their own clothes at the dime store if need be so that their child can dress in the latest fashions. In fact, they will literally give their child the shirts off their backs whenever asked. They attempt to shelter the child from as much of life's adversity as they possibly can and consider themselves to have failed to live up to their obligations as parents if the child should ever feel bad about anything. Let us suppose further that the parents who share these beliefs live during a time when the virtues of selfishness are being extolled by the media. All around them are magazine articles and television shows describing the exhilaration of females liberated from the caretaking role, the pleasures of acquisitiveness enjoyed by young urban professionals, and the satisfied feelings of the "me generation."

What becomes of the child in such a situation? Keep in mind that a child's sense of potency starts out with a major strike against it even in the presence of the most perfect parenting possible. A child comes into the world in a completely helpless state. One of the major results of proper parental mirroring is the development in the child of a sense of personal potency, self-esteem, and self-respect. In situations with a favorable outcome, the blessings of powerful, godlike parents are bestowed upon the emerging environmental mastery of the child's budding self. If a daughter's increasing control of her world and her enlarging ability to take care of herself are not mirrored, she is never quite sure of the reality of them, and a constant sense of inadequacy will plague her every move. An early boon to her developing sense of personal mastery occurs when she becomes able to do something that pleases or in other ways positively affects those around her on whom she is ordinarily dependent. If she can do something for the gods, then by definition she is not as helpless as she once was and thought herself to be. If this new power is mirrored, she comes to appreciate that she has the ability to help others who are far more powerful than she. She will feel very pleased with herself.

What then of a child of our worst-case-scenario parents? In this instance, a previously helpless son with a shaky sense of his own significance would be confronted with parents who refuse to allow him to do anything for them; he receives no mirroring for being able to be helpful. His parents refuse to allow this because it violates their conviction that a parent is supposed to take care of a child, not the other way around. If their son wants to pick out a gift for them, they beg off or say that they expect nothing. If he wants to help around the house, the parents end up taking over the chore in one way or another. He begins to feel rather useless; he begins to think he has nothing worthwhile to give. Not only is he prevented from doing things for his parents, he is also prevented from learning how to do very much for himself. No sooner does he experience discomfort than his parents step in to remedy it, so he does not learn how to be resourceful or to tolerate pain. If he fights with a sibling, the parents step in to stop it, so he does not learn how to settle differences with others. They never let him fail, so he does not learn how to succeed. The child of such parents begins to develop a lack of confidence in his ability to function autonomously.

The feeling of powerlessness to help self or others in the child would be bad enough by itself, but it is hardly the only result of the kind of parental behavior I am describing. The feeling of inadequacy that is generated unfortunately has the nasty side effect of generating a good deal of resentment and anger as well. Despite the common misperception that being constantly babied and protected is a rewarding experience, the actual effect of being overprotected is the unpleasant sensation of having one's legs cut out from underneath. If a daughter in this predicament expresses her resentment about being treated like an incompetent, parents who believe in sacrifice for the sake of the children usually begin to feel inadequate. Their child is telling them that she is unhappy. They have failed. If only they were

better parents, their child would be content. Since their definition of a good parent is one who does things for children, they
attempt to make up for their deficiencies by doing even more.
This, of course, makes their child feel even more inadequate, in
a vicious circle. She quickly learns that any direct expression of
anger toward her parents not only makes them depressed, it
exacerbates the very process she is protesting.

The parents do not escape from these negative developments. The daughter attempts to hide her anger, but children
have not had sufficient time to develop their acting skills. The
parents cannot help but notice that their child seems to be resentful toward them, even though she is attempting to hide it.
The resentment is inexplicable to them. Are they not doing
everything possible for their child? Have not they made sufficient sacrifices for her? They begin to feel unappreciated. They
begin to resent their child right back. The resentment the parents feel toward the child increases exponentially from that
point because of a second, outside factor—the messages that the
parents are receiving from the outside world. Self-actualize! Be
assertive! Go for it! Live with all the gusto you can! Search for
personal fulfillment and do not stop until you find it—and no
mere housewife and mother can really be fulfilled! Individualistic messages seem to scream out at the parents from all sides at
once. These messages conflict with the value system of the parents as much as any messages can ever conflict, but nonetheless
they do hold for anyone a certain degree of attractiveness. They
are indeed seductive, tempting, even reasonable. The parents
start to question the validity of the sacrifices they have made
and cannot help but feel that they have missed out on something. If only they had had no children at all, all of this self-
denial would have been unnecessary. Life is passing them by.
What a drain and a burden those lovable kids really are. They
get everything and we get nothing. Damn them!

The altruistic parents are naturally appalled by the
thought that they might despise and at the same time envy their
own children. Given their value system, such a thought is hor-
rifying, nay, unthinkable. It just cannot be. What would the
child think? The parents are forced to put on an act of their

own. Because of their altruistic self-sacrifice, these parents have created a situation where everyone is a loser. They have made both themselves and their child completely miserable, all in the name of being helpful. In a later chapter, I will argue that my "worst-case scenario," rather than being a reductio ad absurdum argument, is in fact a quite common phenomenon in the American culture in the middle to late twentieth century and is the major cause of the borderline personality syndrome. I will later show how and why children born of this situation develop pseudo-selves of their own in order to solve their dilemma.

The fact that "borderlines" are putting on a purposeful act and are quite aware of what effect their behavior is having on others was driven home to me during the psychotherapy of the first patient I ever treated in my residency training. She had been assigned to me after having spent almost a year in therapy with another resident, who happened to have been a woman. As borderlines are wont to be, she was especially distraught at having to change therapists, and she was particularly miffed at having been assigned a male therapist. During this period of emotional turmoil, she behaved as if the prior physician was the ideal therapist, perfection personified, while I was undoubtedly the worst doctor who ever disgraced the face of the earth. In the process of splitting her two therapists into the good female therapist and the bad male therapist, she simultaneously undid any good that the prior therapist had done and any potential good that I might have done. The "good" therapist was actually bad because she had abandoned the patient. Worse still, she had left *me* as her replacement. As for me—well! I was totally useless in her eyes.

Sensing my inexperience, she zeroed in for the kill. In the first few sessions, she correctly pointed out that I did not know what I was doing and added that I was damaging her. She criticized everything about me, from my speech to my looks. This was definitely a trial by fire for me. My first patient was spending our entire initial sessions insulting me. If it had not been for the fact that the head of the clinic insisted that she work things out with me, while providing me with excellent supervision in the meantime, she would have switched to a third resident.

With great difficulty for us both, she and I stuck it out. After a time, we actually began to make some progress. By the end of the year, she managed to consolidate gains from both her previous therapist and myself. When she had settled down and worked in the therapy, she stopped splitting and began to react to me on a realistic level.

The end of the training year came upon us, and she was then faced with yet another termination experience. At that point, she admitted that, at the beginning of therapy, she had consciously and purposefully tried to be just as mean to me as she possibly could. She apologized for her rude behavior. Then— and this was the eye-opener—she told me how impressed she had been with me *at the time* because I had put up with her garbage and had not dismissed her from therapy at once! How might I have seen through the ruse much sooner than I did? In the next section, I will examine methods for finding the real self behind the camouflage.

Unmasking the Self

Since people are so into deception, not only of others but of themselves as well, determining the motivation behind human behavior is an extremely difficult thing to do. Indeed, how is it possible to know for sure whether the assertion that we are all actors is even true? The various psychotherapies all seem to implicitly believe that what people say about themselves is not always what is really true. Still, since we cannot read minds, how can we ever really know that a subterfuge is occurring? The answer to this question resides in my earlier assertion that it is always impossible to completely hide the true nature of the self. Individuals will always do something, no matter how subtle, that if noticed gives them away. Indeed, this is how Freud came up with the idea of "unconscious" behavior in the first place. Experience in psychotherapy of all sorts later confirmed this, though many therapies do not refer to the difference between overt and covert behavior as residing in an "unconscious."

How, then, does a therapist get at the truth? One method that I have found useful is the refusal on the therapist's part

simply to believe an assertion that is ludicrous on the surface.
This does not always work, but it works often enough. For instance, I once began treating a young woman for a second episode of anorexia nervosa. Although the woman had remained
quite thin since the first episode, she had not been starving herself for quite a number of years. We began discussing the first
episode, wherein the patient had become so severely emaciated
that she had been in very real danger of starving to death. The
patient related that she had been hospitalized and had been very
annoyed that people seemed to think that she was crazy. Nonetheless, she absolutely insisted that she had not been aware that
she was as thin as she now knew herself to have been. I told
her that I agreed with her in that I knew beyond a shadow of a
doubt that she was not crazy. I also observed that she was also
quite bright. How, then, would it have been possible for her not
to have known that she was too thin? She insisted that she just
had not been aware that this was the case. I looked at her in-
credulously for several seconds. Finally she looked down at the
ground and said, "Well there was one time that I looked down
at my arms and saw the veins popping out and asked myself,
'What are you doing to yourself?' "

I would now like to briefly discuss some of the information-gathering methods used traditionally by the major psychotherapeutic schools in their attempts to understand human
motivation. The implicit assumption behind all of these methods is, once again, that what people say about their motivation
may differ significantly from the truth. I believe that all of the
traditional methods can function to sort out true self from
persona.

In *psychoanalysis* and psychoanalytically oriented psychotherapies (Langs, 1973; Greenson, 1967; Sloane, 1979), the
primary investigative technique is the search for metaphors in
free association, dreams, and the transference situation. The
analyst listens for indirect or hidden references to thoughts and
feelings that are not explicitly described by the patient. Dreams
contain symbolic references to these unwanted aspects of self,
and the analyst tries to translate them. Unexpected defensive reactions or feelings about the therapist that interfere with treatment can signal that the therapist has touched on an area that

the patient would rather avoid. Parapraxes, or the well-known "Freudian slips," also expose the patient's true feelings.

Gestalt therapists often pay close attention to body language. Discrepancies between verbal content and nonverbal behavior often indicate a discrepancy between the message that the patient verbally conveys to the therapist and the patient's true feelings.

Behaviorists attempt to ascertain the environmental stimuli that cue the client to exhibit maladaptive behavior (Wolpe, 1973). The behaviorist uses a "behavioral analysis." Clients keep a record of what exactly has been going on whenever they find themselves exhibiting the behavior in question. The behaviorist assumes that the trigger that elicits the behavior is invariably present immediately before the behavior occurs. Behavioral analysis can provide clues as to what clients are "really" reacting to whenever they behave in certain ways, even when they indicate some other reason.

In *family systems therapy,* the therapist observes the family interaction firsthand in order to discover discrepancies between overt and covert directives. One or both of these conflicting directives issued toward a family member can be expressed nonverbally, and they often are. For this reason, the family therapist, like the Gestalt therapist, pays close attention to body language and nonverbal signals. The family therapist also gets at hidden truth by observing the results of verbal directives. If a family member reacts in a way different from what one might expect from the content of the conversation, this is a clue that something is not what it seems to be. These methods can be used to distinguish between true self and persona for each individual in the system. The therapist can assume that the reason individuals within the system give out contradictory messages is that they are experiencing a conflict about how to behave or about what they expect from the others.

In the following sections, I will look at some nontraditional methods for differentiating true self from persona.

Polarized Behavior. When individuals choose to suppress aspects of their true selves in situations where they are ambivalent about doing so, they must constantly be on guard. They must pay scrupulous attention to their every whim and thought, so that any taboo desire is screened out before it has a chance to influence their overt behavior. One way to make this monumental task somewhat more simple is through the adoption of habitual behavior that is the opposite of the wishes of the true self. If people rigidly and compulsively engage in behavior consistent with a role, they are less likely to behave spontaneously. They behave as if on automatic pilot. The role behavior seen in this type of situation is usually an extreme version of the role that the individual has chosen, sometimes nearly to the point of self-parody. The reason for this is that extreme behavior is less likely to contain elements of the behavior it is covering. Of course, as I mentioned earlier, total elimination of the camouflaged self-aspects is an impossibility.

The process of adopting a habitual, compulsive behavior that is the opposite of a true desire corresponds to the psychoanalytical concept of the defense known as "reaction formation" (Freud, 1966), albeit with a modification. When I refer to "compulsive" behavior, I am referring not just to those behaviors ordinarily seen in obsessive-compulsive disorders and addictions but to all behavior that is done invariably. Psychoanalysts usually refer to reaction formation in terms of behaviors that are seen in "anal," obsessive-compulsive personalities; I am applying the concept far more broadly. For instance, histrionic personality traits such as impulsivity are often thought of as being the opposite of compulsive traits. However, if a person *always* behaves impulsively, then the impulsivity is also compulsive and is evidence of an underlying reaction formation as well.

A person's general level of true self-expression may be estimated from an observation of both the rigidity and the excessiveness of his or her behavior. Because reaction formation is involved in determining the compulsivity and severity of role behavior, the types of behaviors that are most frequently affected can be thought of and listed in terms of polarized opposites, which I refer to as parameters of individuation. When people always behave at either one polarity or the other, or when they behave at one extreme for a while and then quickly switch to the other extreme, they are expressing a lower level of individuation than when they tailor their behavior to fit current circumstances. The following is a list of some of the more commonly seen polarizations. Many of the polarizations on the list overlap or are subcategories of one another. The common denominator of all the polarities is a sacrifice of aspects of the true self. The list makes no pretense of being anywhere near complete.

1. Spontaneous versus planned activity.
2. Giving versus taking.
3. Career versus family life.
4. Work versus play.
5. Emotionality versus stoicism.
6. Activity versus passivity.
7. Dependence versus independence.
8. Dominance versus submission.
9. Sexual expression versus sexual inhibition.
10. Caretaking versus care giving.
11. Saving for the future versus spending for the moment.
12. Attention seeking versus remaining inconspicuous.
13. Taking all the blame versus blaming others.
14. Responsibility versus irresponsibility.
15. Competence versus incompetence.
16. Geographical and social mobility versus staying put.
17. Changing unhappy circumstances versus learning to accept them.
18. Change for the sake of change versus constancy and continuity.
19. Togetherness versus allowing "space" in relationships.
20. Ambition versus lack of ambition.
21. Loyalty versus disloyalty.
22. Respect for authority versus freethinking or rebelliousness.
23. Curiosity versus lack of curiosity.
24. Sociability versus preferring one's own company.
25. Priority for children's needs versus priority for parents' needs.

Mental Gymnastics. Ellis, who founded rational emotive therapy, has extensively catalogued what he refers to as irrational ideas (Ellis and Grieger, 1977). Cognitive therapists believe that irrational ideas, because they affect the way people evaluate their lives, are the major cause of emotional disturbance. They believe that people have a natural tendency to think irrationally, which is determined by both their innate nature and the way that their thinking is shaped by the human environment. In a sense, they believe that people are fundamentally irrational beings. If one assumes, however, that the true self of all human beings is fundamentally rational, then the presence of irrational ideas means something entirely different. The irrational ideas become what I call mental gymnastics. In my view, people latch on to an irrational idea, which on the surface appears reasonable, in order to scare or mortify themselves into behaving, thinking, and feeling in certain ways that naturally they would not. They do so in order to decrease the systemic anxiety within a family. The irrational idea can also serve a second purpose: fooling a therapist. Patients often do not want the therapist to understand them the way they really are, for this may allow the therapist to strengthen a true self at the expense of a persona.

Considering the gargantuan proportions of self-destructive, self-defeating, and unnecessarily cruel behavior among the human race at present and throughout history, the idea that people are fundamentally rational may seem a bit farfetched and utopian, if not downright preposterous. However, if one looks at the question of rationality critically, a different perspective can be reached. In order to evaluate the rationality of a given behavior, one has to know something about the goal of the behavior. In other words, one cannot know whether a behavior makes sense unless one knows something about the motivation behind it. We have already seen that the motivation behind behavior is a far cry from being obvious and self-evident, so, likewise, a judgment regarding the rationality of the behavior can be every bit as difficult. For behavior to be judged rational, one must ask the following questions. Is the goal of the behavior a rational goal? Does the behavior lead toward the attainment of the goal, or does it impede progress toward the goal? If the behavior is not having the desired effect, is there a better method for achieving the goal? If there is a better method, is it possible for the individual to know about it?

The evaluation of the rationality of the long-term goal of the behavior is a very tricky business. Ultimately, the "rationality" of a goal will depend on some sort of value system. Is happiness better than misery in a given situation? Most people think so, but the answer does depend on a value system. Even if God himself decreed one set of values to be superior to another set of values, the answer would still depend on a value system—in this case, God's value system. In the last chapter, I described how people highly value the smooth functioning of their family system. If the goal of self-sacrifice is to further that aim, then the goal should be judged as rational.

If the therapist follows our assumption that whenever a patient hangs on tightly to an irrational idea, that patient is engaged in the process of self-suppression, a veritable gold mine of clues as to the true nature of the situation reveals itself. When spotted, such a mental somersault automatically informs therapists that they are being misled in their attempt to understand the problem that the patient faces. Let us look at the forms that irrational ideas can take, in order to see what the presence of each form reveals about the patient's situation. I will first review the irrational beliefs described by Ellis and then turn to the more general topic of logical fallacies. Following my belief that people are rational, I am assuming that these "beliefs" are actually things that patients tell themselves in order to more effectively portray the character dictated by the role they have assumed in the social order. At some level, they know that they are conning themselves.

Ellis (Ellis and Grieger, 1977) tells us that irrational beliefs take four basic forms: First, a person or thing is seen as not being what it should or must be. Second, the person thinks that, because things are different from the way they should be if there were true justice in the world, then the situation is as bad as it can possibly be. Third, such a situation is absolutely intolerable and unbearable. Last, the person or thing responsible for the intolerable situation is worthy of the highest damnation in its essence and totality. A rational person, in contrast, believes that things are the way they are no matter how we feel about them and that things can always get worse no matter how bad they are. He or she believes that one can always tolerate anything no matter how terrible it gets, all the way up to the point where a situation leads to death, and that no one is bad in every conceivable respect.

The sorts of irrational beliefs described here are all overgeneralizations. That one aspect of something is bad is not evidence that the thing is totally bad. That one does not like the way a situation develops is not evidence that any situation is unbearable in an absolute sense. However, not all overgeneralizations of this sort evidence self-suppression, even if they are blatantly incorrect. If a former camp inmate from Auschwitz were to tell me that he considered Hitler to be evil incarnate, I would be the last person on earth to quibble with the ultimate truth of the statement. One can assume that the sort of irrational belief described in rational emotive therapy does indicate self-suppression whenever the belief leads to an inhibiting emotional reaction. That is, if the emotional response to the belief leads to such despair, shame, or feelings of inadequacy that individuals make no further effort or only a halfhearted effort to rectify an unsatisfactory situation, chances are that they are convincing themselves that they simply must put up with it. For example, people often apply to themselves the irrational belief "when someone does poorly, this means that they are a 'screw-up' in their entirety." Such an attitude is frequently seen in people who cannot seem to hold a job. If they get themselves fired once, they believe that they will inevitably get themselves fired, and they therefore give up. If such people truly wish to hold a job, the rational alternative would be to closely analyze what factors led to the poor performance and work as hard as possible on not making the same mistakes again. The next step would be to actively search for another job, doing whatever it takes to get one.

If a person instead takes the irrational position, this usually means one of two things. First, the true self of the person does not really want to hold a formal job but wishes to appear to want to work. Alternatively, he or she really does want to work but wishes to appear to be incapable of doing so. As an example of the first situation, a woman might genuinely want to be a mother and genuinely believe that a mother should be home with her children but be unwilling to openly dispute her feminist sister. As an example of the latter, a son might appear to be a failure as a breadwinner in order to divert the attention of both of his parents away from the father's own inadequacy as a breadwinner.

The overgeneralizations described by Ellis are but one form of mental gymnastics. I will now go on to describe additional varieties of irrational thoughts, the logical fallacies. Again, I will be making the assumption that whenever an irrational idea is held on to tenaciously, an act of self-suppression is occurring. People do engage in faulty reasoning in the normal course of everyday living, of course, and many people are not in the habit of questioning their beliefs too strongly. This does not necessarily mean that they are self-suppressing or neurotic every time they think foolish thoughts. However, when patients maintain an idea in the face of obvious conflicting data, or especially if they maintain an idea when faulty reasoning has been empathetically pointed out to them, the actor's paradox is at work. In general, the more severe the psychopathology, the more tenaciously the patient hangs on to the irrationality.

Familiarizing oneself with the major logical fallacies can help a therapist to recognize sophistry. Sometimes a faulty idea can really fool even the most experienced logician, especially if it is presented in the middle of an emotionally charged exchange. Therapists are not immune to the process of fooling themselves either, so the critical examination of one's own thinking can also be greatly enhanced by searching for these patterns. Major logical fallacies include the non sequitur, post hoc ergo propter hoc, begging the question, ad hominem attacks, and the use of worst-case scenarios.

A non sequitur occurs when a conclusion is drawn deductively that does not follow logically from the preceding propositions. *Non sequitur* literally means "it does not follow." All of the logical fallacies, with the possible exception of begging the question, are based on non sequiturs and are essentially just subcategories of non sequiturs. I will concentrate here on a brief description of the basic principles of logic that make up the non sequitur and then discuss non sequiturs as they are seen in therapy. After that, we will examine the subcategories, also for the purpose of recognizing them as patients use them in therapy. Correct deductive reasoning can best be demonstrated using syllogisms, which in turn can be understood through the use of set theory. Let us look at the famous syllogism:

> All men are mortal.
> Socrates is a man.
> Therefore, Socrates is mortal.

The first thing one needs to understand, if one is to correctly evaluate deductive reasoning, is that this is a logical syllogism whether or not the initial statements "All men are mortal" and "Socrates is a man" are correct. A deduction—the last statement in the syllogism—can be judged logical if the structure of the syllogism is correct. This means that a conclusion can be completely wrong but the deduction can still be valid logically if the conclusion follows correctly from the initial propositions. The truth of a proposition, as opposed to its logical validity, depends upon the truth of the information from which the proposition is deduced. For purposes of the type of psychotherapy advocated in the present work, the therapist does not assume that self-suppression is occurring if the patient makes a valid deduction from incorrect data and therefore strongly believes an incorrect proposition, unless the incorrect data continue to be believed in the face of strongly conflicting information.

In a valid syllogism, if the first two statements are true, the conclusion *must* be true. The presence in the syllogism of the word *all* is extremely important. If some men are not mortal and some are, Socrates might fall outside the set of "things that are mortal," and the syllogism would become invalid. This is precisely why the equally famous fallacious syllogism

> The Virgin Mary was a virgin.
> My name is Mary.
> Therefore, I am a virgin.

is invalid. The set "people named Mary" falls both within and without the set "virgins." Therefore, Marys may or may not be virgins, and the conclusion is thus invalid. It is not true that if the first two statements are true, the conclusion must be true, as would be the case with a valid syllogism. In set theory, only a subset of "all people named Mary," not the entire set, is a subset of the set "virgins."

A word here regarding inductive reasoning is in order. Inductive, as opposed to deductive, reasoning attempts to go in the reverse order. One attempts to make a generalization by examining several phenomena that seem to have something in common. One then makes the leap of faith that because all observed instances of the phenomena have this characteristic in common, therefore all instances of the phenomena, observed and not observed, share the characteristic. For example, every time an object of whatever size or shape is dropped on earth, it falls down. The inductive conclusion is that the set of "things that fall down" entirely subsumes the set of "things that can be dropped" and that anything droppable will fall down if dropped. One makes the prediction that any new object that can be dropped will head earthward if one picks it up and lets it go.

Now the deduction "since all observed instances of a certain phenomenon behave a certain way or have certain things in common, therefore all future instances of the same phenomenon will continue to behave in the same way and have the same things in common" is in all instances a non sequitur. One might come upon an exception to the rule at any time. In other words, all inductive conclusions are invalid! Nonetheless, inductive conclusions are not necessarily unreasonable and are frequently correct. I have in my hand a pencil, which I plan to hold up and then let go. Will it fall? I predict, on the basis of inductive reasoning, that it will. Let me see. Yes, it did it again!

The reasonableness of an inductive conclusion is evaluated not by logic but by whether enough instances of the phenomenon have been observed to make a generalization possible and by whether there are any instances that contradict the generalization. Deductive reasoning, or reasoning based on proof, would not be possible without inductive reasoning. It would be impossible to conclude that Socrates was mortal if one could

not make the generalization "All men are mortal." The determination of how many instances are required to decide whether
an inductive conclusion is reasonable is a very subjective matter,
because no matter how many instances there are, the next one
could always be the exception. For this reason, a therapist looking for mental gymnastics when a patient makes an inductive
conclusion best asks the questions: Are there significant exceptions to the generalization that the patient is making? If so, are
they obvious, if only the patient would look for them?

Knowledge of the mechanics of inductive reasoning is
essential for spotting non sequiturs, for many non sequiturs are
disguised as reasonable-sounding inductive conclusions. Many of
the irrational ideas described by Ellis fall in this category. As another example, take the frequently heard statement, "I do not
like to try new things because I am afraid of failure." The false
inductive conclusion implied by this is "every time I try something new, I fail at it." This is blatantly untrue. Every human
being on earth has succeeded in something. Even if someone has
failed in everything he or she has ever set out to do, most of the
failures undoubtedly stem more from the lack of a concerted effort than from a lack of ability. Another flaw in this line of
thinking is that it assumes that lack of effort ensures success. A
failure during an effort is somehow seen as more disagreeable
than a failure accomplished through the omission of an effort.
Now it is true that people will often say that they feel more devastated if they do something unsuccessfully than if they do not
even try to accomplish the activity, but this feeling of devasta-
tion results from the illogical ideas described by Ellis. The result
in both cases is absolutely identical. In neither instance has the
activity been accomplished. If one is truly afraid of failing at
something, one would keep at it until one was successful no
matter how long and how difficult the effort became. Last, failure is a relative concept. Many people see "failure" if they have
not done something perfectly the first time or if they do not
become the "best." When they do this, the inductive conclusion
is not false. With this definition of failure, they *will* "fail" at
every endeavor into which they venture. In this case, the therapist will smell self-suppression because of the absurd, self-

scaring nature of this definition of failure, rather than through the detection of a non sequitur.

I would now like to describe a case in which the patient presented the therapist with a goodly number of non sequiturs. The remarkable characteristic of this case is that the patient was extremely well educated and had an IQ close to the genius range. I would be making an inductive error if I were to assume that this one fact proves that irrationality does not at all correlate with intelligence or level of knowledge, but it certainly points in that direction! To say the very least, I had a great deal of difficulty believing that at some level this patient did not know she was talking nonsense.

The patient, a single woman in her early twenties, was initially referred by her physician because of agitation and depression that appeared on first inspection to be situational in nature. The patient was being subjected to a series of harassing acts by a co-worker. She had been verbally abused by the colleague almost every day for a year. She was called every name in the book. Not only that, but the co-worker would go out of his way to interfere with the patient's concentration so that she would have difficulty keeping her mind on her work. In addition to playing his radio in the patient's direction, he would gossip loudly about her with his friends so that she would be sure to hear. After exploring the situation for a time, the patient and I were unable to come up with anything she had done to incur his wrath, other than asking him, on one occasion, to turn off the radio. She had surely not done anything deserving of such a level of retaliation.

My suspicion that something other than a situational disturbance was going on was immediately aroused by the observation that she had waited such a long time before attempting to do something about her situation and that she followed a recommendation to see a psychiatrist when she was upset only because someone was doing something to her. I knew for certain that my suspicions were justified when the non sequiturs began.

She first stated that she must have done something besides the request for quiet to make the co-worker behave in this extreme fashion, because people do not hate you unless you've done something bad to them. This was a non sequitur because she had no proof that his behavior was based on hatred of her, and even if it were, she was quite aware that the causes of hate in the world include a great many other things. Hate can be based on prejudice, jealousy, a chip on the shoulder, or any number of things other than what someone has done to the person who hates.

The next bit of curious logic occurred when the patient told me that she just could not seem to make him understand that his gossip was disturbing her. How she could possibly have thought that he was not aware of that was simply beyond my comprehension. I told her I thought it kind of her to wish to give him the benefit of the doubt after all he had done to her, but it seemed that she had too much evidence to the contrary to support this thesis.

The next item that we discussed was what measures she planned to take to put a halt to all this. By the time the patient came to me, she had finally discussed the situation with her supervisor, but from the outset she was certain that this would not help. As it later turned out, a reprimand from the supervisor caused the co-worker to stop his disturbing behavior for months, and when he resumed she was able to get him fired. Now, of course, she did not know that her boss would do this for her, but the pessimism still seemed a bit premature to my way of thinking.

At this point, it appeared that she was trying to justify continuing to be passive in the matter. I began to hypothesize that perhaps her family seemed to her to value her passivity for some reason, and I listened for further evidence to support this. The first clue that I was off the track came when the patient issued yet another non sequitur. She began to get upset with herself for being disturbed by some of the slurs verbalized by her nemesis. She stated that he was just calling her names, after all. Why should just names bother her? Sticks and stones, and all that. She should be able to ignore it, like water off a duck's back. I told her she would be quite an unusual person if she had not found the barrage of insults disturbing.

When faced with a recommendation that we explore why

she was so willing to bend over backward not to cause her tor-
mentor any distress by doing something to fight back, as well as
why she was upset that the whole situation bothered her, she
balked. She told me that if she were to get to the reasons behind this seemingly self-defeating behavior, she might find
something terrible. Well, I supposed she might, but how terrible
could it be? How did she know that she would not discover
something wonderful? The odds were, of course, that she might
find something uncomfortable, but as Ellis says, feeling that one
would not be able to tolerate the discomfort is irrational, especially when the level of discomfort is already so high, and when
bearing some additional discomfort could lessen it over the long
run. She correctly guessed that certain information she had related to me might incline me to think that her parents' divorce
when she was ten bore on her current reactions. She then added
a non sequitur that later turned out to be the essential clue to
what was really going on, although I did not see it at the time.
She told me that she was puzzled by why everyone seemed to
think that a parental divorce had so traumatized her and added
that she had taken the divorce in stride. It was done, and there
was no reason to get upset about it. The event just did not
bother her.

        When she made this statement, she was trying to take
what may sound like a rational position. After all, rational emotive therapy does make the point that the belief that one cannot
stand an unpleasant occurrence makes one suffer more than
necessary. The patient was saying more than this, however. She
was not saying that one should not be depressed over a traumatic occurrence. She was saying that one should not be unhappy about it. No disappointment. No regret. No anything.
Ellis states that regret and disappointment are emotional responses that make sense. She was stating that she was unaffected
entirely. Psychoanalysts would call this isolation of affect. An
experiential therapist would work on "getting the patient in
touch with her feelings." Furthermore, the available evidence
strongly suggested that she was not only disappointed about
what happened but depressed about it as well. She could hardly discuss the matter without breaking into tears.

Much later, I discovered that what the non sequitur really alluded to was the patient's very rational concern about seeming to be bothered about anything. As it turned out, the patient's mother was subjecting her to frequent guilt-ridden harangues about how bad the mother felt about the divorce. The mother would literally badger her with questions about whether she had been upset and traumatized by it. No wonder the patient tried to project an image of not being bothered by things! If she were to admit to being the least bit upset, the mother would feel even guiltier. The mother was already somewhat self-destructive; perhaps she would become actively suicidal.

The next fallacy I would like to discuss is post hoc ergo propter hoc, which literally translated means "afterward this, therefore because of this." Under this fallacy, two events that occur in sequence are assumed to be causally related. That is, if event B follows event A, then an assumption is made that A caused B. This sort of fallacy can be funny when it is obvious but difficult to detect when subtle. No one would believe a doctor who claims that headaches are caused by a deficiency in the body of aspirin, but the debate rages on over whether rapes are caused to a major degree by the effects on the assailant of pornographic movies.

The fallacy of post hoc is most frequently seen in therapy during conjoint or family sessions. When spotted, such a fallacy may reveal the presence of a family myth, a false belief that assists family members in suppressing those thoughts, feelings, preferences, or behavior deemed to be unacceptable or that enables one or more family members to continue playing a specific role. The myth may be believed by an individual, a subsystem of the family, or the entire family. The myth usually takes the form of a causal explanation of a family member's behavior that is not the true explanation. In order to be believable, the myth usually makes use of the post hoc ergo propter hoc fallacy. The causal connection in the myth is based on temporal relation. If the behavior to be explained begins after a certain event, the behavior is blamed on the event. As with other self-suppressive mechanisms, the proposed cause often reveals clues to the true cause, even though the proposed cause is meant to be a smokescreen.

One example occurred in a family being seen under the duress of a probation officer. A young teenager was caught shoplifting. He lived with his father and his siblings. The mother had not only divorced the father but entirely abdicated any family responsibility in order to pursue a career. The father was rarely spending time with the son because the firm that he worked for was demanding more and more overtime. The father routinely worked fourteen-hour days and expressed disappointment that the boys could not take better care of themselves without supervision.

The post hoc fallacy took place in the session following an incident in which the patient picked a fight with another boy who was twice his size. The father theorized that the patient had engaged in this rather dangerous activity because the patient had not had a good night's sleep the night before the incident and was therefore overly irritable. This seemed to me a rather odd explanation. When provoked, overly irritable people will sometimes unthinkingly do or say things that they otherwise might keep to themselves, but they seldom go out looking for trouble. The father appeared to be attempting to veer away from any explanation of the boy's odd behavior that might involve family dynamics, but he unwittingly revealed his own projection. It was the father, not the son, who was irritable from lack of sleep. I later guessed that the boy's acting-out behavior was a feeble attempt to force the father, who was utterly exhausted from working so much, to work less. The father was required to be at home more in order to supervise the misbehaving youngster. The boy was also bidding for more attention, but I believed that he was genuinely concerned about his father. When I suggested to the father that the boy was, at great personal sacrifice, attempting to indirectly demonstrate his concern by forcing the father to insist on more time off, the father never really bought it. However, soon he was spending more time at home, and the patient stopped acting out. No causal connection between my Palazzolian intervention and the subsequent improvement was ever established.

A third major logical fallacy is begging the question. A person begging the question merely insists that an assertion is proved without offering any proof at all. If someone offers some evidence that the assertion is false, the begger states that the evidence must be incorrect. After all, since the assertion is true, any evidence to the contrary must be faulty. It might seem that the absurdity of this kind of reasoning should be quite obvious when it occurs, but it can be quite subtle. Often an intervening argument for the questionable assertion is made by the begger, which is then refuted by the disputer. The begger then goes on to offer yet another argument, which in turn is refuted. This process continues until the begger suddenly announces that he or she has won the case—by reoffering the initial unproved assertion.

I first truly understood this process one day in college when I caught myself doing it. I was engaged in a friendly argument with a fellow student over the relative merits of the space program during the sixties. My friend took the position that going to the moon was a complete waste of money, because there were important human needs here on earth for which the money could be used. I was and am of the opinion that scientific knowledge is valuable for its own sake, but at the time I was unable to formulate a convincing argument for that position. Instead, I advanced the argument that the space program had yielded important scientific by-products, such as Teflon, that were quite useful here on earth. He countered that Teflon could have been invented for far less money by doing research on nonstick surfaces instead of moon flights. I then countered with, "But this way, we also get to the moon!"

Begging the question is a maneuver that occurs most often when clients are being questioned about their motivation but do not wish to reveal their true reasons to the therapist or perhaps even to themselves. They may assert that they behave in the way they do because that is how they truly wish to behave or because they have no other options. If the therapist presents evidence that the behavior seems to be something that is bringing them a great deal of grief or if the therapist offers other options, they will then either just ignore what the therapist has said, invalidate it by making a snide comment, engage in a game of "why-don't-you-yes-but" (Berne, 1964), or begin the process of making further refutable arguments and then returning to the initial assertion as if it had been justified.

A good example of begging the question occurred in the case of a poorly educated employee of a large manufacturing concern. Despite a horrendously abused childhood and the lack of schooling, he had managed to rise to a fairly responsible position with the firm. Then suddenly, through no fault of his own, the position was eliminated. Because of further bad luck complicated by his own aggravating behavior, he was gradually demoted and shifted to a department he despised and continued to go downhill until he had become a glorified file clerk. The more responsibilities were taken from him, the more upset he became. The more upset he became, the more poorly he performed in his job. The poorer the performance, the more responsibility was taken from him, and so on. He felt that his supervisor wished to get rid of him because he was being paid far too much for his present position but also believed that the supervisor was blocking his transfer to another department where he might get a more responsible job.

I wondered why, if it were really true that he was unable to get out of the department and find a job with which he would be satisfied, he did not seek employment with a different firm. I conceded that such a move would be quite difficult considering his lack of education but pointed out that he had not even attempted to look. He replied that he did not wish to leave the firm. He stated that, in fact, he loved working for this company; it was just his department he despised. I pressed on. I pointed out that he had already told me that he could not get out of the department because of his mean supervisor. Why was it so important to stay with the same firm? He replied once again that he would not leave the firm because he loved working for it.

"The firm seems to be very important to you. What is it about working for the firm that you love so?"

"They've been very good to me."

"Well, they certainly have been good to you—in the past. At the moment, however, you've told me that they are not being very good to you at all."

"That is the department that is being bad to me. I have no complaint with the firm."

"I know that, but you have told me that you are stuck

with the department. Don't you think you might find a different firm that you would also like?"

"Yes, I might be able to do that."

"So why are you so intent on staying with your present
firm?"

"I want to get in twenty-five years with the firm."

"What makes that important?"

"It is important to my self-esteem" [a possible non sequitur that I let go].

"So you'll consider leaving when you have been there
twenty-five years?"

"No."

"So there must be another reason why you feel you must
stay with the firm."

"I don't want to give my supervisors the satisfaction of
driving me out." [This is another assertion that does not make
very much sense. Why should avoiding making them smug be
worth daily torture at their hands? I avoided touching on this
also.]

"Do you really think they care all that much?"

"Probably not."

"So why stay?"

"I've told you. The firm is very important to me. I love
working for the firm. Okay?"

The last statement was, of course, merely a restatement
of his initial position that did nothing whatever to shed light on
why the firm was so important to him. This is exactly what is
meant by begging the question.

Let us now go on to another illogical maneuver, the
"worst-case argument." An argument is made that a particular
course of action is ill advised by pointing out difficulties that
might arise in a worst-case scenario. In other words, one asks
the question, "if I did so and so, what would be the consequences if everything possible went wrong?" Posing a worst-case
scenario does not always mean that the poser is engaged in an
illogical maneuver. Indeed, for certain questions, such as whether
to build a nuclear reactor near an earthquake fault, looking at
worst-case scenarios can be a matter of potential life and death.

I have used worst-case scenarios to clarify points in this book. The worst-case argument becomes logically suspect if it is being used as an excuse to avoid some action when either of two conditions is present. The first is when the worst case is so unlikely to occur as to be almost meaningless. The second is when the worst case is preventable.

The most common usage of the maneuver in psychotherapy cases occurs when patients attempt to suppress some self-aspect by frightening themselves with the thought of dreadful consequences should the characteristic of self ever be expressed. One of the most often seen examples of this involves the question of whether to express anger. I once was the therapist in a group where every single member was in complete agreement that anger should be kept to oneself. They all painted a most shocking picture of dire results that might ensue if their anger were ever unleashed. The anger would be destructive to the nth degree. Everyone present had so much anger inside that if some of it got out, a dam would burst and a flood of violent fury would come pouring out. They might murder all of their loved ones and bomb government buildings. They would all suddenly become completely crazed, and each might end up in a mental institution or worse. They might tear the objects of their rage limb from limb and end up on death row. If thoughts like that did not scare them into keeping their anger quiet, nothing would.

The worst-case scenario that was proposed by the group members is illogical for several reasons. First, it is based on the non sequitur "if I let out some of my anger, I'll let it all out." Forgetting for the moment the unlikelihood that the rage they fear is as extensive as they believe it to be, how did they come to the conclusion that they would have more difficulty restraining themselves once some of the anger had emerged than before the process started? They were each masters at self-restraint. The situation is not really analogous to the Dutch boy with his finger in the dike. One can always catch oneself. Indeed, the extra guilt these people probably would feel for having exhibited angry feelings might make it even easier for them to restrain themselves in the future. This worst case, in which all of a

limitless amount of anger would come out in a deluge, is a highly unlikely worst case. Furthermore, this worse case is preventable. As discussed earlier, acting out the anger is not the only
way to express it. This is a very clear example of what I mean
by self-scaring. In this case, an aspect of self, the emotion of
anger, is suppressed by frightening oneself with horrific consequences.

   One last fallacy that I would like to briefly mention is ad
hominem. This translates from the Latin as "to the man." This
fallacy is based on the non sequitur "if a person is reprehensible in
some respect, then everything that person has to say is incorrect." This fallacy is frequently encountered outside the psychotherapy realm in the area of politics. Politicians can have re-
pulsive views on certain issues or may be self-serving liars.
Nonetheless, any single assertion that they make might still be
true or correct. One cannot reason logically that because their
views are unpopular or because they have lied in the past, any
current assertion they make is false. From the standpoint of inductive reasoning, one can be highly suspicious of their statements because of their past behavior and motivation, but in
order to actually disprove their thesis, one needs corroborating
evidence. Just because Castro is a Communist, one cannot conclude that he is always lying whenever he makes accusations
against the United States government. In therapy, patients will
frequently discount an idea because of the alleged motivation
of the person making it, as if any idea that may be self-serving
must also be false.

   Before leaving the subject of logical fallacies, I would like
to discuss one additional type of mental gyration that is somewhat a combination of twisted logic and a parapraxis. I refer to
it as illogical word usage. This involves instances in which a patient expresses an idea using an odd word that is almost, but not
exactly, synonymous with another word that would make better
sense. The word that should have been used would make the
patient's idea perfectly reasonable, but the word that is actually
used makes the idea sound strange. Most listeners, on hearing the
off-key word, assume that they know exactly what the speaker
means; they assume that the speaker merely chose the word

carelessly. Such a listener substitutes what should be the correct word, or the concept signified by the correct word, in formulating her or his ideas about what the speaker has said. In therapy, I find that taking speakers at their word and assuming that they mean exactly what they say often reveals an illogical thought. The illogical thought then can be considered to be, following our assumption about such thoughts, evidence for an act of self-suppression.

A good example of this occurred in the initial stages of therapy with a middle-aged woman who had lost her husband six years earlier and who had become depressed just prior to making her first appointment with me. Since the death of her husband, she had not gone out on a single date and had seldom spent any time away from her family for any reason. She self-lessly devoted her entire life to taking care of her children, the youngest of whom was just about to enter kindergarten. Her justification for spending so much time with the children to the exclusion of time for herself was that she wished to spare the children any deprivation that they might experience as a result of growing up without a father.

This justification was based on non sequiturs. First, spending twice as much time with one's mother does not entirely substitute for the unique aspects of a relationship with one's father. Second, even if both parents were present, there might be a certain amount of time during which neither was involved with the children. They might both work or spend a night on the town together or spend time simultaneously engaged in their respective hobbies. Provided that they did not engage in these activities excessively, they would hardly be described by most people as "depriving" their children. The absence of a father did not justify the devotion of our patient's every waking hour to her children. A major thesis of this volume is that such devotion is actually quite harmful.

During the course of inquiring into her reasoning on this matter, I heard an example of illogical word usage. This reinforced my suspicion, generated by the presence of the logical fallacies mentioned above, that an act of self-suppression was taking place. She had mentioned that her dysphoria was worse during the short hours when her youngest was in nursery school than it was the rest of the time. I wondered aloud whether her depression had been precipitated by the impending departure for daily school of her last child. She allowed that this might be a possibility but then added that she would still need to spend most of her time devoting herself to child-rearing activities even after the youngest started school. She then stated, "the youngest has always been an excuse not to go out."

Excuse? Why on earth did she need an "excuse" not to go out? The presence of a toddler might have provided her with a *reason* not to go out, albeit a rather poor one in and by itself. But an excuse? An "excuse" in this context strongly implies a made-up reason that is covering up a real reason. Since the patient had no other apparent reason for staying home, using the child as an excuse made absolutely no sense. When I inquired about what she meant by "excuse," the patient did not exactly deny the implications of the word. However, when I made the mistake of further explaining my question by pointing out the difference between a reason and an excuse, she told me that she had really meant to say that the child's presence was, in fact, a reason. The patient's sudden decision that she had misspoken turned the illogical word usage into a parapraxis. Clearly, more exploration was required to uncover the real reason for the patient's lack of social life.

The usage of a word in an odd manner may also be an example of what is called "communication deviance" in the family therapy literature. Looking for communication deviance can be yet another tool in the therapist's quest to find the patient's true self.

Communication Deviance. Communication deviance (see Schultz, 1984) signifies those interpersonal transactions that prevent the participants in a conversation from sharing a focus of attention. When these maneuvers are used, the various individuals can never be sure that they are all talking about the same thing, that any speaker really believes what he or she is saying, or whether any agreement has been reached on a bone of contention. The listener is caused to puzzle over one or more of the following questions: What is this man talking about? Does he really believe what he says, or is he saying it merely for effect? How exactly does he wish me to interpret what has been said? Is he trying to confuse me? Did he just change the subject, or are we still on the same topic that we were discussing a minute ago? Is he trying to reach agreement on an issue, or is he trying to avoid reaching an agreement? Did what he just said really answer the question that I just asked?

Therapists who find themselves reflecting on such questions should not be shy about requesting clarification. If the consistent answer to such requests is more unenlightening communication deviance, then chances are that the original subject involves an area in the person's life where self-suppression is occurring. I believe that the purpose of persistent communication deviance is to directly obscure the true nature of the self or to throw the listener off of a line of inquiry that might, if followed to a conclusion, reveal a suppressed aspect of self. Communication deviance is a subtle form of defensiveness. I am not stating that people are fundamentally wizards at syntax in the same way that I am asserting that people are fundamentally rational. Self-suppression is suspected only when patients do not attempt to clarify confusion when they know that confusion exists, do not appear to be able make themselves clear, or are continuously confusing. Communication deviance includes unclear references, questionable commitment to ideas, abnormal syntax, outright contradiction, and subtle changes of subject.

As an example, a patient in her early twenties came to therapy complaining of depression and inability to get involved with men for even brief periods of time. After a psychodiagnostic evaluation, psychotherapy was recommended, to which the patient agreed. Therapy was framed as an attempt to understand why she had to behave in ways that were depressing her, so that whatever was prompting the behavior could be dealt with in a more satisfying manner. I told her that she had to have good reasons for behaving in ways that she herself clearly knew to be leading to her celibate existence, when being celibate was distressing to her. I stressed the importance of finding out what they were. She seemed to accept the frame but within a very short period of time expressed concern that she had a tendency to overanalyze the motivations behind her behavior. She did so without questioning the efficacy of the analyzing approach I had just recommended. This represented an example of a commitment problem and a contradiction. Had she truly accepted my recommendation, or was she dissatisfied with it? I speculated that she had accepted it but was afraid to proceed with it. Later in therapy, her concerns came to light, and my speculation was confirmed.

A second patient demonstrated several instances of referent problems and subtle subject changes. Again the chief complaint was depression. When it came to discussing the factors in her life that she found depressing, the patient mentioned several areas. She was concerned about her marriage, her daughter's recent delinquent behavior, and the appropriateness of her choice of career. She would quickly flit from one of these areas to another as she discussed her depression. I could not come to a complete understanding of any one of the areas because she would change to a different one before allowing me to complete any one line of inquiry. A referent problem occurred because she switched from one area to another rapidly and without saying anything that indicated that she was about to make a transition. This created confusion over which problem area she was referring to with any given statement. The various areas all dovetailed neatly into one another in such a way that she was not overtly changing the subject, making it difficult for the therapist to stop her and point out to her what she was doing. For instance, she was concerned that her daughter's acting out resulted from inconsistent discipline by her husband. This concern led back to the marriage problem. Additionally, the daughter's problem was evidence to her that she was spending too much time at work. Thus, when she discussed her daughter's difficulty, elements in the discussion could refer to the other areas as well. Where I might be inquiring into where she and her husband disagreed, she might be taking my question as evidence for a wrong career choice. To which problem any given statement she made referred was always a matter of some question.

We will now leave the topic of communication deviance

to discuss one last method for uncovering the true self of a patient. Traditionally, psychodynamic theorists have attempted to understand motivation by looking at what a person's behavior seems to say about the person himself or herself. An entirely different perspective is obtained if we try to understand the motivation behind a person's behavior by looking at the effect the behavior has on other people. I refer to this process as the study of the net effect of behavior.

The Net Effect of Behavior. If we once again start with the assumption that Homo sapiens are basically rational animals with eyes and brains, then we can hardly escape the conclusion that they must at some level see and understand the effect that their repeated, stereotyped behavior has on the people around them. They may certainly be able to act as if they are unaware, or may attempt to look the other way, but if they continue in the behavior, sooner or later they will have to notice that they tend to produce similar reactions in a lot of people when they do certain things. The exception to this would be any behavioral maneuver performed for the first few times, which could have a trial-and-error quality, or whose effects on others might be initially interpreted, incorrectly, along the lines of preformed expectations. After that, unless most of the people they encountered behaved in a completely random fashion in reaction to a particular behavior, they would learn what reactions to expect.

I would now like to advance the idea that producing certain reactions is the goal and the motivation behind stereotypical, repetitive behaviors that are directed toward other people in the context of interpersonal relationships. If a certain act usually leads to a given response in others, then the person engages in the act in order to produce that response. The overall outcome that results from the recurrent induction of this response is the "net effect" of the behavior. This idea is not a new one. The analytical concept of projective identification, which postulates that people can induce others to act out unwanted aspects of themselves, is based on it. A similar idea advocated by psychoanalysts is that making use of "countertransference," or monitoring one's own reactions to the productions of the patient, can be a productive method of understanding the patient's "unconscious" motivation. In my opinion, however, this idea has not been taken far enough.

A potential criticism of this idea is that it represents a teleological, functionalistic approach to the question of personal motivation. That is, it assumes that the motivation and the end result of behavior are connected. The statement "the presence of a particular result produced by a given behavior means that the motivation behind the behavior must have been to produce that result" is a non sequitur. However, I am saying that when people *consistently* produce a similar, *immediate* reaction with certain of their behavior, then that is the effect they wish to produce. This is not a non sequitur but a question of fact. I am not saying that motivation must be present in this type of situation, only that it is present.

Looking at motivation in this light can lead to an opposite interpretation of behavior from that drawn traditionally by looking at motivation in terms of what the behavior seems to say about a person observed in isolation. To understand this clearly, we will look at two common personality profiles, keeping in mind this perspective. Every therapist has encountered the clingy, suffocating, childish patient—more frequently female—who constantly demands to have all of her needs met but for whom nothing is ever enough. The interesting thing is that this sort of behavior is commonly interpreted as dependent behavior. That is, the patient is seen as avoiding self-reliance like the plague and as needing others to satisfy all needs. Theoretically, this behavior is viewed by psychoanalysts as reflective of *conflicts* over dependency, an idea with which I wholeheartedly agree. In practice, however, only one side of the conflict receives the bulk of analytical attention. The patient is usually likened to a creature, the baby, who is overly dependent.

This idea stems from looking at the patient's behavior in isolation. If the patient is demanding and refuses to act self-reliantly, then she must be overly dependent. If we choose to look at what effect such behavior has on others, however, a completely different picture emerges. Does clinging, overdemanding, childish behavior motivate strong others to take care of people who behave in such a manner? No! As a matter of fact, this type of patient usually attracts and becomes involved with poorly functioning alcoholics, spouse beaters, and other assorted deadbeats—people who are downright terrible when it comes to caring for the needs of others. People who would be able to take good care of others are, in all cases except the never-say-die helping professional, *driven away* by this sort of behavior. Both the good provider and the poor provider are enraged by the whining, helpless, bottomless-pit style of draining and belittling behavior acted out by such people. The difference is that poor providers feel that it is their sacred duty to continue to attempt to take care of the "dependent" person, handling their anger in a passive-aggressive manner, while healthy good providers, unafraid of selfishness, go on to look for someone with whom they can have a more mutual relationship.

The net effect of overdemandingness is that no one actually takes care of the patient's needs. The net effect is not overdependency. It is *counterdependency*, reflective of a desire to *avoid* having one's dependency needs met, expressed through the mechanism of spoiling behavior, which devalues the help that is given. In contrast to a real baby, who can be satisfied, these patients never appear to be happy with their lot, no matter how much is done for them. All this is not to say that such patients are not needy. Indeed, they are extremely needy. However, this is not because they are overly dependent. It is because their needs are not being met. Their needs are not being met because of counterdependency. As with all other self-suppressive behavior, the method used to fight an aspect of self reveals something about that very aspect of the self. In this case, what I feel are attempts to discourage others from being helpful use the patient's own legitimate needs for help as a modus operandi. Such a patient has a true psychodynamic conflict. Her or his behavior is simultaneously both reflective of a need for caretaking and an attempt to prevent the fulfillment of that very need.

An interesting corollary to the principle of the net effect of behavior is an idea that I call the principle of opposite behaviors. In the example of the clinging, demanding patient, one can see that one of the effects of asking for too much is in all respects identical to one of the effects of asking for nothing at all. In both cases, others usually do not or cannot help satisfy the needs in question. In the former, helpers are either driven off by obnoxious behavior or fail in their efforts to help. In the latter case, helpers are unaware that needs are even present, so do nothing. Two seemingly opposite behaviors have the same net effect. Conversely, a behavior that seems to have one effect can, in reality, have the opposite effect. Patients will engage in this sort of chicanery in therapy quite frequently. In order to fool a therapist into thinking that a real change has been made in their behavior, patients will sometimes do the opposite of what they have done previously. Instead of being unassertive in asking for the fulfillment of legitimate dependency needs, the patient asks —and asks and asks and asks and then asks some more. The behavior is opposite; the net effect is the same. What seems to be a major shift in behavior is nothing more than an exercise in running in place.

A clear example of this is sometimes seen in counterdependent patients who are thought to have psychosomatic problems. One patient with a herniated lumbar disc, documented by medical tests, continued to complain of pain long after surgery was done to correct the problem. After considerable questioning of the patient, I was able to ascertain that the reason that the patient could not heal was because she was not following proper postsurgical activity restrictions. She was in effect continually reinjuring herself. The reason for that self-destructive behavior was counterdependency. The patient simply would not ask for assistance. She would carry heavy packages from the market and stoop to vacuum the carpet, to name but two of her reinjuring behaviors. If she had questions about what she was allowed or not allowed to do, she would not call the doctor for fear of being a pest. When I confronted her with this pattern, she seemed to understand immediately. Afterward, she would still not call her orthopedist but had no trouble asking her psychotherapist to run errands for her!

The narcissistic personality disorder provides a second syndrome ripe for exploration of the net effects of behavior. The DSM III, the handbook of psychiatric diagnoses published by the American Psychiatric Association (1980), lists several features of this type of personality. One of these is an "exhibitionistic need for constant attention and admiration" (p. 315). Unfortunately for the ultimate satisfaction of this need, these folks, most usually males, are also characterized by "a grandiose sense of self-importance or uniqueness" and "characteristic disturbances in interpersonal relationships, such as feelings of entitlement, interpersonal exploitativeness, relationships that alternate between the extremes of over-idealization and devaluation, and lack of empathy." Not only that, but the overinflated sense of self-importance "may be manifested as extreme self-centeredness and self-absorption." Gracious! If one "needs" people to like, admire, and attend to oneself, I cannot think of a worse way to get them to do so than by acting self-centered, exploitative, deficient in empathy, and unpredictably devaluing. Most people are positively repulsed by this sort of behavior because they want at least a minimal amount of attention and empathy for themselves, the attainment of which the narcissist's behavior prevents. The narcissist is far too self-involved to pay attention to the needs of others.

Taken in isolation, the narcissist's attention-seeking behavior appears to be motivated by a desire for attention. Taken in the context of interpersonal relationships, the patient's behavior is reflective of a desire to avoid getting attention. Again, this is not to say that the narcissist does not need attention. Indeed, he needs it desperately, precisely because his behavior prevents him from attaining it. Kohut (1971, 1977) has demonstrated convincingly that narcissism stems from poor mirroring behavior by the parents of the narcissist. Mirroring is entirely lacking in the upbringing of these patients. Looked at in this way, the narcissistic male's characteristic behavior could be interpreted both as reflective of a need for attention and mirroring and simultaneously as an attempt to prevent the fulfillment of that very need. In short, this is evidence of a true psychodynamic conflict, just as a conflict exists in the dependent woman who needs caretaking and works to avoid receiving it. Looking at the behavior in isolation leads to knowledge only of the underlying need, and not of the side of the conflict that wishes to be free from the need.

4

DYSFUNCTIONAL
INTERACTIONS
IN FAMILIES

Now that we have examined the ways in which individuals attempt to hide aspects of themselves, I would like to look in more detail at the disturbances in family homeostasis that induce individuals to do this. What conditions make a smooth-functioning family unstable? In Chapter Two, I looked at the way that the biological tendency to be concerned with the survival of the species is expressed at the family and individual levels, and I noted that the biological tendency toward evolution is also expressed at these levels. In order to understand malfunctioning families and individuals, we must first understand how this takes place.

Adaptation to Cultural Evolution

If a family has not adjusted to changes in its cultural environment, the smooth functioning of the system begins to break down. In many cases, changes in the cultural milieu can be handled by minor changes in system functioning, a sort of fine tuning, if you will. However, if the change is too threatening, too great, or too rapid, fine tuning alone will not handle the problem. The type of cultural change that is most likely to cause breakdown in either the system or one of its members is the development of a requirement for a level of individuation that was previously unacceptable. This is, of course, the main thrust of cultural evolution. The family first attempts to deal with this type of change by hanging on even more tenaciously to its previous modes of functioning, in the hope that if they just do the same thing more often or with more vigor, then the old system will still work. When any combination of family members sees that this is not working, they may find this process extremely difficult to stop, for reasons that will later become clear. Nonetheless, the family is in a position where it simply must evolve, or else the level of distress for the individual members will increase until at least one of them suffers an emotional breakdown of some sort. The reason for this is that the needs of the larger holon, the culture, will exert a pull on the individuals within the system for a level of individuation that will conflict with the needs of the family system for homeostasis. The result will be an increased level of anxiety for the entire family.

Erikson (1963) provides an example of an entire culture being partially absorbed into a larger, more individualized one, with the result that the level of distress for the entire group increased in a manner exactly identical to the process I am discussing at the family systems level. Erikson may not have conceptualized the process in quite the manner I have in mind, but his descriptions are quite consistent with my view. He describes the difficulties experienced by the Sioux Indians in the 1930s, a few decades after the Indian Wars, when White educators set up schools on the reservation. Originally, Sioux culture was based on a collectivist structure. Competition for and the accumulation of personal wealth were highly discouraged. Indians would, in fact, compete with one another to see who could give away the most. In fact, if Brave #1 had more of something than Brave #2, and Brave #2 needed it, the Indian in need would take what he wanted without asking, and no one would think the less of him. This philosophy worked well in an environment where men were hunters, buffalo were plentiful, and most of the needs of tribal members were simple and easily filled.

Along come the Whites. The buffalo are killed off, the Indians are placed in reservations under government control, and well-meaning educators descend on the tribe with well-meaning intentions of providing the Indians with the skills appropriate for American cultural needs. The Sioux were then in what could be considered a time warp. The state of their culture had not evolved to the point where occupations were highly specialized and where personal ambition was highly adaptive, yet their children were placed in schools where these cultural norms were accepted as givens. The children were expected to compete for grades and on the athletic field and to think about eventually training for occupations that did not even exist within the tribe. Once the Indian children were exposed to this rugged individualism, they could not just forget about it and return to tribal ways. For one thing, the occupation of hunter was no longer available to them; even if it had been, these Indians were now aware of themselves in a whole new light. They were aware of themselves as unique individuals. When they returned to their homes, however, the needs of their family for homeostasis would cause the family to discourage this newfound identity. This resulted in the children pulling away from the competition in school and doing quite poorly academically. Even so, they were not able to return to a role that would be satisfactory for their family because of what they had seen. The final result was apathy and a high rate of alcoholism. This in turn gave rise to the Whites' image of the "shiftless Indian," which would further reinforce the apathy.

Let us now look at this process at the family systems level. As culture evolves, it will usually be the children, adolescents, and young adults who are most subject to the pull of increased separation-individuation forces within society. This is because older adults tend to be more conservative, in the sense that they are usually more settled into patterns that were appropriate for the earlier level of cultural evolution. Particularly if their job situation and social circle have remained constant, their contacts with subsystems of the culture that are significantly different from their own will be highly limited. Younger people, meanwhile, are exposed to many more elements of the culture at large, because they are going to school with a large mix of people or are in occupational circumstances that are subject to a high degree of flux. This inequality of exposure is the primary source of the "generation gap," and it is likely to be particularly pronounced during times of cultural transition, such as the late 1960s.

Whenever parts of the family are exposed to a degree of separation-individuation that threatens family homeostasis, the level of anxiety within the system rises to disturbing levels. The persons or holons within the family who have had the most exposure, usually but not always the younger members, are then the ones disturbing the equilibrium within the family system. As an example, let us look at the situation of a hypothetical American woman who grew up before World War II. Let us say that cultural norms in her particular environment dictated that her role functioning be limited to the duties of a wife and mother. Along comes the war, and suddenly women are encouraged to take outside jobs in order to support the war effort. This woman responds to the patriotic calling and goes to work. Once she has had this experience, she begins to realize that the idea of a career appeals to her. However, when the war ends, her family expects her to give up any career aspirations she has had and to return home. Further down the line, in the 1960s, the presence of an ambitious, feminist daughter could represent a problem for family homeostasis.

In the American culture prior to World War II, as in many other cultures today, a woman who had career ambitions could sacrifice their direct expression and still remain relatively comfortable. Even if, through the inexorable progression of individual development, she had reached a stage in her own life where her level of separation-individuation made it highly unlikely that the interests of her true self were limited to wifehood, motherhood, and those other pursuits allowed to women of her time, she could still be somewhat satisfied, for three reasons. First, the wider cultural holon told her that what she was doing was valuable in and by itself. Being involved in a satisfying interpersonal, sexual relationship and being a parent are important considerations for most everyone, regardless of their uniqueness in other respects, so this particular cultural message had at least some validity for each and every woman. Second, birth control, day-care centers, washing machines, microwave ovens, and such were nonexistent or not readily available, so wifehood-motherhood really was a full-time job, with little time for many other concerns anyway. Both having a full-time job and taking care of a family was extremely difficult, unless the family was quite wealthy. A division of labor along sexual-role lines was a very workable solution to this problem, and the woman's biology made her the likely candidate for the caretaker role.

Finally, the culture at that time provided for various mechanisms by which more aggressive, "masculine" urges could be "sublimated." For example, if a pre–women's movement female had strong propensities to run a business, she could instead become involved in the politics of a charitable organization and run it without causing homeostatic difficulties, such as threatening her husband's role-model identification as breadwinner. Chances are, her husband had to sacrifice some of *his* natural propensities, such as some of his dependency needs, to fulfill the expectations of his family and cultural system. Part of those expectations may have been to avoid "masculine," aggressive women. ("Who wears the pants in your family, anyway?") Of course, he too had been provided by the cultural system with mechanisms to sublimate his repressed needs, such as allowing his wife to take charge when he was ill or otherwise indisposed. If the wife were suddenly to come home and say to her husband, "I want to run a business, not a charity, so I can get paid for what I'm doing," the whole delicate homeostatic balance would be upset, but because of the availability of culturally acceptable outlets for partially expressing suppressed aspects of self, there was no need to do such things.

What might happen to upset this happy state of affairs? Because of the rapid rate of cultural evolution characteristic of recent American culture, a mother and a grown daughter could be at different cultural levels. When this happens, the grown daughter is exposed to a cultural "message" that is completely at odds with the cultural message received by the mother when she was young. The daughter learns that it is now possible, because of new technology and new ways of taking care of the family that were simply unavailable to her mother, to "have it all." She can have family and a full-time career as well. Granted, this is a rather new possibility, and the logistics for having it all are far from being completely worked out, but nonetheless the opportunity is there. As the daughter hobnobs with her peers, she hears that not only is it possible to have it all, it is desirable as well. Being a wife and mother is no longer valuable enough; time exists for other pursuits, and limiting these pursuits to unpaid charitable work is denying one's own creativity and satisfaction.

If the daughter comes home from the outside world excited about all the new possibilities for being a more well-rounded, more fulfilled individual, she will usually want to share her excitement with the rest of the family. She has seen the world and herself in a new light. The mother, on the other hand, has had no support from any other parts of her system for expressing this new possibility and is capable of doing so only at the price of an existential crisis. The functioning of her family system is built entirely around the old way of doing things, and to change would be to upset the apple cart, to threaten homeostasis.

The daughter will often become irritated with the mother's attitude, rather than empathetic with her situation, because she does not understand it. To her, there seems no logical reason that would preclude making changes in the way that the system operates. If the daughter acts out the anger, this will prevent a meaningful interchange on the new ideas. If, on the other hand, the daughter were to become empathetic, she might be able to provide her mother with a whiff of the new possibilities. The mother then might wish to consider them for herself but would immediately be met with disqualification from her husband and perhaps her own parents, because of the threat to family homeostasis. The mother's first inclination, whether or not she fully appreciates the message her daughter is bringing to her, would be to avoid upsetting the family homeostasis, as well as the awful feeling of groundlessness that would come from the resultant disqualifications of her family system. One way to do this would be to try to ignore the daughter's ideas, and to quiet the daughter by disqualifying her attempts to communicate them.

Disqualifying the daughter may at first glance appear to be a rather mean thing to do. In doing so, the mother is avoiding an existential crisis for herself and the rest of the family by inducing a sense of groundlessness in the daughter. The daughter becomes the subject of doubt, incurred by the mother's refusal to mirror her, instead of the mother becoming the subject of the doubt that might come out of the daughter's ideas. However, the mother is not ignoring her daughter's sensibilities as much as might appear. The daughter has received some mirroring for her ideas from the larger cultural holon—in the media, from her friends, her teachers, and her mentors, and so on. She will not give them up easily. The mother's disqualification, particularly if done in a provocative style, can have the effect of angering the daughter. If done correctly, the disqualification of the daughter's communication can result in the actual strengthening of the daughter's resolve to be the woman of the new cultural age. The mother in this case provides a form of covert mirroring to the daughter's ideas and life-style while appearing to do the opposite! The mother's anger-provoking behavior has the net effect of disqualifying the daughter's *communication* about the new ideas, not the ideas themselves. The daughter may therefore resolve to live the newer life-style but to pretend in front of the mother to be more traditional than she really is. Additionally, the mother may pretend to be unaware of what actually goes on with the daughter, in order to protect her own position.

The mother's action has the effect of pushing her daughter forward, much the way a mother bear abruptly abandons her cub when the time has come for the cub to function on its own. At the same time, the mother is protecting herself from being disqualified by the larger system and protecting the larger system from threats against its homeostasis. In this way, the family system attempts to concern itself with helping later generations adjust and adapt to cultural changes, while maintaining its homeostasis. This is one mechanism by which the biological concern for evolution is expressed at the family systems level.

The method thus chosen for balancing these factors may

leave the daughter feeling very conflicted, which will make her appear to others to be very neurotic. Should she pursue her own ideas, without the support of and to the apparent distress of the rest of her family? Should she just leave her parents in the lurch, stuck in an old pattern that might not be as fulfilling as a new one, and go on to selfishly enjoy it unshared? The family may wish to help her to make the adjustment. She may be allowed (and by being *allowed,* I mean that her decision will be mirrored, overtly or covertly) to consult an outsider, to see a therapist, for instance. If the rest of the family system is in no acute distress because its homeostatic mechanisms continue to work, the therapist will be able, through individual therapy, to help her continue the process of learning to express her separation-individuation by helping her to resolve her conflicts.

In at least two situations, things cannot be worked out as smoothly as I have outlined in the above example. First, if the homeostatic mechanisms of the family are not working, the daughter will not be able to just leave her distressed family to go "do her own thing." Children care far too much about their family system to just ignore high levels of systemic dysfunction. The survival of their family system is at stake, and they will attempt to come to the rescue. As we shall see, this is true even if, to outward appearances, the child has nothing to do with the family. A second, related type of difficulty occurs when the child's welfare would be threatened, or the family perceives that it would be threatened, if the child were allowed to partake in the new stage of cultural evolution. Cultural evolution does not proceed at exactly the same rate for all segments and classes within society, even within one nation, and this can lead to dangerous situations. I would like to now spend some time describing a model for such an occurrence, in hopes of providing a model for the development of disturbances of personality.

Cultural Change and Personality Disturbance: A Model

Educators and social workers working with Black youths in urban ghettos have long been disturbed by an apparent callous disregard for the value of an education by many poorer

Black families. Granted, the quality of the schools in the inner city is terrible, but only a few of the parents of the Black children who go there complain about it, as many White parents might. This has been true even since government in the United States began to pay attention to Black complaints. To the White liberal, it is obvious that education is the royal road to the middle class and that poor Black youths will never be able to participate in the general upward mobility allowed by American culture unless they are qualified for jobs that require this education. The efforts of well-intentioned professionals to relay this message are routinely ignored by many Black families, much to the mystification of their would-be teachers.

To many White educators, the apparent resistance is completely baffling and appears to be downright irrational. Many have to fight in themselves the racist notion held by some of their colleagues that Blacks on the whole are dumb and lazy. They search for better explanations. Is it perhaps that years of being second-class citizens have destroyed Black pride and self-confidence, and the unfortunate victims ignore education because they have just plain given up, in the cultural equivalent of mental depression? All right, let us work on reinstilling pride in them. We will tell them that Black is beautiful. We will emphasize Black contributions to American history and make "Black studies" a college major. The Black pride movement helped some families, but the interest level of significant numbers of Black schoolchildren continued to lag way behind that of their White counterparts. Education advanced very little on the list of priorities for the average Black in the central city.

This behavior does appear at first glance to fit the criteria for irrationality. Certainly a higher standard of living is a desirable goal. A bias against education clearly impedes progress toward this goal. Is this, then, a prime example of the fundamental irrationality of human behavior? I think not. The behavior can be seen in a light that makes it appear far more rational. A major causative factor for this behavior that has been ignored is the fact that just a few generations ago, Blacks trying to get an education were in a most precarious position. They would frequently be whipped and beaten, if not lynched. A Black try-

ing to get an education was an "uppity nigger." A majority of
Whites thought of Blacks as poor and dumb and aimed to keep
them that way. Threats of violence from the Ku Klux Klan and
other organizations were made as loudly and as frequently as
necessary to make the children of slaves frightened of trying to
get ahead in life. No wonder Black people were not falling over
one another trying to climb the social ladder.

But, one might object, this situation no longer exists, at
least in most of the country. The bright, educated Black is no
longer threatened with such consequences. Avoiding education
may once have been adaptive, but now it is a terrible hindrance.
Doing so once made sense; today it is just not the logical thing
to do. In answer to this, I would say that subtle and not-so-
subtle forms of racial discrimination, the continued existence of
which no one seriously or convincingly disputes, serve as a constant reminder to Blacks that their newfound position as
"equals" in society remains suspect. Any gains made must appear to them to be insecure. However unlikely a resurgence of
Jim Crow is to have the kind of impact it once had, Blacks can
never quite be sure that it will not again take place at any time.
The White majority may appear to be accepting, but are they
really? No one can read minds; perhaps the "accepting" Whites
are trying to lure Blacks into a false sense of complacency. Perhaps they are looking for the first opportunity to push them
back down. Give them a taste of better things and then humiliate them. Pat them on the back and then laugh behind it. This
sort of thing was done to Blacks as a matter of course as recently as the 1960s.

A vicious circle develops. The doubt by Blacks that they
would really be secure in becoming educated leads to much reluctance to make the attempt. Should they decide to press forward, they will do so tentatively, as if to test the waters. This
gives Whites the impression that they really are incapable of
doing so, or really do not want to, reinforcing the racial stereotype that Blacks actually prefer to be poor and dumb. Even the
most enlightened Whites cannot entirely free themselves of the
suspicion that this may after all be true, because so many Blacks
do not apply themselves enthusiastically. The White has no idea

what is actually motivating the Black to behave in this manner. The strengthening of the racial stereotype reinforces Black suspicions that they are not really safe in proceeding with their education.

The vicious circle becomes what Watzlawick, Beavin, and Jackson (1967) have dubbed a "game without end"—a stereotyped pattern of interaction in human systems—at any level—in which any attempt by one of the constituents of the system to change the interaction is interpreted by the rest of the system as just another way of doing the same old thing. Particularly, if any systemic constituent attempts to change the rules by which the "game," the pattern of interactions, is played, the rest of the system responds as if he or she had merely made another move in the same game. Because of prior experiences, no member of the system trusts the change made by any other member of the system. In the example of our model, any attempt by Whites to treat Blacks as equals could be interpreted by suspicious Blacks as an attempt to set them up for future humiliation. The Whites could suddenly show their hand and push the Blacks back into the mud. As I mentioned, that sort of thing was done frequently in the days of Jim Crow. Conversely, any attempt by Blacks to communicate that they truly value education could be interpreted by the prejudiced White as the move of an Uncle Tom. Blacks might be saying that they value education only to please whitey, not because they really mean it.

The way out of a game without end would seem to be metacommunication. If the participants in the game could talk about the rules, rather than acting them out, misunderstanding could be avoided. If the Black said, "I may appear to be unenthusiastic about education, but this is because I don't trust you and I am afraid of what might happen if I act like what you used to call an 'uppity nigger,' " well-meaning Whites would gain insight into how White behavior is holding Blacks back, even in the absence of obvious discrimination. A White might then respond, "My apparent view of you as preferring to be poor and dumb stems from your mistrust and the resultant lack of enthusiasm for education." Gradually, mutual trust and understanding could develop, as each found ways to reassure the other that their suspicions were unwarranted.

Attempts at such dialogue are made from time to time, but they are few and far between. Is this lack of effort at the resolution of conflict, then, a true example of the fundamentally irrational nature of the human animal? If they were rational, could they not work things out in this manner? Not so. An attempt at metacommunication involves a great deal of risk. Because of the game-without-end aspect, Blacks can never be sure that their efforts to clarify things would not be just one more thing used by Whites to humiliate them. A White could appear to be very understanding and even sincere in efforts to metacommunicate back, but it could all be an act. It could all be just a disguised invitation to a lynching. A Black who attempts to challenge the status quo would stick out like a sore thumb and might be asking for trouble. Conversely, Whites could never be sure that the Black was not putting one over on them. Blacks could be viewed as trying to trick the Whites into more welfare or something similar, and not really be intending to take better care of themselves at all.

Would it not be possible for somebody, particularly a younger person who had not experienced back-of-the-bus racial segregation firsthand, to go ahead and take the risk? The answer to this question is that ability to perceive the situation realistically, as well as the courage to take the risk, does indeed exist. However, there is a major complicating factor. In times of rapid cultural change, the earlier generation will have had ample experience with how the old system operated, and it will be they who prevent the younger generation from taking the risk. The parents of the younger Black will become alarmed if their child sticks his or her neck out, and they will not provide the kind of gentle, pushing-out-of-the-nest, provocative disqualification with which our mother of a feminist felt comfortable. Instead, they will disqualify the youngster in a way that truly induces a sense of unmirrored groundlessness in the risk taker. Additionally, the elders' anxiety level will increase to such an extent that it threatens family homeostasis, providing the second reason that can cause children to stop efforts to express their individuation at a level consistent with a new stage of cultural evolution. This formulation does not mean that current cultural factors do not contribute to the educational problem; it means

only that resistance from earlier generations makes it more difficult for younger generations to cope with the current factors.

   A Family Saga. Let us now see how this process might affect members of a hypothetical individual family over several
generations. Let us suppose that a Black great-grandfather-to-be
is a young man in or around 1880. He was born a slave in the
Old South and is now free but is surrounded by hostile White
southerners, banded into various groups such as the Ku Klux
Klan. Any attempt by this Black gentleman to get ahead of the
"poor White," such as attempts to get an education, would be
met with extreme violence. Even learning to read might be a
potential death warrant. Naturally, this man is going to wish to
protect his child from death and will diligently teach this child
to avoid any appearance of wishing to advance himself through
education. This child, the grandfather in our saga, will have a
clear understanding of the necessity of this teaching, as well as
the line of reasoning that led to it. Still, when he reaches adulthood, he wishes for a better life and decides to emigrate to Chi-
cago, where the Klan is not quite so powerful. He has heard that
he can make money working in the munitions plants during the
World War. Once there, however, he is naturally confronted
with a negative Black stereotype. All around him, he is thought
of as potentially no better than a janitor. While going to school
is not quite as dangerous as it was in the South, most doors to
advancement remain closed, and "uppity" Blacks are still subject to danger.

   We note here that the danger of getting an education for
our Grandfather is not nearly so great as it was for Great-grandfather. Grandfather can see this despite what his father had
taught him, and might be tempted to take a risk, but the response set of the surrounding culture reinforces rather than
undermines the lessons that he learned from Great-grandfather.
He has received mirroring for self-advancement neither from
the family holon nor from the larger cultural holon. If he were
to proceed according to his own personal assessment of the risk,
he would be subject to an immediate sense of groundlessness.
Rather than face that awful feeling, he plays it safe. He teaches

his own child, directly or indirectly, to be extremely careful about any appearance of self-advancement.

Even so, he will not be completely blind to the decreased risk in the culture about him. A doubt, small but significant, will remain with him. For this reason, he will feel unsure whether he is really teaching his child something that might be a hindrance rather than a help, but he will nonetheless become fearful and will experience groundlessness if he does not teach the child according to the old rules. What he might *not* do is tell his child all the reasons *why* the thought of getting an education makes him so nervous. He is not completely sure of the validity of these reasons, and he may be annoyed with himself for not being able to take a chance.

Meanwhile, his child, the father in this family scenario, will be subject to a somewhat different message from the surrounding culture regarding the risks of education. Father is now going to school at a time when opportunities for Blacks are starting to increase. World War II has just ended; Black army units have acquitted themselves well on the battlefield, and Blacks are becoming more vocal in demanding a piece of the American pie. The Brooklyn Dodgers, tired of playing second fiddle to the Yankees in their hometown, sense an opportunity and decide to risk signing Jackie Robinson. Whites everywhere, faced with postwar prosperity, are less threatened by the advancement of their less fortunate brethren, for it appears possible for everyone and anyone to do well.

Father looks about him and thinks that trying to better himself might not be such a bad idea after all, but enough evidence abounds that danger is lurking behind the corner. He thinks twice. Schools in Black neighborhoods are consistently underfunded compared to schools in White neighborhoods, and the White majority seems to prefer it that way. Attempts to integrate schools in the South are met with state-sponsored violence. Companies that are beginning to hire Blacks to positions of increased responsibility do so on a token basis and continue to block the doors to true corporate power. To Father, the ideas of Grandfather seem old-fashioned, but he has some understanding of them despite the lack of explanations. With all this, however, he has still experienced some mirroring from the larger cultural holon that the time is ripe for some taking of risk. He may decide that it is too late to educate himself but that his son should go ahead. He preaches to his son the value of education, but every time the son does well in school, Father's anxiety level rises. Father continues to be subject to fear that the old rules still apply. He continues to be subject to ground-lessness, for the mirroring he has received for the idea of striving to get ahead is incomplete at best. Ashamed of his fears, he tells his son nothing about why the son's doing well increases the tension level in the family.

The son is in a very strange position. Around him, things continue to change. The Voting Rights Act has been passed, and some Whites have even died in the civil rights movement helping Blacks advance. Bear Bryant goes ahead and integrates the University of Alabama football team. Black power advocates are everywhere. Some are put in jail, but others rise to take their places. Peers are saying that Black is beautiful. At home, Father is currently preaching education, and indeed gets quite angry if Son does not do well. Simultaneously, however, every time Son does do well, Father becomes a nervous wreck, threatening family homeostasis. The son is in a classic double bind, damned if he does and damned if he does not. He is far more concerned with family homeostasis than he is with being an object of his father's ire, so he opts to avoid the education. Because of the conflict, he also becomes somewhat apathetic, which in a sense helps him to suppress his own desires to make something of himself.

Again, one might wonder why Son does not attempt to solve the double bind through metacommunication. Why does he not go to Father and say, "Gee, why is it that every time I do poorly you get angry, but each time I do well you get nervous?" Obviously, if this book is to maintain that humans can clearly see what goes on about them despite appearances of ignorance, then it would follow that Son can see the contradiction in Father's behavior. Son should have all the motivation he needs to ask for clarification. Father's behavior has direct and severe consequences for him, and Father's behavior is incomprehensible to him. Father says one thing but seems to prefer the opposite. What Father says makes sense; how he acts does not. Father is offering no explanation for this curious state of affairs. Why does not Son go on and demand one? The reason that Son does not demand an explanation has to do with the reason that Father is not offering an explanation in the first place.

Potency, Shame, and the Altruistic Paradox. I have previously alluded to the fact that a sense of personal mastery is something that people value highly, but that the development of a sense of such mastery is particularly vulnerable to the input of the family system. We have seen how concerns with autonomy and personal potency are part and parcel of a stage of the evolution and development of each and every human being, and I have expressed the opinion that this concern is never lost, no matter how little it is expressed by individuals who appear to be big babies.

The refusal of parents to mirror autonomy does not result in a loss of concern for it. In discussing how a poor sense of one's own autonomy is related to existential doubt, I borrowed a page from Erikson (1963), but Erikson also tied another feeling in with the doubt. He spoke of the sense of shame. Shame is an emotion that stems from a sense of helplessness, particularly in relation to the relative strength of other people in the environment. Indeed, the existence of the emotion of shame at all is a mark of the importance to everyone of a sense of personal potency. Shame emanates from the self, with the role of others being their relative potency and their power to mirror. In effect, the sense of shame is a statement about the power of the potent, controlling adult over the dependent, helpless child. A person feels ashamed when *found* to be doing something that others find reprehensible, not because the shame emanates from their disapproval but because they *see* him or her and can then exercise control.

Shame does not motivate an individual to quite the extent that doubt does. Shame is a concern with an issue of individual development, whereas doubt stems from concerns that are more systemic in nature. Because of the biological concern with survival of the species, systemic concerns are more power-

ful than and take precedence over individual concerns in determining motivation. This does not mean, however, that the effects of shame are inconsequential. Far from it. Indeed, a sense
of shame over one's assumed lack of potency is a particularly
depressing feeling. A sense of helplessness, rather than "anger
turned inward," as some have postulated, might even be at the
heart of depression. While not as devastating as the anxiety of
disconnectedness, shame is hard to tolerate.

Let us now return to the question of why, in our model,
Son does not go back to Father and ask for clarification as to
why Father is putting Son in a double bind. If Son were to do
so, he would unwittingly be holding up to Father Father's relative impotency in the face of White discrimination. In a sense,
the raising of the whole question about why the idea of getting
an education makes Father feel upset rubs Father's nose in a
sense of shame. Son, who in contradistinction to his father has
only minimal fear of the White, would seem to others to be
more powerful than Father in this respect. This would be a role
reversal. The situation is akin to the situation of being "caught"
discussed above. Father would not only be caught, he would be
caught by someone who is supposed to be below him in the
family hierarchy.

Any attempt by Son to metacommunicate with Father
about the difficulty would immediately expose Father's shame
and therefore raise his distress level. The rise in distress level
would be obvious and severe enough to precipitate a parental
depression, which in turn would be a threat to family homeostasis. Son quickly gets a message to back off from Father as well
as from the rest of the family. Others in the family also respond
to the threat to family homeostasis and therefore move to protect Father from the shame and the subsequent feelings of helplessness and depression. The family may reactively disqualify
Son in a way that discourages him through groundlessness rather
than in a way that might push him forward through anger. More
than likely, the entire family system would deny that the problem even exists. Father could say, in fact quite honestly, that he
wants Son to get ahead. How dare Son even question Father's
sincerity? Father defensively becomes indignant.

In order to protect Father from an apparent but unclear

threat, and himself from an existential crisis, Son backs off. Trying desperately to make sense of all this, he attempts to guess why Father behaves so irrationally, why Father preaches the very values he appears in actuality to find rather distressing when followed by Son. Son must make his guess without asking Father outright. One possible guess that he might make, and a reasonable one considering the information at hand, is that Father really dislikes Son—that he does value education but secretly wishes to see Son fail. Such a guess would not be at all dissimilar to the interpretation, made by many therapists in such cases, that Father is unconsciously subverting the success of his son.

In order to protect Father from bad feelings and himself from the anxiety of groundlessness, Son opts to do something that has the effect of taking on for himself the shame of impotency in the face of whitey. He sacrifices his own education and with it his chances to improve his economic status. If he did not, and went ahead with the education that Father overtly advocates, Father might get in touch with a sense of shame even in the absence of metacommunication. Father might become envious of his son, even while at the same time being happy for him. The envy might lead to a self-assessment on the part of Father that could lead to the sense of impotency and would most certainly lead to a lot of regret. In light of the presence of a value system that mandates that an individual give highest priority to her or his basic biological propensity to be concerned with the survival of her or his family system, and that maintenance of family homeostasis is the major way to accomplish this goal, Son's decision is an entirely rational one, despite its inherent self-destructiveness.

One possible way out of the bind might be for the son to try to be a star athlete, for athletic competition was one of the first areas of lucrative endeavor opened to Blacks. Father might feel that Son was in less danger and would therefore become less alarmed if Son went this route than if he chose education as his vehicle to get ahead in life. Many Blacks have indeed made this choice, but, unfortunately, openings for athletes are rather limited in number.

The apparent "solution" of the family problem by the

son's sacrifice of his own best interests is the only one that seems available to him, even though better solutions do exist, because he does not know the true nature of the problem he is trying to solve. This would be a sad enough state of affairs, but it is made even sadder by the fact that the son's solution not only is a poor one but actually has the effect of making things worse in the long run. It backfires. Not only does it make things worse for him and for any children he might have, it makes things worse for the rest of the family as well. This is the heart of the altruistic paradox.

The fact remains that the rule by which the family operates, in this case the fear of education, is no longer appropriate for the stage of cultural evolution of the society in which the family lives, despite the presence of continued racial discrimination. Everyone in the system is aware of this to some extent; they just do not know how to go about changing things without the development of an existential crisis. By refusing to allow Father to experience distress, the rest of the family is actually having the effect of *increasing* Father's sense of impotency. For one thing, the family's protectiveness keeps the issue from being put out on the table, where it could be bounced back and forth between the family members. If such discussions could take place, the various factors contributing to the fear level in the family could be weighed and measured. When such a process is carried out by the system collectively, it has the effect of mirroring new ways of looking at reality for all the individuals within that system. The new way of looking would in turn have the effect of renewing the father's sense of potency, by opening up new behavioral options and increasing understanding of the factors that prevented him from expressing his potency in the first place.

A second, far more subtle blow to Father's sense of potency comes from the family's protectiveness. Father can sense that the rest of the family avoids a subject when he becomes upset about it. The message that this gives is that the family thinks he is too weak to tolerate pain. If the going gets tough, he cannot handle it. This is the reverse of the process by which a parent creates a whining, dependent child who cannot tolerate delay of gratification—the type of parent who tries to protect his child from all of life's frustrations and thereby undermines the child's sense of mastery.

In this discussion, I hope to have demonstrated a model for a process in which the difficulties that a family system encounters when its own adaptive mechanisms lag behind revolutionary changes in human culture lead to the development of an irrational-appearing character trait, a disdain for education in this example. In the next section, I would like to expand on the ideas inherent in the model to see how this process might account for the development of a full-fledged personality disorder.

Constellations of Personality Traits

In chapter nine of their groundbreaking book *Paradox and Counterparadox,* Palazzolli, Boscolo, Cecchin, and Prata (1978) describe in detail the case history of an Italian family in which the forces of cultural evolution and family homeostatic mechanisms combined to create a case of anorexia and depression in a young girl. The "Casanti" family descended from tenant farmers who lived for many centuries under a feudal system in rural Italy. Because the people in this cultural milieu were traditionally poor and the work on the farm was hard and time-consuming, the more family members that were available to help, the better off a family as a whole was. For this reason, large families were highly valued by the peasants. Male children were particularly prized, since they were the ones who had to do the work in the fields. The women were completely occupied with having babies, taking care of them, and, since they were there already, running the home. Each family member knew his or her place. No one thought that the distribution of roles in the family according to sex was unfair, because alternatives were clearly unfeasible. Having lots and lots of children had survival value, and no outsider was available to look after them. When they were old enough, the children began to work with the family, but there were usually younger ones to take their place, so the women got very little reprieve from their caretaking duties. The children spent little or no time in school, because their services were needed at home. The common good of the family—sometimes its very survival—was served well by this system. Everyone's role was culturally sanctioned and made sacred by the Catholic Church.

At the head of the family at any given time was a patriarch, who made most if not all of the major decisions for the family group. The decisions that he made were based primarily on the need for the family to work together as a unit. Since almost all available time was spent in activities related to putting food on the table, no one thought or cared much about individualistic activities. All the sons pitched in to work in pretty much identical jobs. Competition between them would have been both pointless and destructive. When they married, their wives were brought into the family, with the purpose of enlarging the labor pool still further and providing assistants to their mother.

Palazzolli alludes to the forces of groundlessness working on the family: "To leave their family meant emigration and uprooting, without any means or preparation. It meant doing without help and support in case of illness or hard luck. Needless to say, most families . . . chose to remain together" (p. 84). She goes on to conceptualize the family process in terms of a family myth: "The survival, safety, and dignity of its members depend on the family. Whoever separates himself from the family, is lost." In terms of the original cultural situation, this idea was hardly mythological. It was accurate. Living according to this rule was quite adaptive. Alternatives were unworkable.

Along come two cultural developments that turn the world topsy-turvy: World War II and the widespread use and availability of the radio. The youngest son in the Casanti family, Siro, goes to the war and is exposed to a whole new world, including a new trade. When he returns to the family at the conclusion of the war, he finds himself "depressed and estranged." This is not in the least surprising; he had received mirroring and support from outside of the family for a completely different, somewhat more individualistic life-style, and forgetting about such a possibility is something most people have trouble doing. Nonetheless, after a time, he readjusts and resumes his former position. Five years away from the family prove to be no match in influence for continuous and at that point unopposed exposure to the family system. However, the forces of cultural evolution refuse to leave this well-functioning family to its own devices.

Through the radio, women in the family begin to learn about how city women are now able to do things about which a country girl would never even dream. These city women do not exist as servants to their men; they can "go to town," both literally and figuratively. The wives of the Casanti sons begin to complain about their newly perceived restrictions. When they do so, the men circle the wagons, joining with their parents in a silent coalition to oppose changes in the way that the family functions. Along with challenges to gender role models, the family begins to experience but will simply not tolerate jealousy, the making of comparisons between family members, and rivalry among them. The family has to stick together at all costs, lest everything be lost.

The barriers to "progress" that the family attempts to erect prove to be of no avail. The forces from the outside culture continue to impinge on the family to a greater and greater degree: "The fascist era with its glorification of the graingrowers is over . . . democracy arrives . . . political rallies . . . tenant farmer defined as exploited . . . inevitable contact with people who can make money fast" (p. 87). The Casantis think that the rest of the world has gone crazy. Eventually, however, they are forced to leave the farm and attempt to re-establish the family in the city. They form a business, still united, and attempt to run the family system in exactly the same manner as it had been run on the farm. They persist in doing so despite a significant gain in family resources, continuing to act as if the survival of the family depended on family unity.

The problems caused by this pattern multiply manyfold for the next generation. In school, Siro's daughter is exposed to a steady barrage of competition, comparisons, judgments, jealousy, and gossip. Such things would have destroyed the family had they occurred in the situation of nineteenth-century tenant farmers. At that moment, however, the family consists of twentieth-century city dwellers. The daughter, Nora, is also confronted by a jealous and backbiting cousin. Of course, no one else in the family will believe that the cousin is behaving in such a manner. The cousin's behavior is always circumspect in the presence of the rest of the family, and the family believes that cousins are no different from sisters, and sisters always stick together. Nora receives no support for commenting on her situation and learns to remain silent. She attempts to refrain from competing with her cousin, to avoid the chance of challenging her family's view of reality. However, an unexpected problem develops. Nora blossoms into a stunning beauty, far more attractive than her cousin. In response, she develops a severe case of anorexia. Her illness transforms her appearance from beautiful to frightful. Additionally, her anorexia causes her to take absences from school.

One way to look at this process is that Nora made herself unattractive in order to follow the family rule against intrafamiliar competition. The cousin was secretly in league with her own mother in breaking the rule, challenging Nora, but Nora could not handle the situation overtly in her own nuclear family. The reason for this was probably that Siro was particularly sensitive to any breach in the family rule. He had challenged it himself on a prior occasion and had experienced emotional turmoil in the process. He had had the experience of being a more individuated human being trapped in a system with no room for individuality. This may have left him particularly vulnerable to any behavior in his family that suggested that he need not have given up the new freedom he had tasted. His powerlessness in the face of systemic forces may have made him ashamed.

One might ask why the arena of the competition was physical attractiveness in its concrete manifestation. The attractiveness might have been a factor only in the competition for boyfriends, for instance. In order to avoid competing with her cousin, Nora could have developed a fear of being with boys instead of developing anorexia nervosa. Palazzolli gives us a clue as to why things turned out the way they did. She notes that Siro was "fiercely proud" of Nora's appearance. He would constantly show off photographs of his then-attractive daughter. In doing so, one might imagine that Siro was engaging in a bit of personal pride that was inconsistent with the family rule against making comparisons between family members. Nora found herself exposing her father to existential groundlessness not only when she openly competed with her cousin but also by merely existing with the body she happened to possess. Her attractiveness made it difficult for Siro to avoid the temptation of engaging in the individualism he had first experienced in World War II. In becoming ugly, Nora helped her father avoid such temptations. Attractiveness may play a role in the genesis of many cases of anorexia.

I would now like to expand on the model for maladaptive personality traits to provide a model for the development of complete personality disorders. Personality disorders are clusters of maladaptive personality traits that tend to be found together in many individuals. In order to play the role of an anorectic, with the purpose of solving a problem for family homeostasis such as that described above, an individual cannot merely refrain from eating. To engage in this behavior creates additional problems, as we shall see. An entire constellation of personality traits—a personality disorder—often becomes necessary in order to maintain the major trait. One trait alone simply does not fill the bill. I will refer to these additional traits as "ancillary traits."

First, the behavior of the anorectic is naturally bound to lead to countermeasures by the rest of the family, who will no doubt become alarmed by the threat to the health and well-being of the daughter. Even though it appears that it is the behavior of the family that maintains the symptom that is threatening the girl, in reality the family does not wish to see the child remain sick, as some theories would seem to imply. The daughter, our little actress, is far less disturbed by her family's worries over her health than she is with the threat to family homeostasis, but she must nonetheless do something about her family's efforts to get her to eat. In order to resist these efforts, she turns every family effort on her behalf into a power struggle. She develops a stubbornness and tenacity that would be the envy of anyone prone to criticize themselves for giving up too easily. A power struggle occurs over every bite of food the anorectic is given. This serves two purposes. It discourages her family from continuing their efforts to get her to eat, and it distracts her from the constant hunger that she must be feeling, particularly since food is being placed under her nose.

The anorectic must deny that she is hungry, just as she must deny that she is too thin. If she were to admit to the presence of a problem, she might be in danger of metacommunicating about her true motivation. In the case of Nora, this would risk exposing her father to shame. The denial is also another way of putting off anyone attempting to help her get over her "problem." As she will not acknowledge that a problem even exists, efforts to get her to "change her mind" are futile. Despite the denial of hunger, the anorectic is literally starving to death. The denial, however, is taken by some at face value. Many theoreticians have advanced the idea that anorectics have somehow not developed an ability to "pay attention" to somatic sensations such as hunger. Some have even gone so far as to say that awareness of hunger sensations is a learned behavior, and that anorectics have never learned how to know when they are hungry and when they are not. This idea ignores the behavior of anorectics when they are babies. No evidence exists that babies who eventually become anorectics do not cry when they are hungry. For that matter, it also ignores the fact that no evidence exists that any neurologically intact infant has to *learn* how to cry when it becomes hungry. Given the survival value of eating, if any behavior is instinctual, then knowing when one is hungry must surely come naturally.

Anorectics are, in fact, known to be preoccupied with food. Some anorectics decorate their walls with pictures that contain depictions of food in one guise or another; others prepare elaborate meals for their families, of which they themselves do not partake. If it be true that the appetite of the anorectic is present, and that she is preoccupied with food, then how is it that she seems to possess such extraordinary will power that she can go without food? Such is the power of family homeostasis and existential isolation that they can induce people to perform remarkable feats. Clearly, however, the anorectic must develop mechanisms to disturb her sense of hunger so that it is not so troublesome, in order to make her role playing at least somewhat less painful. One such way has already been mentioned—distracting herself with power struggles. A second way involves exercise.

Many anorectics compulsively exercise (Sours, 1980). Some theorists assume that the exercising represents yet another mechanism by which the anorectic hopes to lose more weight. It is assumed that this results from the current cultural emphasis on being thin and being physically fit at the same time. Indeed, exercise does serve the purpose of helping the anorectic to lose more weight. An additional purpose is to decrease appetite. Any runner will tell you that, after completing a ten-kilometer race or a marathon, the last thing one feels like doing is immediately sitting down to a large meal. The mechanism responsible for this phenomenon is thought to involve the substance pyruvate, a product of muscle metabolism that is released during long and strenuous exercise. Pyruvate is thought to decrease appetite. Of course, in the long run, exercising increases one's appetite. The pyruvate dissipates, and energy stores demand replacement. In order for the anorectic to get a continuous pyruvate effect, she exercises until she drops. This mechanism explains why exercise can be used as a reward in a behaviorally modeled inpatient program for anorexia. After the anorectic has reached starvation level, the effects of the starvation itself help her to continue to avoid craving food. At a certain point, the starved individual has difficulty eating.

As mentioned earlier, the anorectic also denies that she is too thin. She tells everyone that she views herself as being too fat. Any fat, even the slightest trace, is described as an unsightly blemish that must be dealt with immediately. She will even insist that her gruesome cachectic state is an attractive one! Besides being a way to frustrate potential helpers, such a statement is also a cryptic reference to the underlying conflict over attractiveness. As with the denial of hunger, the denial of unsightliness is also interpreted concretely by some experts on anorexia. They theorize that the anorectic has—fundamentally—a "distorted body image." This seems to imply that the anorectic does not really know how she appears to others. In the chapter on self-suppression, I gave an example of an anorectic who admitted otherwise in a candid moment brought on by a therapeutic double bind. In my opinion, that case is representative of most if not all anorectics. The fact that anorectics really seem to believe the nonsense that they are espousing is a reflection of the actor's paradox.

An anorectic, in order to stay in character, must develop a whole repertoire of behaviors. These include stubbornness, a tendency to engage in power struggles, use of denial, an apparent inability to perceive how she appears to others, and preoccupation with exercise. The necessity of ancillary traits—those traits required in order to play a role more effectively—is one reason that a whole constellation of personality characteristics might develop in response to cultural lag. These characteristics would tend to be found together in similar patterns in all those people who developed a particular response to a given problem of family homeostasis. A second reason for the development of a full-fledged personality disorder is that many traits may be required in order to cope with a particular stage of cultural evolution. The next generation is then forced to deal with all these traits in a new milieu in which none remain appropriate.

A good example of a cultural event that generated a whole host of personality traits that were then seen together in a subsequent generation is the Great Depression of the 1930s. This event can be seen as the driving force behind the creation of many obsessive-compulsive personalities. Many traits were necessary for survival during this period, not just one or two. During this historical era, people were brought abruptly to the realization that one could lose, with little warning, everything one had worked a lifetime to accumulate. Stock markets crashed, businesses failed, farms were repossessed, crops were destroyed by dust bowl conditions, jobs were lost, life savings were wiped out by bank failures, and so on. If you lost your job, you were out of luck. Employers were not keen to offer you another position. If you had a job, your employer considered you a lucky person. He was not sure himself whether he had the money necessary to pay you. Telling off the boss when you were angry was hazardous to your health. Complaining about the job was an invitation to poverty. No matter how capricious or unreasonable your boss, you kept your mouth shut and you took it. People were waiting in the wings to take your place the minute you stumbled. If you did not enjoy your job, you did not concern yourself with your pleasure. You did not have the luxury of being able to look for a job you liked; you were fortunate to be employed at all.

In such an environment as this, several traits were adaptive. One learned to keep angry feelings toward authority figures—such as a boss—inside, lest one be fired. One worked whenever one could; pleasurable experiences that one missed were irrelevant or of low priority. One saved one's money for a rainy day, since financial disaster was always just around the corner. One could not afford to waste resources on trivialities. In fact, one watched every penny; even little savings here and there add up. One would certainly not be foolhardy enough to engage in speculative investments such as the stock market; even banks were not safe. Indeed, were it not for the advent of federal deposit insurance, many of the Depression-era folks still with us would be saving their money by stuffing it into mattresses. In 1985, runs on state-insured savings and loan institutions indicated that fear can reign long after a feared occurrence disappears.

The culture of the Depression era cultivated in many men habits that are prized by employers. Among these are punctuality and orderliness; a willingness to work overtime whenever requested no matter what sacrifices are necessary in order to do so; dedication to one's work; loyalty to the company; and a willingness to do what the boss asks no matter how unreasonable. When these traits are seen in a period of relative abundance and affluence instead of during a depression, what we have is precisely an obsessive-compulsive personality. At such times, watching every penny becomes cheapness; holding in your anger at authority becomes isolation of affect; punctuality becomes obsession with time; heightened concern with risk becomes indecisiveness; a willingness to put in long hours becomes workaholism; refusal to quit an unsatisfying job or an over-demanding boss when job opportunities are readily available be-

comes downright silliness. Nonetheless, such traits would continue to stabilize a family in which the parents continue to feel
that economic disaster is always lurking around the corner.
Such fears are not entirely unreasonable; after all, the Great Depression did follow a period of affluence and abundance.

The forces of cultural evolution do not operate in an even
fashion throughout the globe but affect various groups of people in different pockets around the world differentially. Important historical events have repercussions over only a limited geographical range. Conversely, national and ethnic groups will,
more frequently than not, share a wealth of common experience as they are collectively brushed by the winds of history.
As individuals, families, and larger societal holons attempt to
adapt to the same changing environmental conditions, it is not
surprising that clusters of similar personality traits will develop
and be shared by most members of the particular cultural
group. As historical conditions change still further, these adaptive traits might in some cases become maladaptive, leading to
personality disturbances that are common to many individual
members of the ethnic collective.

This phenomenon is readily apparent among the descen-
dants of the various immigrant groups in the United States, as
described by McGoldrick, Pearce, and Giordano (1982). For
example, the emphasis on family loyalty common to many Italian families stemmed originally from the fact that the Italian
state and the wealthy landowners changed alliances frequently
as various groups of invaders occupied the country. Trust put in
a person with whom one did not have personal connections was
dangerous. In many Irish families, a pervasive belief in fatalism
and human powerlessness against nature stemmed from experiences in their homeland, an island lacking in natural resources,
frequently subjected to disastrous famines, and oppressed by a
dominant foreign power.

Having shown how a whole pattern of personality traits—
a personality disorder—might develop in a manner consistent
with the model of the Black family's attitude toward education, I must now address two obvious points that might call the
model into question. First, why is it that some families can go

through periods of cultural transition without generating a personality disorder? In the example of the Great Depression, how is it that some families—even those who suffered major financial reversals—did not produce obsessive-compulsive offspring? Second, why is it that some families go through periods of cultural transition and produce several different personality disorders, often of a kind exactly opposite to the one the model might seem to predict? Many Depression-era families do not produce compulsive cheapskates, for instance, but instead produce impulsive spendthrifts. In order to answer these questions, I must enlarge the model to include two more concepts: the cultural micropattern and the unstable parental role function.

Micropatterns

The forces of cultural evolution do not act evenly on all segments and classes within a particular culture. The same can be said about even smaller holons within the larger society. The forces of cultural evolution do not impinge on all family systems or all individuals with equal intensity. These forces interact with random events at different places and different times, and also interact with human selves of different predispositions and interests. Therefore, the experiences of any two households, or even any two individuals within a household, are never even remotely the same. I call the patterns of interaction among cultural evolution, random forces, and personal predilections as they affect particular families and individuals "micropatterns." In the model of the Black family, as an example, one might expect that a family that had actually experienced the lynching of one of its members might react more forcefully than a family whose neighbor was lynched, who in turn would react more forcefully than a family with no direct experience with lynching. Another family might even have been fortunate enough to have had only good experiences with Whites and have no negative reaction at all to the idea of getting an education.

The experiences of different members of a family may interact to heighten concern over a particular character trait, or they may serve to balance one another out, leading to differential effects on the progeny. In one family, a tendency toward overconcern with saving for a rainy day, leading to penny-pinching, was caused by two separate cultural events on two different continents. The father in the family had nearly had to quit college because of a shortage of funds partially caused by the Depression in the United States, while thousands of miles away in Russia, large sums of money were suddenly needed to save the mother's brother from a firing squad. This uncle had been arrested for anti-Communist activities, and only the bribes submitted by the grandfather saved his neck. Another sum of money was necessary a few years later to provide a bribe needed to arrange exit visas for the family.

The forces of natural disasters or disease can interact with cultural events in ways that give added significance to certain types of personality traits. As an example, Inga had conflicts over choosing between a career and a family. These conflicts appeared to be related primarily to the change in the culturally accepted role model of the female. Her conflicts over having children turned out to be much more complicated than that, however.

Inga had had five children in quick succession when she was in her late teens and early twenties but eventually left her family and allowed her husband to retain custody of them. She described to me her feelings and reactions. She stated that at first, she loved taking care of children. After a while, however, she began to have quite a different experience. She started to feel that the children were little leeches, sucking her lifeblood, draining her, constantly taking and giving nothing in return. When these feelings became oppressive and caused her to abandon her family, she felt extremely guilty, and she tried to make up for her leaving by showering the children with as much attention as she was able to muster during her frequent visits. (The frequent switches between over- and underinvolvement from their mother left her children with a feeling of uncertainty regarding their role in the family, leading to behavioral difficulties in some of them, but that is another story.) After leaving her family, Inga put a lot of energy into training for a career but tended to make decisions that made it difficult for her to find employment in her chosen field of marketing.

Inga's ambivalence regarding choosing between the caretaking and the career-woman roles, a conflict that she shares with many others because of the need to adjust to a new cultural stereotype, was a particularly charged one in the family of this patient. The reason for this had to do with two random, unrelated factors: the ordinal position of the maternal grandmother in her family of origin and a particularly vicious family confrontation with the grim reaper. Her maternal grandmother was the eldest of a horde of children born to a family in the Ukraine. As so often happened with big families at that time and place, the eldest daughter functioned as the mother's primary assistant in raising the rest of the children. A female in such a position was, in effect, forced to give up her childhood at an early age in order to assume a position of responsibility that is nearly adult in scope. She had to sacrifice some of her own mothering needs in order to be a little mother herself.

When such suppression occurs, it must be maintained in order to avoid an existential crisis. If the grandmother suddenly were impressed by the idea that her sacrifice was unnecessary, she would be overcome by a sense of meaninglessness. The major purpose in her life—being a caretaker—would become suspect, and she would have nothing to take its place. Her life would no longer have a point. A similar process would take place if she were to be robbed of the opportunity to be a caretaker. If she were unable to bear children, for instance, she would be exposed to existential groundlessness. Her purpose in life would be unfulfillable, at least until a suitable substitute for children of her own could be found. Additionally, an opportunity for sublimation of her dependency needs would also be unavailable. As ultimately unsatisfying as such sublimation may be, it does provide some gratification and helps maintain self-suppression. If taken away, suppressed aspects of self threaten to expose themselves to consciousness, with no means of expression that have been mirrored.

Not surprisingly, the grandmother set out to have a brood of her own, in order to continue her role as caretaker for large numbers of children. Unfortunately, disaster struck. For various reasons, only one of the large number of children that she carried to term survived. The surviving child was Inga's mother.

These events caused the grandmother to focus all of her energies on the one child in a particularly tenacious manner. The child was her only link to her purpose in life. Additionally, the grandmother may also have felt indirectly responsible for the deaths of the other children—after all, it had been her job to look after them—and she might have been determined to make sure no untoward happening befell the remaining child. This would have caused her to be more anxious than she might otherwise have been when the child was out of her sight.

Needless to say, whenever this child—I will refer to her as Mother—left home, Grandmother would be subjected to more than just an average empty-nest syndrome. Grandmother's entire raison d'être would evaporate, and additionally, her anxiety would increase because of worry that some disaster might strike her baby. Mother simply could not tolerate exposing her own mother to such levels of distress. Mother's attempts to establish a life of her own away from Grandmother were haphazard and halfhearted. She would limit the degree of true intimacy in her relationships with the men that she married, and the relationships would invariably fail. Time and time again, she returned to live with Grandmother. Later in life, after Grandmother had passed away, Mother expressed the belief that men were nothing but trouble.

Here I must stress the important point that, in this situation, Grandmother's intent, consciously or unconsciously, was not to "keep her child dependent on her" or to "force her child to provide the caretaking that she had missed as a child," although both of these things eventually transpired. Variations of these two interpretations are frequently made by therapists, and they have the effect of painting Grandmother as the villain in the story, rather than as the victim of unfortunate circumstances. Such a view leads to unproductive blaming. In fact, Grandmother was undoubtedly distressed at Mother's inability to form a satisfying outside relationship, and probably blamed herself for being a poor parent who hung on to her child too tightly. The decision to stay close to Grandmother was made by Mother. Mother was not forced by Grandmother to do so. Her decision was rational, based on the goals of preventing Grandmother from becoming anxious and avoiding in herself a feeling of existential groundlessness. Had Mother allowed Grandmother to get anxious instead of protecting her, and had Mother weathered her own existential anxiety, everyone would have ended up better off. Unfortunately, Mother had no way of knowing that.

Only one of Mother's romantic encounters produced a child—Inga—and that occurred late in Mother's life. Thereafter, Mother was a little bit more free to wander off to pursue her own interests. Whenever she went off to her job, Mother left the little girl with Grandmother. Inga accompanied her grandmother everywhere she went. (Grandfather had since died.) Inga was told that her father had died, even though he had not. He had nothing to do with the family, so the lie could easily be rationalized as necessary to protect the patient from feeling bad about a deserting parent.

This example illustrates how an adjustment to cultural change, difficult enough all by itself, can become nearly impossible for a family because of a set of experiences that are unique to that family. Historical events and natural calamities, fortuitous meetings, epidemics, birth order, varying proportions of male and female siblings, and a host of other factors can interact to give particular meaning to certain changes in cultural expectations and evoke different constellations of personality traits. These experiences combine in patterns that are never identical for any two holons at any level. Additionally, these micropatterns have differential effects on selves with differing propensities. The grandmother in our example, depending on whether or not she had been naturally inclined to enjoy taking care of a large contingent of children, might have reacted differently to her role as the oldest female sibling and might have had a different reaction as well to the deaths of her own children. A completely different sequence of events could have been set into motion.

In the case of Nora Casanti, random factors that may have contributed to her development of anorexia include her being the youngest child of a youngest child, which gave her the most exposure to cultural changes of any member of the family; her father's experiences in World War II; her being born a female; the success of the business venture by her father and uncles; the level of her own natural competitiveness; and her own exceptional physical beauty.

Different siblings within the same nuclear family are often exposed to different mirroring by the parents, leading each to learn a role that is unique in the family. Each will develop a unique persona, on top of his or her unique self, and therefore will have a markedly different personality. Before discussing this further, I must first address myself to the second of the two questions I posed earlier: Why is it that some families produce offspring who seem to behave in a manner exactly opposite to the way that the model seems to predict? How does one explain the studious Black or the spendthrift son of a dust bowl farmer?

Unstable Parental Role Function

Although it is the younger members of the family system who are most exposed to new ideas and possibilities for lifestyle changes in the evolving cultural system, the older members are hardly immune. A woman who had sublimated her career ambitions after World War II to become a housewife, for example, hears the feminist message just as surely as does her daughter. Such a woman may already be subject to doubts as to the need for all aspects of the role model she has chosen for herself. Mirroring is not an all-or-none phenomenon; this woman's mother may have herself expressed some ambivalence regarding the traditional female role. Such expressions can modify the mirroring that the woman received. Perhaps her mother, or some of her older female relatives, had been involved in the women's suffrage movement. The mother may have supported the traditional role halfheartedly, or may even have covertly encouraged aggressive behavior in the female children, leading them to develop an unstable role identification. Additionally, our war bride may have briefly entered the work force during the war while her husband was fighting, thereby getting a taste of pursuits that appealed to her true self. This woman, whenever she turns on the evening news, will be bombarded with messages that remind her of the "masculine" aspects of herself that she has long submerged.

The forces of cultural convention and cultural evolution do not occur separately and in sequence; both take place simultaneously. Earlier in a period of cultural transition, most families will experience the forces of convention as having more of an impact, while later on the forces of cultural change predominate. In the example of Black education, the old fears of White retribution will gradually lessen as the events that inspired them become more and more distant in time. This process can be conceptualized as a balance between the opposing forces of cultural stability and cultural change. The balance gradually shifts over time.

As mentioned earlier, Sheehy (1974) and others have pointed out that as adults reach the stage of midlife, they experience increasing difficulty suppressing aspects of themselves in order to play a role in their family. This is true even in the absence of exposure to cultural evolution. Even in the most conventional of historical circumstances, suppressed self-aspects will occasionally push through. When change is in the wind, however, the forces operating within the self at midlife interact with the forces of cultural change, giving rise to a powerful disturbance. Unmirrored, suppressed aspects of self that emerge, instead of being unsupported, may then be reinforced by the culture. Thus, a midlife crisis will tend to be more severe during times of rapid cultural transition. This will be especially true if the mirroring one has received for one's role model had been weak to begin with, because of parental ambivalence. The latter factor is also more likely to occur during periods of cultural transition. All these forces are intensified still further in today's world of mass communication. Messages concerning new life-styles and other new possibilities are seen nightly on television and trumpeted in a wide variety of reading material.

What becomes of midlife adults whose own mirroring had been plagued by parental ambivalence during a time of cultural transition? Ambivalent as it may have been, mirroring had been given to the role that they have chosen. They may have had no mirroring, ambivalent or otherwise, for a more individualistic life-style. Such people would remain subject to groundlessness were they to attempt to make a change but would also be subject to suddenly strengthened forces from within themselves that would trip up their efforts to maintain a persona. To add insult to injury, many midlife adults reach that plateau just as their own children either are leaving home for the first time or are in the middle of establishing their own life-styles as young adults in their early twenties. This is precisely the time when, by their example if not their overt verbal messages, the next generation is most likely to challenge the role models set by their parents.

If the mirroring that the parents had received from their own parents had been particularly ambivalent, or if some mirroring had been covertly supplied for an alternate life-style, this type of confusion could easily occur even earlier than the parents' midlife and affect their children prior to adolescence. The child of parents with an unstable role identification during a period of cultural transition is in a different position from that of the child of parents who are comfortable with their choices in life. Unstable parents are less able to resist the pressure, coming from their own true desires and encouraged by the cultural milieu outside, to expose suppressed characteristics. This pressure subjects them to the dangers of an existential crisis. Family homeostasis is threatened. In contradistinction to the situation of the family in which the role the parents have chosen is more stable, the child in this family cannot restore homeostasis by adopting a role that is consistent with the earlier stage of cultural evolution. This is because the threat to family homeostasis is not coming from the child's more individualistic behavior alone, as it might be in the other situation. In fact, the threat may have nothing to do with her or his behavior at all. The parents are in a dilemma created by pressures that are independent of the child.

Despite being peripheral to the problem, such children are nonetheless highly concerned with either parent's unstable behavior and the resultant threat to the family. They will be motivated to do all that they can to restore homeostasis. One way that this can be accomplished is for the child to somehow find a way to alleviate the pressure on the parent to unmask suppressed, threatening self-aspects. Children often find, through trial and error, that they can accomplish this goal by taking upon themselves the task of giving expression to the repressed aspects of the parental self that are the root of the systemic trouble. If the child acts them out, parents can gain some vicarious satisfaction of the urge to be what they are but are not supposed to be. In other words, the child can be the one expressing the troubling aspect of the parental self so that the parent does not have to. The parent then identifies with the child's action. Because of the parent's identification with the behavior, he or she may find it difficult to avoid acting in a way that seems to give approval to the child's acting out. This serves the function of providing the behavior with mirroring.

Because the child's behavior gives some vent to the parent's troubling self-aspects, the parent has an easier time maintaining a persona. The parent can then avoid the existential crisis, and family homeostasis is restored. The child has then accomplished the goal that the acting out was meant to achieve, and the behavior is reinforced. The child therefore continues the behavior. Doing so is quite sensible, given the motivation of the child.

The more conflicted the parental persona, the more the child will have to exaggerate the parent's impulse in order to restabilize the situation. This can lead to situations where the child's attempt to restabilize the parent leads not only to self-suppressive behavior but to behavior that is actively self-destructive. Slipp (1984) discusses two paradigms that, although described using object relations terminology, can with a few alterations serve as models for important variations of the acting-out process that occurs in families with a parent or parents who exhibit an unstable persona. These models are useful in understanding certain types of personality disorders. Depending on whether the repressed aspect of the parental self acted out by the child is destructive or constructive, the child will assume one or the other of the roles that Slipp has called the "avenger" and the "savior." A child who acts out parental ambitions is a savior;

one who acts out parental rage is an avenger. Let me begin with the avenger.

The "Avenger." In the extreme, when a child acts out against a wide variety of objects of repressed parental hostility, the model of the avenger is the prototype of the sociopath. In less severe cases, the model of this role can explain the presence of antisocial traits or milder forms of delinquency.

Many individuals appear to be mild-mannered, meek, and wary of their own anger. While some are naturally inclined to this behavior, others adopt it as part of a role. They learn at an early age that expressions of hostility or even annoyance are unacceptable in their families. The reason for the initial development of such family rules most likely involves some problem of cultural adjustment. Many Jewish families, for example, discourage aggression because of their heritage as a dispersed people. For generations, they were minorities in cultures in which they were outsiders. They were under constant suspicion by a frequently violent majority. Faced with such a situation, one would not wish to call attention to oneself by behaving in a threatening manner. For a time, sociopathy among Jews was relatively unusual, probably because not many Jewish parents were ambivalent about the role they had developed. It had survival value. Their children would not need to act out parental hostility in order to stabilize the parents' role function. Black families in the United States, on the other hand, were more numerous and less dispersed. A contemporary Black child acting out a parent's repressed rage against Whites would not be an unusual occurrence.

When a person represses hostility and is ambivalent about doing so, it tends to build to higher and higher levels. Sooner or later, the hostility threatens to break through the defenses of the self and express itself. This in turn leads to a strong desire to behave in a fashion that has not been mirrored sufficiently. Thus, a crisis of existential groundlessness is threatened. Children of a person in this situation can alleviate the crisis by volunteering to give vent to the feelings of rage. They serve, in a sense, as the parent's proxy. The parent thereby gains the satisfaction of striking back at the enemy without ever having to behave in a way that would be existentially unfeasible. Such parents probably would not be happy about their children's behavior, but their delight at the end result would be hard to mask. A psychoanalyst, focusing only on the child's behavior, would see "super-ego lacunae"—holes in the child's conscience—corresponding to the suppressed destructive impulses of the parental self.

The children in this scenario might appear to show no guilt or remorse over their actions. There are two reasons for this. First, they would rather harm an outsider than see their family suffer, so they are apt to view their behavior as the lesser of two evils. Second, if they were to allow themselves to feel bad for their victim, it would be far more difficult for them to play the role of avenger. Any identification that they felt with the victim, with whom they personally may have no particular quarrel, would have the effect of creating sympathy that would undermine their efforts at destroying that victim. Such children, bound and determined to carry out the parental vendetta, must suppress any such feelings that may be generated and appear to be cold, unfeeling, and guilt free.

This implies that being conscience free, as the sociopath appears to be, is in reality just an act, and that the true self of all individuals is at least capable of identifying with the pain of others and feeling guilty about having caused it. Is it not possible that some people are natural sadists, with no such capacity? I suppose it is, but I have doubts. It would seem to me that everyone is aware that other human beings have feelings, whether they pay attention to them or not; at some level, all people know that the pain experienced by others is equivalent to the pain with which they, of necessity, are personally acquainted. Therefore, it must be possible for each and every one to identify with the victim of pain and feel bad for them, no matter how cruel or uncaring they may appear to be. To say that they are incapable of imagining how their victim might feel is to once again posit some sort of undetectable defect in the wiring of their brains. In any event, I have found it clinically useful to be unbelieving of any patient who claims total lack of concern for the golden rule.

Let us now return to the model of the Black family, to

see how it might illustrate the creation of the role of avenger. What we have in this model is a family who, over several generations, has been systematically emasculated and humiliated by the White majority. Earlier on in American history, and up until recently in the South, any expression of Black rage against Whites was handled by the Whites in a most severe manner. Whereas an "uppity" Black ran some risk of being attacked, the violent Black would almost surely be subject to the lynch mob. Worse still, Whites not only blocked the expression of impulses toward retribution in Blacks, they would often attempt to *provoke* Blacks into expressions of anger, in order to humiliate them all the more. They would call the Black man "boy" and "nigger" to his face, laugh at his ways, and make him walk to the back of the bus. If Blacks showed pride, Whites would try even harder to humiliate them. If Blacks reacted, they or their families would be attacked. Black self-suppression was difficult to maintain under these circumstances but was absolutely necessary.

In the North, a different situation began to develop. Unlike the position of "uppity" Blacks, whose attempts at self-advancement made them stick out, angry Blacks in the city gradually found themselves in a position where destructive acting-out behavior could be done anonymously. They could commit criminal acts under cover of darkness and retreat to the ghetto, leaving the victims of the crime no way to identify the criminal. They could become faceless members of gangs. Although some random harassment of Blacks by the White-controlled police was still possible, mob violence by Whites against Blacks to frighten the offenders was not common.

An older contemporary Black father, who still felt the rage against the humiliation suffered by his family but whose parents might have been too frightened to mirror any expression of it, would feel groundless if he were to express his hostility in this manner. He might be destabilized by his own repressed, forbidden rage. His son, whose education and mirroring in these matters had been more ambivalent, could, in order to help his father, partially solve this problem by acting out the anger. The son could act out the rage against the humiliation felt by the father or even the grandfather, even though it was not the son who was subjected to the original insult. Each time the son acted out, the father might criticize him for it but nonetheless seem to be calmed by it. The rage that threatened the father with existential panic were it to be expressed directly by him would have found an outlet. The more rage felt by the father, the more difficult it would be to hold at bay, and the more frequent would be the occasions during which it threatened to break out. This, then, would lead the son to more extreme and more frequent acting out.

The son might believe deep down that the father's reaction indicated that the father actually supported the violent activity, but he would probably not admit to this belief. If he were to express it, he would get nothing but denial and defensiveness from his father, for two understandable reasons. First, just as in the education example, the father would feel ashamed of his and his family's inability to protect itself. An admission of vicarious satisfaction at the son's behavior might bring this into the open. Second, even though the father might get vicarious satisfaction out of the son's behavior, he would not truly wish his son to become a criminal. Far from it. The father would protest that he was unable to control his son, and add that he was appalled at the son's behavior. He might criticize the son unmercifully. The son, in truth ignoring his father's wishes in order to make the father less anxious, would in turn feel misunderstood. Angry exchanges would follow, and attempts at discussing the situation would appear fruitless to all concerned. Metacommunication would be impossible.

The reader might wonder why it is, if this model is correct, that many of the victims of Black sociopathy in the ghetto are other Blacks, instead of just Whites. I can think of at least two possible reasons. First, as the cultural situation that gave rise to the rage in the first place becomes more and more distant in the past and becomes more generations removed, the object of that original rage becomes less and less identifiable, particularly in light of the absence of metacommunication. The Black avenger might attack other Blacks because they are convenient targets. The second reason has to do with the development of another systemic problem in many Black families. Many Black males have been unable to become good family providers because of the combination of external racism and their own once-adaptive but now dysfunctional character traits. The Black woman often has been forced to compensate for this lack by taking over the role of the breadwinner in the family. It is somewhat easier for a Black woman to find work as a domestic than it is for a Black man to get a job.

Some Black males leave their families altogether. The reasons that they do so are complex. First, they are ashamed of their inability to protect their families from the "White devil" as well as of their inability to be adequate breadwinners. They feel belittled in the eyes of their women. Second, the idea of close-knit family ties was frightening to members of earlier generations of Blacks because of the treatment of slaves on the plantation. Slave families would routinely be broken up for purposes of the slave trade. A certain degree of distance became self-protective. This attitude was passed on to later generations in the manner that I have suggested. Today in the ghetto, family support systems tend to include neighbors and other members of the community, rather than just family members, to compensate for this behavior (Hines and Boyd-Franklin, 1982). When the Black man leaves his family, the woman becomes both mother and sole breadwinner. Not surprisingly, such a woman would often become quite angry about having been placed in this predicament. She would have to contain her rage, however, in order to provide the family with some stability. In this situation, the child's acting out is prompted by the mother's rage against Black men as well as White, rather than by the father's rage.

The mechanism by which an "avenger" is generated in a family explains why a family in a situation where changes are occurring often produces an offspring whose behavior seems to fly in the face of the cultural norms appropriate for the earlier stage of cultural evolution. The child of a Depression-era father may become a lazy, chronically late spendthrift, instead of an overly frugal compulsive, in order to act out his parent's repressed wish to be a spendthrift himself. Which type of child the Depression-era family produces will depend on many factors, including the propensities of the selves of the parent and the child and the events and their timing in the micropatterns that had affected the various holons before, during, and after the Depression. As I shall show later, a situation may even come to pass where the best solution for a particular family is for one sibling to express one side of the conflict and another sibling to express the other side. Before going on to that, I would like to discuss the role of "savior," which follows a pattern similar to the role of "avenger."

The "Savior." In past generations, the role of the father as breadwinner in the family was a particularly important one in determining his position in society as well as his sense of self-esteem. When a father was conspicuously unsuccessful in this role, or perhaps even relatively unsuccessful when compared with his peers, he was often viewed by himself, his wife, and perhaps other family members as being a failure. Slipp notes that this situation often leads to the development in a child of the role of "savior." This role would develop in a manner parallel to the development of the role of avenger, based on the child choosing to act out repressed aspects of the parental self in order to stabilize parental role function.

Slipp goes on to point out that a failure in the role of breadwinner was not an unusual occurrence in the United States because of two cultural events: the influx of immigrants in the early and middle parts of the twentieth century and the Great Depression. An immigrant to this country often did not know the language or had only skills that were no longer in demand. He would have difficulty supporting his family because of these factors alone. Add to this a shortage of jobs, and the difficulty became insurmountable.

Because the father in an immigrant family in this situation considered himself a failure, his wife might attempt to compensate for the lack of "strength" in the family by assuming the dominant role. She in fact might be more skillful in many respects than her husband. Unlike the situation of the Black woman, however, she would be unable to translate her abilities into becoming a breadwinner herself, because of the limitations placed on females working outside the home by many European cultures. She would have to avoid being career oriented because, were she to be successful, her husband would feel even more that he had failed in his role as family provider. He would feel that he had not provided well enough to prevent his wife from being forced to work, and he would also be humiliated by the fact that he was outshone by a "mere woman." The mother would have to avoid being career oriented in order to avoid upsetting the homeostasis in her patriarchal family of origin as well.

Instead of going out and getting a job, the mother might provide the family with strength and satisfy her secret ambitions as well by, almost covertly, running the affairs of the home with extreme competency. Unfortunately, even this expression of potency could have the effect of further enhancing her husband's sense of failure. He could see that his wife appeared to be more competent, while at the same time believing that women are supposed to be the weaker sex. Seeing her husband's mortification at this, the mother would then feel obliged to hide her abilities even more to protect her husband from shame. She could not sacrifice them completely, because the family would fall apart if she did. Any attempt to metacommunicate about this dilemma would aggravate the husband's sense of impotency. She would have no way of knowing that this effect would be temporary if only she persisted in her attempts to discuss the whole problem.

A child in a "savior"-generating family, perhaps the brightest or the most talented of his siblings, might take it upon himself to stabilize the mother's repression of her own ambition by acting it out, thereby allowing the mother to vicariously experience her sacrificed wish for mastery and success. He would be spurred to high achievement, academically and professionally. This is the savior role in a nutshell. As Slipp indicates, this child would experience an apparent pressure to succeed that would come from the mother, not the father. The process by which a mother identifies with the success of her youngster was summed up succinctly in statements reported by two of my patients, who were not related to one another. Both of them reported statements by their mothers about a child's newly earned diploma along the lines of "your diploma has your name on it, but it belongs to me." When pressed, each mother indicated that what she meant was that it was her insistence on academic performance that motivated the child. In a way it was; however, the underlying identification is strongly implied.

Children adopting the savior role might seem to be the beneficiaries of a situation that was quite good for them. They could be seen as being groomed for success, as it were. Unfortunately, self-suppression is more often than not involved in these situations. Savior children choose a field of endeavor that corresponds to the mother's ambitions, not their own. As Slipp points out, this often leads to resentment on the part of the children, who feel that they have been used. I would add that they feel this way even though they have volunteered to be in this position. They have sacrificed autonomy—the right to choose one's own interests—in order to perform for the mother. Because they live in a culture that prizes individualistic strivings, they can never be completely comfortable with that sacrifice.

In some families, a successful child will at first stabilize family homeostasis but then threaten it. This situation develops as follows. The child gives vent to the mother's urges to be ambitious and successful, helping her to avoid in a position that is supposed to belong to her husband. If she were to step into the position, the husband's sense of inadequacy would initially increase, and he might become depressed. While it is true that the mother's covert competency causes this anyway, it does so to a lesser extent. After a point, however, things begin to unravel. If the child becomes too successful, his or her achievements increase the father's sense of inadequacy. The father compares his own accomplishments with his child's, and comes up short. This reminds the father of his own shortcomings. As the child pushes ahead in her or his chosen field, the father starts to become depressed. This alarms the mother, who then reacts to the child's achievement with increased anxiety, instead of increased equanimity, as she had earlier. In addition, the mother might begin

to react negatively to the child's success because she becomes
envious.

Slipp calls this sort of pattern a "double bind on achievement." Outwardly, both parents continue to preach success, as
they really do wish to see their child be successful. If a daughter follows that advice, she finds herself upsetting family
homeostasis. She is in a situation analogous to that of the Black
child whose family preaches education but becomes alarmed if
the child follows their directions. Since a desire to protect the
family always takes precedence over individual concerns, the
child opts for failure, while attempting to appear to be making
an effort to succeed. She might somehow subvert herself just
when she is about to make a major career advance, for example.
An alternative way out would be for the child to attempt to
find a field of endeavor in which to succeed that was stabilizing to the mother but not threatening to the father. For example, the son of a father who had been unsuccessful as a trades-
man might become a successful fashion designer. This would
allow the father to remain jealousy free, as the father could devalue the son's job as being suitable only for homosexuals. This
type of situation is analogous to that in which a Black child
climbs the social ladder by being an athlete instead of a scholar;
a plan is devised by which the child can follow both the overt
and the covert family rules simultaneously. Such ingenious solutions are not always possible, of course.

Children in a double bind on achievement do not understand the reactions of the parent. They see the parent's conflicting reactions, and then become confused about what is expected from them. Because of the lack of metacommunication,
they guess—incorrectly—that the parent *wants* them to fail.
This idea is particularly devastating to children in this position,
because they have already sacrificed their autonomy for the sole
purpose of being a success for the sake of the mother. They feel
exploited and then betrayed. This, in turn, leads to confusion,
anger, and a sense of helplessness to boot. As in all cases where
a child chooses self-suppression as a solution to a culturally induced problem of family homeostasis, the adoption of the role
of the savior or the avenger provides only a temporary cure and

ultimately makes the situation much worse. To truly adjust to new contingencies, the family must be able to put the problem out on the table and discuss it, no matter how painful the discussion may prove to be over the short run.

Within a single family, the number of permutations and combinations of the various patterns seen in this model of the development of disordered personalities and personality traits is almost limitless. Children in a family can turn out to be completely different from one another, despite having come from a family dealing with the same existential issues. A patient in therapy will often notice this and protest, when his own pattern is elucidated, "why doesn't my sister seem to have problems like these?" So that the reader will be prepared to answer legitimate inquiries such as this, the following section is addressed to that question.

Role of the Sibling

A culture often assigns a particular function to a child on the basis of sex and ordinal position within the family. Particularly in less evolved cultures, the distribution of these role functions is often quite rigid, so that the status of individuals is immutable from the moment of birth. Some cultures even use separate words to describe the eldest son and the youngest son in a family. The eldest son is often the major heir to a family estate and assumes a patriarchal role. In some cultures that value large families, such as Chicanos in the United States, the eldest daughter is routinely assigned the duty of being the substitute mother whenever the actual mother is incapacitated or otherwise occupied. The forces of cultural evolution can create difficulties for a child who fulfills one particular function, while leaving the others relatively untouched. The feminist message that women should have careers as well as families will, for instance, be more unnerving to the eldest daughter of a Chicano family than to the youngest, for the oldest probably has already sacrificed some of her own inclinations in order to take care of her younger siblings. Toman (1961) wrote a fascinating book about how certain clusters of personality characteristics regularly turn up in people who share the same ordinal position in their respective families.

In addition to their culturally determined destiny in the family, dictated by their ordinal rank and their sex, the various sons and daughters in a family also have special, individualized meanings for their parents. If the mother is herself the youngest in her own family, she may identify most strongly with her own youngest daughter. If one son looks more like Grandpa than another, he can be an especially potent reminder of a particular family conflict. If a child exhibits a certain temperament—and the research of Thomas, Chess, and Birch (1970) shows clearly that infants come into the world varying widely in this characteristic—he or she can become the focus of increased parental concern or scrutiny. Microevents have differing significance for different siblings in the family. As an example, the youngest child's leaving home often represents the end of the caretaker role for a mother; the significance of this child would be different for a woman who had given up a career in order to be a caretaker from what it would be for a woman who had given up the caretaker role to a nanny in order to have a career. A change-of-life baby might have more of an impact on a couple who had lost a child than it would have on one who had not suffered such an occurrence.

One other major factor may explain why one sibling will act out a difficulty caused by cultural change while the others do not. By virtue of being born at different times, the exposure each child has to cultural forces varies. This factor will be of greatest importance during times of rapid cultural transition, when siblings may seem to have grown up practically in different eras. The exposure that one child has may activate a suppressed aspect of a parental self, causing the parent to focus on the child who is responsible for creating this disturbing situation.

Some or all of these factors—cultural dictates, the ordinal birth position of the parents, other microevents, random genetic predispositions, the time when a particular child is born, and so on—work together in determining why one child may be important for a specific role in maintaining family homeostasis, while another child plays a different role or even escapes a specific role in the family homeostasis altogether. Not infrequently, one child acts out one side of a family conflict, while a second acts out the other. One of two brothers may be a workaholic, the other a bum. The family therapy literature is filled with anecdotes about how one child becomes the "identified patient" while the other children seem to be on the road to escaping the family unscathed by the distress in the family system.

Another point I would like to make regarding the role of the sibling is that once a child—say a son—assumes a personality trait or role in order to alleviate systemic or parental anxiety in his family, and if he performs this chore admirably, his siblings may leave the job entirely to him. They may appear to be uninvolved in and perhaps unconcerned about the family troubles. However, if the "identified" child then abdicates the role—say because he has been to a therapist who has taught him to "get in touch with his feelings"—the level of systemic anxiety naturally rises. Under these circumstances, it is not at all unusual for a formerly unaffected sibling to step into the role vacated by the abdicating child. As we shall see later, this can cause difficulties in psychotherapy.

The reader will undoubtedly have noticed that in discussing the generation of maladaptive personality traits and their distribution among siblings, I have focused mostly upon the interaction between the child and only one parent. This was done in the interest of simplifying the model I am presenting so that it can be easily understood. Before going on to give case examples that are illustrative of the role of siblings in a family troubled by inability to adjust to cultural change, I must first complicate the model by addressing the obvious hole in it created by my oversimplification. To state the obvious, a child has two parents. If a mother has engaged in the process of self-suppression in order to play a role for her family of origin, and if she is having some trouble in doing so that is affecting a child, where exactly does the father fit in?

Role of the Spouse

If individuals maintain a persona in order to fit into a particular cultural or familial role expectation, they will naturally feel uncomfortable with people who do not share that expectation. They will seem to have very little in common with and understanding for people or cultures that expect overt functioning that is either more or less highly individuated and differentiated in the evolutionary sense. If they attempt to adjust to another's viewpoint because it seems more satisfying than their own, they will experience groundlessness. In societies in which the state of cultural evolution is relatively advanced, in which the level of individuation is significant, and in which cultural changes are proceeding at a rapid clip, individuals will come in contact with people who exhibit a wide variety of behaviors. Some of these behaviors will be at a level of individuation comparable to their own, and some of them will be at level that is quite different. Similarity in the overall level of expression of individuation, particularly regarding behavioral parameters that are deemed important by one's family system, is a highly significant factor in the process of mate selection.

The most important factor in mate selection in families that are disturbed by cultural change, aside from the degree of similarity in the level of expression of individuation, is the sharing of all major conflicts over role-specific behaviors in a complementary manner and to a similar degree. In cultures lower down on the cultural evolutionary ladder, and in times when cultural evolution proceeds slowly, brokered or arranged marriages are not uncommon, and they often work out quite well. The reason for this might be that less evolved cultures tend to be considerably more homogeneous when it comes to the level of individuation and that individuals within these cultures will be in less conflict about traditional role behavior. A matchmaker would have only to be familiar with a manageable number of characteristics of the families of clients—social class, general level of intelligence, and so forth—in order to make a compatible match. For a modern-day matchmaker, the number of characteristics relevant for compatibility would be astronomical, and many of them probably could not be identified at all.

A man and a woman will continue to be attracted to one another after an initial screening based on superficial characteristics if they provide mirroring for one another on matters of concern common to both. Specifically, the concerns that are important for mutual mirroring are those related to role behavior. If a potential partner attacked or challenged, rather than mirrored, the persona of a date, most likely few additional dates would be arranged. People who find that their role functioning is being questioned by a date with a less individuated persona will tend to look at the partner as being much like a primitive African tribe—quaint but terribly backward. If the challenge came from a date who tended to be more individualistic, they might view the partner as licentious and immoral or as having unrealistic ideas. The relationship would eventually prove to be irritating and would go nowhere. On the other hand, if their partners validate and mirror, overtly or covertly, their views on how people should approach life, the relationship will feel very comfortable.

People having trouble maintaining a persona will often be attracted to someone who will help them to strengthen it. If a mate provides pressure to continue to act out the persona, they may have less trouble avoiding the expression of self-aspects that might produce an experience of existential groundlessness. Since the avoidance of groundlessness is an extremely powerful, if not the most powerful, motivating force, they will value highly a partner who is willing to provide, overtly or covertly, this service. They will hang on to this partner tenaciously and do whatever it takes to maintain the relationship. The type of partner who is willing to provide mirroring and support to the persona of a spouse who is having trouble maintaining it will most likely be someone who is already used to providing a similar service in his or her own family of origin. Because self-sacrifice is usually necessary to strengthen the role stability of another, such a partner will also have an unstable persona.

If a woman were covertly stabilizing her mother's unstable role functioning, for example, she would find herself attracted to a man with a complementary type of instability. Let us say that the woman had been sacrificing her own ambitions for a career and appeared to be a docile housewife, in order to avoid alarming her mother, who had done the same thing. If she receives a positive response from a man when she follows the demands of her role by allowing him to be the dominant force in the relationship, this has the effect of reinforcing *her* unstable persona. She will find herself drawn to this man, assuming that there are no other major conflict areas on which the two of them differ. As she is already making a difficult sacrifice of important aspects of herself in order to maintain homeostasis in her family of origin, she is happy to receive mirroring and support for her persona.

As I mentioned above, the man she chooses for a husband will invariably be a person with a complementary conflict over his sex-role functioning. Her choice may, for example, be a man who is unhappy with the role of being the always responsible macho head of the household. The reason for her attraction to a man with a complementary conflict again relates to the difficulty in maintaining a less individuated persona in an evolving culture. In order for the woman in our example to maintain her persona, continuous pressure from her husband to stay home to take care of the house will be helpful in allowing her to avoid expressing career-oriented aspects of her true self. Her mate would have to provide this pressure to an almost compulsive degree, constantly and consistently making an issue of how important it is for him to have a wife who does not work. A man who was comfortable with the traditional male role model would find her continuous need for this to be irritating and would immediately suspect that his potential partner was not comfortable with her role. Her discomfort would be a threat to the relationship.

What we arrive at in these situations is an unspoken marriage contract, a tit-for-tat agreement that each spouse help the other maintain the role that each learned in her or his family of origin. This is one way of looking at what is referred to by systems theorists as the *marital quid pro quo*. The role of spouses in a family that is having difficulties caused by cultural change is to help one another maintain family homeostasis in their families of origin by helping one another maintain an unstable persona. Once a pattern of tit-for-tat responses becomes established, it can become impossible to stop. A game without end often develops. If one spouse has seemed to prefer one way of relating for as long as a couple have known one another, the other spouse can never be sure that any request for a change in the relationship is sincere, unless effective metacommunication can take place. Once again, however, metacommunication is extremely difficult, because of the issue of shame.

Unfortunately, the very quality that first attracted these spouses to one another can eventually prove to be the major irritant in their marriage. Self-suppressive behavior in the face of cultural evolution is the cause of maladaptive character traits. They are maladaptive because they are no longer appropriate for the new circumstances in the culture. Since they are not adaptive, they are ultimately self-destructive and self-defeating. They may appear to stabilize the family system, but in the long run they produce nothing but misery for the individual who has adopted them. Ultimately, they produce misery for the family system as well. By maintaining the old family homeostasis, they retard the adoption by the family of new ways of functioning that are more appropriate to the new environment.

The spouses who help one another maintain maladaptive character traits are, in a sense, devoting their entire relationship to making one another miserable—not as miserable as they might be, temporarily, if they were exposed to existential groundlessness, but miserable nonetheless. The need for stabilization of a shaky persona is to me the rational explanation for the otherwise mystifying propensity of many couples to hang on to their relationship when on the surface they seem to hate one another, and also for why, after they split, the members of the couple proceed to hitch up with new mates not much different from their old ones.

So that I might clarify the concept of spouses helping one another maintain their respective personas, I would like to compare and contrast this view with an idea that is similar in many respects but different in others. I refer here to Wile's (1981) concept of "interacting sensitivities." Wile discusses how the behavior of one spouse in a dysfunctional relationship almost always plays into a conflict area of the other. He labels this conflict area a special "sensitivity." When Husband treads upon the sensitivities of Wife, Wife almost always reacts in a way that happens to play into a special sensitivity of Husband. Husband then reacts by doing more of the behavior that had originally offended Wife, who responds with more of the behavior that offends Husband, and so on. A vicious circle of interaction takes place, which eventually leads to one or more of three states commonly seen in dysfunctional couples: mutual accusations, mutual withdrawal, or a situation where one spouse pursues and the other withdraws.

As an example, he cites the case of Dick and Susan. Dick had felt rejected by both his parents and his first wife. He had, in fact, found his first wife in bed with another man, despite the fact that the wife had never given any indication that she had been dissatisfied with her relationship with Dick. "Dick expressed this sensitivity [to rejection] by complaining in a bullying manner whenever he thought Susan had been a little rejecting. Susan, who had a domineering father and an abusive first husband, responded to Dick's bullying by withdrawing, which Dick then took as further indication of rejection. To put the problem simply, Dick was sensitive to rejection and responded with bullying; Susan was sensitive to bullying and responded by rejecting" (p. 125). Each time Susan withdrew, Dick increased his bullying, Susan withdrew even more, and so on. This is an example of the demanding-withdrawn couple interaction.

Wile, whose criticisms of the work of Murray Bowen were the major inspiration for my own ideas about psychotherapy, does an admirable job in trying to positively reframe what many therapists would label as pathological behavior indicative of some sort of developmental defect. Traditionally, therapists view patients as receiving "infantile gratification" from their dysfunctional behavior. Wile, in contrast, accurately sees members of a dysfunctional couple as deprived rather than gratified. In the example of Dick and Susan, Dick is not receiving gratification from his bullying, he is experiencing loneliness and rejection. While Wile's efforts to view patients as inhibited instead of defective and infantile are impressive and important, they have the unfortunate side effect of also portraying them as being rather stupid. Are Dick and Susan so oblivious to how their behavior affects one another that they cannot see that it is the *way* that they are expressing their distress that makes the problem worse? Wile himself brings up this question: "An irony of Dick's behavior was the unloving manner in which he was trying to get Susan to express her love. He was condemning her . . . for her failure to express love in the way that he wanted . . . the mystery was why Dick did not notice this. He was able to discount his continuous carping" (p. 210).

Wile correctly discards the common explanation that Dick's behavior is based on fantasies of narcissistic omnipotence. Dick's efforts to control Susan were in fact ineffectual—hardly reinforcing of omnipotence fantasies. Wile tries to explain Dick's lack of insight with the fact that underneath his bluster, Dick was desperate: "He needed continuous signs of affection from Susan to be able to maintain even the slightest belief that she cared for him. As discussed, his long-standing doubts about his lovability had been traumatically reinforced when he discovered his former wife in bed with another man" (p. 210).

I agree that Dick is desperate, but the difficulty with this explanation is that Dick's bullying behavior is not caused by his desperation; his desperation is caused by his bullying behavior. He is making himself very unlovable by behaving so boorishly, thereby depriving himself of the gratification that would come if he induced his lover to feel kindly toward him. Undoubtedly his former wife allowed herself to be discovered with her lover as a response to Dick's behavior in that relationship. One might guess that Dick was just as bullying with her as he was with Susan. In the vast majority of cases where a spouse is caught red-handed in the middle of an affair, that spouse has deliberately allowed him- or herself to be caught. If a spouse really wished to conceal his adultery, he would go to great lengths to avoid detection (even though his better half would on some level be aware anyway that something was amiss). The former wife was giving Dick what his nasty behavior seemed to demand—hostility. Apparently, she had her own problems with the direct expression of hostility and chose a passive-aggressive method by which to communicate it—much as Susan's withdrawal can be seen as a passive-aggressive method by which Susan expressed hostility.

The actual explanation of Dick's irrational-appearing behavior can be understood by use of the principle of the net effect of behavior. If one assumes that people are not stupid, one is forced to the conclusion that Dick knew very well that it was the way he expressed his demands that was driving Susan away, rather than the demands themselves or Susan's own coldness. Likewise, Susan must have known that her withdrawal was aggravating Dick's bullying behavior. This is not a case of the behavior of each unwittingly causing reactions in the other that then reinforce that behavior. Dick and Susan were deliberately reinforcing the behavior of *each other*. Dick was helping Susan to avoid a satisfying, intimate relationship, while Susan was helping Dick to play the role of an unlovable bully.

Since we know only sparse details about what went on in their respective families of origin, we do not know the function that these roles served. What we do know is that each maintained a role, with the help of the other, at considerable personal sacrifice. Their sacrifice of their own gratification is the cause of the desperation that they feel.

Having explored the question of where the spouses fit into the cultural-lag model of the development of a personality disorder vis-à-vis each other, I must now turn to the question posed in the lead-in to this section: where do the spouses fit in vis-à-vis their acting-out child? When a child is acting out the conflict of parent *A* in order to maintain family homeostasis, where does parent *B* fit in? The answer to this lies in two connected facts. First, parent *B*, for the reasons discussed above, usually has a conflict that is complementary to the conflict of parent *A;* second, both parents attempt to support the persona of the other. These two facts combine to strengthen the resolve of the child to sacrifice some of the wishes of his or her true self in order to maintain a single persona that seems to maintain family homeostasis.

The complementarity in the parental relationship allows the child to be able to develop one role that can stabilize the personas of *both* parents simultaneously. As an example, let us again look at the case of Dick and Susan. The dysfunctional behavior of both Dick and Susan prevents them from having a close relationship. Let us assume for purposes of this discussion that they really want to be closer to one another, but for some reason related to the homeostasis in their respective families of origin, they feel that this is impossible. They apparently also feel, again for a reason related to family-of-origin homeostasis, that they cannot break up. Dick and Susan are stuck in a bad marriage that they do not feel free to change or to discontinue. Dick's bullying behavior causes Susan to conclude, incorrectly, that he does not really want to be close; Susan's withdrawal misleads Dick to the same conclusion about her. Both are very unhappy and angry in this situation, so it is likely that their role functions are unstable.

Suppose that they then have a child, whom we will call Ricky. After Ricky becomes old enough to gain some feel for the family problem, he might wish to provide his parents with additional role-function support in order to maintain family homeostasis, which is threatened by the marital discord. Depending on the reason for the lack of closeness in the parental relationship, he can provide this help in a number of ways. One is by siphoning off some of the parental anger by making himself the target of it. He can do this by adopting the role of a person who behaves in a hateful manner. This behavior provides a significant distraction from the parental battle. Ricky's provision of an outlet for their anger helps each parent to remain in character more easily. He functions like a lightning rod. Dick has an outlet for the anger that builds up in him when Susan withdraws; Susan has an outlet for the anger occasioned by Dick's bullying. It becomes less taxing for each of them to put up with their relationship, and they can continue in their unhappy roles. Since both of the parents are angry, Ricky can stabilize the persona of each parent with the same role.

Ricky's resolve to play this role would also be strengthened by the reaction of each parent to him whenever he plays the role with the other parent. When Dick is having difficulty remaining in character, this threatens the family homeostasis, because the homeostasis is partially built upon Dick's bullying demands. If Ricky's behavior helps Dick to resume his role, not only would Dick seem to relax, but so would Susan. Dick's role playing helps Susan maintain the persona that she developed in her own family of origin. If he has trouble with it, she loses this support and may begin to experience existential anxiety. If Ricky can help Dick resume his old behavior, Susan regains this support, and her persona is therefore stabilized. The same process occurs with Dick when Ricky helps Susan stay in character. Ricky receives unintentional reinforcement for his role from both parents whenever he acts hatefully with either one.

Dysfunctional Family Roles: Case Examples

Case 4-1

What follows is an example of a family in which two children were assigned different roles on the basis of sex and ordinal position. The younger child, whose role was the more important of the two, was supported in her role by her husband. When she began to abdicate that role, her older sister began to step into it.

The basic pattern in the family could be traced back for at least three generations in the families of both the mother and the father. The ethnic background of the family was American Indian, but the family was considerably Anglicized, and they told everyone that they were from South America. The family pattern developed as a reasonable outgrowth of the experiences of early family members, who had left the Indian reservations at a time when doing so was fraught with considerable danger. This danger was particularly relevant for the mother's family. The mother's grandfather had left the reservation to marry an Anglo, and his son, the mother's father, was stigmatized by his "half-breed" status. In addition to being subjected to confusion over his cultural identity, this man experienced considerable difficulty with the role of breadwinner—a role considered important for males in both cultures. He suffered racial discrimination by the Anglos, and by the Indians as well, because his family had left the tribe and had adopted many Anglo ways. He suffered a considerable loss of pride and eventually became ineffective. His wife then gradually stepped in to fill the void in family leadership. She became dominant; a matriarchy was established. However, in order to avoid further exacerbating the father's sense of shame, the family developed mechanisms for minimizing the appearance of the female dominance to outsiders. The women in the family appeared to the world to remain proper squaws.

In each generation, the younger of two sisters took over the position of dominant female in the family. The older sister became a childish and demanding individual who helped out in the family very little and who, after she got married, fell under the thumb of a matriarchal mother-in-law. Men in the family were viewed as impaired and tended to live up to this expectation in one way or another. Most worked at relatively low-paying jobs in construction, turning over their paychecks to their wives. The matriarch tended to do all the thinking in the family, making most of the minor everyday decisions as well as the major ones—even decisions concerning the husband's working life.

My patient, Maria, was the youngest daughter in the family of the matriarchal sister from the previous generation. She was being groomed by her mother to be the next matriarch. Her mother, Laila, the current matriarch, was extremely overburdened by her responsibilities in the family, as she had many children. Her husband, Maria's father, seemed almost to act as if he were one of them, and added to Laila's workload. He was trusted with as little responsibility as possible, as he was viewed as defective.

Maria's primary job in the family was to assist her mother as much as possible. In addition to making most of the decisions concerning her own husband and children, Maria served as the family resource whenever Laila had to handle any family business that involved the larger Anglo culture. If Laila were to deal with the Anglos herself, she would run the risk of exposing her dominance and subjecting her husband to shame. Maria became a sort of go-for for Laila. In contrast, Maria's sister Tanya, in line with the family expectations, helped her mother hardly a whit. In fact, Tanya was used to making extra demands on Laila, keeping her busy rather than helping her out.

The roles of both Tanya and Maria were stabilizing the role functioning of Laila, and in different ways. Laila's true self clearly was exhausted with all her responsibilities and yearned to give them up. Tanya, by being a chore for her mother, assisted her "helpless" father in making sure that Laila would remain in the matriarchal position. If Laila backed off from her role, they would threaten to fall apart. Tanya was also available to be a person in need of her mother's assistance after the sons in the family grew up and left home, thus making sure that Laila would be protected from the temptations of an empty nest. As long as Laila was needed by the family, she would not leave it.

Maria's job, in addition to serving as the heir to the matriarchal mantle and as mediator with the Anglos, was to function as a safety valve. Should Laila's responsibilities become too unbearable, Maria was always around to ease the pressure by assisting her. Maria's responsible position as a helper to the mother also helped simultaneously to stabilize the role of her father. He could continue to appear to be helpless during times when Laila would otherwise have been, were it not for Maria's help, too busy to look after him.

The role functioning of Maria's husband, Derek, was complementary to that of Maria. Derek, a painter, had been tyrannized by an overworried, overprotective mother, and consequently felt that females expected him to be unable to do anything right. Once married, he allowed Maria to make most of the family decisions—just as he had done with his mother. This was in deference to Maria's apparent need to be in control. He assumed that Maria was just like his mother. Derek's mother had gracefully given up some of her authority over Derek at the time of his wedding, secure in the knowledge that Maria was competent to take care of her baby. Derek's father, though alive, seemed so unimportant to the rest of the family that he was rarely mentioned.

Although clearly unhappy with their respective roles, Derek and Maria helped to stabilize the role functioning of each other. Derek helped Maria to be responsible by being rather ineffectual; Maria helped Derek to be ineffectual by always taking over responsibility the moment Derek faltered.

This unusual family homeostasis worked fairly well until Maria fell ill and became temporarily incapacitated. Most of the rest of the family refused to believe that she was really ill and acted as if, as a strong matriarch, she was indestructible. Because of the family's denial of her illness, and because of their overall mistrust of doctors, Maria was not able to follow all of her doctor's orders (the negative family feelings toward doctors stemmed from traditional Indian stoicism, mixed in with their understandable distrust of the Whites). Because of her hesitation to completely trust the doctor's instructions, coupled with the family's interference, Maria ended up inadvertently prolonging her own disability. This added to the building crisis in the family. Maria would impair her own recovery because she did not feel free to rest. She did her best to respond to the continuing requests from her family, who made no effort to ask for less. When Maria could not drive her own children to school or needed a baby-sitter to go to the doctor, no one in the family would agree to help her out, despite the fact that Maria had never refused a similar favor for one of them. Tanya was especially nasty whenever Maria asked her to help out, thinking that Maria really believed her to be incapable of doing so. After all, that was what the rest of the family seemed to think.

The stress created by this situation caused Maria to suffer from an emotional breakdown. She became anxious, depressed, and easily enraged. Because she was unable to function effectively in her previous role, she began to take on the characteristics of an individual who was totally incapacitated. This behavior represented the flip side of her previous hyperresponsibility. Her new role was somewhat similar to that of her sister. At first, the rest of the family refused to accept the change and acted as if she were still able to do all the things that she had done prior to the illness. When she refused, they assumed that it was only because she was angry at them—which she in fact was—rather than because she was ill (a game without end). Nonetheless, as the crisis became an extended one, the idea began to sink in that Maria was unavailable to perform the functions demanded by her family role. Gradually, Tanya quit making demands on Laila and began to step into Maria's old role. She started to help Laila in the same way that Maria had done previously.

Case 4-2

    This case is an unusual example in which the father in the family, Jack, had undergone an apparent personality change at the age of twenty-one upon the death of his own father. Because of new family requirements brought about at the time of the death, Jack had needed to change his persona to one that differed significantly from his previous one. Neither the "before" nor the "after" personality made an especially good fit with all of the inclinations of Jack's true self. The complexities of Jack's persona affected, in different ways, the later role development of Jack's children.

    Jack and his wife Petra had two sons, each of whom adopted a different role. The factor that seemed most important in determining which son played which role was the innate temperament of each child. One son, Waylon, had as a toddler been the more timid and passive of the two. As he grew, Waylon tended to take on some of the character traits that his father had had before his transformation. The second son, Eric, originally the more adventuresome brother, seemed as he grew up to become similar to his father as he was after the change.

    When Jack was a young adolescent, he behaved like a goof-off and a clown. He did poorly in school and always kept everyone guessing and amused with outrageous antics. After the death of his father, he was suddenly commissioned by his mother to take over the family business. Jack continued to do poorly in school but changed from being a goof-off and a clown to being a workaholic. He worked long hours at the family business, a habit he later carried into his own business. After this switch, he continued to show evidence of being the cut-up he had been previously, but only at parties.

    As his father had before him, Jack became a person who always seemed to have a need to prove his worth. No matter how successful he became, he was always anxious to reach the next level, working as much as was necessary to do so. The behavior of Jack's mother had helped his father to play this role, and after the father died, she apparently set out to push Jack toward success in a similar manner. Her methods were rather peculiar. In order to spur Jack on, she constantly told him that the business was losing money, when in fact it was doing quite well. She would hide the actual financial state of the company by playing with the books. She refused to hire an accountant. She would write personal checks from the business account and hide the money. Jack had no idea why the business always seemed to "lose money," and tried harder and harder to make it do better. One other trick Jack's mother used in order to provoke him to high accomplishment was to call him up to ask for advice—usually at an inconvenient time—which she would then never follow.

The actual reasons for the genesis of this family pattern were never discovered. One might speculate that the mother's behavior was meant to maintain traditional gender-role functioning within an ambivalent family. As a female, she might very well have sacrificed her own ambitions for success and sublimated them by using her skills covertly to force reluctant male family members, who had conflicts about work, to become successful breadwinners. While appearing to be an incompetent, she would be in actuality the power behind the throne. The hostile manner in which she performed her role indicated a great deal of underlying distaste for it.

In keeping with such a family theme, Petra's father was a man who had conflicts over work and success. He considered himself to be a failure in life already. He had been taught, and strongly believed, that if he just worked hard, then he would be rewarded. When he was suddenly laid off from his job, he realized that his hard work had not paid off, and he became a depressed and bitter man. Perhaps out of a sense of being a poor role model, he began to drive his children away from him by being critical of them, to the point where he appeared to be picking on them.

Petra felt sorry for her father because he was depressed, but nonetheless took on the role of protector of her siblings. Her mother, meanwhile, attempted to prop up her husband's position in the family by making excuses for his ill-mannered behavior. This "propping up" behavior can be viewed as having a similar net effect as Jack's mother's manipulations.

The presenting problem in the case was Waylon, who had quit school and refused to work at a job. When his parents threatened to withdraw financial support, he became depressed. Petra had in the past always rescued Waylon whenever he seemed to be faltering in some achievement. She believed that his passivity provided a good justification for doing so. She would, for example, do his homework whenever he complained that it was difficult. Eric, on the other hand, did not seem to need this service.

When Petra became frustrated because all of her good-natured help failed to motivate Waylon, Jack would attempt to step in. He would harshly criticize Waylon—much as Petra's father had criticized her siblings—calling him lazy and irresponsible. Waylon would respond to the criticisms baitingly, causing Jack to become provoked and angry and therefore even more harshly critical. Occasionally Jack and Waylon would nearly come to blows. Jack's criticisms would then alarm Petra, who did not want Waylon to go through what her sisters had. She would in turn criticize Jack, who would consequently feel that Petra did not really believe he could handle a difficult situation —just the way Jack's mother had seemed to believe that he was incapable of handling the business. Petra had an additional habit that resembled some of the behavior of Jack's mother, although to a much less vicious degree. She would ask Jack for assistance in some activity and then criticize him for how he handled the task.

When the couple socialized, Jack would begin to act silly and clown around, as he had done as an adolescent. Petra, who secretly believed that Jack was depressed much as her father had been, would enable this to go on by being a mother hen around him in a way that would prevent his clowning from getting him into any major trouble.

Eric was a hard worker like his father. He went to school, though he did rather poorly, and also held a job. Like his father and grandfather, he always seemed to need to prove himself. He would also act silly in social situations.

My interpretation of the role function of Jack was that, prior to his father's death, his primary job in the family was to stabilize his father's persona as a workaholic by expressing his father's suppressed true wish to dump responsibilities and clown around. Jack was assisted in this job by the apparent approval of his mother. After the death, this job became obsolete. Instead, by taking his father's place, he helped his mother to continue to play her role as a demanding woman who pushed males in the family toward great success. He became a workaholic like his father, with the safety valve that he could continue to clown around, but only in certain situations.

Petra's role in her family of origin was to express the suppressed wish of her parents to criticize an overbloated family work ethic. Apparently, the family dynamics of the parents had made them afraid to even dare to doubt the view that work was the be-all and end-all of existence, even though the father had learned the hard way that this was not the case. Petra expressed the taboo feelings by covertly sympathizing with her father's depression and overtly criticizing him for the harshness in his perfectionistic demands on the other sisters.

Jack and Petra, at great personal sacrifice, helped one another to continue in their respective roles. Petra helped Jack play the role of "a male who pushes himself to the limit because of a woman" by being provocatively critical of the way Jack went about his life. Jack helped Petra play the role of "a rebel against the work ethic and a protector of the weak" by being a person who harshly criticized his son for being lazy. At the same time, he helped her to play the covert role of sympathizer and mother hen by seeming to need her to watch out for him when he was clowning.

Waylon stabilized the role functioning of both parents. His refusal to work served two purposes in the family. First, he was acting out his father's repressed wish to dump responsibility and clown around, helping his father continue the role of workaholic. Second, his behavior provoked his father's criticism, allowing his mother to rescue him and continue the role she had played with her father and siblings. Waylon became depressed when both parents suddenly, though ambivalently, demanded more responsibility from him, because he felt helpless to maintain the family homeostasis.

Eric functioned as a safety valve. He remained in a position where he could be a workaholic like his father or a goof-off like his brother. In fact, when Waylon finally got a job and began to do better, Eric began to get into more and more trouble at school.

5

PERSONALITY DISORDERS IN A SYSTEMS CONTEXT

This chapter is devoted to an exploration of the cultural changes that have led to the creation of specific personality disorders and a discussion of why the traits that characterize these disorders develop. I will look at the family systems of the hysteric, the narcissist, and the borderline; I will touch on the dynamics of the agoraphobic, the bulimic, the hypochondriac, and the patient who is apparently estranged from her or his family.

Oedipus Revisited: The Hysterical Family

The theory of personality encompassed by psychoanalysis was based on inferences made from the observation, using the technique of free association, of predominantly middle- and upper-class individuals of late-nineteenth- and early-twentieth-century Vienna who had emotional problems that were common in that time and at that place. Freud's Vienna was a place in transition, from the point of view of cultural evolution. The Industrial Revolution was moving forward, creating a need for more highly evolved technical skills and more specialization.

177

These skills, which were particularly necessary for middle- and upper-class males, required longer and longer periods of education to achieve. More education meant the postponement of full-time employment, with longer periods of financial dependency on one's parents. At the same time, the length of the workday was gradually being eroded by advanced technology, with the result that people began to have more free time to develop their own unique life-styles. Life expectancy was beginning to increase significantly. Because of the increase in free time and the resultant increase in individuation, people seemed to have less in common with one another, leading to the demise of easy partner selection. People needed to go out with a larger number of partners before they could find a compatible spouse with whom they could settle down.

All of these developments combined to cause people to postpone marriage. In earlier centuries, marriages that occurred not long after the onset of puberty, which on average began at a later age than it does today, were the rule rather than the exception. Because of new cultural conditions in Europe during Freud's historical era, such early marriage for middle- and upper-class individuals, who made up the bulk of Freud's practice, became unfeasible financially and unappealing aesthetically. People who wait until they are eighteen, twenty, or even older to get married have a problem that the person who marries at fifteen does not. What does one do with his or her sex drive in the meantime? The sex drive kicks up under the flow of advancing hormones at puberty and is difficult to ignore for long. This is an especially difficult problem for a woman, who is always at risk of becoming pregnant. This problem may account for the fact that women traditionally married at an even younger age than men.

Cultural norms mandating that sexual activity be limited to a marriage that took place early in a person's life had been adaptive in the days when competition among members of the same society was counterproductive and effective birth control was unavailable. Competition for mates was as undesirable as other forms of competition, and the society adopted mores that kept it to a minimum. Once married, the partners were, at least in theory, off limits to the rest of the society, so the sooner the better. Competitive feelings about previous sexual partners would also be nonexistent. Additionally, in the absence of birth control, children born under a system of sexual exclusivity within the context of marriage were invariably provided with one parent to support the family and another parent to raise them. This division of labor was necessary for survival; being a bastard was a major disadvantage. This became a moral standard, and illegitimate children were ostracized.

With the advent of delayed marriage, a new problem— what to do with the adolescent and young adult sex drive—was created. The culture had not yet had time to adjust to the new contingencies. Competition, including competition for mates, had now become acceptable. Furthermore, many of the old problems, such as how to prevent an unwanted pregnancy, remained as problematic as ever. Women could suffer disastrous consequences were they to have an unwanted pregnancy. Abortion was no option. Middle- and upper-class women had not yet been generally accepted into the work force; thus, they would have difficulty raising a child without financial help from a family who would often be in no mood to give it. A woman had but one choice—sexual abstinence. Although premarital sex was frowned upon by the larger society for males as well, society could look the other way if a male engaged his whims, for men did not get pregnant.

The sex drive is an especially powerful one for women as well as men, despite the claims of the Victorians that women are less sexual than men. In fact, in the Middle Ages, women were actually considered to be the lustier of the two sexes. Because of the power of the sex drive, a severe reaction formation is required in order to contain it. In order to force themselves to abstain for the sake of family homeostasis, many of the women of Freud's time had to find a way to make themselves, in effect, frigid. They did so by forming a powerful, conditioned association in their minds between sex and the emotion of disgust. Their families helped them to perform this herculean task by drumming into the minds of little girls the idea that sex was wrong and that the human body was an object of shame and loathing instead of desire. Since the original cultural contingencies that had led to this attitude were often not discussed, because of the difficulties that cultural lag creates for metacommunication, that attitude could and frequently did become a major and permanent component of the female persona. Once frigidity became compulsive and habitual, it became difficult to unlearn, even after marriage. Little mirroring was available for an opposite attitude.

Men were not immune to the effects of this problem. The attitude among men that "nice girls don't," a statement that was in fact true in Victorian times, also did not automatically reverse at the altar. A strange situation developed in which women came to be seen by both sexes as normally asexual. The women of the time, due to the actor's paradox, all seemed to believe it. Because they did believe it, and acted accordingly, men would have no way of knowing that it was not true. Women who allowed expression of a strong sex drive were thought of as diseased. If a man found that his wife enjoyed sex, even after marriage, he was forced to the conclusion that she was highly disturbed or even mentally ill, in addition to being morally unsound. Since a good woman—the only kind worth marrying—not only did not enjoy sex but found it distasteful, if the man then insisted upon it, he would have to begin to think of himself as insensitive and selfish. Since he, unlike the woman, had not needed to teach himself to be asexual, abstinence for him was undesirable. The only alternatives seemed to be to suffer, to subject his wife to something she found distasteful, or to defile himself by having affairs with prostitutes or "loose" women, who by definition were sick and undesirable! The "good" wife was in a similar predicament. If she allowed her husband to feel himself to be unselfish and sensitive by enjoying the sex he demanded, she would then become undesirable as a wife for him. If she allowed him to feel good about his choice of mates by not enjoying sex, then she would have to begin to feel herself to be cruel and depriving.

This bind often led to ingenious but rather peculiar solutions. One possibility was for the woman to routinely "fake" orgasms, while subtly letting on that she was not really enjoying the sex. The man could never be sure whether she enjoyed it or not. He was free to think of her as not enjoying it whenever he was concerned with whether she was a good woman, and think of her as enjoying it whenever he became concerned with whether he was selfish and insensitive. Another possibility was for the woman to look the other way when her man had affairs. Her continued presence despite the affairs could be used by the male to convince himself that he was still worthy of a "good" woman even though he continued to involve himself with a "bad" one. The female, in the meantime, could continue to avoid sex without depriving her husband.

Considering the true strength of the female sex drive and the lack of acceptable outlets for it in Victorian society, it is no accident that Freud found many metaphorical references to missing penises in the associations of his female patients. Freud was not completely successful at fighting a tendency to believe, as did most of the population of his time, that healthy women did not normally have a strong sex drive. Having seen omnipresent references to castration anxiety in his male patients for reasons to be discussed, he naturally assumed that any reference to a missing penis by his female patients indicated that they unconsciously feared that they already had been castrated. If this was true, then Freud was being only logical when he thought that any associations indicating a desire for a missing penis meant that a woman felt that she was "missing" a prized possession. Naturally, she would want to have it back and would envy those who still had one—hence, "penis envy." The problem with this formulation was that, although a penis was indeed missing, it was missing not from the female anatomy but from the female sex life.

One clinical feature that is prominent in the presentation of the classic grand hysteric is her tendency to dress and act seductively and then deny that her behavior is an invitation to the male for sex. The net effect of this behavior is to push away any male interested in a satisfying sexual relationship. The men who witness this spectacle invariably feel themselves to have been teased, and generally become annoyed and look elsewhere. Pseudo-seductive behavior, then, can be seen as serving three functions. First, it allows the hysteric to continue her persona as an asexual being, for not only is she saying no, she is also causing males to stop pursuing her out of irritation at her behavior. This ensures that she will never have the opportunity to be tempted to say yes, and therefore makes it easier for her to keep her sex drive under wraps. Second, the behavior is an obvious expression of her true underlying desire to be sexual. Third, it allows her to express some of the hostility caused by the need to repress such an important self-aspect, through the mechanism of being aggravating to others.

The strange situation created for both sexes in many Victorian families by the belief that "good girls don't" was often combined with the belief that children are asexual. The effects of this combination on the children in these families accounted for the high incidence of associations relating to an oedipal conflict found in Freud's patients. Freud is credited with dispelling the belief that children are asexual, but he did not see all the ramifications that this belief had for his clientele. Neither a wife nor a husband in the hysterical family could feel good about openly expressing her or his sexuality around adults, including each other. They also believed that children would have no reaction to sexually suggestive activities. Therefore, many Victorians who had not been able to devise other ways of sublimating their repressed sexuality found themselves acting in a very seductive, sexual manner when their children were around. This applied as much to hysterical mothers as fathers, since the mothers were already used to behaving seductively in general. Although we can never be sure that the seductive behavior of adults in hysterical families toward their children did not usually progress to the stage of actual incest, my feeling is that generally it did not. Child abuse, sexual or otherwise, is related more to the phenomenon of spoiling behavior than it is to the issue of sexual repression. As Slipp (1984) points out, seductiveness is not a single traumatic event but a continuing style of relationship.

Unbeknownst to these parents, however, their seductive behavior was actually quite sexually stimulating to their children. This had the effect of sexualizing the relationships between mothers and sons, as well as fathers and daughters, to a degree far greater than normal. It is no accident that children from these families had great difficulty resolving their otherwise normal and normally destined to be unimportant sexual attraction to their opposite-sexed parent. Resolving those feelings, though difficult, would not, however, be impossible. Such resolution is not, in fact, the main problem created by this unfortunate family pattern. By allowing themselves to be a passive focus for the repressed sexuality of the opposite-sexed parent, children can stabilize the family homeostasis in a hysterical family. Slipp (1984) refers to a role pattern in females that he calls the "go-between," in which a female child takes over the job of attending to the demands of a narcissistic father when the mother abdicates this responsibility. The pattern that I am about to discuss in regard to both male and female children is in essence quite similar to that pattern. Children in this role function much like an extramarital relationship, giving to the true self of the opposite-sexed parent something that the same-sexed parent cannot give.

What the child in the go-between role may often give to the opposite-sexed parent is warmth and affection. Parents who avoid sex as much as possible frequently also avoid excessive coziness, because affection can be sexually stimulating. This therefore tends to be missing from their relationship as well. Avoidance of sexuality is one of the reasons that Victorians tended to be undemonstrative generally in their interpersonal relationships. When a child supplies this ingredient missing from the parental relationship, a role reversal has taken place. A son or a daughter acts like a parent to a mother or a father. Nurturance normally is supposed to travel from the parent to the child, not the other way around. When such children are thus parentified, they must sacrifice something of their own needs for parenting. This becomes the basis in the child of a serious dependency conflict, which explains the frequent linkage of "oral" issues to the sexual ones seen in disturbed children from hysterical families.

The go-between child has volunteered to maintain family homeostasis by filling a covert need of the opposite-sexed parent. This type of situation can lead to the transmission of sex-

ual repression from one generation to the next. When the covert
parental need is primarily sexual, the child must sacrifice his or
her own genital sexuality. Being a passive focus for the repressed
sexuality of a parent is a role that can be played without creating too much of a fuss. Being an active focus is, of course, totally unacceptable. Being a passive sexual focus, unfortunately,
is sexually stimulating. These children were therefore faced at a
young age with the very task that was bedeviling their parents.
They had to find a way to repress their sexuality. For female
children in Victorian times and up to the recent past, devices
for the accomplishment of this goal were already readily available. For male children, more innovation was required.

The male child actually had two tasks to accomplish. Not
only did he wish to avoid becoming too stimulated by his mother, but he also was concerned about the feelings of his father.
Because of the mother's conflicts over sexuality, the father
often developed a sense of inadequacy regarding pleasing his
wife, because he could never seem to satisfy her needs. If he
avoided sex as she seemed to demand, she would actually become more frustrated. The source of the frustration would
never be clear, so the father would be totally bewildered. If the
son were able to solve this puzzle too well and fill the needs of
his mother, the father would feel even more inadequate than he
already did. Family homeostasis would again be threatened.

The male child in the hysterical family would be able to
accomplish both of these tasks with great ease if only he could
avoid becoming sexually stimulated by his mother during those
times when he was engaged in partially fulfilling her covert
needs. For this reason, he would often harbor a secret wish to
be rid of his penis. However, since he really felt his penis to be a
rather valuable possession, this wish would cause a great deal of
anxiety. In addition, because he continued to possess his geni-
tals, his mother's seductive behavior would lead to strong inces-
tuous feelings. If this whole process continued into adulthood,
and he then went to a psychoanalyst, he would exhibit in his
associations a sexual attraction for his mother, anxiety about
losing his penis, and a concern for the reactions of his father.

Another possible result of hysterical dynamics is that the

male child might find most pressing a need to act in ways that gave vent to the father's rage against "depriving" women. This would help stabilize the father's persona as "a man satisfied with an asexual woman." In this case, the boy would be functioning as an avenger and would exhibit some sociopathic tendencies. The mother might seem to support this role, because stabilizing her husband's persona would stabilize hers as well. This dynamic may be part of the explanation for the observed epidemiological link between hysterical females and sociopathic males in families.

Freud was correct in his formulation that "repressed libido" was central to the genesis of the psychopathology of many of his patients. Unfortunately, his ideas were overgeneralized because of the prevalence of hysterical dynamics in his practice. It is a supreme irony of history that the man who did the most to help destroy the antisexual notions of the Victorians was himself trapped by them. Freud's theories, in effect, made sex seem more pernicious than even the Victorians thought. Whereas before it had been merely distasteful, it was now, if not handled carefully, neurotogenic as well.

As the need to repress sexuality diminished, and cultural evolution proceeded, different types of problems created by other forms of conflicted self-suppression began to predominate. The loosening of the connectedness of the nuclear family itself, caused by the individuating forces in society, created the widely acknowledged increase in prevalence of borderline psychodynamics that has been noted in America in the late twentieth century. This is the subject of the next section.

The "Spoiler": The Borderline Family

In the 1970s and 1980s, the popular press abounded with essays and analyses of the forces at work in our culture that seemed to be tearing apart the nuclear family. Skyrocketing divorce rates, marriages between couples with completely different interests and life-styles, untended "latchkey" children, two-career families, absent fathers, step-parents and step-siblings, half-siblings, unmarried parents, and so forth thrust individuals into a new state of existential loneliness and confusion. No longer do they learn the ways of the world from a constant perspective. No longer are they supported by an unchanging systemic framework. Mirroring provided by multiple caretakers playing musical chairs—or absent caretakers—is insufficient and inconsistent, leading individuals to feel ungrounded most of the time. They learn to alter their role functioning like a chameleon to fit whoever happens to be most significant in their systemic context at the moment. The formation of an "as-if" personality, where individuals seem to blend in temporarily with their immediate environment but also seem to have no self-constancy or stability, is hardly surprising given current contingencies. Given the fact that the primacy of the nuclear family itself over the extended family was itself a rather recent phenomenon, the number of major adjustments that individuals and family systems have recently been forced to make in relatively short periods of time is staggering and unprecedented.

Because of the rapidity of these cultural changes, we are now in a situation where broken families and families composed of independently functioning individuals are common but where the larger culture cannot seem to make up its mind whether such families are inferior or undesirable. Even people who intellectually agree that it is desirable for one to be concerned about leading one's separate life, apart from the family, still feel guilty about paying less attention to the needs of spouses and children. For a while in the 1970s, young adults born during the postwar baby boom were scorned as the "me generation." Supposedly, their concerns had been transformed from the more collectivist, humanitarian concerns of the sixties to selfish ones. Posters with the famous quotation from Fritz Perls stating that people are not put on earth to meet the needs of one another were a common sight. The trouble was that, despite appearances to the contrary, very few people were actually persuaded to that idea. Many put it on their wall to read over and over again so that they might convince themselves that they did not feel guilty when they tried to live up to it.

Given the course of cultural evolution, forces that would gradually tear the individual further and further away from his or her context, to the point where the nuclear family became involved, were inevitable. Such a transition could be expected to be traumatic. In some families, a polarity developed out of the conflict between the needs of the family to maintain itself and the pull of the larger culture toward individuation. Parents in such a family, especially the mothers, who were the culturally designated caretakers, vacillated between sacrificing all of their own desires for the sake of their children and attempting to unload their burdens and be concerned only with themselves.

The latter polarity tended to be short-lived, because these people were overcome with guilt and groundlessness at the thought of giving priority to their own needs. This then led to a severe reaction formation. The parents would go without all but the most basic necessities and give everything they had to their children, expecting absolutely nothing in return. The act of sacrificing so much for their children in a cultural context in which individual aggrandizement was considered admirable naturally led them to experience a certain amount of resentment and anger. Anger about being overburdened and going without was, predictably, destabilizing to the persona of the "self-sacrificer." To really be convincing in that role, one has to appear to desire to act the way one does, not appear to be unhappy about it.

Children of a parent who is having great difficulty with maintaining the martyr role and with containing the resultant hostility are faced with a situation where family homeostasis is threatened by that parent's role-function instability. As in all cases of parental-role-function instability, they experience strong motivation to help stabilize the role functioning of that parent and do whatever is necessary to effect this goal. Since they are the center of the parent's reaction formation, they find that they exert considerable power. The behavior that they will eventually choose must be designed to accomplish certain important goals. First, it should allow the parent to keep giving and making sacrifices. Second, in cases where parental resentment is dangerously high, the behavior should help the parent give vent to it without betraying the underlying source of the parent's anger, namely, the ambivalence about self-sacrifice.

Additionally, any behavior that accomplished these goals would need to be behavior that had been mirrored for the child, so that the child would not experience existential anxiety.

The child comes to find, by trial and error, that one way that the level of systemic tension in the family can be reduced is for her or him to engage in certain hate-provoking behavior. The reason for this is that some types of purposeful behavior by the child allow the expression of pent-up parental hostility and anger but do not subject the parent to the danger of exposing the true source of that anger—the underlying parental desire to be more selfish. If the child does things that make the parent angry, then any expressed parental anger would seem to be reactive in nature. It would appear to stem from the aggravating behavior of the child, rather than from the parent's difficulties with martyrdom. By providing a parent with a safety valve for the built-up resentments, the child stabilizes the role functioning of the parent. The child develops the role of "lightning rod." In addition to, or instead of, providing the parent with a pseudo-rationale for resentment of the child, the child adopting this role can also use it to deflect any anger that one parent feels over sacrifices made for the other parent. The child designs a behavior that makes it appear that he or she is the one draining the affected parent, rather than the spouse. This pattern is frequently seen in families with a martyr mother and an incompetent or frequently absent father.

If the child behaves hatefully, the parent becomes angry and upset but does not experience an existential crisis. Children who provide this service do not understand why behavior that draws hate from the parents decreases family anxiety. They probably believe that the parent prefers them to behave in a hateful manner because the parent really does hate them and needs a convenient excuse for expressing it. If the child made a comment imputing such motives to the parent, the parent would, of course, deny it, and rightfully so. The parent would point to all the things that he or she was doing for the child as proof that love, not hate, existed between them. The parent would also deny that any hostility existed, except where it was a natural reaction to the child's provoking behavior, because the hostility and its real sources would be a threat to the parental persona. The child would soon learn that metacommunication was impossible. I once again must emphasize the point that the parents are *not* "using" children as scapegoats for the family, or for their own problems, out of their own immaturity or defectiveness. The children are volunteering to behave the way they do in order to maintain family homeostasis. The parents are genuinely perplexed by their infuriating behavior.

One can make oneself the object of hate in a variety of ways. Children of a parent who exhibits an extreme form of martyrdom have many factors to consider before making a choice on how to do this. As mentioned, they must behave in ways that have been mirrored for them. They have to help the parents continue to perform the role of self-sacrificer for the children even while they are behaving in a manner designed to make the parent hate them. A behavior that meets all of these requirements may seem at first impossible to design, but the solution to the bind is both relatively simple and quite elegant. These children have received mirroring only for taking what the parents give—not for giving anything in return. The parents, because they are having difficulty staying in the role of giver, tend to tell themselves at one level or another that they are not giving enough, in order to prod themselves into giving more. They tell themselves that they are inadequate whenever they are tired of doing for others, in order to make themselves feel bad about their desires to rid themselves of their burdens. Children can prod the parents to give more and more while making the parents furious at the same time by adopting what is commonly referred to in the psychotherapy literature as spoiling behavior.

Since they have already received mirroring for being takers, children can wholeheartedly embrace this role and become extremely demanding. They tell the parents through their behavior what the parents are already telling themselves: the parents are not doing enough for the offspring, and what is being done is not very good. They take everything the parent has to give and demand more. They appear depressed and unhappy and make the parents feel to blame for it. They go so far as to misuse or destroy what the parents do manage to give, im-

plying that everything that has been given is worthless and un-
worthy of respect. They appear to be completely helpless, so
that the parents must constantly do more and more. They get
into trouble, so that the parents are constantly busy rescuing
them. They never grow up, so that the parents always have them
around. When they have nothing left of their own to destroy,
they begin to damage their bodies, cutting or burning them.

The insufferable demandingness and troublemaking from
such a child infuriate the parents, who do not understand that
the behavior is designed to help them. To them, the child appears lazy and stupid. They berate their child angrily. The an-
grier they get, the lazier and more stupid the child becomes, as
the behavior is having the desired effect. It is successfully drawing parental wrath. The role is reinforced. If the parents attempt
to change their selfless behavior, the child helps them to regain
their original personas by attempting to force them to continue
their self-sacrificing ways. For example, if they attempt to follow the advice of a parent effectiveness teacher or a "Tough
Love" group, and refuse to rescue the child when she or he gets
into trouble, the child gets into even more trouble. If thrown
out on the street, the child stays there and becomes a prosti-
tute, a drifter, or a junkie. The advice the parents had received
then appears ill advised, at best.

In addition to acting the part of selfish, insufferable, insatiable ingrates, children in this type of family have to force
themselves to become helpless in a different sense of that word.
The act of giving anything to the parents is very risky. It re-
verses what is supposed by the parents to be the natural order
of things: that parents give everything to their children. The
children must become people who can *give* no help, incompetent as well as ungrateful. They must sacrifice their own sense of
potency. Spoiling behavior produces the added bonus of helping
them retain this impotent persona. Spoiling behavior is an extreme form of counterdependency, in terms of its effects on the
rest of the world outside of the spoiler's family. Any potent
helper—including and especially the psychotherapist—is made
powerless by the spoiler. Nothing a bona fide helper can do
does much good. Everything is devalued, trivialized, or used in a

way that causes more harm than good. In particular, psycho-therapists' usual techniques designed to give added "ego strength" to the patient seem to make matters even worse than they were before therapy started. If therapists try to be empathetic, they are accused of being condescending. If they try to be neutral, they are accused of being uncaring. If they try to be caring, they are accused of caring only because they are paid to do so. Therapists may then feel as helpless and resentful as the patient's parents do, and are prevented from strengthening the true self of the spoiler.

The type of family that produces this sort of offspring is the borderline family. While borderlines have developed the role of spoiled, spoiling children, they have also lived up to the notion, which has been force-fed to them throughout their lives, that one should sacrifice everything for the sake of the all-important family. Despite their apparent "selfishness," they have sacrificed their true selves, with their need for potency. What on the surface appears to be a contradiction—a "selfish" self-sacrificer—is really no contradiction at all. Anything gained through phony selfishness is ruined or devalued, and the borderline ends up with nothing.

To make such a terrible sacrifice, a good deal of mental gymnastics is required. Borderlines convince themselves that they deserve all of the hatred that they draw. They learn to hate themselves, focusing on all of their shortcomings and ignoring all their good points. They blame all of the family problems on themselves, while at the same time blaming everybody but themselves. They paint the world in black and white, and vacillate from one extreme to the other. They engage in "splitting." Patients who split suffer no developmental defect that renders them incapable of forming an integrated concept of self or other; they simply cannot afford to be able to see both the good and the bad simultaneously. If they were to do so, they would not long be able to remain in character.

When the spoiling borderline female reaches an age where marriage becomes feasible, a new bind develops. For all of her life, she has received mirroring for being childlike and selfish, but she has also been taught that the family is the be-all and end-all of human existence. She has been taught that the individual means nothing; what is important is the next generation. If she were to avoid having children, she would be violating a basic rule in her family and threatening family homeostasis. She will feel herself to be under great pressure to have a baby. The female is traditionally the family member most dedicated to producing and caring for the family heir; a woman who has no children is viewed by the family and by herself as "incomplete." This explains a part of borderline behavior that has perplexed many a therapist: how is it that a person who appears to wish to be nothing more than a child can also possess, admit to, and act upon such a strong desire to burden herself with a child of her own?

If the borderline goes ahead and produces children, she suddenly finds her family seeming to expect her to be able to switch back and forth between two contradictory roles. To maintain family homeostasis, she must somehow develop the ability to transform herself in an instant from a person who does nothing but take—from her parents—into a person who does nothing but give—to her children. Even worse, she must somehow become a person who has the power and ability to meet all of her children's needs while remaining entirely impotent to assist her parents.

When faced with this riddle, which is enough to challenge Solomon himself, the borderline has a number of options. First, she can develop an ego-dystonic symptom that allows her to be labeled as "too sick" to have children. This option will be explored later in the chapter. A second option, frequently used by female borderlines, is to purposely or "accidentally" have a child but give it up to her parents to raise. In this situation, the new grandparents are sometimes assisted in raising the new baby by one of their other children. This sibling of the borderline usually already lives with the parents and volunteers to be a parental child. This allows the family to continue into the future while leaving everyone in their original roles. The parents continue, with some much-needed assistance, to make sacrifices for both their child and the new grandchild, and the borderline continues to appear to be an irresponsible leech who cannot delay the gratification of her drives for either sex or affection long enough to obtain some sort of birth control. This scenario permits the borderline to follow the family rule about having children without needing to face the dilemma of switching back and forth between being a taker and a giver.

Yet a third option for the borderline faced with a desire to have children is to go ahead and have them and do the best she can when she must switch back and forth between the roles of "demanding child" and "giving parent." Before considering what becomes of a child of a borderline when this option is chosen, a discussion about the father of such a child is in order. In many instances, of course, he may be just a casual acquaintance of the mother who is not involved with the child at all, but frequently he is very much involved or is replaced by a man who plays a similar role.

The Narcissist. A man who is attracted to a spoiling borderline woman will of course invariably be someone who is playing a role that is complementary to the role of the borderline. The role that most closely fits this bill is that of the narcissistic personality. A man who would go so far as to live with or marry a borderline woman usually comes from a family in which he has learned that it his duty to live up to the demands of family members, no matter how unreasonable. This is a variation on the collectivist theme with which his prospective partner is grappling. A complicating factor in a narcissistic family is that this ideal is taught to the child by parents who prevent him from living up to it in relation to themselves.

In the most extreme version of this kind of family, the mother appears to be extremely needy herself but is appalled by the idea of a child of hers helping her. She may have borderline tendencies herself, or she may be struggling to rebel against the traditionally passive female role. In the latter case, she might use a reaction formation to force herself away from passive tendencies and become uncomfortable when anyone tries to take care of her or help her. One narcissistic patient whom I treated in therapy was raised by a mother who was forced by the death of her husband to take care of a large family without the tra-

ditional help of a male breadwinner. The patient was the youngest of six siblings, and the family had been rather poor even
when the father was alive. After his death, the mother bravely
moved her brood to a large city and took on the combined role
of caretaker and breadwinner. The patient always felt obliged to
ease his mother's formidable load but somehow never felt supported in his efforts.

       As Kohut (1971, 1977) pointed out, the narcissistic per-
sonality is frequently a victim of poor or absent mirroring and
suffers from low self-esteem. I believe that the mirroring that is
missing in these cases, rather than being global, pertains specifically to the child's emerging sense of personal potency and mastery. The narcissist has never received mirroring for being helpful to his mother. In light of the fact that his mother seems to
need such help desperately, he begins to feel himself to be rather
worthless as well as completely powerless, and his self-esteem
suffers. Kohut also discussed how the narcissistic patient's sense
of self-esteem can be enhanced if he is able to turn to the father
for the mirroring that he had not received from his mother. Indeed, the father in some such families may provide a source of
positive identification and mirroring, but unfortunately the father in most narcissistic families does not do so. Not infrequently, Dad is as ambivalent about the traditional role of the male as
a macho breadwinner as a borderline female is ambivalent about
her traditional role as selfless caretaker of children. To combat
his ambivalence, he too adopts a reaction formation; he develops an exaggeration of the male role in which he fancies himself to be completely independent, supercompetent, and never
swayed by emotion. He is appalled by anything that smacks of
weakness or neediness. Others must depend on him, never the
other way around.

       This persona, based on reaction formation, is also inher-
ently unstable given current cultural conditions. The cultural
message advancing the cause of individuation is just as loud for
males as it is for their wives. One currently popular metaphor is
that men should no more be Prince Charmings than women
should be Cinderellas. Men are entitled to indulge their dependency needs! Women resent being treated as if they were help-

less! These cultural messages play into our superman's suppressed self-aspects, strengthening any cravings for dependency that he may—and almost always does—possess. This, in turn, leads to a great deal of existential anxiety as his reaction formation begins to crumble. In this situation, his son may find that he does not receive any support from his father when he behaves in a potent, caretaking way. In fact, he finds that the level of his father's anxiety decreases when he acts in an impotent manner, even though his father may be simultaneously criticizing him for being a sissy. The reason for this has to do with the general situation, discussed previously, of the family with a parent who exhibits unstable role functioning. The father's persona becomes stabilized if the son acts out, and therefore gives vent to, the father's threatening suppressed self-aspects—in this case the father's suppressed wishes to drop the burdens he takes on when he assumes the macho role.

Once again, the son in such a family is faced with an impossible bind. Overtly, he is being criticized for being weak and ineffectual, while covertly, he is being mirrored by both parents for being just that. The family becomes anxious if he becomes powerful but becomes ineffective if he remains weak. In some cases, this dilemma is handled by the narcissist through an attempt to be both weak and powerful simultaneously. He may become a successful businessman who is also an alcoholic, or a tyrant at work who is sexually impotent.

In general, the narcissist is a male who has taken on the role of someone whose help is needed and whose duty it is to provide that help but who is ultimately incapable of supplying it. By forming a relationship with a borderline woman, he provides himself with a mate who is ideally suited for the job of helping him to maintain this persona. She accomplishes this unusual assistance by furnishing a never-ending torrent of unreasonable and unfulfillable demands, which he then feels obligated to attempt to satisfy. He strives for and fantasizes about omnipotence because omnipotence is what it would take to satisfy the demands of the apparently insatiable borderline—and because striving for the unattainable is one way to make oneself feel incompetent. For his part in the dyadic relationship, he supports his wife's role by supplying her with the hate that she is attempting to draw onto herself. Her unreasonable requests, belittling manner, and accusations of incompetence, coupled with his frustration over the impossible task he has set for himself with his mate's assistance, lead him to episodically spew his rage at her. This is the paradigm of the wife beater, who is often an alcoholic as well.

Family Violence. When a woman with borderline tendencies, with or without a narcissistically inclined partner, elects to have a child and care for it herself, she must attempt to fulfill both the giving role of a parent and the taking role of a child. This usually results in the production of a child who is a carbon copy of the borderline parent or her spouse. The level of disturbance in a family in which a spoiling borderline mother and/ or a frustrated, inadequate, violent father square off against a spoiling borderline child is fearful. It frequently results in parents abusing children, adult children abusing parents, or both.

The role functioning of those who are spoilers in their family of origin demands that they think of themselves as powerless. When one is used to thinking of oneself in this light, suddenly being saddled with the demands of a helpless child leads to an even greater level of resentment, anger, and hostility than would be found in a martyr who was not used to thinking of himself or herself as globally impotent. Nonetheless, borderline or narcissistic parents feel duty bound to provide as much as they can for their children. This pattern puts the children in exactly the same position that each parent had been in within the families of the grandparents, but to an even greater degree. Such children will eventually stumble upon the role of the spoiler themselves. This can become an extremely dangerous situation, for the nastiness of the parent, who has learned to express rather than repress all hostility, reinforces the nastiness of the child, who is trying to infuriate the parent in the first place. The parent's hateful behavior likewise reinforces the child's view that the parent really does hate her or him. If the family has not developed ways to dampen the vicious circle that results, it will spiral out of control, and physically damaging violence or even murder can take place, as the parent and child continue to take turns egging on one another.

Violence against infants and toddlers occurs through a far less complex feedback loop, which superficially resembles the scenario described above. These children are, of course, too young to formulate and act out a role in order to solve a family problem. However, they are not too young to be tied into the family system—indeed, at their stage of development, they are more tied into it than they will be at any later time in their lives. When faced with an angry, agitated, and frustrated parent, babies will reflexively and instinctively become more and more agitated. They will begin to cry and carry on. The more they do so, the more inadequate the borderline parent begins to feel, because such a parent believes that it is his or her duty to protect the child from all adversity. This leads to another vicious circle. The more agitated the child becomes, the more agitated the parent becomes, which then further agitates the child, and so forth. Again, if the feedback loop is not in some way checked, tragedy can result.

The "Defective"

Yet another way for family members to prevent themselves from behaving in ways that threaten nuclear family system unity is for them to develop some sort of defect that renders them *incapable* of behaving more individualistically. Alternatively, they might develop a defect that prevents them from behaving in ways that threaten the traditional role function of other family members. Behavior that subverts the role function of another family member, who is perhaps already ambivalent about it, might help that other individual behave in a less enmeshed fashion. This would also loosen the bonds of family interconnectedness. The avoidance of such behavior through the development of a symptom is, in a sense, a variation of role-function support. Psychiatric symptomatology can serve the function of making the individual seem to be defective, and in a way that appears to be involuntary, so that the "defective" individual does not appear to be putting on an act. Good examples of the role of "defective" are the bulimic, the hypochondriac, and the agoraphobic.

When people experience anxiety, depression, or a psychophysiological reaction, such as an asthmatic attack, they may find that, because of the reaction the symptom produces in significant others, the symptom is a quite useful possession. It may help them to have a desired effect on certain family members. They can incorporate that symptom into a role that they have devised to solve an evolutionary problem in the family system. If the symptom goes away, and the role playing is thereby interfered with, the sufferer can pretend to continue to experience it, in order to continue to produce the same effect.

Individuals will find an incapacitating symptom useful, and will pretend to continue to have it, in situations where family systemic homeostasis is undermined *no matter how they willfully behave.* In other words, a defect is useful when a person is in a double bind that precludes either wishing to engage in some activity or wishing to refrain from it. Such a dilemma can be solved through the mechanism of appearing to remove the problem-creating issue of personal desire from the equation. The person's behavior must appear to be determined by factors other than personal preference. For instance, the hysterical female described earlier in this chapter was in a nasty bind. She needed to maintain the persona of an asexual person in order to fulfill cultural requirements and be worthy of her husband. However, if she avoided giving her husband sex, she would be seen as cruel and depriving. If perchance she happened to develop an incapacitating headache and begged off sex for that reason, she might notice that her problem concerning sex was temporarily solved. She would see that she had been able to avoid intercourse without appearing to be willfully depriving her spouse. The headache, being involuntary, rendered her unable to have sex, through no fault of her own. This temporary solution could easily be turned into a long-lasting one if the woman continued to take advantage of any incapacitating headache she happened to have and pretended to have one whenever she did not.

A symptom becomes part and parcel of the persona of

the person in such a predicament. As with any act that is alien to the true self, it must be supported by a variety of mental gymnastics. Additionally, symptom bearers make use of the actor's paradox to be convincing and so act as if they really believe they are continuing to suffer from the symptom even when, in actuality, they are not.

Bowen (1978) has pointed out that the development of an "involuntary" defect in any family member temporarily solves conflicts in the family relationships and can make less differentiated behavior more comfortable. The defect stabilizes and rigidifies previous role functions and prevents the system from advancing to the expression of new, dangerous levels of individuation and role choice. For instance, a woman's capability and ambition toward a successful career might make her husband's wish to be a househusband more feasible, exposing him to existential anxiety and role-function instability and threatening family homeostasis. If she were to attempt to solve this problem by denying her ambition, she would fail, because the husband already knows that it exists, and in any event he has already come in contact with his own disturbing desire to give up the role of breadwinner. If instead she has, say, a nervous breakdown, she may apparently become incapable of having a career. Her husband would then be forced to continue in his previous role of breadwinner, or the family would starve. Since he has no other choice, he will not be as troubled—again, temporarily—by thoughts of "what if?" Of course, if she were perceived by her husband as sacrificing her ambition and becoming defective on purpose to force him to remain in his previous role, this would tend to increase his misgivings about it, rather than to make it more comfortable.

In order for an individual with a symptom to deny willful intent, it must somehow appear to be involuntary. A psychosomatic symptom is ideal in this regard, since a physiological reaction is something over which a person is generally thought to have no control. The confusion in many quarters over whether, say, an asthmatic has a "physical" or "emotional" problem, already high because of the tendency of the symptom to be brought on by the physiological effects of anxiety, is further in-

creased by the fact that some asthmatics will at times pretend
to wheeze, or force themselves to do so, when they are not in
fact experiencing a physiological asthmatic attack. They do so
in order to continue to play the role that they have designed for
themselves. A psychologically minded but otherwise naive observer might suspect that a given asthmatic attack was a charade
because of its timing or some other peculiarity, and might then
erroneously conclude that the asthmatic never really had a
physiological problem, when in fact at other times he or she did.

An individual who feigns a low IQ can appear to be disabled. Likewise, an affective symptom can appear to render an
individual involuntarily incapacitated. A person who is "too depressed" to engage in some activity cannot in good conscience
be blamed for avoiding it. The person avoiding an activity by
this means may or may not in fact be depressed. In addition to
affective and psychosomatic symptoms, the various forms of
self-destructive compulsive behavior can also function as "involuntary defects" in many instances. Binging and purging buli-
marexics, hand-washing compulsives, and so forth appear to be
utterly distressed by their "ego-dystonic" and "uncontrollable"
behavior. In addition to pointedly making a verbal claim that
they do not like and cannot control their behavior, these patients bolster the case for these otherwise unbelievable assertions by convincing other family members that they are ashamed
of their behavior. The reason that this works is because shame is
the emotion that people feel when they are powerless to control
their fate. Compulsives often do everything they can to "hide"
the behavior from others, thus demonstrating shame, but usually also manage to leave clues around that something is amiss.
Claims that they have no control over their behavior allow compulsives to deny responsibility for it much as ulcer patients can
deny responsibility for the holes in their intestines. Haley (1963)
put it this way: "The patient does something extreme, or avoids
doing something, and indicates that *he* is not doing it because
he cannot help himself" (p. 5).

This sort of mental gymnastics has one additional feature
that increases its versatility. No matter how much the rest of
the family might wish to believe that compulsive behavior is in-

voluntary, a doubt about it will always cross their minds. We all have the intuitive feeling whenever we do something as specific as, say, washing our hands that we intend to do so. How can anyone deny such an intention? As the compulsive engages in ritualistic behaviors, other family members will wonder whether the behavior is deliberate. This doubt-inducing feature allows compulsives to change their personas as the homeostatic conditions in the family system change. In order to solve family conflicts, an individual might need sometimes to appear defective and at other times to appear to be a willful, vindictive spoiler. If others can never be certain whether one's behavior is willful or involuntary, one can switch back and forth as conditions dictate. Compulsive drinkers, for example, may on some occasions hide bottles, thereby appearing to be embarrassed about their lack of control, while on other occasions go out of their way to flaunt drunkenness. They may loudly blame all of their misdeeds on being intoxicated, and then turn around and insist that they do not drink too much.

Occasionally an individual can discover a useful defect through the reactions of a psychotherapist. A good example of an iatrogenic induction of a defect, one that can be a nagging difficulty in the type of psychotherapy described in this book, occurs when the therapist successfully unmasks a symptom as a voluntary maneuver before adequately dealing with the reasons for the necessity of the symptom in the first place. The "defective" may then take on the role of "immature individual," in order to continue in the same role. The client begins to appear to be someone pretending to be ill to shamelessly manipulate others for selfish purposes rather than altruistic ones. Being seen as "immature" can serve the same function that the original defect was meant to serve, since being immature is just another kind of defect.

Case Examples

A beautiful and intelligent woman (Case 5-1) works in a job far beneath her capabilities; although rather thin, she ritualistically attends Overeaters Anonymous for three years without ever conquering her tendency to episodically stuff herself with ice cream to the point where she feels ill. A brilliant government employee in his twenties (Case 5-2) is severely depressed, passes up promotions at work, spoils his relationships by being unreasonable, and accepts his father's description of him as a person who never completes anything he starts. A woman in her thirties (Case 5-3), whose own father was a compulsive gambler, develops agoraphobia after the death of her father-in-law, the "only father" she ever had. A middle-aged man (Case 5-4) with no major medical problems constantly runs to doctors for a succession of inconsequential back complaints, demanding tests and procedures. The tests always prove unremarkable, but their negative results, instead of providing reassurance, cause him to worry even more. He concerns himself with the question of what it was that the doctors were unable to find.

The personalities of these four disparate patients were as superficially different as any four personalities could be. The first patient was a smart-mouthed, streetwise ethnic from Philadelphia. The second was a soft-spoken, self-deprecating sort who could suddenly turn stubborn and quietly hostile. The third was a somewhat obsessive, rigid woman who showed a minimum of emotion. The last was a self-absorbed, pesty individual, whose constant complaining was never matched by any objective appearance of distress. The chief complaints of each of these people varied as widely as their personalities. Yet in each case, the significant parameters of individuation that proved to be important in their families were oddly similar—in four important ways.

First, each of these people experienced difficulties separating from his or her family of origin. The first three patients were estranged from their families, living hundreds of miles away and keeping interpersonal contacts minimal or nonexistent. They were bitter about the way their families had treated them and wished to have as little to do with their parents as possible. The fourth patient, in contrast, appeared to have remained firmly attached to his mother's apron strings. The patients who were alienated from their families may seem to have established independent life-styles, with only the last having

difficulty doing so. However, we can invoke the principle of opposite behaviors and hypothesize that either over- *or* underinvolvement with one's family of origin is evidence that one is
having problems establishing a life separate from them. I believe
that humans are not yet at a stage of cultural evolution where
they can completely divorce themselves from family systemic
considerations. As I will shortly illustrate, when people are apparently estranged from their families, their absence is somehow
needed in order to maintain family homeostasis. Their behavior
remains highly contingent on systemic considerations, and they
are not truly free to express their individuation.

The second similarity in these cases, related to the first,
was that in each case the parents of the patient seemed to have
a conflict about how close they should be to one another. Each
pair had a characteristic way of handling the problem that involved either over- or underinvolvement, and none of the eight
parents appeared to be particularly happy with the way things
turned out. The parents of the bulimic divorced when she was
fifteen. Her father then kept the children, turned their care over
to his dominating aunt, and never remarried. He remained isolated from relationships outside of his own family of origin. His
wife went home to live with her mother after the divorce and
likewise never again ventured away or remarried. In contrast to
this underinvolvement, the parents of the depressive seemed to
be overinvolved with one another. The father would invariably
go along with all of his wife's whims and desires, no matter how
unreasonable, and would act as if he were merely an extension
of her. He seemed to have no individuality.

The parents of the agoraphobic had a ritualistic dance
that kept them at arm's length from one another. The father
would go out every night until the wee hours of the morning,
gambling and womanizing. As soon as he came home, the mother would pick a fight over his behavior, which the father would
then use as a pretext for going out gambling and womanizing
the next night. The parents of the hypochondriac were overinvolved similarly to those of the depressive. The father would
passively allow the mother to worry and fuss over the health of
all the family members, including himself, and would escape

from her carping by isolating himself in a room and reading. The mother would spend all of her time worrying about everyone in the family; should things be going well for them, she would herself fall ill.

The third similarity in the family dynamics of these four patients was that each considered her- or himself to be grossly inadequate and defective. The bulimic was so obsessed with her aberrant behavior that her "treatment" activities permeated all aspects of her existence and destroyed her relationships. Her failure to get well was, to her, prima facie evidence that she was incurably mentally ill. At the beginning of therapy, she considered changing therapists because she thought that I was expecting her to get better too quickly. The depressive considered his behavior to constitute obvious proof that his father was correct in labeling him as a person who could never complete a task. His problems at work and in relationships seemed to him to be clear indications of that. The agoraphobic thought that her general fearfulness—she was unable to stand up to her unreasonable co-worker, for instance—was evidence that she was constitutionally weak. She continued to maintain that she was disabled even after her panic attacks were controlled with imipramine. The hypochondriac knew that his obsession with his health was unreasonable and concluded, with the concurrence of his former psychiatrist, that he was hopelessly immature.

The fourth similarity was related to the third, similarly to the way that the second was related to the first. At issue within the relationship of the parents of each patient was the question of relative competence in spousal or male-female relationships. One parent tended to overfunction in various activities while the other exhibited incompetence in those areas. The incompetence of the "weaker" spouse was invariably belied by some evidence of hidden strength.

The father of the bulimic was an alcoholic who, although he was strong enough to work a demanding job to support the family, would come home each night and appear to fall apart. He would drink and wring his hands endlessly. His aunt ran the household and took care of all the family affairs outside of his work. In the family of the depressive, the mother had done extremely well in school but had worked only as a file clerk, apparently to avoid earning more than her husband, who had always been considered the lazy one in his family of origin. The mother appeared to be insecure, and the father would appear to paternalistically humor her.

The mother of the agoraphobic refused to leave her gambling, cheating husband. When asked why, she would answer with the statement, "I'm not going to let some whore get his money." This turned out to be one way of saying, "a woman cannot survive without the presence of a male" or, in this case, without his financial support. This idea of a woman's need for a man presumably applied to fathers as well as husbands—the agoraphobic became "weaker" when her substitute father figure passed away. Of note was the fact that the patient's maternal grandmother had been deserted by her husband and was forced to work long hours at a low-paying job to support the family—at a time when working women were the exception and not the rule. Last, the mother of the hypochondriac appeared to be completely helpless without her husband. She did not know how to drive, handle money, or even call the local bus company for information. If her husband did not wait on her hand and foot, she became ill. Despite her apparent weakness, she had been able to induce her husband to alter his career choice to something more lucrative before they were married.

Each of these families was troubled by discomfort over the amount of emotional fusion or, more accurately, the degree of systemic interconnectedness expressed within the context of the nuclear family. As in the borderline family, the forces of cultural evolution were at work, ripping apart the nuclear family system. In each case, cultural change created psychopathology. The anxiety caused by the lack of mirroring for more individuated behavior was so great that the old system was maintained through homeostatic mechanisms despite great suffering on the part of the individuals concerned.

In cases where severe psychopathology results from cultural change, one expects the presence of some micropattern that has rendered individuation and family disunity even more threatening for the particular family than might be expected from the normal progression of cultural evolution. The historical context of a given problem is not always available, but in cases where a good family history can be ascertained, I have found such patterns in every case. For example, in the case of the depressive, family unity for the mother was important because the family was the only Jewish family in a hostile gentile neighborhood.

What, then, is the relationship of family system interconnectedness and the issue of personal competence? I have discussed previously how a personal defect can draw other family members back into enmeshment. Stated simply, competent individuals are far more able to survive independently of their support system than are incompetent individuals; if they can take care of themselves, they will free up the other family members to pay more attention to their own inclinations. A crippled individual requires the family to put more energy into systemic considerations and less into the expression of the differentiation of the individual selves. The development of an involuntary defect is a homeostatic mechanism by which an individual can altruistically decrease the temptation faced by other family members to abandon their enmeshment behavior.

The type of family system conflict that is most usually alleviated in such a manner involves inflexible gender-role functioning. As I have discussed previously, in pretechnological days, strict division of labor within the family along sexual lines was necessary for the survival of the system and was the hallmark of family systemic functioning. Gender-role choice is the hallmark of the decline in family interdependence and is experienced by many as a major threat to family system survival. A defective spouse will help the family to maintain the old rules of sex-appropriate behavior. In a sense, the presence of a cripple increases the need for family interdependence in just the same way as did the previously existing lack of technological alternatives, and in so doing maintains family homeostasis.

In times of rapid cultural evolutionary transition, the picture of the family with a defective becomes even more complicated. Role-function choice during such times may be somewhat freer than it had been traditionally, but it will still have many limitations. A woman may feel comfortable with a career, for instance, but not with making more money than her husband. A family member might then develop a defect that serves the specific function of limiting the amount of time a woman can devote to her career, hampering her chances for career advancement, rather than the function of helping her to avoid having a career altogether. In a situation where one spouse is assisted in maintaining traditional role functioning through the development of a defect by the other spouse, a great deal of marital tension invariably develops. The dysfunctional behavior of one mate may decrease the existential anxiety felt by the other, but all the same, it is exasperating. It may aid the functional mate in keeping his or her system-sanctioned role, but it also makes the role more difficult. A wife who is unable to drive, for example, creates many headaches for her husband. Who will do all the errands that need to be done when the husband is at work? This frustration works to enhance the husband's sensitivity to the individuative messages that continue to bombard him from the outside culture and causes him to resent his wife for her impairment. Why should he have to do all the driving? The agoraphobic wife keeps the resentment in bounds, because she does not appear to be avoiding driving "on purpose." The functional spouse, being somewhat more comfortable with expressing his individuation than a member of a borderline family, stays in the relationship only because the dysfunctional spouse "can't help herself" and "needs him."

Nonetheless, and even though he is deathly afraid of expressing less interdependent behavior, this man will in almost all cases have a suppressed wish to say "to hell with the family." His spouse, being impaired, is a burden and a nuisance and prevents him from paying more attention to his own inclinations. Of course, if he were comfortable with his true inclinations, he would not need nor would he stand for a dysfunctional wife. She would have no motive for being dysfunctional. If her role in her family of origin demanded that she be defective for the sake of a spouse, she would leave and find someone more in need of her services. As is so typical of disturbed families, this is a case wherein the very traits that attracted this couple to one another in the first place become the major source of friction in their relationship. Ironically, the defective spouse's efforts at maintaining family cohesiveness have the ultimate effect of undermining the emotional warmth and closeness in the marriage. This is yet another example of the altruistic paradox.

The alarming quantity of resentment in the marital relationship that can be generated through this mechanism is almost as much a threat to family homeostasis as the groundlessness that would be experienced if the members of the couple further expressed their individuation. The danger that the marriage will become so intolerable that a divorce is contemplated is ever present. Whenever family homeostasis is threatened as it is in this instance, the children in the family become intensely interested in finding a method by which to restore it. One way a child can diffuse the situation and decrease the interspousal resentment is to take over the role of defective from the dysfunctional parent. A dysfunctional child is just as effective as a dysfunctional spouse at inducing guilt in a family member—maybe even better. After all, you can divorce your spouse; you cannot divorce your child. When a parent is bound to a customary, comfortably mirrored fate because of a defective child, the spouse who had been serving this function becomes free to be less defective. The persona of the functional spouse is stabilized without the help of the mate. Becoming less defective, the formerly dysfunctional spouse is no longer as burdensome to the functional one as before. The functional spouse then has much less reason to be angry at the mate, and the threat of divorce is greatly lessened. The child playing the role of "defective" helps maintain the parental persona and deflects the tension in the family from the marital relationship onto the parent-child relationship.

By becoming defective, these children become lightning rods for the parental hostility, deflecting the resentment that had existed within the relationship of their parents. The manner in which they serve the lightning rod function, however, differs significantly from the way in which borderlines serve it. Their goal is not specifically to draw anger onto themselves but to make the functional parent guilty and to take the heat off the dysfunctional parent. If they were to play the part of the vindictive spoiler, they would strengthen the resolve of the functional parent to leave, rather than weaken it. Such parents are more comfortable with differentiated behavior than are borderlines and have rationalized maintaining the traditional role function as something that they do because they "have" to. A vindictive child would be a good excuse to leave, rather than a justification for staying. The behavior of a "bad" child might be comfortably blamed on the dysfunctional spouse, strengthening the case for a divorce. For this reason, the child playing the role of defective must appear to be doing so "involuntarily," just as the defective parent had done.

In some families, the borderline issue of sacrificing for the children and the "defective" issue of traditional gender-role functioning are both present. In this situation, the child may on some occasions play the role of vindictive spoiler and on other occasions play the role of defective. The aforementioned confusion about whether a given defect is voluntary allows them to move back and forth between these roles. In still other families, a child will develop the role of defective, but the spouse who was dysfunctional will continue to play the role as well. In such families, the degree of ambivalence regarding traditional sexual-role functioning is so high that it takes more than one family member to contain it. I once had the pleasure of treating a patient whose family contained a dysfunctional parent and *three* dysfunctional children. In many families, of course, the development of a defect in one of the children allows the other siblings to feel free to lead relatively normal lives. The pattern that I have been describing here is another way of looking at what Bowen (1978) refers to as the "family projection process," but with a stronger emphasis on the following point:

The child's behavior relieves the dysfunctional spouse from the burdensome necessity of being defective, while the functional parent receives much needed role-function support. Both will have difficulty disguising their relief; they might appear to be pleased with the current state of the family and threatened if the child behaves competently. However, they are not actually happy with their child's defect but only with their own markedly decreased distress. In fact, the child's impairment in life skills is of tremendous concern to them. Since they do not have a clue to the reasons for their child's defectiveness, they do not know how to deal with it. They read books on child rearing, go to lectures, and so on, to try to learn how to solve their child's difficulty. They worry about whether they are to blame for the way their child is turning out. The guiltier they feel, the more involved they become in interdependent family activity. This is precisely the goal the child's defective behavior is designed to achieve. In behaviorist terms, the child's impairment is continually reinforced by the very parental behavior that is meant to stop it. To the naive but psychologically minded therapist, the parent's behavior looks as if it were meant, unconsciously or perhaps even purposefully, to keep the child in the impaired state.

The parents gradually become more and more frustrated over their impotence in helping their child become an independently functioning, self-supporting individual. This sometimes leads to harsh, punitive behavior toward the child, often by the more functional spouse. He or she will attempt to motivate the child toward success through a relentless torrent of biting criticism or through the use of shame. The parents of a teenage bed wetter might hang the soiled sheets out of the window, for example. The child will grin and bear what may have become, by this time, emotional abuse from the parent. The other parent, meanwhile, will become alarmed at the abuse the child is receiving, and will attempt to blunt its effect by secretly subverting the disciplinary moves of the harsh parent. To the family systems therapist, this once again appears to be a move on the part of the dysfunctional parent to maintain the impairment in the child, rather than to protect the child from the punitive parent.

Because the defective behavior in individuals playing this role has been so thoroughly reinforced, their tenaciousness in hanging on to the view that they are sick or inherently flawed is utterly remarkable. If they are challenged on this point by a psychotherapist, they can resort to a full negative split of the self. I learned this truth the hard way. At the time of my lesson,

I had been reading about the technique of "positive reframing" employed by systems therapists who use paradoxical techniques (Weeks and L'Abate, 1982). In an effort to practice what I had learned, I attempted to praise the actions of a patient (Case 5-5) whom I later realized was a pro at playing the role of defective. She was a woman of high intelligence who had been a miserable failure at work, love, and leaving her family. When I attempted to focus on her strengths, she told me that she knew for a fact that she would never be successful at anything; she had never grown up, could not tell a winning relationship from a losing one, and always took the easy way out in any endeavor. I dutifully pointed out all the obvious flaws in the reasoning that she was using to maintain these dubious beliefs. She countered, of course, that the clearly disturbed reasoning that I had just described was evidence that her cognitive functioning was inherently defective. Either that, she reasoned, or else she must be some kind of "sicko" who was manipulatively playing games with me, and wasn't she awful for doing that?

No matter how hard I tried to describe her character traits as positive, she found a way to see them as negative. When I pointed out how skillful and clever she was at doing that, she replied, "Well, I like to be the best at *something!*" This was yet another statement of her defectiveness—she wanted to be the best at doing something bad—but at the same time, it was also a statement of how miserable and frustrated she was about not feeling free to live up to her considerable capabilities.

The Estranged Defective. Individuals playing the role of "defective" may sometimes also adopt a variation on the role of "savior." The child of a parent who has a repressed but nagging wish to be less enmeshed with family can provide additional role support to the parent by electing to act out the wish. The parent can then vicariously experience the freedom from family responsibility that he or she longs for by identifying with the child. The savior option can in most instances be adopted only by a child in a family in which one of the other siblings has already taken over the role of defective from the dysfunctional parent. The lightning rod function of the defective is more im-

portant in maintaining family homeostasis in these families than
is the role of savior. However, the adoption of the additional
role of savior can add further stability to the family and decrease the load on the impaired sibling.

An overenmeshed parent may even initiate the savior role
in the child by electing to altruistically push the child out of the
nest, hoping that the child does not make the same mistake of
family overinvolvement that the parent has. Such a decision on
the part of a parent is not uncommon, particularly in the
United States, where the culture at large places high value on
the pioneer spirit, independence, and "elbow room." A parent
may not be able to avoid being "tied down" him- or herself because of existential anxiety but may be able to help a child to
do so. Whether or not the parent has initiated the process, the
adoption of this form of the savior role leads to the estrangement of the affected child. The child may still become defective, however, as we shall see.

How might a parent who feels stifled by overinvolvement
with the family attempt to prevent a child from making the
same mistake, while not exposing his or her own true feelings?
One of the most common means chosen to accomplish this goal
is for the parent to make closeness in the family so uncomfortable that the child gets angry and cannot wait to leave. The parent demonstrates—without coming right out and saying it—that
family closeness is obnoxious, and covertly mirrors the child for
rebelliousness. The parent does not have to change his or her
behavior very much in order to get this point across; in fact, it
can be made emphatically merely by showing off the already
existing patterns within the family. The mother of the agoraphobic (Case 5-3), for example, would constantly complain to
her offspring about the father's behavior and about how miserable she was in the marriage. Her inability to leave her husband
served as a warning as to what might become of an individual
who could not avoid becoming too involved with a spouse. She
would have the patient spy on the father on the pretext that a
wife needed to keep tabs on her husband, so her daughter could
see firsthand what one might expect from marriage. The joyless
atmosphere pervasive in the house was blamed on family dis-

cord in general. The mother herself hovered over the patient's every activity. The overbearing quality of the mother, who was intrusive yet not supportive, allowed the patient to experience the stifling quality of overenmeshment firsthand. The patient could not wait to leave home.

The mother of another agoraphobic drove away her daughter, the oldest of her children, by showing gross favoritism to the younger children. The patient was expected to help take care of them without any thanks or support. This constituted an impressive demonstration of the exploitative nature of family ties, in a way guaranteed to make the patient angry about it. The mother also demonstrated the lack of appreciation one might expect from one's family by allowing her daughter to watch the abusive behavior of the father. Yet another of the mother's tricks was to gossip about the patient to the other children in the family, creating discord and infighting. In this manner, the mother attempted to make sure that the patient wanted nothing to do with anyone in the family.

With behavior like that of the parents in the above examples, it is hardly surprising that these patients developed a strong wish to keep contact with their parents at a minimum. They know, of course, that close family relationships have not led to such disasters in the kinship systems of all of their peers. Nonetheless, they have received no mirroring for close family ties that are characterized by warmth, affection, and mutual caring.

Children who provide vicarious satisfaction of a parental wish to individuate will nonetheless in many instances become defective anyway, just as if they had stayed at home and played the role of defective there. The reason for this is that few people at our stage of cultural evolution really want to live lives devoid of the ties of marriage and family. In order to avoid relationships, estranged defectives will often convince themselves that they are incapable of forming close ties. They tell themselves that they are incapable of doing so because of some defect they invent. Alternatively, estranged defectives might marry dysfunctional spouses. The reason for this is a double bind on achievement. If they were to succeed at establishing satisfying and non-burdensome family relationships, not only would they bring upon themselves a great deal of existential anxiety by doing something for which they have received no mirroring, they would also make the parents feel depressed and envious about not having been able to do what their children had done.

This mechanism explains the otherwise illogical tendency of many individuals, particularly young women, to escape from an unhappy home through the process of marrying into another one. Such individuals are acting out the suppressed wish of the family to bolt from stifling family enmeshment but cannot do so successfully. Such was the early fate of the agoraphobic in Case 5-3. To get away from the miserable behavior of her family, she married at a young age, but the relationship lasted only a short time. The marriage did result in one child. Interestingly, after the divorce, the patient's mother insisted on taking over the care of the baby while continuing to act in ways that alienated the patient. The patient, who was the youngest child in her family, eventually became estranged from her parents. Nonetheless, they continued to raise her child.

Once a maladaptive patient persona is identified and understood by a therapist, the next step is for the therapist to help the patient solve the family problem through some less destructive mechanism. The question arises of whether this can be done with individual psychotherapy, or whether family therapy is necessary. In the next section, I will recommend a method for inducing change within the patient's family system through individual psychotherapy.

6

SYSTEMIC CHANGE
THROUGH
INDIVIDUAL THERAPY

I have always found family psychotherapy to be a rather cumbersome process and have preferred to work with individuals. The number of permutations and combinations of resistances, diversions, disqualifications, dyadic interactions, existential and evolutionary issues, and so forth seen in a given session increases exponentially with every additional member of the family present. I am well aware that many therapists have become adept at following complex patterns of interactions among multiple individuals, but I personally have had a difficult time seeing the forest for the trees. Keeping track of everything an individual does in a session is difficult enough!

A second problem with family therapy is that getting a nuclear family together weekly at a single time and place, in these days of two-income families and children going to different schools, is often a logistical nightmare. The very same forces that are tearing apart the nuclear family make the assembly of all significant family members for a series of therapy sessions extremely difficult. Granted, many times this difficulty represents a resistance, as when different combinations of family members show up with no warning for various sessions. In other cases, however, getting everyone together represents a legitimate hardship for the family. Some employers, for instance, will not allow for weekly absences. A husband and wife may even work different shifts. A therapist's schedule cannot accommodate many such people in a manner that is reasonable for the therapist. If the cast of significant others includes grandparents, two sets of step-parents, and in-laws, one is pretty well forced to exclude them from the sessions, which undermines the justification for having family sessions in the first place. Essential relatives may even live in a different city. Even if it were possible to get them all to agree to come, and find a time when they all might get there, many therapists have office space limitations that make such large gatherings impractical.

On the other hand, when the therapist is attempting to deal with the patient's problems from a systemic perspective, the pitfalls of individual therapy are legion and well known. The first problem is that descriptions of interfamilial interactions reported by individuals can either be outrageously biased or leave out the most important data. Individuals may not know which occurrences in their families are significant and which are not, or they may conveniently forget or overlook important events. As I shall show, however, there are methods for ascertaining with sufficient accuracy significant systemic patterns during the course of an individual session. The information can later be corroborated by inviting other family members in, one at a time, for a session or two.

The second major problem with individual therapy, it is widely believed, is that individual and systemic change is difficult or impossible if the therapist can have a direct effect on only one family member. Are single family members powerful enough to effect a change in themselves, let alone in the entire system, in the face of powerful systemic forces? One might enlarge this question to ask whether a nuclear family has enough power to generate change in the presence of a powerful extended family system, or even whether an extended family has enough power to make changes in the face of a powerful cultural or subcultural system.

In my experience, I have found that it is indeed true that children and most adolescents do not have enough power in their families to make a significant impact on the systemic dynamics, so that individual therapy with them is pointless. From a theoretical standpoint, this observation makes much sense. As I have described, I believe that human beings begin to develop the ability to seriously challenge the family system's view of the universe only when they reach adolescence, and that this ability is not developed completely until adulthood is reached. The exact age at which this stage of self-development comes to fruition is undoubtedly a variable, and it is not an all-or-none phenomenon. As a general rule, individuals under the age of twenty-one or twenty-two have not developed a self powerful enough to challenge and change the family homeostasis. When a child or adolescent is presented as the identified patient, one must make an attempt to engage one or perhaps both of the parents in psychotherapy, or do family work. I have also thus far had no luck with helping schizophrenic patients individually to make systemic changes in their families, even after their psychosis is stabilized through medication. I do not know whether they have the power to do so. The therapeutic methods that I will describe do not work for them.

As for nonschizophrenic adults, I believe that individuals are powerful enough to make the most far-reaching kinds of systemic changes, and I have seen them do it. I believe that they possess a self that is a center of initiative and that exists outside of and apart from their systemic context yet is unalterably enmeshed within that system. If one member of the system can change the way in which he or she interrelates with the others, the rest of the system must change in order to accommodate that person. Each individual is too much a part of the system for such changes to have no effect on it.

The name most associated with the idea of helping patients individually to make systemic changes, indeed to become therapists for their own families, is that of Bowen. He advocates a method by which he coaches his clients in the art of derailing the homeostatic mechanisms that are creating problems within their families of origin. He literally sends his patients on trips back to the family. The main goal of these trips is for patients to learn to differentiate themselves from their system, but in the process patients usually help other family members to do the same. Bowen himself used the techniques he advocates on his own family (Bowen, 1978, chap. 21).

Wile (1981) made a very interesting observation about Bowen's work: "What I find most striking in Bowen's discussion is the dramatically different tone in the relationship between the coaches and clients and between the clients and their families. Bowen, as coach, uses nonmanipulative means (education, logic, collaboration) to instruct clients to manipulate or deal with their families. . . . Certain of the tactics he recommends seem similar to paradoxical interventions, therapeutic double binds, and strategic maneuvers of the Jackson-Haley orientation. It is not immediately clear why Bowen does not coach individuals to be therapists of the Bowen type—that is, to be the same sort of therapist to their families that he is to them" (pp. 44–45). The type of psychotherapy that I am about to describe was designed to enable the therapist to do just that.

This form of therapy is designed for use with adults within the age range encompassing the early twenties to the early fifties who exhibit self-destructive or self-defeating behavior, affective symptomatology, or overt family discord. The methods are not as well suited to the post-midlife adult. The therapy is relatively long term, averaging about forty sessions, with a range of between twenty-five and eighty sessions. The length of therapy is determined by the degree of family system disturbance, how hard the patient and the therapist work, and the number of significant family members that are contributing to the patient's problems.

In order for a successful outcome, the method requires therapists to be able to form and maintain specific attitudes about the problems that they have set out to solve. Attitude is perhaps the most important ingredient in helping the client to report accurately during individual sessions the processes occurring within a family.

Principles of General Attitude

People Are Not Defective. Far and away the most important attitude a therapist must convey to a patient is the therapist's firm conviction that neither the patient nor any member of the patient's family system is either defective or inherently evil. The therapist must believe that the problem that the patient brings for solution is not a problem *with* that patient or with anyone else, but a problem *for* all of them. To anyone trained in the traditional methods of psychotherapy, the maintenance of this attitude does not come easily. A therapist must constantly guard against interpretations and judgments based on a belief in the existence within the true self of the patient—though not in the patient's persona—of immaturity, irrational fears, impaired development, masochism, cognitive impairment without convincing evidence of an organic abnormality, innate evil, stupidity, or a lack of perceptivity. Likewise, a therapist must avoid attributing such characteristics to the essential being of other members of the patient's family system. He or she must believe that there are no villains in the family drama and must always be careful to distinguish between appearances and reality.

The attribution of evil intent or defectiveness to patients always brings forth one of two reactions. Either they become defensive and begin to cover up rather than clarify, or they pick up on the defectiveness theme and present themselves as worse than they actually are. Likewise, the attribution by the therapist of evil intent or defectiveness to the parents or other family members of the patient invariably induces one of two possible responses. Either the patient defends and protects them by painting a rosier picture of them than is realistic, or, if the other family members are portraying themselves in a negative light, the patient picks up on that theme and wastes time becoming indignant. In any event, the descriptions of family process that the patient will give to the therapist under those conditions will not be accurate.

When patients describe behavior that either is inherently horrendous—such as child abuse—or has disastrous consequences, therapists will find it difficult to avoid resorting to old thinking habits. They will be reminded of various clichés that they have learned, such as "poor ego controls" or "family scapegoating." It matters not at all that therapists keep these ideas to themselves; the patient will know about them. Therapists must maintain the discipline necessary to force themselves to search for

the altruistic intent behind the behavior, the factors that provoke it, and the hidden rationality behind it. They must get past
the emotional revulsion they feel for the behavior, though without globally denying the existence of their negative reactions. In
order to do this, they learn to use a skill that they will be teaching to their patients. They learn empathy, the ability to understand why individuals feel that they must behave in a certain
way, without the additional conclusion that the behavior is
right or good. One can find behavior understandable without
agreeing with it. I sometimes find it useful to contrast the concept of empathy, which is useful, with that of sympathy, which
is not. I define the latter to mean understanding *plus* agreement.

Another way of looking at this is to think of behavior in
terms of goals as opposed to means. The therapist assumes that
the ultimate goal of all behavior is ultimately good, insofar as
the family system is concerned, although not necessarily as far
as outsiders are concerned. Specifically, patients want to do
what will ultimately be the best for the entire family system or
its individual members. Only the means by which they attempt
to reach these goals are questioned. These means, despite being
questioned, are thought to be the best means that the clients
could possibly have chosen, *given the limitations of what it is
possible for them to know about human behavior.* If they knew
more, they could have picked better ones. Nonetheless, the
means that the patient has chosen are not having the desired results. The outcome has unexpectedly gone sour. The attempt to
solve a family problem has backfired. The patient comes to the
expert for assistance. The rationality of patients is to be respected at all times, no matter how inappropriate or stupid or
ridiculous their behavior might appear to the therapist, the outside world, or even the patients themselves.

One consequence of the therapist's belief in the patient's
lack of defectiveness is that the therapist will find that it becomes much easier to discuss the patient's family situation
using, to use Wile's (1981) terms, education, logic, and collaboration. When the therapist believes that unpleasantries can be
discussed rationally, frankly, and directly, although empathetically, with a patient who is capable of effective problem solv-

ing and who can tolerate discomfort, she or he will actually exert a calming effect on the patient. Character resistances are minimized. For a change, patients experience being treated as the competent, strong human beings they really are. The therapist who altruistically protects patients from unpleasant truths or sadness does more harm than good.

One of the central ideas advocated in this volume is that psychological problems are ultimately caused by the inability of a family system to change interdependent behavior that once had tremendous survival value, in situations where the culture has evolved to a level requiring more individuated responses. Indeed, the reason that interdependent behavior is so difficult to change is precisely because it was, at one time, so important. Because of the temptation of less enmeshed behavior dangled in front of the family by the culture at large, the old rules of conduct often become even more inflexible than they had been generations ago when they were useful. As I mentioned earlier, any discussions within the family about the disappearing necessity for maintaining these behaviors will naturally generate a great deal of existential anxiety, as well as regrets and misgivings about lost opportunities for the parents and untoward effects on the children. If the patient is able to make a breakthrough and begin behaving differently, other family members may become quite envious.

The attempt by the patient and his or her family to avoid subjecting various members to these feelings is precisely what blocks the resolution of the family problem. Worse still, the protectiveness of the family backfires and ends up making the protected individual feel even worse. When patients are coached to deal effectively with their families, they, like the therapist, will do more harm than good if they protect the family from negative emotions. However, the therapist must address the patient's concerns about harming the family. How the pain and discomfort of metacommunication can be minimized will be discussed later.

The Therapist Is an Expert. Implicit in the attitude toward the rationality of patients described above is the idea that if

they could find a better way to solve their problems, they would
do so. They would have no need for a therapist. They come to
the therapist because the therapist is an expert; in other words,
the therapist is supposed to understand the science of human
behavior and know things that the patient does not know. This
is what an expert is paid for. The ability of the expert to help is
not based on superior objectivity or maturity. It is not necessarily contingent on the therapist's self-understanding, although
such understanding is useful in preventing the therapist's own
persona from interfering with the therapeutic function. The
ability of the therapist to help is based on three factors: factual
knowledge, which consists of an approximately correct scientific paradigm; the ability to apply that knowledge to the solution of the patient's problem; and the ability to involve the patient in therapy and to motivate the patient to solve the problem
in the way that the therapist suggests.

　　If this idea is valid, one can conclude from it that it is just
as important or even more important for the therapist to gain
insight into the patient's problems than it is for the patient her-
or himself to gain this insight. A therapist who understands the
problem has the knowledge necessary to suggest a better solution to it than the patient has been able to devise and to answer
the patient's legitimate questions and objections to the therapist's advice. A patient who merely understands why he or she
has a problem may still not know enough to come up with a
better solution for it. The primacy of the therapist's insight over
that of the patient will find a parallel when I discuss helping patients to work with their own family. In order for them to be
successful in that endeavor, they will need to understand the
motivation of other family members as much as or more than
they will need to understand their own. Only through an empathetic understanding of the motivation of significant others
can clients define a solvable problem and motivate their families
to work on it with them.

　　The Problem Has a Solution. John Spiegel (1982) describes the predominant attitude of the American middle class
toward the question of the relationship between humans and

nature: "the assumption that there are few (if any) problems that cannot be solved. . . . We have conquered infectious diseases, gone to the moon, and split the atom. Although we have not mastered chronic illness, especially cancer and long-term mental illness, there is hope. And while a few imbalances, like war and weather, are more elusive, they are not impossible to control. Problem solving is where it's at" (p. 41). In contrast to the beliefs of other cultures, humans are not expected to suffer.

This attitude, which does not always come naturally to even a middle-class American, is quite a useful one to convey to one's clients. No matter how hopeless a patient's situation may seem, no matter how bogged down the family system may be in games without end and mutual disqualifications, the therapist must believe that a solution can be found. If nothing the therapist suggests seems to work, it must be because the patient has overlooked an important aspect of family interactions or because the therapist has failed to understand a significant point. The therapist does not give up easily, does not become discouraged, and remains optimistic. If the patient becomes pessimistic, the therapist can state, "I guess I'm more optimistic about these things than you are." The therapist is outrageously persistent.

This is not to suggest that any therapist can help any patient. Indeed, for various reasons, one may fail, and it can eventually become time to refer the patient elsewhere. A therapist may simply dislike a client and be unable to generate any empathy for the patient's position; in that case, the therapist may be *unwilling* to be persistent. One does not have to feel guilty about referring the patient away under such circumstances; in fact, an attempt by the therapist to suppress these feelings will ultimately damage the patient. In other cases, therapists may have completely exhausted their bag of tricks and got nowhere. There is no point in keeping a patient in therapy for years if no progress is being made. With these exceptions, however, the therapist's general willingness to press forward in the face of adversity is essential if the patient is to do likewise. Unlike the therapist, the patient is not in a position to send her or his family on to somebody else. A therapist can do a certain amount of modeling, particularly if a patient comes from a culture in which people are supposed to accept their fate rather than attempt to control it.

The Family Problem Is Best Solved Within the Existing Family System. Therapists can often become frustrated and angry with a patient's family when they perceive that the family seems to be engaging in behavior that maintains and reinforces the patient's symptomatology. This is a particularly common occurrence with individual therapy in which the therapist takes an eclectic approach and in family therapies that stress the idea of the "identified patient." The whole idea of scapegoating is probably the result of systems theorists being induced to help patients get rid of anger at the family, and thereby maintain their personas, through projective identification. Patients who can vicariously experience the therapist's anger will have less difficulty suppressing their own.

In one way or another, patients in these therapies are often advised to divorce their families. In individual therapy, the patient may be pressured to avoid family members who are perceived as manipulative. In the family therapy of disturbed young adults, Haley (1980) concerns himself only with helping the identified patient establish an independent life; if the parents continue to suffer marital problems after the child leaves, that is their problem, not the primary focus of therapy. Haley will deal with the marriage per se only if the parents take it upon themselves to ask for help.

I believe that human beings have not reached the evolutionary stage where a complete divorce from the family system is possible; nor do I believe that such a separation would be desirable. Since I do not find parents or other family members defective or evil, I find the concern that children have for them to be praiseworthy, a mark of love and caring for one's fellow human. Even more important, I believe that only through the mirroring and support of the family system can a person learn to comfortably express the individuation that is gradually and unceasingly crystallizing out of the family system matrix. Those who learn, through therapy or through some other means, to defy family system homeostatic mechanisms and to write off other family members always seem to feel that something is terribly missing from their lives; they are more troubled by feelings of being cut off, of being groundless, than are those who individuate while maintaining contact.

For this reason, I always take the side of the client's ambivalence that wants to remain in contact with the family. I often remark that the client does not seem to be the type who can just write off the suffering of parents and siblings, no matter how mean they seem to be. If such clients then reply that they want to learn how to do that, I respond that if that was what they really wanted, they would not be having so much trouble doing so. They are unwilling to leave because they care for and wish to be helpful to the family; this is admirable. They need to learn a better way to do so, as the methods that they have been employing are failing.

The question of whether to stay with or leave the family becomes more complicated when applied to the nuclear family, as opposed to the family of origin. When confronted with a patient in a bad marriage, should the therapist work to solve the marital problems or to end the marriage? If the spouse is physically abusive, advice to work on improving the relationship can be hazardous to the patient's health. In these situations, I once again assume that the reason that abused spouses are willing to put up with abusive behavior at great personal sacrifice—indeed, they will do what they can to provoke it—is because they are unwilling to write off the mate. They are willing to help the mate in any way possible, even by being a punching bag, so that the mate can maintain a persona. Furthermore, since they are receiving support for their own role behavior, should the relationship break up, they are very likely to find another relationship that is not much different from the first. An abused spouse may just as well learn to stop being a punching bag within the context of the relationship that already exists. Only when the patient's life is in actual danger or when the patient has already decided to leave the spouse will I work enthusiastically on helping the patient to first end the relationship, and leave the systemic problems for later.

Therapists Will Not Sacrifice Themselves. Therapists are present to help the patient, but they are also there to make a living—the best that they possibly can. They are entitled to lead a normal family and recreational life and work reasonable hours. The nice part about taking such an attitude is that, since therapists are helping their clients deal with the altruistic paradox, it sets a proper example. Therapists need have no guilt about their high fee, which is commensurate with the staggering degree of responsibility they are assuming, their level of training, and the relative cost of other professionals. They must remind themselves that if they were amateurs instead of highly paid professionals, they would be too busy making a living doing something else to have time to be very good therapists.

I do not mean to imply that therapists may not compassionately reduce or even waive fees in the presence of sudden unemployment, incapacitating illness, or major natural calamity. If they have open hours or if they really enjoy it, they may donate time or agree to work with poor people at a low fee. They must remain aware, however, that they are far more valuable to the patient than are cigarettes, drugs, alcohol, and gambling—money spent on which causes many people to be considerably poorer than they might be otherwise. A therapist's fee deserves precedence over those other expenses.

One other way to reduce the monthly cost of therapy to people who legitimately cannot afford it is to meet with the patient every other week instead of weekly. The kind of therapy I will describe works quite well on this basis, although it may take somewhat longer than if weekly sessions were held. Multiple sessions per week are usually unnecessary and may even be counterproductive.

The Goal of Therapy

The overall goal of the type of therapy that I am advancing is to help patients to give up unnecessary and destructive aspects of their personas and to express their true selves, while remaining in close, helpful contact with their families. This is accomplished by helping them to learn to help their family to solve problems of cultural change through empathetic discussion and metacommunication, rather than through self-destructive acting out. Patients learn to react differently to any family behavior that had previously caused them to experience existential groundlessness, or that had once had the effect of preventing intrafamilial metacommunication.

The rationale for this procedure comes from the idea that altruistic self-sacrifice, which I see as the cause of most chronic psychiatric symptoms and almost all maladaptive behavior, is reinforced by the groundlessness that patients experience whenever they behave in a certain individuated fashion within the context of the family system. The groundlessness, in turn, is brought about by the family's disqualification of any differentiated behavior that challenges the family homeostasis. Disqualifications, which are actually distress signals sent out by the disqualifier, are built into the homeostatic mechanisms of the family system. They are designed to protect the leaders of the family system from existential anxiety, depression, or shame. If a patient were to react to any apparent disqualification in such a way that family members were induced to change their response from disqualification to a mirroring or even a neutral response, the patient's feelings of groundlessness would diminish, and the patient would feel more comfortable with the new, self-expressive behavior.

The power of a holon to mirror behavior for an individual is directly proportionate to how closely enmeshed the individual is within that holon. At the current stage of cultural evolution in Western culture, the individual is less closely enmeshed with the system outside of the family of origin and the nuclear family than at any time in the past. Larger systems of which the nuclear family is a part have far less power than they once did. In particular, authority figures such as therapists are less an integral part of the patient's systemic functioning than they were even a generation ago. Mirroring provided by the nuclear family and especially by the family of origin is far more powerful in diminishing the patient's feelings of groundlessness than is mirroring by outsiders—far more effective than mirroring by a therapist. If the system in which the patient is closely enmeshed can be induced to respond differently from the way it has in the past to the patient's individuation, behavior change can be rapid and significant.

Not only can the family system provide individuals with mirroring, but individuals can provide it for the rest of the family as well. Indeed, individuals are such an interconnected part of the family system that their response to the disqualifications of other family members often has the consequence of disqualifying more individuated behavior from the others! For instance, let us examine what might happen to a daughter if she were to attempt to initiate a family discussion of the continued need for a division of labor within the family along the lines of traditional gender-role functioning. Such a discussion might strike a responsive chord in the true self of a mother who had always been bored being a housewife. However, the emergence of the desire by the mother's true self to escape her traditional role would lead her to experience existential anxiety at the thought that perhaps she might be able to alter it. She might then react negatively to the daughter's attempt to begin the conversation, and this negative reaction would probably have the effect of disqualifying the daughter in some way. The disqualifying effect of the mother's negative reaction, the reasons for which are unknown to the daughter, might then cause the daughter to find a way to quickly end the discussion that she had started. This retreat would have the effect of disqualifying any impulse the mother might have had to question the necessity of remaining a housewife. A chance for the mother to step away from her persona would have been lost.

If, instead of protecting the mother from existential anxiety, the daughter pressed forward in the discussion in an empathetic, noncondemnatory way, making the mother's impulse to question her own persona as comfortable as possible, then the daughter would be, in effect, mirroring the desires of the mother's true self. This would be a great help to the mother. Additionally, if the daughter could help the mother express the reasons for the initial disqualification, the daughter would better understand it. The daughter would see it for what it really was—a response to the apparent family rules in the mother's family of origin—rather than an attack on her personally. If the daughter then went on to honestly and frankly discuss the effect that the mother's reactions had on her, the mother might become more careful about explaining such responses and avoid future disqualifications.

I see my job as a therapist as understanding the reasons for the various manifestations of individual self-suppression and intrafamilial disqualification that take place within the context of a patient's family system, as well as understanding what barriers to effective metacommunication are there. I then help patients to share in this understanding and send them back to the family to metacommunicate in a way that will be effective in reducing the overall level of self-suppressive behavior. Eventually, if the process can be continued long enough, patients become able to shed the unnecessary aspects of their personas, and their psychological symptoms disappear.

One additional point must be stressed. Patients must understand, at some point, that they are not ultimately responsible for making any other family member change his or her own maladaptive behavior, although they must help in any way possible. What they can do is to stop protecting the others in a self-destructive manner. If individuals change the way that they relate to other family members, this forces family members to change the way they relate to individuals. Patients can learn to respond differently to the family's disqualifying behavior that had previously led them to decide to behave in a self-destructive manner. Luckily, in most instances this will help the other family members to change their destructive patterns of behavior. The patient, however, cannot *make* them change, any more than the therapist can force the patient to follow advice. In the last analysis, the family members have decided to behave the way they do for various reasons, and it is they who must decide that they should stop. This does not mean that the patient should become oblivious to their suffering if they elect to continue as they have in the past—far from it. They must continue to remain involved and help as much as possible, but without self-sacrifice.

In the process of helping the patient deal with problems

at their source, therapists will find that they must also deal with transference phenomena, but in a way that is diametrically opposed to the way transference is dealt with in psychoanalytically oriented therapies.

Dealing with Transference and Transference Resistances

From the theoretical standpoint advocated in this volume, transference can be defined and conceptualized as patients acting out a persona in the relationship with the therapist. The "neurotic" or defective behavior that they exhibit in the course of the therapy is presumed to be an act, rather than a manifestation of the inclinations of a patient's true self. If a therapist finds that transference behavior by a patient is increasing in frequency from one session to the next and is interfering with a systems approach, the chances are very good that the therapist's behavior is supporting the patient's persona, rather than contributing to its diminution. The reason psychoanalysts are eventually confronted with a full-blown transference neurosis is because they purposely foster it. Analysts have come to believe that the patient's fantasies determine behavior, rather than that, as I believe, the behavior that the patient wishes to exhibit determines the content of the fantasies.

In the therapy under discussion here, in contradistinction, the therapist wishes to behave in ways that encourage patients to express their true selves. The therapist also wants patients to report the happenings in their lives realistically, rather than to report on and to act out the fantasies by which they maintain a persona. The only fantasies I encourage the patient to dwell upon are those that concern the patient's beliefs about the motivation of other family members. I assume that the patient is misinterpreting the reasons for the disqualifying responses of the family and wish to suggest more empathetic explanations. I discourage the development of the transference, for I am not attempting to divert relationship problems on to the therapeutic relationship, as is the analyst. In this type of therapy, the therapist wishes to avoid such diversions.

To minimize the fostering of transference reactions, the

therapist must avoid certain procedures that are essential to psychoanalysis. Patients are to focus their attention on dealing more effectively with their families, not on the relationship with the therapist. For this reason, seeing patients more than once a week is usually counterproductive. If patients see the therapist too often, a danger exists that the relationship itself will become more important than the task at hand. Additionally, the therapist wishes patients to have time to think about the issues raised in a session and to try out new ways of relating to their families. At the beginning of therapy, patients need time to observe the behavior of the family with a more discerning eye, while in later stages, they need time to try out new behaviors practiced in the role-playing phase of therapy.

The therapist does not try to be a blank screen for the patient's projections. To do so is to encourage the patient to act out a persona rather than to talk about it. When patients are met by silence from the therapist whenever they attempt to have a two-way conversation about problems, the silence reinforces their belief that talking about problems does not solve them. Despite the analyst's admonition to talk about what is on their minds, patients abandon any notion they might have about the usefulness of an open discussion. Since they know of no way to solve the family problem other than the one they have already been using—the therapist has not given them one—they continue to act out a persona as they always have.

As in analytically oriented therapies, I do not discuss details of my personal life; this is not because I want the patient to fantasize about them but because they are irrelevant to the task at hand. The patient is paying too much money for the session to waste time focusing on me. I may respond to a personal question by stating that I am there to talk about the patient, not myself. Alternately, if the patient asks a question about me that is not overly personal, I may decide to quickly answer it, precisely so that the patient does not fantasize about the answer.

Sometimes, however, a personal question may indicate that the patient is looking for a way to become emotionally involved with the therapist as a resistance; that is, to divert attention away from the answers to the questions that the therapist is posing about the patient's family. The patient may be looking for information about the therapist that can be used to "push the therapist's buttons" and distract him or her from current lines of inquiry. A transference *resistance* is not the same as transference as defined above. Rather than an acting out of the patient's current persona, it is a way to disqualify the therapist that is a reflection of the methods by which the patient has been disqualified by a family system. Transference resistances and how to handle them will be discussed further, but I would like to make one point here. A transference resistance, like any resistance, cannot be ignored, for it will block the work of therapy. In analytically oriented therapies, the analysis of resistances is an important part of the therapy. In the type of therapy here under discussion, the understanding of resistances can be helpful but is not all-important; transference resistances should not be encouraged. When I suspect that the answer to a personal question will be used to create a transference resistance, I may respond with a more analytical-sounding "why do you ask?" and refuse to answer. The therapist is free to be warm and responsive, to appear to be happy to see the patient if she or he really feels that way, and to share personal emotional reactions to the patient if such feedback will be valuable in helping the patient to understand the family dynamics. Once again, however, the therapist must be constantly watchful to make sure that this openness is not fostering a transference resistance.

At the beginning of therapy, it is frequently possible for the therapist to nip potential transference reactions in the bud. All of the interactions and behavior that occur in a given session take place within the context of the dyadic therapeutic relationship, and anything patients say can be a metaphor for their concerns about that relationship, as well as or in addition to being an objective discussion of the problems they are having outside of the sessions. (A pure discussion of outside problems that is not a metaphor for the transference is possible, because the context of the dyadic relationship with the therapist includes—primarily, if it is going well—problem solving.) I listen carefully to the patient's verbalizations, just as I would if I were an analytically oriented therapist, for anything that might indicate the development of a transference reaction. If I hear such a statement, I quickly move to head off the reaction.

In the first few sessions, patients have no idea what to expect from therapy. They are concerned that giving a description of their self-destructive behavior either will elicit from the therapist the kind of response that it elicits in their family or will be cavalierly dismissed by the therapist as foolish. They hope that the therapist will react in neither of these ways. As I discussed earlier, the reason that individuals develop a persona is because it induces or prevents certain kinds of reactions in the family system. Not surprisingly, the behavioral manifestations of the persona induce these reactions in other people as well. Patients come to therapy because the problem they are trying to solve is not being solved, despite the fact that they have been successful in inducing those desired reactions. They are afraid that the therapist will not appreciate the reasons why they must maintain their self-destructive behavior, but they are also afraid to act differently.

Such concerns will usually be expressed in the form of a metaphor about what usually happens to the patient in relationships. After an initial description of presenting complaints, patients will describe, in one way or another, how their relationships ordinarily develop and how this displeases them. Most of the time, they will not state directly that they are worried that the relationship with the therapist will turn out the same way. The reactions of their families have generally discouraged this kind of metacommunication. If they could metacommunicate, they would probably have no need for therapy. When I hear a statement that indicates what the patient dreads yet expects from relationships, I waste no time in indicating that I will react differently from any person with whom the patient has yet come in contact and that metacommunication will be encouraged in the therapy.

I quickly inform the patient that a chance exists that, at some point during the course of therapy, the patient may start to think that the uncomfortable problems that he or she experiences in relationships outside of therapy are taking place in the relationship with the therapist. I add, as might an analyst, that should such an event transpire, it could be helpful for the therapy. The therapist and the patient could explore what is happening as it occurs, rather than through a secondhand discussion of what happens outside of the sessions. What I am really saying is that I will metacommunicate about any problem that comes up in my relationship with the patient, knowing full well that one of the patient's biggest fears is metacommunicating. The way that this intervention is phrased paradoxically diminishes the likelihood that patients will have the reaction toward the therapist and increases the likelihood that they will discuss how the interaction develops within their family system. (While the intervention has a paradoxical effect, it is nonetheless honest, up-front, and straightforward.) Should patients go ahead and have the reaction, they have implicitly committed themselves to metacommunicating about it, a procedure that can eventually lead to a diminution in the transference and a discussion of family patterns anyway.

When I warn patients about potential reactions that they might have, they usually counter with a statement that they do not believe that such a reaction will take place. I then respond, "Okay, but we'd better keep an eye out for it just in case." As an illustration of this process, a hysterical patient might complain that men always seem to make sexual advances toward her. A male therapist might respond, "You know that in therapy such an event will not transpire, but I am a man, and you may begin to fear that it will. If you start to feel that way, it might help us to understand why you always seem to find yourself in these situations." This kind of statement, assuming that it is spoken in truth, has the added benefit of reassuring the patient that the therapist is not going to be taken in by the inappropriate seductiveness of her persona. The patient will usually respond with a statement such as, "Oh, I know you'd never do a thing like that."

Now let us turn our attention back to transference resistances. Transference resistances can occur at any time during therapy; they are most likely to arise when the patient is feel-

ing uncomfortable with the questions that the therapist is raising. These uncomfortable questions are usually the very same
ones with which the patient's family is uneasy. Therapists can
identify a transference resistance by monitoring their own reactions. Whenever they feel uneasy about bringing up a particular
topic that seems meaningful, and the discomfort is not coming
entirely from their feelings about the topic as it applies to their
own lives, then chances are good that a transference resistance
is taking place. The patient is indirectly indicating that a negative reaction would occur should the therapist proceed with an
exploration of the subject in question.

   In general, any kind of resistance to discussing a particular subject can usually be diminished by treating it in the same
way that the therapist treats any seemingly illogical or inappropriate reaction, whether of thought or behavior (these methods
are elucidated in Chapter Eight). When these methods fail and
the patient acts out a transference resistance, all is not lost. The
reaction can be turned to therapeutic advantage. As the analysts have pointed out—although they do not conceptualize it in
quite the manner I have in mind—any sort of transference phenomenon that the therapist does see can always be thought of
as a replay of the family problem. It can therefore be used as a
valuable source of information concerning the systemic dynamics. I believe, as do the analysts, that the nature of the therapist's uncomfortable reaction to the patient's transference resistance, the countertransference, provides particularly valuable
data about the family system.

   The therapist can assume that the patient is developing a
transference resistance for the purpose of inducing in the therapist a particular counterreaction that will stop the therapist
from pursuing certain lines of inquiry. I base this assumption
on the net effect of the behavior, which is in this case, almost
by definition, resistance to therapy. I believe that patients are
aware of what they are doing and that they are diverting the
therapist's attention on purpose, because the topic in question
induces in them a highly unsettling sense of groundlessness. Patients will generally pick a method for discouraging the therapist that they have learned from their families. They will at-

tempt to disqualify or induce groundlessness in the therapist in a way that parallels the way that their own families induce groundlessness in them. Patients actually attempt to engineer a very specific type of countertransference reaction from the therapist. If they do get a countertransference reaction, they will get the reaction that they are intending to get. I do not mean to imply that countertransference reactions are not also determined, in large part, by the therapist's own idiosyncrasies. Psychoanalysts would burn me at the stake for voicing such an opinion. However, the therapist's idiosyncrasies are taken into account by patients when they design the transference resistance. They will use trial and error to make minor alterations in their habitual ways of responding, depending on how the therapist responds to them, in order to get the desired effect.

Keeping in mind the notion that all transference phenomena, including tranference resistances, contain references to the family problem, and that the patient is attempting to get a specific response from the therapist, one can use transference resistances to understand how the family disqualifies the patient and to empathize with the reasons why the patient feels a need to avoid certain subjects. I carefully monitor my own emotional response to the patient when a transference resistance does occur. I ask myself how other people besides me might respond to what the patient is doing, to make sure that I am not misreading the situation. I then move to decrease the transference resistance while simultaneously clearing up any remaining confusion about the family dynamics. The form the intervention takes is a variation on the following statement: "When you made those statements, I had such and such a reaction, which made it difficult for me to continue to discuss the subject we were talking about. I wonder if sometimes your family makes you feel that way. If they do, I can certainly understand why you might wish to avoid this subject." The "avoid this subject" part of the last sentence can refer to the patient's avoidance of a subject in sessions with the therapist or, later in therapy, to the patient's avoidance of a subject in attempts to metacommunicate with the family.

Once the therapist can empathize with patients' need to

resist, they will become less defensive about it, as well as more willing to discuss alternate ways in which they might be able to solve the problem of the family's disqualifications. Thus, the transference resistance is turned from a transference phenomenon back into a realistic discussion about systemic difficulties.

Case 6-1

In his second session with me, a young man who had recently dropped out of medical school was describing his experience with a previous therapist: "I think the therapy did me more harm than good. The therapist told me that I had no self-confidence and that I always set myself up for failure. Whenever I hear something like that, I really latch on to it. I became convinced that I would never be able to make it in school."

Students who have been turned away from medical school would no doubt wonder how anyone who did well enough in college to be accepted in the first place could consider himself an academic cripple. Clearly, this patient did not "always" set himself up for failure. However, at this point in therapy, I was somewhat more interested in the transference implications of the patient's statement than I was in the mental gymnastics.

"So it sounds like you had a tendency to get carried away with what your therapist told you. You know, I don't know if you will do that with me, but there is a chance you might find yourself accepting something I say without examining it critically. Or you might start applying what I say to areas of your life where what I say does not apply. We'll have to watch for that."

As the therapy progressed, it became apparent that this patient was an expert in the principle of opposite behaviors. Rather than behaving in the way that I had successfully prevented—blindly accepting everything I said—he exhibited trouble committing himself to *any* idea that I came up with. Whenever I would make an interpretation of the patient's behavior and its function within his family, he would reply, "That sounds really reasonable and like it might be right, but I'm just not sure." Since he could not commit himself to an explanation, we could not proceed to working on how to change his situation. This behavior functioned as a transference resistance.

After several sessions of this, I became more and more convinced that my ideas about the patient's family dynamics were on the right track but that the patient could not go along with me. Nor could he *not* go along. The patient stopped this behavior after I incorporated it into my understanding of his position in his family. "For some reason, you seem to have real trouble taking a firm stand on the issues we are discussing. This makes it difficult for us to work on improving things; if we can't agree on what is going on, we can't figure out how to change it. I wonder if there might be some negative consequences for your family if you were to suddenly become very decisive in these matters." As it turned out, indecisiveness was a significant part of the patient's persona and applied to many areas in his life. My straightforward but empathetic confrontation with the behavior allowed the patient to realistically think about its function and to stop acting it out in the transference.

In some cases, the fear that patients express in metaphor represents a fear that they will *not* be able to maintain a persona in the therapeutic relationship, rather than a fear that the therapist will react just like everyone else. Patients in this case are saying that they are afraid that the therapist will strip away a part of their personas that serves an important function, without providing them with an alternate means of handling the problem. Such a belief can be a transference resistance, but it may also be a valid fear. Therapists often do attempt to induce change without attending to the systemic consequences.

Case 6-2

A patient expressed a fear that she would become too dependent on anyone from whom she might ask for help. In actuality, she was a counterdependent individual who always took charge in every relationship she had and who seemed indeed to be allergic to asking for help. Her fear of leaning on the therapist made it likely that she would be prone to early termination. This kind of potential transference reaction was handled in the following manner: I first expressed my admiration that the patient was able to overcome her fear and make an appointment with me for the help she needed. "It must have been really difficult to do, feeling the way that you do." This statement indicated that I was very aware of her sensitivities and would take them into consideration. I then went on to say, "I don't think there is any danger of you becoming overly dependent. If anything, you seem to err on the side of not depending on people when it would be beneficial to you. This may be part of the difficulty that you are having." This statement framed the patient's problem as counterdependency rather than dependency, without making the patient feel that I was going to attack her for it. It also contained an implicit value statement that would later be an important issue to be explored with the patient: dependency need not be a negative in all situations.

Case 6-3

A patient had the habit of touching on several important themes in her family dynamics whenever she described the kinds of interactions that took place within her family. These themes were brought up practically all at once, in such a way that I was unable to get a complete fix on any one of them. A related difficulty was that she seemed to be unable or unwilling to relate a complete family transaction in the chronological order in which it took place. She would skip from one part of a sequence to another in her descriptions, and she would not clue me in that pieces were being left out or that sequences were being described in reverse order. Often I had the impression that I had heard a chronological description when in fact I had not.

I realized that I was having a hard time putting all of the information that I was getting together into a usable formulation so that we could work on changing the family patterns. I asked myself whether I was having this problem because of my own blind spots or because I was not being presented with a complete picture. Between sessions, I reviewed my notes and concluded that I had probably not been misunderstanding what I was hearing, but that what I was hearing was confusing.

As it turned out, the way that members of the patient's family handled discussions of important issues paralleled exactly the way that she discussed them with me. Major conflicts were touched upon in groups, and none was settled. Past and present events were brought up interchangeably in a most confusing manner. If the patient brought up a problem that she was experiencing with her mother as it occurred, the mother would usually counter with, "Well, what about the time you did such and such to me?" This kind of time-shifting statement would make the discussion of the present interaction difficult enough even if the past problem were analogous to the present problem. In every case, however, the mother's analogy seemed to the daughter to be off the mark. The past difficulty that was mentioned usually seemed to concern a different bone of contention from the one the patient was trying to clarify.

Actually, the mother *thought* that the situations were analogous, because she misunderstood what the patient was talking about in the first place. The patient and her mother had conflicts over gender-role functioning that involved three interrelated issues—sex, women living alone, and women having careers. The mother would become anxious if the daughter discussed going out with a man, because she viewed men as an impediment to her daughter's career and felt that a woman's sex drive practically enslaved females to their traditional role. The mother, a widow, was concerned about the daughter dating for another reason as well. The daughter was the last child living at home, and the mother was uncomfortable with the thought of living by herself should her daughter get married. The elder woman did not wish to remarry herself, did not wish to live with a married child, and did not really want to move into a retirement home.

The daughter did not know what to make of the mother's unexplained anxiety over her dating. Was it an indication that the mother had no faith in the daughter's ability to handle her sex drive maturely? Did the mother wish to keep the daughter all to herself? Since the different issues were all interconnected, neither the mother nor the daughter necessarily understood to which issue any statement might refer. If one or the other reacted to a statement negatively, a misunderstanding of the reason for the reaction was inevitable.

For instance, if the daughter said to the mother, in reference to the issue of sex, "Whenever the topic of my attractive- ness to men comes up, I feel like you are putting me down," the mother would become defensive and answer with a criticism of her own. The mother's thoughts probably went something like this: "Daughter seems to think that I want her to be sexually unattractive. First of all, even though I am concerned with the consequences of any move toward marriage that she might make, the assertion is not really true. But even if it were, what possible motivation is she attributing to me? Everyone else seems to think that I cannot live by myself and need her to stay with me. She probably thinks that is what I am trying to do." The discussion would seem to shift back and forth be- tween the issue of sexuality and the issue of the daughter's leav- ing home, because any statement that referred to one issue could just as well refer to the other. The issue of the daughter's career would also get tossed into the salad every so often for good measure. Past interactions involving one issue were brought up as examples of interactions that actually involved another.

The attempt to discuss the issue led to a situation where mutual understanding was more muddled than it had been be- fore the discussion began. One would hardly be surprised to learn, under these circumstances, that the patient thought that my recommendation to clarify the issues with her mother through talking about them was nonsensical and that she wanted to induce me to bark up some other tree. I handled the situation by sharing with the patient my confusion. I indicated that sev- eral different issues seemed to be causing problems between her and her mother, and they all seemed to get muddled together when we attempted to get a good handle on them. Perhaps this was what happened when she and her mother attempted to clar- ify things. No wonder the two of them did not really under- stand one another! "Let's try to figure out a way to prevent this from continuing to happen, although it sounds as if that will be no easy task," I added. My acknowledgment of the difficulty in- herent in the situation, coupled with my confidence about find- ing a way out, helped to induce the patient to work on teasing the various issues apart, instead of continuing to jumble them all together.

7

INVOLVING
THE PATIENT

I have always found it useful to have an overall plan in mind when I begin therapy, a step-by-step approach that will be useful in most cases that I am treating. To some, the overall plan may sound like what has come to be disparagingly referred to as "cookbook therapy," since the basic sequence of steps is the same in the majority of cases. However, even the most creative chefs have a methodology, even if they are unable to explain how they do what they do. They become creative because they can devise variations on a basic pattern, but they learn the basic pattern before devising the variations. The following is a useful sequence of steps for conducting psychotherapy:

1. Assess the need for therapy and involve the patient.
2. Elicit the exact nature of the problem.
3. Establish the altruistic motive behind the patient's troubling behavior.
4. Discuss how the patient's attempts to solve problems in the family backfire.
5. Offer an alternate solution.
6. Explore the difficulties the patient might encounter with the alternate solution.
7. Role play.
8. Terminate therapy and arrange follow-up.

This chapter is devoted to a discussion of the first step, involving the patient in therapy; the other steps are discussed in the remaining three chapters of this volume.

I have found that one useful way to quickly involve patients in therapy is to proceed in the first two or three sessions in a way that is similar in some respects to a psychoanalytically oriented approach (Langs, 1973). The biggest difference from that approach is the way I frame patient problems: I make it a point to stress that they *have* a problem to solve, not that they or their families *are* a problem. Framing the problem thus is very important in this method of treatment, but what follows is just one of many possible approaches for involving the patient. Any useful method of doing so with which the therapist is comfortable can be employed at the beginning of therapy.

The Initial Session

I usually begin, as does Langs, by asking patients how I can be of help to them, in order to establish the nature of the therapeutic relationship. I wish to convey the idea that I am an expert who is going to aid them in getting to the root of whatever it is that is really upsetting them. This opening question usually leads patients to a discussion of a chief complaint or to a description of what is transpiring in their lives that is causing them stress. If patients do not clearly state a problem, but instead begin a meandering discourse that alludes to several interrelated difficulties but does not clearly define any of them, I move quickly to ask specific questions. What was it exactly that made them decide to see a therapist? Had they been thinking about a consultation for some time, or was the appointment prompted by some sort of crisis? If a crisis exists, what is it? If they had been considering coming to see a therapist for a long time, what was it that finally made them resolve to pick up the phone and schedule the visit? Even when patients clearly state a problem, they may often neglect to mention why they came to therapy at the moment that they did. The therapist should ask this question whenever a patient does not address it, as the answer is often helpful in understanding the family problem.

Case 7-1

A twenty-six-year-old post office employee came to therapy on the advice of her friends. In response to the question of how I could be of help to her, she replied that she was not really sure. Her friends were concerned about her because she seemed to be overreacting to the death of her pet cat three months earlier. She could not seem to stop thinking about it. She was not sure whether this was even a problem at all, but since her friends thought it was, she decided to come. She had no other thoughts on the matter.

I then asked her whether she was perhaps also feeling a bit depressed.

"Well," she replied, "my friends have said that I look depressed, and I haven't felt much like going out. But I don't think of myself as depressed."

I pressed on. "Have they told you what is making them think that you are depressed?"

"I guess I just look depressed."

"Well, do you think they might be right?"

"Probably."

"Well, if you are, do you think it is just over the cat, or are there other things going on as well?"

"I can't think of anything else, although I have been having some trouble with my boyfriend."

The patient did not seem to think that the boyfriend problem was very significant, but since she had brought it up herself, I was able to ask more questions about the relationship. The more questions I asked, the more difficult it became for the patient to deny that the problem had something to do with her looking so depressed.

If a patient continues to be vague and circumstantial even in the face of clear and concise questioning, I do not hesitate to make a statement to the effect that "It sounds like a lot of different things are going on, but I am having some trouble getting a fix on exactly what is upsetting you the most." How this statement is said is as important as the actual words. I do not wish to sound overly critical, but I want to communicate to the patient that I am not afraid of metacommunication and that I can best help the patient if the patient can be frank and straight-forward. In doing this, I let the patient know that I will react differently from the way the patient's family has and set the tone for a relatively transference-free therapy. (This type of statement might be considered a "confrontation"; it is similar in many respects to the type of confrontation advocated by Masterson, 1981, in his work with borderlines.)

History Taking. After the patient's presenting complaints are clarified, I take a careful history. This is, of course, the first step in eliciting the problem, but it is also, in those cases where therapy will be recommended, necessary for obtaining the information that will be used to frame that recommendation. The medical model for history taking can be a useful one. In this model, the history is broken down into the history of the presenting problem, past history of emotional problems and treatment, and social history. Using the medical model, I ask the most far-reaching questions in a matter-of-fact way. I can inquire into all areas of the patient's life under the guise of learning as much as I can about the patient and leaving no stone unturned, without implying that any of the information about which I am inquiring *necessarily* relates to the patient's current problem. (With borderlines, a therapist may sometimes need to make an overt statement to this effect.) If a therapist takes the history in this manner, the patient's natural defensiveness is diminished. The patient is often more open about family problems during history taking than at any subsequent time in the initial stages of therapy. Often I have brought up weeks later something the patient told me in the first session, only to have the patient deny ever having told it to me.

As I take the history, I pay special attention to anything patients say that bears upon the family's involvement in the problem. At first, I do not necessarily indicate that I believe that the family is part of the problem, unless the clients themselves define the problem as a family one. I steer the formulation of the problem in the direction of the family only after I have sufficient information to make a case for this. It is rare that such a case cannot be made.

The history of any past psychotherapy that patients may

have received is important in the therapist's evaluation of possible transference resistances. Did they have a bad experience? If they had a good one, why did they not return to the original therapist? In some cases, the previous therapy may have failed because of the uncooperativeness of the patient, who may not have been ready for therapy of any kind, but in other cases the patient may have received bad therapy. If so, the patient may fear that the new therapist will be no different from the old. Therapists are ill advised to state that they are going to be better than the last one. They cannot yet be sure that the patient is correctly describing what transpired with the former therapist, and in any event, claims of superiority are sure grist for the transference resistance mill. However, therapists can acknowledge the patient's concerns and indicate how they view the issue in question. For example, one patient described how his former therapist kept telling him that he was an immature individual who used his symptoms to run away from his problems. I remarked that, in my experience, people choose their behavior for a good reason, not because they are immature.

When I obtain the social history, I unabashedly ask specific, probing questions about the patient's family relationships. My behavior indicates that I am not afraid to ask delicate questions. In particular, I may ask whether there has been any history in the family of origin or in the nuclear family of physical or sexual abuse, extramarital relationships, divorces, alcohol and drug problems, antisocial behavior, lack of emotional expressivity, or lack of openness in discussions of family problems. Other important areas to cover are the siblings, including their birth order, and the patient's education, medical problems, job history, and marital history. Later in therapy, when I have established the family contribution to the problem, I get as detailed a history of the grandparents as is available.

While on the subject of history, I would like to make some additional comments about the importance of the past in understanding the present. A few systems theorists dismiss the past as unimportant. They believe that the history of how the family homeostasis developed into its present form is unimportant, that only the currently operating systemic forces are of

significance. To me, this is a surprisingly naive view of the nature of systems. Time is intimately connected to the fabric of
human systems, as space and time are considered intimately
connected in physics. Physicists speak, in fact, of a "space-time
continuum." To ignore time is to ignore a major component of
the system. Moments in time do not cease to exist as soon as
they pass. If this were the case, if the present and the future
existed independently from the past, then existence would have
no continuity but would consist entirely of unconnected instances. Knowing how one got somewhere is important for fully
understanding where one is. Residues from the past are to my
mind the primary cause of impaired system functioning. Cultural lag might be considered a sort of time warp.

Occasionally a patient may become annoyed that the
therapist is digging up skeletons from the past. Why, the patient
demands to know, does the therapist not focus attention on the
here and now? The answer is simple. The problems that took
place in the past have not been resolved. In many different
ways, they are still taking place. In fact, the reason that they
have not been resolved is precisely because no one has brought
them out for discussion. In some instances, the patient will
counter this explanation with a statement that discussion of
past problems invariably leads to a sense of beating a dead
horse. The therapist can answer by asserting that this result
stems from *how* the discussion proceeds, rather than from an in-
trinsic worthlessness of discussion.

After I have taken a complete history, I make a preliminary formulation of the patient's problem and decide whether
the presenting difficulty is one that is amenable to psychotherapy. I do not generally prescribe therapy in the first session. I
like to think about what I have heard from the patient before
recommending a treatment that involves so much time, effort,
and money. Additionally, most patients do not seem to like
being rushed into something as frightening as psychotherapy. I
tell patients that their situations sound like complex ones but
that I think I can be of help to them. I tend to use the word *situation* rather than *problem* because upon hearing the latter
expression, many patients jump to the conclusion that I think

that there is something horribly wrong with them and are frightened away. I tell patients that their situations are complex because I know for a fact that they are not simple. I respect patients' intelligence; they would not be coming to me if a solution to the problem were easy to figure out. I do not say I *know* I can be of help, because I do not offer guarantees.

Next, I tell patients that I would like to schedule an additional appointment to explore their difficulties further before I make any specific recommendations as to how I can help them. I assure them that after I know a bit more, I will have something for them. Patients almost always agree, and I end the appointment by setting up the next one. The major exception to this is the narcissistic male patient, who frequently demands some immediate feedback, knowing full well that the therapist might be way off the mark after just one meeting. Fortunately, such patients have generally at some time during the session made metaphorical references to how they have been disappointed in other people throughout most of their lives. The "feedback" I give at the end of the session, if I am asked for it, is a paradoxical prediction phrased something like, "From just what I have heard thus far, it sounds as if people have always been a disappointment to you, and they do not appreciate all you do for them. Sooner or later, you cannot stand it and you want to leave. I am concerned that this will make it difficult for you to come to me for help, as you will constantly be looking for evidence that I am going to fail you." As with most paradoxical predictions, the patient will deny that he will do this and will make the next appointment.

Symptomatic Treatment. In those cases in whch the patient exhibits distressing affective or psychosomatic symptomatology, I see no contraindication to prescribing medication to help relieve it. The major exception to this is the prescription of a drug that might encourage a patient to act out a persona. One would not give abusable medication to a patient prone to drug abuse or a potentially toxic drug to a patient who may be suicidal. To do so would also support the development of transference reactions. Many therapists oppose the use of all medications, because they have seen problems related to misuse of them, but any good thing can be misused. Medications have their place. Symptomatic treatment can be prescribed in the first session. In my dealings with the patient, I define the drug-responsive symptom as just that—a symptom—and go ahead to suggest the additional explorative session so that I might recommend a way in which I can help the patient address the root cause of the symptom.

Many analysts fear that "covering up" a patient's anxiety or depression with a drug removes her or his motivation for treatment. I find, on the contrary, that the prescription of medication can be a lever for inducing patients to return for more sessions. They will come back for a refill if the medication is helpful, and in the meantime I can help them to become comfortable in getting involved in therapy. Additionally, when one takes a problem-solving approach, affective symptomatology that is left untreated works to the detriment of therapy. One cannot solve problems well when one is in a panic or so depressed that one can hardly speak. The nonmedical therapist can work closely with a cooperative psychiatrist on those patients who would benefit from organic therapies. In addition to medication, relaxation exercises or biofeedback can be a useful adjunct to therapy. If therapists are adept at psychological testing, they may feel free to proceed full speed ahead with that. Traditional testing results can easily be reinterpreted using my theoretical framework. When therapists report the results of these tests to the client, they can often use the "objectivity" of the tests to advance a useful formulation of the patient's problem that would normally stir up a transference resistance early in therapy. After all, they are reporting only what the test showed, not their own interpretations.

Hospitalization should be reserved for major affective disorders and psychoses that are untreatable at home and for patients with a significant suicide potential who do not have a good support system. Putting people in mental hospitals is guaranteed to increase any sense of defectiveness that they have about themselves. If the therapist is forced to hospitalize patients who have a tendency to play the role of defective, they must be warned that they may start to think that the therapist finds them mentally ill. This is a transference-reducing warning that is phrased in the same way that I described in the section on handling the transference. Borderlines also tend to do very poorly in a hospital setting, although hospitalizing them is sometimes unavoidable. They act more regressively than ever once they find themselves in an environment dedicated to "helping" them; what they often need is for people to stop helping them so thoroughly.

The Second Session

The goals of the second session are to frame the patient's difficulty in a useful way, to make the recommendation for psychotherapy, to explain a bit about how therapy will proceed, and to begin the process of reducing the potential for transference acting out. Psychotherapy is defined to patients as a treatment method designed to help them understand and modify the distressing situation in which they have found themselves. I usually begin the second session by asking patients whether they have had any further thoughts about the problem areas identified in the previous session. This question is meant to indicate to patients that they are expected to think about what we discuss and to work on their difficulties outside of as well as during the sessions. This question is also quite useful later in therapy, when patients are having trouble getting started in a session. I am not interested in the reason for a patient's silence unless it is because the patient is so uncomfortable with what I am doing that he or she is either planning a transference resistance or thinking of discontinuing treatment. Otherwise, I assume that the silence is based upon existential discomfort and that the patient is capable of proceeding in spite of it.

Framing the Problem. I listen for information to add to my preliminary formulation that supports one of three possible frameworks for a recommendation of appropriate psychotherapy: (1) self-destructive behavior, (2) family, marital, or relationship difficulties, and (3) anxiety or depression of unknown or unclear cause. If patients discuss behavior that is self-destructive, I recommend psychotherapy as a method for understanding why they feel that they must behave in this manner and for helping them accomplish their ultimate goals in a way that brings them less grief. I often set this up with the following statement: "You must have a good reason for doing what you are doing, when it brings you so much unhappiness (or exposes you to such danger, makes you so nervous, ruins your chances for a successful career, prevents you from being satisfied, destroys your relationships with the opposite sex, and so on).

Case 7-2

When the patient was asked whether he had given any more thought to the reasons for the chronic anxiety he had complained about in the first session, he replied that the most pressing worry (of the many we had touched upon) was his fear of losing his job. He was so nervous at work that sometimes he had to leave in the middle of a shift, and this was jeopardizing his job. Because he sometimes worked nights, he was also afraid of falling asleep at work. He was taking large numbers of caffeine pills to prevent this.

I gave him a surprised look. Did he not realize that the caffeine was making him far more nervous than he might be otherwise? After some initial denial, he reluctantly admitted that this possibility had crossed his mind. I told the patient that he seemed to be making himself more nervous and was risking getting fired. I knew he liked his job and really was concerned about losing it. "You must have a good reason for taking such a risk." The patient agreed that he must have such a reason but said that he did not know what it was. I replied, "This is the kind of situation where psychotherapy can be helpful."

Self-destructive behavior is usually obvious, and therapists must presume that the patient knows that it is obvious. If the patient succeeds in defining self-destructive behavior as non-self-destructive, therapists cannot recommend therapy on the grounds that they can help the patient to stop it. If what a patient is doing is not harmful, why bother coming to therapy to change it? For example, a young female patient assured me that taking long walks through the city alone at three in the morning was not a dangerous activity. Although she had experienced a rape, the assault had taken place in the middle of the day. "One cannot live in a closet to avoid danger," she added. I replied that she might be able to get away safely with these nighttime walks for quite some time, but it seemed to me that she was sophisticated enough to know that she was really tempting fate. Additionally, she seemed to be taking risks unnecessarily. There was no particular reason why she had to walk at that hour.

The therapist also presumes that patients are in control of their behavior. Compulsive patients will often frame their difficulty as lack of control. They "cannot stop" themselves, they say. The therapist can agree with them that they cannot stop the behavior but indicate that there must be a good reason *why* they cannot stop. The therapist does not come right out and say that the patient has control over the behavior, but the implication is there. Patients cannot stop the compulsive behavior *because* adverse consequences would ensue. Generally, patients will not argue this point, because if they really believed that they were incapable of stopping the behavior, why on earth would they be coming for help?

When patients indicate that a family or relationship problem is the primary difficulty, psychotherapy is recommended as a method for helping them learn to better handle the relationship or relationships in question. I usually remark that they must care a lot about their families in order for them to want to stick around and put up with all this trouble. I imply that the family is worth caring about but somehow they cannot seem to get along. Psychotherapy can provide the answers.

When patients are unable or unwilling to tell the therapist about the source of their nervousness or unhappiness, or when the apparent source does not really explain the full extent of their symptoms, psychotherapy can be recommended as a method for figuring out the source of the difficulty, so that something can be done about it. The therapist can refer to ideas, feelings, and fears about which the patient is unaware but that are contributing to his or her distress, much in the way an analytically oriented therapist talks about the unconscious. Patients who ask why they do not know the cause of their distress can be told that the reason is that thinking about it must be hard and uncomfortable. Nonetheless, if the problem can be brought out, it can be solved, and they will feel better in the long run. The implication of the last statement is that the patient is really strong enough to deal with it.

Case 7-3

In the first session, the patient complained of having felt depressed for the previous three months but could identify no precipitating stress. I asked her specific questions about what events had transpired in her life around the time of the onset of her symptoms; her answers revealed several tantalizing leads. She had recently got married, moved away from her family of origin, and quit school. She insisted, however, that none of these things felt like the "real" cause of her upset.

In the second session, she recalled that she had felt the same depression once before, when she was in high school. She thought that there was some relationship between the first and second depressive episodes. Whatever the cause of the depression, it must have been present for years. What could it be? The patient's statement that the cause of her depression existed before the current episode seemed to me to be an indirect challenge to the implications of the line of inquiry that I had pursued in the first session. If the cause was already present before she made the recent life changes, then it might seem to follow that these events were unrelated to the depression.

I nonetheless agreed that there probably was a connection between the first and second episodes but added that I was a bit reluctant to also conclude, as yet, that her recent decisions did not figure in somehow. I recommended psychotherapy as a way to make sense of all this, so that we could figure out what to do about it. "When people are depressed and they can't understand why, psychotherapy is the treatment that can help."

Telling the Patient What to Expect in Therapy. After framing the recommendation for psychotherapy, I recommend regular meetings and then go on to tell the patient about how I work in therapy. The initial instructions that I give are similar to those given in a psychoanalytically oriented treatment. Patients are told that they should come into the session and talk about whatever thoughts, feelings, fantasies, dreams, and so forth seem to be foremost in their minds, without deciding in advance what is relevant and what is not—with a general focus on the problem areas that we had discussed when therapy was recommended. They are told that, in everyday conversation, people censor their thoughts. They label their ideas as irrelevant, offensive, or embarrassing. The idea in therapy is for them to avoid making such decisions in advance and to say everything that comes to mind. They are told that doing this is quite difficult, especially in light of the fact that they are talking to a stranger whom they do not know at all. This last statement, in addition to being an acknowledgment of the truth, is a transference-reducing maneuver.

The patient is then told that, in the beginning, I will be relatively quiet—not unlike the stereotypical therapist one sees in the movies—just listening and asking a few questions. The reason for this, I indicate, is that I have to understand a lot before I can say anything that will be helpful. In reality, I am not very quiet most of the time at all but am quite active in questioning, probing, and hypothesizing right from the outset. Nonetheless, the truth is that I will not be able to offer any solutions until I understand the problem. The statement is also made so that I retain the *option* of sitting back and listening whenever my usual activity seems to be leading to nothing but dead ends. Sometimes a therapist's current working hypothesis is way off the mark, and he or she needs to be quiet and listen to what the patient has to say.

I give one final instruction to patients. I inform them that we will be talking about a lot of very uncomfortable subjects. Usually the most uncomfortable areas turn out to be the most important. I let them know that patients often become so uncomfortable with what is being discussed in therapy that they find that they have a hard time getting to therapy sessions. Cars seem to break down, memories slip, and so on. This may happen to them. They may even decide to quit. If they do, for whatever reason, they should come to therapy at least one more time to explore this decision. They may wish to quit because, in truth, no progress is being made, but it is important to see whether the decision is really based on discomfort. Once again, this instruction is, in addition to being the truth, a paradoxical prediction meant to use the patient's fear of metacommunication to decrease the probability of a premature termination.

After the last of these instructions, if time remains, I tell the patient to get started. I then listen to what the patient brings forth and begin the next step of therapy, eliciting the exact nature of the problem. I also listen for potential transference reactions and move quickly to keep them to a minimum.

FRAMING
THE PROBLEM

To begin the next step of therapy, I listen to the patient's associations and ask questions in order to obtain information that will allow me to make a useful hypothesis about the family problem. The initial formulation must of necessity be an educated guess, for it cannot be confirmed without feedback from the rest of the system. The hypothesis consists of my speculation about the motivation behind any disturbing or maladaptive behavior presented by the various members of the patient's family system, including the patient, as well as speculation as to the reasons for any misunderstandings that are taking place within the system. I do not pretend to be able to read minds; the only member of the family system who can confirm the therapist's earliest speculations about her or his motivation is the patient. Confirmation from the other family system members must await the patient's attempts to metacommunicate, which will come after the therapist presents the initial hypothesis. The information gained from the patient's interactions with the family may later alter, or even completely negate, the therapist's ideas, which must then be modified to incorporate the additional information. When the time comes to present the patient with the early ideas, they are clearly labeled by the therapist as an educated guess based on the information available at that time.

I develop my hypothesis by first listening to the patient's

256

descriptions of patient and family behavior. Early in therapy, patients may omit any mention of their family in discussing problems and focus entirely on other matters, such as symptoms or practical problems with career or financial matters. The therapist's job is to steer the patient's associations to the role of the family without stirring up major transference resistances. I assume that patients would have no symptoms, and would be able to handle career and financial problems, were it not for the reactions of their families, even when they and the family no longer seem to be in contact. In the case of work problems, a safe assumption is that the family's behavior discourages the patient from doing whatever he or she has to do in order to solve them. If the patient's inability to solve a practical job problem were based purely on a lack of knowledge, a career counselor or attorney would be consulted, not a therapist.

In those cases where the patient does not include information about the family, I move the early discussions in that direction by asking specific questions about how the rest of the family is reacting to the patient's troubles. Are they supportive, or do they seem to get in the way? How does the patient's behavior affect them? If the patient focuses on interpersonal difficulties outside of the family, I listen for evidence of behavior on the part of the patient that provokes negative reactions from others. I can then ask the patient where he or she learned this particular method of coping with people. Did anyone in the family present the same type of difficulty?

When the answers to my questions do not seem to be yielding significant clues to the family dynamics, I sometimes resort to indirect information-gathering methods. I may ask clients about their dreams or perform a behavioral analysis. In doing so, I am looking for evidence that their chief complaints are indeed related to processes that are taking place within their families. I use the patient's associations to dream elements and information regarding the timing of symptoms selectively to make a case for that idea. This kind of indirect information often provides new leads that allow a therapist to open lines of questioning that may not have been previously apparent.

After listening to a description of the family behavior and

establishing its role in the patient's problem, I move to get more family history. What was the parents' relationship like, and how did each of them relate to the patient? What were the grandparents like? Did the patient know them? What was he or she told about them? How did they relate to one another over issues with which the patient has problems? A therapist can then apply knowledge about what motivates human behavior to ask questions and pursue ideas that will continue to shape an overall hypothesis. A therapist can make use of the various paradigms that were discussed in Chapter Four, as well as knowledge of the patient's cultural background and family history, to generate possible explanations of the family behavior, and can then ask questions that will confirm or refute these ideas. In particular, I pay attention to the patient's family and cultural attitudes toward gender-role functioning and sex, raising children, solving problems, careers and education, and family loyalty. Significant microevents, such as immigration, deaths, and disasters, are also carefully noted and incorporated into my impressions. I am not shy about pursuing any possible lead and feel free to explain to the patient why I am asking the questions that I am posing.

As the reader can see, my conduct in the session is straightforward and actively probing. I fairly quickly make known my prejudice about families always being involved in emotional problems. If the patient protests that the family has nothing to do with the problem, the protestation will invariably be based on the patient's wish to protect them. The patient's fears may be based on illogical propositions or other kinds of mental gymnastics, which can be handled in ways to be described shortly. Alternatively, clients may be resisting because they feel that a family member is being blamed unfairly for the difficulty. In this case, I make clear that I believe the family is unwittingly contributing to the problem, not causing it out of spite or defectiveness. The family members bear responsibility for their contribution to the problems but are not to blame in any moral sense. Any appearance of moral culpability is probably based on the client's misunderstanding of the motivation of the involved family member.

Case 8-1

A patient in his forties complained almost exclusively of insomnia. He agreed with me that his sleeplessness might be caused by anxiety but added that the only thing he was nervous about was his inability to sleep. His fear of insomnia was also making him anxious during the day. Outside of this problem, he was not upset about anything.

In obtaining the patient's social history, I learned things about him that made it appear quite likely that his anxiety about sleep masked a more significant fear. His father had suffered from manic-depressive illness. When the father was not sleeping, it meant that he was crazy. The patient had often been compared to his father by his brothers and sisters; this angered him so much that he had to a major degree cut off communication with them. The patient insisted that his family was not causing him any distress, because he had very little to do with them. However, when he discussed his estrangement, he became tearful. I commented that, despite his distance from his family, they still seemed to provoke a highly emotional reaction. Perhaps his anxiety was related to them in some way.

In eliciting the problem, I also wish to get a feel for how the client's family system handles or does not handle metacommunication. In order to do so, I need the client to recount important transactions as accurately as possible. I must sometimes make my needs clear by asking questions such as "What exactly did she say? What did you say next? And how exactly did she respond to that?" Many times, a patient will report an evaluation of what was said rather than the actual content, and therapists might be fooled into thinking that they have understood the nature of the transaction when in fact they have understood absolutely nothing. Descriptions of transactions related to the therapist by a patient such as "He blows up over the most trivial things" or "She acts like she hates me" are useless. What were the trivial things he blew up about, and what exactly did he say about them? What took place right *before* he blew up? What exactly did she *do* that made the patient think that she hated him?

Not surprisingly, most patients' knowledge of their family history, particularly the nature of the interpersonal relationships in earlier generations, contains large gaps. Indeed, if they were more aware of how family problems got started, they would better understand and be more empathetic toward their family members and would probably respond to family anxiety with less maladaptive behavior and self-suppression. As I mentioned earlier, an understanding of family history is the first step in understanding the family problem, which is in turn the first step in finding a solution for it. When I come upon an important gap in the patient's knowledge about his or her family history, and the patient knows of a living family member who might be able to shed some light on it, I instruct the patient to go to that family member for more information.

This instruction is not only meant to help elicit the problem but is also the first step in the alternate solution. In asking their families for history, patients are initiating metacommunication about the current family problem in metaphor. The remote family history about which they inquire will contain a metaphor for the current difficulty, because the current difficulty results from leftovers from the way the family system operated in earlier generations. Because this initial discussion of the problem takes place in metaphor, the chances are better that the family will be able to discuss it nondefensively than would be the case if clients brought up an interpersonal problem directly. Later, when the family defenses over the issue in question are down because of increased understanding of where the problem came from, patients will be able to bring the discussion out of the metaphor. They will be able to discuss how the historical problem is affecting the family relationships in the present. This process is analogous to the way the analytically oriented therapist discusses transference issues in metaphor before bringing the discussion around to the more threatening transference.

Of course, not all families will react to even metaphorical discussions nondefensively. If clients react with resistance or anxiety to the therapist's advice to ask the family about certain areas in the history, or if they report a negative response from the family when they do ask, I explore the nature and causes of these reactions. This information assists me in understanding the blocks to metacommunication that exist within the patient's family system, so that I can help the client anticipate them and work around them. Even when patients are agreeable to speaking to the family about history and anticipate no problem in doing so, I warn them that they may encounter a negative reaction, and should this occur, they should back off and report in detail what took place to the therapist. I tell them that this information is valuable and that I will be able to help them to deal effectively with any negative reactions that they do encounter.

Many times, patients who are told to ask the family about family history will want to know how to go about bringing up the subject. They worry that, if they were to start asking questions out of the blue, the family might start to wonder what they were up to. In these instances, patients are instructed to be truthful. They can at first say that they have been thinking about the family lately and were curious about the family tree. If the family is not satisfied with that answer or even asks the patient whether the therapist has set her or him up to ask questions, the patient can reply that the therapist has indeed indicated that understanding more about the family will be helpful in solving the patient's problems and will probably be informative to the rest of the family as well. If the family reacts with indignation over what they perceive to be blame for the patient's difficulties, the patient is instructed to back off and report back to the therapist for further instructions.

In the latter eventuality, a precise recounting of what was said helps me to know whether the negative reaction was set up by the patient—who may have brought up an issue in a blaming tone—or came from the family or both. I then work with the patient on being more empathetic to the family, thereby decreasing both blaming behavior and family defensiveness, so that the important history may be obtained. The methods for doing this are the same as those that will be described when we discuss coaching the patient in the alternate solution (see Chapter Nine). I always assume that the patient can give an accurate report about the difficulties with the family that have been encountered. If the patient does not, I usually know it, because something will seem unclear about what transpired. I then share my confusion with the patient, in order to induce a more accurate or complete description. This intervention is similar to the way that I generally handle mental gymnastics and communications deviance.

Handling Mental Gymnastics

The best weapon a therapist has against illogical statements made by a patient is the therapist's own attitude. The therapist must believe that everybody is capable of logical thought and must assume that any patient can be induced to discuss a situation in a rational manner no matter how unreasonable that patient appears to be at the outset. The therapist must, of course, be able to identify an illogical statement when he or she hears it. This is not always easy, but with a little practice, anyone can learn to listen for the logical fallacies and errors of inductive reasoning discussed earlier.

Upon being confronted with an illogical explanation for a problem or for the motivation of a significant player in the family drama, my initial intervention is to point out the error in the patient's reasoning in a reassuring, noncondemnatory way. The best way to accomplish this aim, I have found, is to be very matter of fact and to act as if I am assuming that the patient had made the illogical statement innocently—the patient was just not thinking as clearly as he or she might have been, or perhaps had merely neglected to think about the evidence that contradicts the idea, despite how obvious it was. Had the patient thought about it, he or she would have taken it into account and would never have made the illogical statement. When I mention the reasons why the patient's statement does not hold up, and if I am certain that I am correct and am aware of all the relevant data, I confidently expect that the patient will easily see and acknowledge the error in thinking, without further ado.

When a therapist intervenes in this manner, patients will generally respond in one of three ways. First, they might respond in the way that the therapist expects of them. When patients agree that their explanation does not hold up, I then invite them to join in a search for a better one. Second, patients might react by pointing out the error in the therapist's reasoning. Perhaps it was I who was not thinking straight, or perhaps I was not aware of a relevant fact that would alter my ideas about the question being discussed. If I have been operating with incomplete information, an incorrect intervention can serve the useful function of eliciting more data. If I have been illogical myself, I admit my error and then pursue the patient's ideas.

The third possible type of response is for patients to dig their heels into the role of "illogical person." They might maintain an explanation with even more farfetched arguments than the ones they have already given. They might pout and beg the question, refusing to discuss the therapist's arguments, and adopt the attitude, "My mind is made up, don't confuse me with the facts." These responses are resistances and nothing more. They do not prove that patients are fundamentally irrational. I cannot emphasize too strongly that the therapist must convey the attitude that she or he *knows* that patients can do better. Whenever patients react in these ways, I respond with surprise and bemused consternation. In those cases where patients escalate with more and more preposterous reasoning, I often refuse to accept that they really believe the nonsense they are espousing. I might say something to the effect that "I don't understand why you are saying this when I know you understand what is wrong with it." When patients ignore my counterarguments, I might say, "I'm puzzled by your reaction. I know you understand what I just said, and you seem to be ignoring it." If patients beg the question incessantly, I often state, "You seem to have a need to hang on to that idea even though you know it is wrong. What's going on?"

Case 8-2

During the course of therapy of a young woman who was depressed over her inability to decide whether she wanted to be a pampered housewife, a self-sufficient career woman, or a little of both, a pattern in her interactions with her husband was clarified. She seemed to be putting him in a double bind. If he encouraged her to pursue a career, she would conclude that he really didn't want her to but was merely trying to cater to her whims. If he encouraged her to remain a housewife, she would accuse him of trying to dominate her. No matter how he behaved, she seemed to think of him as preferring the traditional gender roles, and she would then become angry about it. Because of the bind, the husband would try to hide his true feelings and would go along with whatever plan she happened to favor at a given moment. The patient would then become upset that she did not know where her husband really stood and was therefore unable to take his feelings into account when she made her decision.

After I had discussed this pattern with her, she agreed that this was happening. She even went home and discussed the pattern with her husband. Nonetheless, soon thereafter she began to escalate her binding behavior. She demanded that her husband wait on her hand and foot.

I puzzled aloud over what she was reacting to that caused her to want to do this. How had her husband responded to their conversation about the binding pattern? She immediately countered that the problem that was creating this behavior resided entirely within her own psyche. She was immature; her husband and the rest of her family had nothing whatsoever to do with it.

I observed that she seemed to be saying that her behavior existed in a vacuum and added that I thought it did not. She would not be behaving in an "immature" fashion just for the hell of it. "I hope you don't think that I'm trying to blame it all on your husband, either. Something must be prompting him to behave in the way that he does, also. Perhaps some problem would be created for both of you if you made a decision about a career. Perhaps there would be some negative consequences no matter which way you went."

The patient reacted favorably to this intervention and began to give the matter some thought. This led to the elucidation of the family-of-origin problems that both the patient and her husband were experiencing.

The therapist does not have to induce patients to give up a particular instance of illogical reasoning quickly. Especially with borderlines, the process can go on for many sessions before they begin to act reasonably. I hold my ground, refusing to accept that such patients really believe what they are saying, without getting bogged down in an extensive argument. A long and involved argument has no point, because patients already know that what they are saying is nonsense. For a therapist to go on ad nauseam with an argument is to presume otherwise. I simply agree to disagree about the point in question and go on.

In some cases, a therapist may get the feeling that patients are taking an illogical position not merely to get the therapist to stop asking certain questions by stonewalling but in order to anger the therapist. The therapist must not, needless to say, act out an angry response. If one were to do that, one would surely become embroiled in an even more complicated transference resistance. When I feel myself getting angry, I instead share my reactions: "You know, it's very annoying when you ignore what I say and continue on like that, and I think you know that. Why do you think that you're doing that?" Patients, who in my experience will seldom go on to protest innocence when confronted with such a statement, then have a choice. They can metacommunicate about the transference resistance, in which case I handle the situation as I would any other transference resistance, or they can stop trying to anger the therapist.

Another maneuver that is useful for both handling mental gymnastics and gathering useful information about the systemic family problem is the intervention that I call "Why I can't–yes but." An example of this was presented in Chapter Three. This intervention is a variation on the theme of the game "Why don't you–yes but" (Berne, 1964). However, it is not a game in the transactional-analytical sense, because it is meant to be transacted "adult" to "adult," to use Berne's terminology, on all levels. In fact, it is a countergame. The patient may start with "parent" or "child" behavior but will be induced to end up with "adult" behavior.

This intervention is used when patients present a problem

to the therapist that has a seemingly obvious solution but they maintain that they cannot use it. It can also be used when patients are resisting following the therapist's advice to metacommunicate with their families but are afraid to clarify the precise nature of the reasons for this reluctance. The therapist presumes that patients indeed have a good reason for not adopting the logical and readily apparent course of action or for not wishing to follow the advice. Indeed, they have probably been advised about what to do by many of their acquaintances, who do not understand the true nature of the problem. They no doubt feel frustrated that people think they are so stupid. However, they feel that they must avoid explaining the negative consequences of the "obvious" solution to the outside world because it would compromise an important aspect of their personas or would make their families look bad.

The aim of the "yes-but" intervention is for the therapist to learn the real reason behind the patient's inability to solve a problem in the obvious way or to follow the therapist's advice. I begin the process by remarking that the problem the patient has presented seems to have such and such an obvious solution, which the patient has no doubt considered. He or she must have a good reason for not employing it. If the patient responds by giving a plausible but logically flawed excuse for being unable to do so, I reply with "yes, but" and go on to give a logical reason why the patient's excuse does not really prevent the course of action in question. If the excuse is blatantly absurd, I also express puzzlement over why the patient is giving excuses that are clearly invalid. The patient may then respond with another improbable excuse, and I refute it. The process continues until the patient either reveals the real reason for the unwillingness or agrees to try out the "obvious" solution.

If patients elect to try out the solution in question, the therapist must make sure they are really convinced and do not have any unspoken reservations. This is best accomplished by merely asking them whether they are truly convinced. The therapist expects an honest reply. If patients are not convinced, the therapist has not yet found out the real reason for their reluctance and must continue probing. When patients finally give the real reason for their resistance, the therapist will recognize it as truth because it is logically valid, concerns the patient's family in a way that is consistent with the known facts of the case, and consists of a feared potential outcome that is both likely and onerous. The therapist goes on to get even more information about the family dynamics on the basis of the new lead. Later in therapy, she or he may be able to work with the patient on avoiding or minimizing the feared outcome. The way to do this is described in the section on role playing in therapy in Chapter Nine.

Patients will often give invalid excuses when advised to metacommunicate with their families on emotionally charged subjects. Common ones include "If I say that to my mother, I'll be disowned," and "If I say that, I know I'll get so angry that I won't be able to be as empathetic as you say I need to be. I might even get violent." To the first of these, I answer, "But your mother seems to be so involved in your life. Do you really think she'd disown you just for trying to talk to her about something that's bothering you?" To the second, I answer, "But we can practice it in here so you'll be sure that this won't happen." The patient may reply, in response to the therapist's yes-buts, "Yes, but if I bring up this subject, my mother will get upset." This statement indicates, in most instances, the patient's real fear. The therapist must then press for a more detailed explanation. "In what way will mother get upset? What do you think she'd really be upset about?" The kind of answer the therapist is looking for is something like, "She would get depressed because she'd feel bad about having given up her dreams of having her own career." The therapist can then work on helping the patient to be less protective while keeping the mother's depression over the issue at a minimum. The mother *already* feels depressed about having sacrificed her dreams. An empathetic discussion might make her more depressed temporarily but can only be beneficial in the long run.

One type of excuse that cannot be handled with logical argument is one that hinges on a question of fact or a judgment. For instance, what if the son in the above paragraph replied yes to the question about whether his mother would really disown him. The validity of that statement depends not on logic but on the accuracy of the patient's prediction about his mother's response. Perhaps mother had disowned a family member at one time. The therapist will no doubt be correct in assuming that mother's disowning behavior had not occurred in response to an attempt by the disownee to empathetically metacommunicate but has no way of proving this to the patient. The patient may not be aware of the full story of what transpired during the disownment. An example of an excuse that hinges on a judgment is, "I'll get nowhere with empathy because mother enjoys being cruel to me." As the reader by now is aware, I do not believe that anyone really enjoys being cruel to family members, but once again, whose judgment of mother is correct?

I have found that the simplest way to handle these kinds of excuses is for the therapist to say, in a matter-of-fact tone, "I don't agree with you." This simple statement often has a stunning affect on patients. They seem to stop in their tracks. They are not used to someone disagreeing with them without either putting them down for an opinion or disqualifying them. The family may have acted as if disagreement were somewhat akin to treason. At other times, the family may have condescendingly humored them when a disagreement existed and treated them as little children who must be protected from judgments about their opinions. For an authority figure to *respectfully* disagree with them is a breath of fresh air. Patients may then ask me why I disagree, and I answer straightforwardly by sharing my knowledge of how human beings generally behave.

Communications deviance is handled in much the same way as mental gymnastics. The therapist matter of factly points out exactly how and why the patient's descriptions are confusing and expects the patient to clarify what is being said. If the patient's speech contains referent problems, I state, "It's a little unclear to me what you were referring to when you said such and such." If the patient exhibits commitment problems, I say, "The way you said that made me think that you really do not believe it." If the patient contradicts himself or herself, I say, "I'm getting confused. Earlier you said something entirely different." The therapist *never* assumes that patients are incapable of speaking clearly or saying what they truly believe. When patients have a pattern of confusing speech or do not respond to my requests for clarification, I treat the problem as a transference resistance. The transference resistance described in Case 6-3 consisted of referent problems.

Establishing the Altruistic Motive

The aim of this step in the therapy is to present clients with an interpretation of the function that their maladaptive behavior serves within the context of the family system. The therapist tells clients what the "good reason" behind their destructive behavior or troubling affect is and praises them for their wonderful intentions. In the next phase of therapy, the therapist will question the means that clients have chosen to achieve their goals.

The gist of the interpretation is that when patients engage in the behavior in question, then various holons within the family system feel better in some way. Patients sacrifice aspects of self or agree to be defective for altruistic reasons. They care about their family and want it to function smoothly, and their personas help it to do so. On the one hand, they want to minimize the overall level of incapacitating anxiety within the family system. On the other, they want to minimize the overall level of shame and depression. Not infrequently, behavior that minimizes shame increases anxiety, and vice versa. Their self-destructive behavior is designed to strike the proper balance.

Patients do not know the real reasons why the family reacts to them in the manner that it does. The problem that has created the tension in the family is a matter about which they can only speculate. They are not aware that the family is contending with individuative forces external to itself that are ripping apart the old family homeostasis. The system may have engaged in behaviors designed to bring back the old homeostasis or to devise a new one; members may have hung on to their children or spouses too tightly, or they may have pushed them out into the brave new world too quickly or too harshly. They may have alternated between these two extremes. Patients can react only to the negative energy in the family that has resulted from these processes. They attempt to determine what they can do to decrease the level of family anxiety and depression the most, and they design a persona accordingly. The therapist will help them to understand the reactions of the family in the next step of the therapeutic process. Let us now, however, look at this step in more detail.

The form that the therapist's interpretation takes is as follows: "When you behave in such and such a manner, certain family members seem to become a lot more comfortable. They may tell you that they want you to behave differently, and get angry at you when you do not, but when you act as you do, they seem to have more peace of mind (become calmer, become less depressed, stop fighting with one another so much, quit threatening each other with divorce, become more free to do or avoid doing certain things that they prefer, and so on). You must think that they really want you to behave in these ways that are making you so unhappy. You're very kind to give them what they seem to need. You have given up so much; you must care about them a lot."

The first part of the above intervention, concerning the patient's self-destructive behavior, may refer either to the behavior per se or to the net effect of the behavior. In the majority of cases, the family system homeostasis is maintained by one of the effects of the patient's actions, rather than by the actions in and by themselves. The therapist would be wrong in saying, for instance, that the hand washing of an obsessive compulsive makes a family more comfortable, for clearly it does not. The hand washing, however, *prevents* the patient from doing, being, or appearing to be something that *would* make the family uncomfortable. Its net effect is to keep the patient from expressing certain threatening self-aspects. The link between the defect or the self-destructive behavior and its net effect should already have been established by the therapist by this point in the therapy. The process of establishing that link begins when the therapist frames the recommendation for therapy and continues as the patient provides additional information during the problem-elicitation phase. The net effect of the behavior can then be used as the subject of the above statements.

After presenting a patient with the above interpretation, therapists can know whether they are on the right track by monitoring the patient's response. This is done by looking for confirmation in a way similar to the way Langs (1973) recommends in his psychoanalytically oriented approach. If the patient responds to the interpretation by bringing up additional memories or other historical family data that seem to underline what the therapist is saying, the therapist is doing well. If the patient responds with exaggerated defensiveness and mental gymnastics, the therapist is probably also on the right track. That type of response indicates that the therapist has brought up an emotionally charged issue that is at the core of, or is at least a significant part of, the patient's persona. The therapist must then go on to work on the patient's defensiveness by questioning it and attempting to understand the need for it.

If the patient nondefensively disagrees with the therapist's interpretation but then goes on to bring up data that seem to confirm the ideas, the therapist may still be correct. The therapist can act puzzled and point out that the patient's ideas do not seem to contradict what the therapist has said. If, on the other hand, the patient disagrees and goes on to present information that logically refutes the therapist's interpretation, then the therapist is probably wrong. He or she needs to sit back and listen for more information in order to reformulate a hypothesis.

Case 8-3

A patient with marital problems was found to be reacting to his mother's unstable gender-role functioning. The mother was a woman who had, on the surface, passively let her husband assume all of the traditional male role functions. She did not handle finances or drive and seldom went anywhere without him. For her part, she immersed herself in worries about the emotional status of all of the members of the family. Unfortunately, her husband was now quite ill and was not living up to his part of the bargain. They were stuck in their home together, getting on one another's nerves. She started to become aware of the fact that looking after the emotional needs of family members was not such a wonderful job after all. Whenever she became depressed or started fighting with her husband, the patient would develop some sort of catastrophe in his marriage, and the mother would spend all of her time worrying about it. This induced the mother to resume her previous caretaking role, thereby stabilizing it, and drew her anger away from her husband and onto the patient.

If the patient expressed concern for her overtly, she would employ one of two disqualifications. She would either change the subject back to her concern for him, in a very provocative fashion, or become even more depressed. The former maneuver started a fight, which was meant to induce the patient to get angry and quit being so concerned about her. She did not want him to be concerned with her emotional health, not only because such a role reversal made her feel groundless and guilty but also because she did not want her son to fall into the same pattern of family enmeshment in which she herself felt trapped. Unfortunately, the patient's lack of concern was always short-lived. The mother's provocative behavior and expressions of concern for the patient misled the patient into believing that she really wanted him to have problems so that she could have something to worry about.

The other disqualification would cause the patient to feel guilty about bringing up the subject of the mother's depression, and he would change the subject himself. He would bring up his own problems in order to get his mother to worry about him instead of being so depressed.

The interpretation to the patient went as follows: "No wonder you do things to cause fights between you and your wife, and she goes along with you. [The things that they were doing had already been established earlier in therapy.] Telling your mother about your problems takes her mind off of her own problems and helps her get along better with your father. If you didn't do this, your mother would become very depressed thinking about all she had given up in order to let your father take care of her. [This had also been previously established; the patient had been instructed to ask his mother about her early life.] She would also start to fight with him. You can't help solve your mother's problem more directly because, if you bring it up, she picks a fight or seems to get even worse. Considering all the trouble this causes you, you must really care a lot about her to do this for her."

The patient responded that he had never really thought of it that way, and he suddenly remembered having developed school problems earlier in his life in response to his mother's depression at that time.

Patients may disagree with the therapist's ideas concerning the altruistic goals of their self-destructive behavior and contend that they do what they do for selfish reasons. They may insist that the behavior is gratifying in some way. Such statements may have a grain of truth and may therefore be difficult to counter, but they cannot be completely correct. Self-destructiveness can never be a selfish act. Such an assertion is simply a contradiction in terms. A self-destructive act may have a variety of consequences, some of which may be gratifying, but on the whole, its effect is to decrease gratification. Insulting the boss might be fun, but losing a prized job is not. The short-term gratification in the former can never counterbalance the long-term loss of gratification inherent in the latter. If patients maintain that it does, they are using mental gymnastics, and the therapist reacts accordingly.

Case 8-4

The family of a young male patient had subjected him to a steady stream of negative commentary regarding people in general and male-female relationships in particular from the time he was small. Not surprisingly, he had become socially isolated and never went on dates. I pointed out to him on a couple of occasions that, even though he knew intellectually that this negativity was exaggerated, he nonetheless acted as if he believed it. It was nice of him not to challenge his family's beliefs in this manner, despite having to sacrifice a social life.

On the first occasion, the patient denied being lonely. "I don't mind not dating."

"You mean you don't even get horny?"

"Well, ye . . . ." The patient suddenly became silent.

The second time I made the interpretation, the patient began making a case for the belief that he was better off avoiding people because people get on your nerves. "They ask stupid questions and pry into your business."

When I asked him on what he was basing this idea, he replied that acquaintances of his were always asking him what he was up to. I gave him a quizzical look and remarked, "Gee, that sounds like they're just trying to be friendly and express an interest in you." The patient reluctantly agreed that my interpretation sounded reasonable. He recalled that his mother was critical of his father for getting involved in the problems of friends.

Patients may maintain that the family would punish them if they were to abandon the self-destructive behavior and that therefore their motivation is a selfish one. In this case, they may be right to an extent. If they were to suddenly start to behave in a more individuated fashion without having first metacommunicated about their intentions, the family would undoubtedly start to disqualify them more and more. They would then suffer from existential groundlessness, the worst of all possible punishments. When patients tell me that the family would make them feel like outcasts if they were to change, or in some other way indicate that the family would induce in them a sense of groundlessness, I agree. I state that their motivation is indeed selfish to some extent but that they *also* seem to be concerned with the rest of the family. If they did not care about the family, they would not care whether they were shunned. If the family were not important to them, it could not induce in them a sense of meaninglessness, lack of purpose, sense of smallness or annihilation, or other any other indication of existential uneasiness.

Many times patients do not understand or are unable to describe the real fear that they have. As common as existential anxiety is, it is something about which most people understand little. Instead of discussing a fear of isolation or a feeling of lack of meaning in life, patients might state that they cannot change because the family would cause them to suffer in some other way. The therapist will know that the patient has not described a real fear, because the patient's statement will be illogical. The fallacy in these instances usually concerns the fact that the feared outcome of change that these patients describe is no worse than what they are already suffering. They have, after all, been spending the first few sessions describing how miserable they are under the current circumstances. How can they be "selfishly" avoiding one kind of suffering through their actions when they are experiencing just as much pain the way things are now? No, they must be going through the suffering for some other reason. They are sacrificing aspects of self for the family, or the suffering that they would experience if they changed is worse than what is taking place at present. Most likely, both of these are occurring. I press them until they either agree with the interpretation of altruism or describe fears of groundlessness.

In cases in which the patient is not already angry with the family or is not engaging in an exaggerated blaming game, the interpretation of a patient's altruistic motivation will sometimes induce anger. The patient may gradually begin a slow burn after having accepted and mulled over the therapist's interpretation. Such patients have avoided anger over their sacrifices up to this point because they have simply ignored the family's seeming contribution to their misery. They have told themselves over and over again that they alone are to blame for their own problems. They have pretended that there is something wrong with only themselves. Now their attention has been forcefully drawn to the real source of the discomfort. They have "insight." Their skill as method actors, while not destroyed, becomes diminished, because they can no longer believe in their script so strongly. They have a harder time concealing the source of their anger. They may even experience a transitory urge to tell the family to go to hell.

The therapist's goal when this happens is to help patients deal with the anger constructively. In the next step of therapy, the therapist will present a hypothesis about the true nature of the behavior of other members of the family system, so that the patient can learn to empathize and to metacommunicate. Patients who are blindly angry will not be able to make systemic changes. They will be blaming and punitive in their attempts to

276 Unifying Individual and Family Therapies

discuss family problems, which will induce the family to avoid metacommunicating even more than before. The therapist must help patients to temper anger with understanding, while at the same time validating the angry feelings.

Before going on to describe that process in detail, however, I must first address the question of what to do when patients become so angry at the family because of new understanding that they inform the therapist that they are going to stop helping family members feel better post haste. They resolve to be more selfish immediately. If dear old Dad will be uncomfortable when they change, so be it. He started it. Let the bastard suffer. They are going off to do their own thing, and his feelings be damned. When I first heard statements like these, I was immediately reminded of those earlier times in my career when I thought the purpose of psychotherapy was to help the patient to *express* repressed anger, and how frustrated I used to become with traditional methods of psychotherapy. When I first began trying to help patients become empathetic with their families instead of trying to help them get in touch with repressed anger, I never ceased to be amazed at how often I would find myself arousing the very anger that I could never elicit when I had wanted to! This phenomenon is, of course, a manifestation of the principle of opposite behaviors. The patient can resist change either by being excessively angry or by excusing and choosing to ignore the misbehavior of others.

When therapists hear a patient finally express that previously elusive anger, they may be tempted to cheer the patient on. They may decide that they have executed a brilliant paradoxical maneuver and should continue to help the patient express the repressed feelings. They forget that the goal is systemic change as well as individual change. They should resist the urge to say bravo! Instead, they should observe aloud that such clients do not seem to be the kind of people who can just write the family off in the manner suggested. The clients care too much for the family to just let its members experience discomfort without helping them to handle it. Clients who did not would have told the family off and left it to its own devices a long time ago. Sure, they are tired of sacrifices and are not sure whether the family deserves their love. Still, they have already decided that the family is worth it. Perhaps they have misread the family and have misunderstood the motivation behind its behavior. Perhaps they can help family members to feel better without making a sacrifice.

Explaining How the Patient's Behavior Backfires

The goals of this step of therapy are two. The first is to present the therapist's hypothesis—clearly labeled as a preliminary formulation—as to the true motivation behind the disqualifying responses of the various members within the family system. The therapist wants patients to be empathetic with their families, so that emotional reactivity will be reduced when they learn to metacommunicate with the family during the next step in therapy. The therapist explains to patients how they have been misreading the intent of the family's behavior. The second goal is to explain to patients why their self-sacrificing behavior not only fails to solve the problem but actually prolongs it. Patients learn that rather than making another family member feel better, in the long run they are making the relative feel worse. Their protection of family members has been preventing the problem from being put out on the table where it belongs, where it might be discussed and solved. Their intentions are good, but they have chosen a method to achieve their goals that does not work. The therapist must also empathize with how frustrated patients feel and explore the reasons why alternative solutions seemed to them to be impractical, so that they do not use their past failure to solve the problem as further evidence for their own defectiveness.

The hypothesis about the reasons why a patient's self-destructive behavior seems to have a beneficial effect on the family will concern any of the evolutionary problems discussed in earlier chapters, in whole or in part and in any combination. The patient's sacrifice may have a calming effect on the system because it supports role functioning in an ambivalent individual, deflects conflict in a troubled holon, draws off destabilizing anger, assuages systemic worries about previously existing but no longer operative external dangers, or decreases envy. By this time in therapy, these ideas may already have been introduced to the patient. The therapist no doubt touched upon them when interpreting the patient's altruistic motives (see Case 8-3). The important additional point to make at this stage in therapy is that the family only *seems* to encourage the patient's self-destructive behavior. They do not really wish the patient ill; in fact, they are probably trying to protect him or her. They disqualify because of their own anxiety. Parents may seem cruel because of their own fears or because of their desires to push the patient into functioning at a more individualistic level than they can. They themselves cannot endorse less enmeshed behavior overtly because of adverse systemic consequences.

Although the therapist's hypothesis is by nature preliminary and requires confirmation by other family members, the patient may still be aware of additional family historical data that partially confirm it and that have not yet come out in therapy. If the patient volunteers such data after hearing the interpretation, therapists can feel more confident about their ideas.

The therapist goes on to explain that, although the patient's self-sacrifice does indeed exert a short-term calming effect on certain family members, in the long run, it backfires. Patients are trying to help, but they are not succeeding. No matter how much they divert the attention of involved family members away from ambivalence, anxiety, or depression, the family members will continue to be distressed by those feelings. The unpleasant feelings come from the true self of the affected individual, and no outside force can take them away. They can be resolved only by being faced, and to face them, individuals need the patient's help. They need mirroring to avoid an existential crisis. They must not be disqualified when they attempt to discuss their feelings; they do not need to be protected from the demons inside of them.

Case 8-5

This case involved a patient, her sister, her mother, and a dependency conflict. The mother in the family was overtly counterdependent. She had always been a supermother, worrying about her daughters' problems and trying to handle them herself whenever possible. This behavior had a different effect on each of the two daughters. The patient, Betty, reacted to her mother's ambivalence about being a caretaker. Betty was worried that her mother would worry herself into an early grave. Since Betty was one of Mother's worries, she tried desperately to have no problems at all. She charged into all of her responsibilities with a vengeance, making sure that any and every potential problem was nipped in the bud. She worked herself into a frazzle. She complained that her family did not help with her work, but she either did not ask directly for assistance or asked in such a nagging way that nobody wanted to comply with her request. Despite Betty's hyperresponsibility, Mother continued to worry about her. In fact, Betty's obsessive behavior induced her mother to worry that Betty was overextending herself. Betty naturally believed that her mother had no faith in her and was bothered by a feeling that she never did anything right. She nonetheless kept trying harder and harder.

The patient's sister, Rosalyn, on the other hand, acted as if she were completely helpless and useless. I hypothesized that the mother's behavior had led Rosalyn to believe that her mother needed her to be helpless, so that Mother could take care of her and feel fulfilled. Mother always gave Rosalyn a lot of financial support.

A problem developed when the mother suddenly developed lung cancer. True to form, Betty took over all of her mother's affairs and ran herself ragged arranging medical consultations, around-the-clock nursing, postsurgical care, and the like. True to form, Mother was very unhappy with any arrangements that Betty came up with, causing Betty to feel that she could do nothing right. True to form, Rosalyn was no help at all.

The patient misread the motivation of both her mother and her sister. As mentioned, Betty took Mother's displeasure with her efforts as a sign that Mother was disappointed in her, did not think much of her abilities, and wanted her to be more responsible. The patient responded by thinking herself inadequate, despite the obvious evidence to the contrary. She used this idea to prod herself into taking on even more responsibility, despite the obvious fact that she was already doing too much. The patient was helped to change her belief with the following intervention:

"I can see why you think your mother feels that way. It's the obvious conclusion. But let me suggest an alternate explanation. From what we've learned about your mother, she probably feels just like you do. She thinks she has to take on all of the family responsibility herself. She, like you, does not always like doing that. This may sound a little off the wall, but I think that when she criticizes you, she is actually trying to discourage you from feeling responsible for her. She does not like it when you do—that is why she worries when you overextend yourself. She does not want you to fall into the same pattern that she feels trapped in. She does not tell you this directly because she has difficulty admitting that she has mixed feelings about being such a responsible mother."

Betty felt that her sister was weak and lazy. She was angry at Rosalyn because Rosalyn did not help her to take care of their mother, but she generally would not ask the sister for much assistance. Whenever Betty criticized Rosalyn for not helping, Rosalyn became extremely angry and gave lame excuses. I surmised that Rosalyn became angry because she really believed that Betty enjoyed taking all the responsibility herself and that Betty wanted her to be helpless just as Mother did. (Mother did, in fact, become alarmed when Betty asked anything of Rosalyn.) Rosalyn had sacrificed her competency for her sister and mother; how dare she be criticized for it. However, when Betty backed off from her request for help, Rosalyn would be more convinced than ever that Betty really wanted to hog all the responsibility for herself. The likelihood that Rosalyn would offer assistance then decreased accordingly. (Interestingly, when this pattern was partially broken and Betty insisted that Rosalyn help out, Rosalyn's daughter did everything she could to prevent her from doing so. The daughter was probably trying to stabilize Rosalyn's persona.)

The whole pattern was explained, in a straightforward manner, to the patient. The explanation was prefaced with the remark, "You must think that Rosalyn doesn't want to help and is trying to pawn off all of her responsibilities on you. I think it's quite possible, though, that Rosalyn doesn't help because she mistakenly believes that you don't really want her to."

After the patient had a better understanding of her family's otherwise inexplicable behavior, it was time to explain to her how her habit of taking on all of the responsibility was preventing resolution of the problem. "You are trying to help everyone, but it is not working." In regard to Mother, Betty's continued efforts at trying to help without commenting on the bind that her mother was putting her in was actually making Mother feel guiltier. Mother saw the efforts and was dismayed that Betty was doing so much; this caused Mother to *escalate* her help-rejecting behavior. Since Mother did need help, this pattern was making her medical treatment more difficult than it might otherwise have been. Additionally, by refusing to complain about Mother's behavior, Betty was helping Mother avoid acknowledging her own ambivalence. Since the issue was never discussed, change was difficult. With the sister, the patient's lack of demands was actually reinforcing Rosalyn's sense of helplessness, rather than easing her lot.

I do not wish to disqualify a patient's anger over the family situation. Patients have good reasons to be disgusted by the whole state of affairs. Although I attempt to help patients to assuage their anger through understanding, they will still feel it. I am interested in helping them express it in a constructive way; that is what is important. Anger must be expressed in a way that diminishes the problem that has created it, not in a way that merely adds fuel to the fire. Blaming is a complete waste of time; it leads only to responses that diminish the likelihood that the family will wish to discuss the situation that is the sore point. Patients must learn to understand the reasons for the family's behavior without condoning it; they must empathize with the family's good motivation but not sympathize with the methods family members have chosen to achieve their goals. In short, patients must learn to behave toward the family the way that the therapist behaves toward them; only then can they effectively metacommunicate.

Once patients start to view the family more empathetically, they may begin to flagellate themselves over their failure to have previously understood the family's behavior. The therapist must then stress that they could not have known what motivated the family to react in the way that they have. If they had known more, they could have helped the family in a better way than in the way they had chosen. They could not have known more because they, like the therapist, cannot read minds. The family members did not explain why they did what they did. They did not do so because they themselves had probably avoided thinking about the reasons for their own behavior. They did this, in turn, because of the unexplained responses that they had experienced from their own families of origin. If the parents had understood more about their own family history and the reasons for the behavior of the grandparents, then they too would have behaved differently.

The therapist tells the patient that the family has not been able to discuss and clear up their situation because they care so much about each other. Any discussion of the problem would naturally lead some family members to experience anxiety, regret, envy, shame, or depression. The family members wish to protect each other from these feelings as much as possible. Since metacommunication brings out the unpleasant emotions, the family chooses, logically, to avoid it as much as possible. Because the short-term effects of metacommunication are negative, the process is cut off quickly. Consequently, the family never learns that bad feelings eventually diminish when they *can* be openly discussed. If any family member were to try to bring up the problem, he or she would most likely be disqualified by other family members alone or in unison, because the other family members would become frightened that permanent, irreparable damage might result. The rest of the family is just as afraid of bringing up the problem as is the patient. The patient knows firsthand how difficult it is to begin a family discussion on sensitive issues; surely she or he can empathize with the fears of the rest of the family. The family is willing to disqualify the patient because that seems to them to be the lesser of two evils.

Case 8-5, Continued

After the therapist had explained to Betty how her efforts at helping the family had backfired, she became very quiet and looked extremely distraught. The therapist responded with the statement, "You look upset. Was there something about what I said that bothered you?" She did not answer.

It occurred to me that the patient was feeling overly criticized. I had, after all, told her that she was not doing things right. I was being, in effect, just like her mother. I handled this problem by bringing it up. "I hope you don't think I'm being just like your mother when I tell you all this. It's very difficult to help you to find a better way to solve this problem without sounding critical of the methods that you have chosen in the past. But really, you had no way of knowing that there were better ways of handling things. If you had merely stopped being responsible, it would have appeared to you that your mother would not have got the help she needed, because it did not look as if anyone else would have stepped in to take your place. And when you complain to your mother about her behavior, she feels angry and criticized and reacts negatively. Actually, she feels even guiltier, just as she does when you try to help, because she thinks that she is making you feel responsible for her. Criticizing her causes her to increase her help-rejecting behavior anyway! You do not yet know that there are ways to bring up this problem that do not cause this kind of response. That is what we are going to talk about next."

At the conclusion of this step of therapy, clients should understand the nature of their problem and something about the reasons why they have been unable to solve it. They will have been told that they care a lot about the family and that therefore they should not fool themselves into thinking that they can now resolve to ignore it. All well and good. They still have no idea about what they can do about all of this.

The Alternate Solution

In the form of therapy that I am advocating, unlike some others, therapists are not afraid to give advice. As experts, they know what the patient can do to change the predicament. They also know the pitfalls and the hazards that the patient might face if and when the advice is followed. Should the advice fail, they are able to determine exactly why and correct the problem, so that the patient can try again and become successful. They have confidence that the patient will be able to appreciate not only the letter but the spirit of their directions and that the patient can carry them out correctly. They are also experts at motivating the patient to follow their advice, even when the patient strongly resists, without becoming embroiled in a power struggle.

Therapists devise an alternate solution to the patient's problem—one that does not involve self-sacrifice or self-destructiveness. They must present it to the patient, convince the patient that the effort will be worthwhile, and then help the patient to implement the plan. They tell the patient not only what to do but also how to do it. They predict the likely ways in which the patient's family might disqualify the patient's new behavior and, through role playing, coach the patient on how to make the plan work despite difficulties and apparent reversals.

In most instances, the alternate solution consists of patients making contact with the living members of the family of origin and initiating intrafamilial metacommunication. (The situation in which no such family members remain alive is discussed in Chapter Ten.) Patients will impart to the family knowledge learned in therapy about the existential dilemma that they all face and metacommunicate about any family interactions that have become maladaptive because of that dilemma. The patient and family must help each other to understand why they are getting reactions from one another that create dissonance. Patients must communicate how they have been perceiving the motivations of the rest of the family, so that the others have a chance to correct any misperceptions. They must also let each family member know how her or his actions have affected them, so that if the other does not wish to have that effect, she or he can change. They must all learn to understand why they get anxious when they veer from previously necessary role functioning and should gain the ability to realistically debate the pros and cons of more individuated activity.

I inform patients that when this kind of family discussion successfully takes place, the pressure that they feel to act in self-destructive ways will begin to diminish, and their psychological symptoms and distress will then disappear. The metacommunicative process within the family must continue after the initial discussions, but the skills that patients learn in therapy will be required less and less as time goes on, as the family learns new ways to cope with the ever advancing march of cultural evolution.

There are two keys to effective metacommunication in the family. The first is empathy, the ability to understand why the family members feel and act the way they do, combined with the ability to communicate that understanding without either condemning the family or agreeing that it is behaving in the best possible way. Patients can achieve empathetic understanding more easily than one might think, because their behavior has been shaped by the same forces that shape the behavior of the rest of the family. They do not have to learn to put themselves in the shoes of the others, because they are already in them! Effective communication about the understanding is, alas, a great deal more difficult.

The second key to effective metacommunication is respect for the potency and integrity of all family members. Human beings are very strong. They can tolerate unpleasantries to an astonishing degree. People have undergone unspeakable tortures and survived. They can certainly live with regret, shame, or envy. They can cope with feeling sad or anxious. They can handle their anger without going insane. These feelings are all natural and normal and become toxic only when they are shunted aside. If family members begin to feel bad because of the subject under discussion, they will get over it. In fact, they already feel bad, and have not got over the bad feelings, precisely because the feelings have never been dealt with. They experience these feelings even if the family never says a word about the uncomfortable subject. No one in the family needs to be protected from his or her own feelings. Collectivist tendencies that dictate otherwise must be overcome.

I have found that the process of metacommunication proceeds most smoothly if the patient follows a planned sequence of steps, from historical, metaphorical discussions of the central issues to here-and-now discussions of the family process. The more disturbed and defensive the family is, the more important it becomes to stick to the plan. With less troubled families, the patient may be able to skip steps or even to jump to the heart of the matter right off the bat. In many instances, the therapist's attempts to slow down patients in their efforts to discuss the current family interactions paradoxically induce either the patients or the families to get right into a discussion of the most immediate and emotionally charged facets of the family dynamics.

The therapist role plays each step prior to sending patients back to the family. After each family encounter, patients return to therapy to give as precise an accounting as possible of what transpired. The therapist uses this information for two purposes. First, it is used to revise, if necessary, the hypothesis about the family system dynamics. Second, if the patients have run into any problems that were not anticipated in the original role playing, the therapist figures out a way to solve them. The therapist then role plays again using the new information and sends patients back to redo the step more successfully. The techniques of coaching the patient to metacommunicate through role playing are the same for each step of the process. Before going on to describe those techniques, I will describe the overall strategy of the alternate solution.

If therapy has been progressing well, patients have already initiated a discussion of the family difficulty by the time the therapist begins to present them with the alternate solution. They will have approached several family members for the historical data that the therapist has used in the endeavor to figure out what is making the system tick. Once a patient and therapist have identified the systemic issues that are most likely relevant to the patient's distress, the patient is ready to advance the metacommunicative process to the next level. The therapist sends the patient back to see important family-of-origin members individually, to continue the discussion of the basic issues. At first, the discussion should stay in the historical metaphor; the patient asks questions about how the family handled the relevant evolutionary problem in earlier times and in past generations. The reason for this is, once again, that metaphorical discussions are less threatening than direct metacommunication. Once the patient is successful in getting the family to talk about the issues in their historical context, the patient will find that he or she has already gained a tremendous understanding of the motivation behind previously mysterious family behavior. A good starting point for the initiation of such a discussion is some significant microevent in the family history that bears on the existential issue in question. The patient may start with inquiries such as

1. "When Grandma died and Grandpa was left with five small children, how did he handle it?"
2. "How did Grandma support herself when she came here all by herself from Ireland? Did people look down on her because she had to work?"
3. "When Dad lost his job in the Depression, how did he feel about himself?"
4. "How did you handle it when that cop called you 'boy' and hit you with his nightstick?"
5. "How did you feel about Dad when he asked you to give up your promising accounting career when you got married?"

These types of questions, concerning qualitative aspects of past relationships and the emotional reactions of various family members, are naturally more apt to induce defensiveness in the family member being questioned than are questions concerning dry historical data. As the patient progresses further in the metacommunicative process, the potential for defensive and disqualifying reactions increases still further. The defensiveness may allude to family members being discussed or may concern someone else. A woman questioned about her mother giving up a career for her father, for example, may jump to the defense of her father as well as or instead of her mother. The family member being questioned may identify with a family member from a previous generation that seems to be under attack or may even defend someone of whom he or she is secretly critical—out of a sense of family loyalty. The patient's empathy for the plight of all concerned family members, including the person being questioned, becomes increasingly important with each succeeding step in the overall strategy. Defensive reactions that might inhibit the metacommunicative process are kept, through empathy, to a minimum.

The next step in the process is, therefore, the expression of empathy for the people being discussed within the context of the historical metaphor. After the family member who has been targeted for metacommunication is induced to discuss the feelings and interactions prompted by the events in question, the patient expresses concern for how difficult it must have been for the various players in the family drama. He or she also expresses understanding or even admiration for the methods by which they coped with the difficult situation. Using the examples of the discussion-initiating questions listed above, the empathetic statements might take the following form:

1. "Grandpa must have had a really difficult time with all those kids; no wonder his sister volunteered to take over. She must have given up a lot to do it, too."
2. "Grandma was sure brave to go to work like she did when everyone looked down on her; I can see why she worked twice as hard as anyone around to prove herself and didn't have much time to be close with her children."
3. "Dad must have felt terribly degraded when he couldn't support the family; I'm not surprised that you thought twice about earning more than he did."
4. "You must have felt humiliated by that cop because there was nothing you could do to fight back; I sure admire you for being able to keep any pride about yourself at all."
5. "I can see why you acceded to Dad's request; both of you were just reacting to what everyone else at the time expected of men and women."

Patients can gradually move the discussion from earlier generations toward the past of the person with whom they are talking or, if they are starting at that point, move it closer and closer to the target family member's current predicament. Continuing with the above examples, sample statements that might move the conversation in those directions are:

1. "Your aunt must have wished at times that she never had nieces and nephews but would have felt guilty admitting it. Maybe she tried to cover any resentment she might have felt by being overprotective of you."
2. "With your mother being so busy all of the time, you must have learned at an early age to avoid depending on anyone but yourself."
3. "Do you still think Dad would lose face if you got a job?"
4. "I'll bet that you really admire the ability of today's Blacks to stand up to the White man, but I wouldn't be surprised if you felt rather envious of them."
5. "I know it looked like you had no choice but to drop your career, but boy, if I were you I sure would have some regrets."

Once the stage has been reached where the current dilemma of the target family member is under discussion, the next step in the process is the discussion of how the issue in question has affected the relationship of the discussants.

1. "I appreciate your worries about me, but the way you question me makes me feel that you have no confidence in me, and that makes me angry with you."
2. "I know you want me to be independent like you and not feel bad when you're not around, but at times I feel like I can't get close to you when I need you."
3. "I know that you want me to get married and have a good relationship, but sometimes I feel that you become alarmed when I get too close to a man. Do you think that a man would be an impediment to my career advancement?"
4. "I felt like I was in a bind when I joined the Black Power movement; on the one hand, I felt like you were kind of living through me, but on the other, if I went too far I

thought I would remind you of how humiliated you used
to feel. I never knew what to do to make you happy."

5.   "I know you want me to succeed, but sometimes I feel like
you were jealous of me when I got my degree, and I become afraid to do well in my career."

This stage is the most difficult of all for several reasons.
First, patients must be prepared to discuss their resentments
empathetically and work to correct misunderstandings. As the
reader can see from the above examples, patients should always
preface their remarks with a statement that gives the benefit of
the doubt to the person with whom they are speaking. This
preface attributes a beneficent motivation to the targeted family member. Patients must make clear that they are questioning
neither the morality nor the intelligence of the targeted family
member. This can be difficult if one is angry about being placed
in a bind. Second, patients must learn to listen to the target
family member's complaints about them and correct any misunderstandings about their own motivation without rancor.
Last, patients must be prepared to let the other family member
experience all the negative feelings that might be aroused by
metacommunication and still maintain contact.

In the last step of the process, patients begin to suggest
better ways to cope with the conflicts that have been brought
out by the discussions. They pose and explore the answers to
the following questions: How can both the patient and the family member alter their reactions so that they do not disqualify
one another? How can they be more aware of each other's
sensitivities? Does the older family member think it feasible to
begin to try out alternate, more individuated behavior him- or
herself? How would the rest of the family react if he or she did,
and why? How might the rest of the family be induced to help
rather than disqualify? Should a family meeting be held? The
patient and the family member learn to metacommunicate and
negotiate any major differences in outlook.

The entire series of steps described above is repeated with
each significant family member. A patient who has had a successful experience with one family member will usually be more

confident with a second, and the process tends to progress much more quickly. The family members who are the most powerful influences on the patient, and who are therefore the first to be targeted if they are living, are of course the parents. If grandparents, step-parents, or siblings are or were functioning in a leadership role in the patient's family of origin, then they should also be targeted. Whether the process is done sequentially or concurrently with each important system member is determined by the logistics of the family, by the relative importance of each family member regarding a specific issue, and by whether one family member might interfere with the patient's attempts to talk to another. Siblings, aunts, uncles, and cousins may be important in the family dynamics, in which case they are dealt with in a manner similar to the way the parents are handled. They can also interfere with discussions with more central family members. The question of how to handle interfering relatives is discussed in Chapter Ten.

After the patient has discussed the important issues with all of the important family system members—effectively, with any luck—the patient may then wish to talk with some of them together. A three-way conversation with both parents might be productive, although often the individual conversations with each parent prompt metacommunication between them, and this step becomes unnecessary.

In the case of married patients, spouses are intimately involved with the patient's problem, whether or not they figure prominently in the patient's presenting complaints. As I described earlier, spouses are attracted to one another on the basis of mutual role-function support. If individuals begin to renegotiate their roles within the family of origin and exhibit more individuative responses than has been their wont in the past, this naturally will be quite confusing to the nuclear family. Spouses who have made sacrifices of their own to stabilize the role functioning of a mate will feel betrayed if the mate gives up this role. They had been giving up their own self-wishes for the spouse, who now suddenly acts as though the sacrifice had been completely unnecessary.

For this reason, I advise my patients that it is extremely

important for the spouse to be kept informed of exactly what is going on in the therapy. The spouse must know what issues are being examined and how they are being dealt with. Patients can elicit the spouse's support in their efforts to deal with their families. This is possible even in situations where there is a good deal of tension in the marital relationship. The reason it is possible is that, even when the members of the couple do not know how to handle each other, they are already experts at helping each other deal with family-of-origin problems. Since the spouse's own situation is reciprocal, the marital pair can be induced to metacommunicate about their own relationship in a manner parallel to the way that a patient metacommunicates with the family of origin. Patients can also be coached to help a spouse look at similar dynamics in his or her own family of origin. Occasionally, patients may find an opportunity go through the steps listed above with an in-law. The process of therapy can help the patient and the spouse to have a "relationship about the relationship," to use Wile's (1981) idea.

A spouse who is not kept informed will invariably interfere with the patient's attempts to renegotiate his or her role regarding the family of origin. A spouse may even induce the patient to discontinue therapy or make it difficult for the patient to keep appointments. If, after being advised of its importance, the patient does not wish to have a discussion with the spouse about the therapy, I inform the patient in a frank but noncondemnatory manner that the therapy may suffer accordingly. If the patient continues to resist, an exploration of the reasons for the reluctance—which I naturally assume to be good ones—is indicated. Therapists must help the patient overcome whatever difficulties might ensue should the patient follow their advice. In order to do so, they must determine what the difficulties really are. In most cases, the difficulty concerns the patient's fear that the spouse will be devastated by any renegotiation of the marital quid pro quo. Because of the spouse's power to scuttle the therapy, helping the patient to keep the spouse informed takes precedence over most other matters.

I often find it useful to invite spouses (or targeted family members) in for one or two sessions (Wachtel and Wachtel,

1986). This serves a number of purposes. First, spouses can be reassured that the patient and the therapist are not ganging up on them and that their interests are being considered. Second, spouses can be an additional source of information about the family dynamics. They may relate data that the patient has forgotten or thinks unimportant. Additionally, the therapist can watch the interactions of the spouses to verify the accuracy of the information that has been reported by the patient and later confront the patient individually with any discrepancies.

Whenever any relative is invited into a session, the question of confidentiality invariably arises. The therapist may wish to ask the relative about information that has been supplied by the patient, in order to help verify a pet hypothesis about the family dynamics. When therapists have to keep secrets, their ability to help the patient and the family system is handicapped significantly. The easiest way to avoid this difficulty is for therapists to inform the patient in advance that they can be most helpful to everybody if they are free to bring up anything they know in the conjoint session. If they are not free to do this, their ability to help will be compromised. Seldom will a patient insist that a therapist keep important information confidential when told this. Occasionally, a patient may specify one event in the past history that he or she would rather keep secret. The therapist can then explore with the patient why this event should be off limits. Even if the patient's objections cannot be answered, however, all is not lost. Often the issue symbolized by the secret event can be brought up without reference to the actual happening. The therapist can get the patient's permission to bring up the issue while agreeing to let the incident itself remain secret for the time being. In most instances, the spouse already knows something about the secret anyway. For instance, a spouse almost always knows at some level when a mate is having an affair. The issues in the marriage that led to the affair can often be elucidated and even resolved without mention of the actual tryst.

If the patient's chief complaint deals specifically with a marital problem, the situation is more complicated. The therapist may have a hard time getting such patients to even think about the contribution that a family of origin has made to the marital problem, because the patients are far more concerned with the immediate relationship difficulty. Patients may, as a resistance, switch back and forth between the marital conflict and the conflict in the family of origin, so that neither can be dealt with effectively. Because the conflicts are so interconnected, the therapist may have trouble confronting patients with the subtle changes in subject. Inviting the spouse to a session will usually lead to marital therapy, which is fine if that is what the therapist wishes to do. The ideas in this book can be adapted for the purposes of developing mutual empathy in the marital relationship through couples therapy, as described by Wile (1981). If the therapist wishes to continue to work with the individual, however, he or she can modify all of the therapeutic steps described above in order to include solving the marital problem on the therapeutic agenda.

As I elicit the problem in such cases, I maintain a focus on the patient's chief complaint of marital discord but look for information that will help me to formulate a hypothesis about how the behaviors of the patient and spouse support the respective role functioning of each. I gather information not only about the patient's parents and grandparents but about the spouse's parents and grandparents as well. This is not quite as complicated as it sounds, since the dynamics of the two families will usually be remarkably complementary. I keep things clear for myself by drawing out a genogram (McGoldrick and Gerson, 1985) on a piece of paper and writing down important information about the relationships. This also prevents me from mixing up the patient's family history with the family histories of patients with similar problems. Eventually, the reciprocal role-function support can be interpreted to the patient using the same methods discussed above in the sections on establishing the altruistic motive and explaining how behavior backfires.

The alternate solution to the marital problem will involve concurrent metacommunication between patient and spouse and patient and family of origin. The steps for the family of origin are no different from those listed above. The steps for the spousal metacommunication are similar. The therapist's

coaching techniques (described in Chapter Nine) are identical.
Patients may begin the process of metacommunication with the
spouse by relating the relevant family history of their own family of origin, as it is learned in therapy. This history will contain
a metaphor for the existential difficulty that is now creating the
marital conflict. Patients then continue to weave the story of
their family until it leads to a discussion with the spouse about
how the difficulties of their parents affected them. Patients may
inquire whether the issues in their family might also have been
important in the past of the spouse's family. The goal is to eventually bring about a discussion of the marital interaction in
terms of how the issue in question affected the marital partners
and their relationship and in terms of the couple's mutual role-
function support. Once this is done, the couple can discuss their
wishes to give up aspects of role functioning that are undesirable and negotiate ways to help each other achieve selfhood.
The patient and spouse must work to clear up any misunderstandings about each other's motivations. In general, each
spouse has learned to support the role functioning of the other
without knowing the real reasons why the spouse appears to
wish to act in certain ways. Let me illustrate this with an
example.

Case 8-6

A woman in her twenties complained of having difficulty
agreeing to her boyfriend's marriage proposal because he had
made no serious efforts to get a job, and she was afraid that she
might end up supporting him. She had come from a family in
which women had always appeared to be the stronger sex. The
idea that women were stronger than men dated back to the
mother's grandmothers, both of whom raised large families on
their own because of the early deaths of their husbands. Coin-
cidentally, the patient's father had also died at a rather young
age. The patient, who was the youngest child in the family and
the only one who had not left home, lived with her elderly
mother.

The bind the patient was in had two components. First, if

she were to have a boyfriend who was an effective breadwinner, her mother not only might become envious but would probably feel herself to be totally unneeded and therefore useless. She would become more depressed. There would be no children left at home to "take care of," and her entire persona was built on the role of caretaker. Second, if the boyfriend were effective, the patient would have no excuse for turning down his proposal of marriage. Unfortunately, marriage would create another major problem. The mother was becoming elderly and frail but was playing the role of "strong woman." She never liked to ask anyone for help and would not like the idea of imposing on a married daughter. Her underlying neediness, of course, caused the whole family to feel imposed upon anyway. The patient felt obliged to look after the mother covertly. In order to stick around but to keep the real reason secret and to support her mother's persona, the patient made it appear as if it were she who was too incompetent to leave home. The patient knew that if she ever did leave home, there was a strong possibility that her mother might need assistance but refuse to call and ask for it. As the mother was so old, this could indeed lead to a dangerous situation.

If the boyfriend were to get a job, the patient would become anxious about the twin problems of providing her mother with a meaning in life and what might happen to the mother were she to leave home to marry. The boyfriend would see the outward manifestations of the anxiety, but because the patient was playing the role of "one-up on males," he did not know the actual reason for it. He assumed, naturally, that she really *wanted* him to be a failure, and so he continued to play the role. Not surprisingly, the role of failure fit in nicely with his role in his own family of origin. She helped him stay in character for his family by nagging him about his unemployment without really expecting him to get a job and by turning down his proposal of marriage.

In therapy, the patient gradually came to grips with the reasons for her mother's strange behavior and began to understand how she was unwittingly inducing her boyfriend to behave in ways that she really did not like. In addition to learning to metacommunicate with her mother, the therapist coached her to explain her predicament to the boyfriend so that he would understand her reactions and to help him to explore his role in his own family so that she would be able to expect more of him without his feeling betrayed. In this situation, the patient had not yet committed herself to a permanent relationship with the boyfriend, so there was a chance that she would choose to drop him and find someone who was not as deeply affected by the relevant existential issue, rather than to work out the relationship.

9

COACHING AND
ROLE PLAYING

The process of coaching patients to metacommunicate with their families has two major components: education and practice. Metacommunication is a skill that does not come naturally to anyone, any more than playing the piano does. There are do's and don't's that are far from obvious. Challenging the behavior of another empathetically without giving up one's own position, in the face of frequent disqualification, takes a great deal of knowledge, thought, and preparation. The patient must learn a set of principles of effective interaction. These principles are similar in many ways to those taught by assertiveness trainers (Alberti and Emmons, 1974). The therapist is the teacher.

Knowing how to do something in a technical sense is a far cry from actually doing it. In any profession, as we all know, the student who has just graduated may know more factual information than an experienced old-timer, but the old-timer is more effective. The value of experience is obvious. The patient who attempts to metacommunicate will, with proper coaching, become more effective as time goes on. More than in other fields of endeavor, however, getting one's feet wet in doing family metacommunication over sensitive topics is very frightening. The family system is felt by any individual to be an immensely powerful force, and challenging it is no easy undertaking. Patients must learn how to step back from an interaction and become an observer as well as a participant. They must learn how to decrease their emotional reactivity without attempting to abandon their emotions.

The bridge between factual knowledge and hands-on experience with effective family interactions is role playing. The therapist, with the patients' help, predicts what difficulties they are likely to encounter when they talk to a particular family member and devises strategies for overcoming these problems. Patients then practice ways to deal with the predicted family disqualifications with the therapist. The process continues until patients have gained enough confidence to try it with their families. At the beginning of role playing, patients play the part of the person with whom they will be metacommunicating, and the therapist plays the part of the patient. This is known as role reversal, a technique used frequently by psychodramatists (Moreno, 1985).

The purpose of role reversal is threefold. First, it allows the therapist to model potential ways to further the metacommunicative process. Second, by playing their "adversary," patients often gain insight into the predicament of the targeted family member and thereby learn to be more empathetic. Last, by observing the responses of the patient, the therapist gains knowledge about what the patient might expect from the targeted family member when the interaction finally does take place. This allows the therapist to plan a better strategy.

After role reversal, the patient and therapist change roles, with the patients playing themselves. On the basis of what I have learned about the possible responses of the targeted family member, I confront patients with worst-case scenarios. I give patients as hard a time as they are likely to get from the targeted family member. They slowly learn how to handle negative reactions. Because I am basing my choice of responses in the role playing on the worst possible eventuality, the reactions that the patients will eventually get from the family are usually far less aggravating than what they have experienced through role playing. This has the effect of causing the patients to gain confidence in their metacommunicative abilities very quickly once they have started to confront the family. Let us now look at some of the components of the coaching process in more detail.

Getting Started

Before teaching specific principles of metacommunication and then helping clients to practice them, the therapist must help clients develop a mind set that will allow them to be persistent even when they seem to be getting nowhere. This is accomplished through the use of reassurance and a prediction about how the whole process is likely to go. I inform clients that no matter how badly they do at first, even if they explode in anger and let loose with a torrent of attacks and hurtful statements that destroy any good feelings that there might have been at the beginning of a family confrontation, they cannot make an irreversible error. They cannot do any irreparable damage, although the repair job might take a bit of work. They can always go back and apologize, and do so in a way that will actually push the metacommunicative process forward. As we shall see shortly, the therapist can teach them how to do this. After a nasty incident, a family member may refuse at first to deal with the patient but will eventually come around if the patient is persistent and anticipates the family member's behavior.

A second, related idea that must be imparted to patients is that if they get an unanticipated response from a family member that they do not know how to handle, they can gracefully back off from a confrontation and return to the therapist for further strategy planning and practice. Beating a dead horse is pointless, if not counterproductive. However, if the nature of their error becomes clear before the next therapy session, patients need not feel obliged to wait until then before going back to the targeted family member. The therapist wishes to encourage patients to rely on their own resources and not to become overly dependent on the coach. Metacommunicative errors can be rectified at any time. Patients are told that they do not have to be shy about returning to a family member to talk about earlier interactions. In fact, waiting until after emotions have cooled before discussing a troubling interaction is often a necessity.

Patients are told that the family may not at first welcome their efforts with open arms, no matter how empathetic they are. At the beginning of the metacommunicative process, the family problem not only may fail to improve but may actually get worse. I predict that patients may find that they are made by the family to feel themselves villains when they initially bring up touchy issues. They may feel that they have made a big mistake by following my recommendations. They may experience groundlessness, a feeling of being wrong, a sense of being a fake or a phony. A particularly devastating family response that they may experience is what I refer to as clustering. Several members of their families may join together to criticize them for either their ideas or their efforts to bring up a touchy subject. They may hear, with remarkable family unanimity, that they are selfish and do not really care about the rest of the family or that they are troublemakers. The full force of the system may be brought to bear on them in an effort to force them to observe the family taboos.

Patients can handle this by reminding themselves that the rest of the family is just as frightened as they are of the consequences of metacommunication. They can look at their own resistances to bringing up the topics in question in order to empathize with the needs of the family to disqualify them. I tell them, in accordance with Bowen's (1978) observations, that if they can be persistent in their efforts to press forward, the family will eventually look up to them. A family member may even express gratitude, verbally or through action, for their efforts. I may add that they have no way of knowing at present that this is true and hope that they will take my word for it. The key idea is persistence. If my patients express doubt that they can be persistent, I tell them that we will practice it in the sessions. One of the keys to effective metacommunication is prolonging effective interaction times.

When warning patients about the potential trouble that they may encounter while metacommunicating, I have sometimes gone a little too far and frightened them away from following my recommendations. Therapists can soften their warnings by stating that they are describing the worst that could happen and that the whole process may in fact go more smoothly than even the patient might think.

The Nature of Negative Reactions

The targeted family member is most likely to react negatively to a patient's attempts to metacommunicate when the issue of blame is not dealt with empathetically or when the target wishes to protect a third member of the family system from anxiety or depression. The latter situation will produce what Bowen refers to as triangulation, which is discussed in Chapter Ten. Here, I will look at the nature of reactions caused by blaming behavior.

The patient must be careful to avoid placing the blame for any family problem on any particular family member or larger holon, past or present, including the targeted family member. This can be quite difficult when the patient attempts to discuss adverse consequences of certain behavior within the family. This kind of discussion naturally lends itself to questions of who is at fault. The patient must be careful to imply that any behavior under scrutiny was not motivated by evil intent, that it was not meant to have all of the consequences that it did, and that it was partially based on a misunderstanding of the motivations of other family members. The patient can imply that she or he is "guilty" of the same miscues that others have made. This temporarily places the patient in a "one-down" position that allows the targeted family member to think that the patient is not being overly critical. Although this move is similar to moves made in strategic family therapy (Madanes, 1981), it is not made in the service of tricking other family members. The statement is the truth—the patient has indeed made the same errors as other family members.

Family members being questioned will become defensive if they feel that they are being criticized for behavior that they consider to have been a necessary sacrifice for the good of the family. They will become defensive about another family member if they identify with her or him—even when they do not recognize all of the parallels between the motivation of that family member and their own. (The parallels may be obscure because of the principle of opposite behaviors—the other person's behavior may seem to be completely different from the behavior of the targeted family member, even when its net effect is identical.) Targeted family members, like the patient, have molded the outward manifestations of their personalities to maintain family homeostasis at great personal cost, and they will become incensed if they think that the patient thinks their behavior was motivated by an intent to harm others.

This anger will come out even if the targeted family members have gone to great lengths to mask their altruistic motivation, and even when they have purposely portrayed themselves as villains! In those cases where the true nature of the altruistic intent must be concealed in order for the family members to maintain a persona, the form that the anger takes will also conceal its true source. If the targeted family members feel that their motivation is being attacked and do not wish to reveal what that motivation really is, they cannot defend themselves by pointing out how the patient's criticism of them is unfair. Instead, they will counterattack in an unreasonable fashion. This has the effect of getting back at the patient by angering her or him, while at the same time, it allows them to continue to look like villains.

Case 9-1

A female patient was attempting to confront her mother about how the mother's help-rejecting behavior made her feel impotent. As a prime example, whenever Mother looked angry, the patient would try to ask what the matter was. Mother would reply, like a broken record, "You don't really care." This would infuriate the patient. Did her mother think she was unfeeling? That her expressions of caring were phony? In her initial attempts to be more persistent, the patient insisted that she did care and wanted to help, if only the mother would tell her what was wrong. The mother again replied, "No, you don't really care." At that point, the patient was not feeling particularly empathetic to the mother's need to be the strong one in the family, and she became caught up in the passions of the moment. She continued to press the mother on the real reasons for her refusal to discuss her feelings. The mother walked out of the room.

My guess was that the mother really felt obligated, despite her own obvious neediness, not to burden the patient with her own troubles. She wanted to protect her daughter from falling into the same oppressive caretaking role in which she herself was trapped. Her method for achieving this aim was to discourage the patient from helping by making the younger woman angry. The mother resorted to this indirect procedure because she could not just tell the patient outright not to take the caretaker role. Such a statement might lead to a discussion of the mother's own counterdependency. This she did not wish to discuss, probably because the discussion might lead to the exposure of the link between the counterdependency and her anger, which would expose the resentment her true self harbored over her role in the family, which in turn would make it more difficult for her to maintain her persona.

Even so, the mother was angry because her motivation was being misread. She was not rejecting the patient's help because she thought her daughter was callous or insincere. She could not reveal her true motivation, so she ended the discussion by a very unreasonable withdrawal. This had the multiple effects of making the mother look bad, blocking a discussion of the mother's anger, expressing the mother's anger, and further discouraging the patient's efforts to help by making the patient angry. Pretty ingenious! Another trick the mother used to similar effect was to accuse the patient of not *really* wanting to help, and proving the assertion with examples of instances where the patient had refused to quickly drop everything she was doing in order to help the mother in a nonemergency situation.

The patient was coached to advance the metacommunication about this interaction by praising the mother's motivation before criticizing its effects: "I know you don't like me to worry about you, and I appreciate your concern for me, but when you don't tell me what's wrong, I worry about you even more." This statement confronted the mother with the problems her counterdependency was creating for the patient, while at the same time acknowledging and expressing gratitude for the mother's need to avoid burdening others. This decreased the mother's defensiveness. Additionally, the statement foiled the basic aims of the mother's passive-aggressive behavior. The patient was letting on that, while the unreasonable behavior did make her angry, it was not discouraging the patient more than temporarily from wanting to help. Furthermore, rather than cutting off a discussion of the mother's counterdependency, the mother's behavior was now having the effect of moving it a notch forward. The daughter's statement brought the mother's ambivalence about her role in the family into sharper focus—the true self of the mother really did want the patient to worry about her. If the mother behaved passively-aggressively in the future, the patient could use it as a starting point for further discussion of the mother's persona. (The technique of turning around a metacommunication-scuttling maneuver by a family member to push it forward instead is an important one.) The patient's statement paved the way for later discussion of the relative merits of the mother's role, where it came from and why it developed, and whether it was still necessary.

The structure of negative reactions to attempts at metacommunication can be thought of as falling into two major categories: fight and flight. The targeted family member will get angry and pick a fight or will withdraw and use the silent treatment or the threat of abandonment. These maneuvers are meant to either frighten patients out of pursuing the taboo subject or get them so angry that they no longer want to pursue it. Looked at in another way, these negative responses fall into the categories of aggressive and passive-aggressive behavior described by assertiveness trainers (Alberti and Emmons, 1974). Fighting and belligerence correspond to the aggressive category, withdrawal to the passive-aggressive. Which combination of specific responses the targeted family member will choose when he or she becomes defensive will depend on the prevailing behavior in the family system. This behavior is frequently determined by the cultural system of which the family system is a part. For example, Irish Americans traditionally resort to an emotional cutoff followed by a sudden rupture in the entire relationship (McGoldrick, Pearce, and Giordano, 1982). The therapist uses the information provided by the patient during the entire therapy process, particularly during the role-reversal stage of role playing, to predict what the patient is likely to face during attempts to metacommunicate with the family.

Principles and Techniques of Metacommunication

In this section, we will look at some of the basic strategies for overcoming disqualifications and other forms of resistance to metacommunication and explore ways in which they can be taught. The reader may note that the techniques that patients are coached to use with the family differ very little from the techniques that the therapist uses with the patients. Many of these ideas have been mentioned earlier in this chapter. The overall guiding principle of effective metacommunication is that one should do everything one can to prolong effective interaction time. The longer the metacommunication process continues, the more likely that mutual understanding and empathy will result. Longer discussions allow for deeper and deeper probing of sensitive topics as the family members provide one another with mirroring for alternate behavior. Any trick that a family member uses to derail a conversation can and should be used instead to further it.

Stepping Back: The Observer Versus the Participant. Emotional reactivity is deadly to effective metacommunication. Knee-jerk emotional outbursts not only prevent the patient from being reasonable but turn off everyone else. Repressing the emotions per se is not, however, a good way to accomplish the diminution of emotional reactivity. Repression of any self-aspect is hardly a basis for initiating a process that is supposed to lead to freedom of self-expression. As I pointed out earlier, there are many ways to express one's feelings. What must be avoided is acting out emotions, particularly in situations where clients are feeling fearful or angry. They must learn the skill of thinking about what effect they would like to have on a family member before merely reacting. The goal is the removal of bad feelings not through catharsis but through the removal of the situations that lead to them.

The first step in learning to reduce emotional reactivity is learning to identify those situations in which it is likely to occur. If patients can become aware that an interaction is leading to strong feelings before it gets too far, they have won half the battle. I coach patients to be on the lookout for statements or actions by the targeted family member that make them feel uncomfortable. As I mentioned above, the inducement of fear or anger in a patient by the targeted family member is *designed* to scuttle metacommunication. Metacommunication will proceed if the targeted family member fails to induce that desired response. When patients notice that the targeted family member is inducing strong emotions, they must learn to step back and look, as objectively as possible, at the entire situation. The coach can help patients learn how to do this by using the technique of having them imagine during role playing that they are watching a movie of the family and themselves rather than participating in a transaction. This technique of coaching is performed during the phase of role playing when patients play themselves. Once they are able to mentally remove themselves from the situation, they can coolly analyze exactly what is happening on the level of cognition rather than emotion.

The process of analyzing the situation is done through a step-by-step series of cognitions that parallels a process that the therapist uses in figuring out how best to play the role of the targeted family member. Before discussing what to teach the patient, let us examine how the therapist plays the role of the targeted family member. When I prepare myself to get into character, I ask myself two questions about this protagonist: What is the targeted family member's motivation for the behavior that is the subject, directly or in the historical metaphor, of the metacommunication? How might this motivation be misunderstood or unappreciated by the patient? Whenever patients playing themselves in the drama say something or act in a way that implies one of these negative appraisals or misunderstandings, I then confront them with one of the disqualifications that the targeted family member is known from the role-reversal stage to use. I almost invariably get a chance to do this, because patients at this stage are new at metacommunicating and have not become acquainted with or developed all of the necessary skills. They are bound to make an error. They may suffer a loss of empathy and make this kind of mistake because they really do misunderstand the target's motivation, but by this point in therapy they should already have insight into it. In addition to the patient's inexperience, mistakes at this stage can also be caused by the patient's failure to effectively become an observer as well as a participant in the role-playing process. He or she may then react on a purely emotional level.

When in the course of role playing I have an opportunity to present the patient with a disqualification, say from a father, I teach the patient to go through the following series of cognitions: I am becoming frightened by or angry at Dad, or I feel that I am harming him in some way. This means that he is becoming defensive and wishes to terminate this conversation. To what is he reacting? What does he think I am saying about his behavior and his motivation? In what way does he feel unappreciated or misunderstood? Through searching for the answers to these questions, patients can attempt to muster some empathy for disqualifications that would ordinarily set them off in one way or another. If they can do this, they are less likely to react with hostility or withdrawal themselves. They can plan a response that, rather than stopping metacommunication, will induce the targeted family member to continue talking.

The idea behind the type of response that will achieve this aim is quite simple. One turns the sequence of interactions that led to a negative response by the targeted family member into the *subject* of the conversation. Rather than being turned off by the disqualification, clients attempt to use it as a vehicle for understanding the motivations of the other. They look for common ground. This type of response subverts the intentions of the other. The targeted family member's disqualification is

meant to cut off metacommunication, but every disqualification now induces the patient to metacommunicate even more.
Because the patient is being empathetic, the targeted family
member cannot reattack without making her or his intentions
so obvious that they can no longer be denied. If the targeted
family member goes ahead and renews the attacks anyway, the
patient makes that maneuver the subject of the conversation,
and so on down the line, until the other is finally induced to
discuss true feelings.

I will now describe some useful techniques for achieving
this end, first discussing how to handle disqualifications that result from the patient's mishandling of the issue of blame and
then going on to describe some techniques of more general ap-
plicability.

Praising Motivation. The key to changing a distancing,
communication-scuttling response into a vehicle for closeness
and the advancement of understanding is the expression of the
empathy that patients have mobilized by asking themselves the
questions described above. I have given some examples of one
of the basic techniques for communicating empathy: one ac-
knowledges the good intentions of an individual before questioning the effects of his or her behavior. When patients feel
that the other is feeling unappreciated, they express appreciation before making any criticisms. This idea follows a well-
known principle understood by many teachers and behaviorists,
which is to always praise a student or client for what he or she
has done well before pointing out errors and suggesting improvements. Hearing something good makes anyone more
amenable to constructive criticism.

This is all well and good, but there is a potential problem
with this approach. I pointed out earlier that any ideas that the
therapist or the patient comes up with concerning the motivation of the significant other are hypotheses only and require
some sort of confirmation by that other. At the beginning of an
interaction, the patient can make only an educated guess about
the intentions of anyone. What if the patient attempts to praise
the motivation of the other, but the targeted family member re-

plies that the patient's ideas about it are incorrect? The patient's attempts to be empathetic in such a circumstance might cause the other to become even more annoyed, and a metacommunication-ending argument might ensue.

How this sort of disconfirming response is handled depends on the willingness of the targeted family member to take the patient's effort at empathy as a sign of good faith, so that the other feels comfortable continuing with a frank discussion of his or her motivation. If the patient's guess concerning the motivation of the target is incorrect, but the family member does not become defensive, then the patient's remark may still have the effect of furthering the metacommunicative process. This is the effect it was meant to have in the first place. This situation will be easy for the patient to identify, because the target will calmly and rationally attempt to correct the patient's misperception, and the patient will not feel threatened in any way. The patient can then use the target's corrective statements as a springboard for a further discussion about how the target had been perceived by the patient up to that point. This exchange increases mutual understanding and can lead to the desired exploration of alternative ways of relating.

If, after an attempt by the patient to be empathetic, the target accuses the patient of misunderstanding the whole situation, and does so in a hostile way, the patient will once again begin to feel threatened or angry. The targeted family member will confront the patient with this kind of reaction for one of two possible reasons. The target is either protecting another family member or is feeling blamed or criticized for some issue that the patient is not properly addressing. In the latter case, the patient not only probably has misread the nature of the target's defensiveness but may also be coming across as blaming rather than as empathetic. Such patients must then step back once again and attempt to ascertain the reasons for the defensiveness by repeating the series of cognitions described above. They must also question whether they are feeling more anger than empathy themselves, and if so, why. If they get an idea about why the target is reacting negatively, and the reason concerns the issue of blame, they can get back on track by saying something to the effect that "I can see that what I am saying is bothering you. Maybe you think I'm being critical of such and such. I did not mean to imply that. Let me see if I can rephrase that."

Case 9-2

The patient in this case, previously described in Chapter Four, was in the middle of separate but concurrent attempts to metacommunicate with her husband and her parents about the family pattern. After much resistance, the patient and her husband had finally learned to discuss, albeit hesitantly, the reasons why the patient acted powerfully while the husband appeared to be less competent. They had also talked about how both of them wanted to discontinue this pattern. The patient had explained some of the parental behavior that had led her to react in the way that she did. The husband, who by then was acting more competently and helpfully than he had in the past, still had his doubts about whether his wife was really comfortable with his newfound strength.

A short time after the last episode of spousal metacommunication, the patient's mother exhibited one of her typical patterns. Rather than waiting for the patient to handle it, the husband took it upon himself to confront the mother. Since the battle with the mother was really the province of the patient rather than the husband, the patient began to feel as if her power were being undercut. Her husband was doing her work for her, thereby protecting her from the distress of the metacommunicative effort. The danger of the development of a role reversal, in which the patient would become helpless and the husband overly powerful instead of both being equal, began to loom on the horizon. The patient was coached to praise her husband's efforts to help but to point out to him that, in this particular case, this was something she had to do for herself. Her initial attempt to do so led to a marked defensive reaction from the husband.

When the patient returned to therapy, we attempted to understand and empathize with the husband's reaction. The problem, we determined, was that the couple was trapped in a game without end. By asking the husband not to help, the patient was playing into his fear that she really thought he could do nothing right and confirmed his fear that she wished to remain in the dominant role. The patient was coached to initiate a discussion of this problem. She told her husband that she was worried that her request to let her handle the mother was being interpreted by him as a criticism of his ability to handle family problems. She informed him that this was not the case but that it was difficult to discuss the husband's actions without making it sound that way.

What should clients do if, after stepping back and asking themselves the reasons for the target's negative reactions, they are unable to come up with any ideas? Should they back off immediately and wait until the next therapy session? Before doing that, there is one additional technique that can be attempted.

Verbalizing Feelings and Expressing Puzzlement. A major principle of metacommunication is that calmly verbalizing feelings is far better than acting them out. When a target, say a mother, becomes defensive and reacts negatively, and patients cannot figure out exactly why and therefore cannot praise the mother's motivation, they can still advance metacommunication by describing their own emotional reactions and by asking the mother why she is doing what she is doing. This class of responses has the following basic structure: "You know, when you react (in the way that you are now reacting), it makes me feel (angry, annoyed, helpless, like dropping this whole conversation). This subject is very important to me, and I think it is important in our relationship. I know you care about me, so I don't understand why you are reacting so (negatively, angrily). What is it about what I am saying that's so (irritating, troublesome)?"

This statement is once again meant to turn a sequence of responses that is ordinarily acted out into a subject of discussion. The statement strongly implies that the mother knows what kind of reaction she is inducing in the patient, without implying that she understands the motivation behind the patient's response. The patient may even say directly: "I think you know that what you are saying will really set me off. Why are you picking a fight?" If the mother denies that she is attempting to frighten or anger the patient, or if she states that the subject under discussion is not troublesome, then she must calm down and continue the conversation. If she does not, she is proving that the patient's observation is correct. If the mother persists in her previous behavior anyway, the patient might then say, "I do not understand. If this topic does not bother you, why do you keep changing the subject?"

Another potential response of the mother to the patient's initial statement of puzzlement is to dismiss the patient's observations out of hand without refuting them and continue to behave in ways that annoy or frighten the patient. The patient can counter this sort of move with what some assertiveness trainers refer to as an "escalation." An escalation involves placing the mother's new response into the same category as her initial response or, alternatively, making a generalization about a whole series of responses. An example of the first type of escalation, which the patient might use at this point, is the statement, "When you ignore the point I am trying to make and continue on as if I had said nothing, it is extremely annoying. I still do not understand why you are trying to pick a fight." The second type of escalation is typified by the statement, "Whenever I try to discuss this subject, you seem to find some way to stop the conversation. I don't like to make you uncomfortable, but I think this subject is really important."

In order to be effective at using these maneuvers, clients must adopt a specific posture. They must remain calm, and they must be persistent. They must always give the benefit of the doubt to the target when questioning his or her motivation. That is, clients must always let on that they are assuming that the intentions of the target are honorable, no matter how provocative the target's behavior. They must fight off urges to protect the other from uncomfortable feelings. If, after a good try with this technique, they are unable to make headway, then they should back off until they have a chance to role play with the therapist.

The following types of disqualifications and blocking tactics may be used by targets not only in cases in which they are feeling blamed but also in cases where another family member is being protected. The countermeasures that I will describe can be used in either situation.

Changing the Subject. When the target becomes uncomfortable with a conversation and wishes to exit the transaction without making a scene, a common method for accomplishing this aim is to merely change the subject. The subject change may be abrupt and obvious, or it may be subtle and insidious. The target may go off on a tangent, intermix two or more issues so that none are fully discussed, use communications deviance so patients become unsure whether they and the target are both talking about the same thing, make jokes, or look for something in the environment that can be used as a distraction. When confronted with these types of maneuvers, patients should first attempt to change the subject right back to the subject at hand. If that fails, they should point out in a noncondemning manner how the target is avoiding their concerns and insist on returning to the subject at hand. If the target still persists in sidetracking maneuvers, patients should handle it in the same manner as they handle any defensive reaction. They should step back and ask themselves why the target is becoming uncomfortable and then either attempt to empathize or express puzzlement over the target's reactions.

Mental Gymnastics. The target may derail an attempt at metacommunication by making illogical statements about the subject a patient is trying to clarify. Mental gymnastics are performed, just as is any other form of defensive reaction, to frighten or anger others or to create confusion. Patients can be coached to react to these maneuvers in the same way that the therapist reacts to mental gymnastics from them (see Chapter Eight). In brief, patients initially point out the absence of logic or inattention to contradictory information inherent in the target's statements. They do so in a matter-of-fact way and expect the target to see the error and make corrections. If the target responds by pointing out an error in a patient's reasoning or strengthens his or her own case with additional valid data, the patient admits the error. If the target maintains an obviously ludicrous position, the patient expresses surprise and puzzlement over why the target is being unreasonable on purpose or attempts to empathize with the reasons for the target's defensiveness.

Unreasonable Behavior. The target may also derail an attempt at metacommunication through some kind of unreasonable behavior, such as walking out of the room or starting to drink heavily in response to the patient's statements. Let me first address the issue of responsive, self-destructive acting out by the target. Such behavior can be particularly frightening to a patient. When confronted by such a reaction, a patient may get the idea that the subject matter that elicited the behavior is more than the target can reasonably be expected to handle and that the target needs to be protected from it. A patient may decide that the idea that people do not need to be protected from distressing feelings is hogwash and that he or she should leave well enough alone.

Fortunately, most of the time the targeted family member has a previous history of responding in these ways, so that the therapist who has done a good job of eliciting the problem can anticipate the problem and warn the patient about what to expect. The therapist can explain that such targets behave in the way they do to achieve a specific response in the patient. They do this for an understandable reason, not because they "can't take it." The patient must learn that backing off in response to self-destructive behavior rewards it, in a sense, by providing the target with one of the intended net effects of the self-destructiveness. By rewarding it, the patient may increase, rather than decrease, the chance that the target's self-destructiveness will be repeated. If the patient does not back off but is persistent about pursuing the subject, the raison d'être of the self-destructiveness will evaporate, and the behavior will eventually cease.

Clients may have a difficult time believing these ideas from the therapist because of past experience. They may have tried to be more persistent in the past, only to see the self-destructive behavior of the target worsen, and have at that point finally conceded defeat and backed off. Readers familiar with the behaviorist concept of reinforcement schedules (Reese, 1966) will recognize immediately that the longer the clients have persisted before backing off, especially if that length of time has varied widely, the more difficult it will be to induce the target to give up the behavior in the future. The target will persist with the behavior for longer and longer periods of time before it is finally extinguished. The clients have taught the target patience. If the target just waits them out, sooner or later they will give up. Past efforts by clients to be persistent may have had the effect of convincing them even more strongly that persistence is futile.

If the therapist is persistent in insisting that patients continue their efforts to metacommunicate with the target despite the target's self-destructiveness, patients who have had these experiences will eventually express their pessimism and the quite valid reasons for it. The therapist can then explain the concept of reinforcement schedules to them so that they can have a better grasp of what is happening. I often use the metaphor of the slot machine to get the idea of reinforcement schedules across. The reason that gamblers persist in pulling the lever for so long is because they never know when the machine will pay off. It pays off just often enough to reward them for their continued efforts. Likewise, the target is "rewarded" when the patient backs off. The longer the patient waits before backing off, the longer the target will persist in the frightening behavior.

Being persistent is not often easy even when patients are strongly motivated. How can they persist if a father walks out of the room or drinks himself into a stupor? One cannot talk to a person who is not, literally or figuratively, all there. Should patients follow the other around like a puppy dog or try to talk to a target who is incoherent? The answer, of course, is no. Patients must be persistent but do not have to be persistent within any limited time frame. The issue they were trying to discuss with the target, because it is so central, will always come up again. After things calm down, patients can look for an opportunity to discuss the sequence of events that occurred in the earlier situation or to bring up the general problem of the other's self-destructiveness.

Another type of unreasonable behavioral response to the patient's attempts to metacommunicate, seen particularly often in cases where the patient is attempting to explore the reasons for the target's self-destructive behavior, is an accusation by the target that the patient is a nag. The "I drink because she nags/I nag because he drinks" merry-go-round is a well-known pattern in couples. On the surface, the nagging complaint sounds reasonable. Everyone hates to be constantly bugged by someone else. While it is indeed true that the nagging behavior of the wife is contributing to the continuation of the drinker's offensive behavior, this is not merely because the nagging is irritating. The flaw in that idea becomes apparent when one realizes that the drinker is stating that he is, in effect, "cutting off his nose to spite his face." If he really wanted to get back at his wife for carping, there are many non-self-destructive things he could do to be irritating right back. What is really happening is that the drinking husband is helping the nagger play the role of the sainted martyr, while the nagging wife is helping the drinker play the role of the no-good drunk. The nagger's nagging is meant to put her in a morally superior position, rather than to stop the self-destructive behavior of the drinker, even though the nagger really is concerned for the well-being of the drinker.

In trying to metacommunicate about this pattern, the possibility for a game without end is high. It is nearly impossible for the wife to discuss the self-destructiveness of the husband *without* putting herself in a morally superior position. One possible way out of this dilemma is for her to discuss her own concerns and worries about the self-destructiveness of the husband, rather than discussing his behavior per se. She can say something like, "I'm really worried about what this drinking is doing to you" rather than "I just don't understand why are you drinking." If the husband replies that she should stop worrying, she can then point out, "If I did that, you would think I didn't care about you at all." The latter type of response will be enlarged upon when I discuss handling double binds in the next section. Before going on to that, I will first address the possibility that a target might use violence to derail a conversation.

In my experience, well-coached patients will not incite a target to violence if they attempt to metacommunicate empathetically, no matter how clumsy the initial attempt. This is true even in families where violence is a routinely recurring pattern. The reason for this is that family violence against adults is invariably cued by the person at whom it is directed. A battered wife, for instance, helps the abuser play the role of abuser. If a victim did not wish to do that, she would leave the relationship as soon as the spouse caused her significant injury, no matter how much financial hardship she would have to bear. This does *not* mean that it is the woman's "fault" that she is being abused. The violent response of the man is totally inexcusable from a moral standpoint; individuals should be able to refrain from violence no matter how much provocation they are subjected to. Nonetheless, a violent response is just that—a response. Its ultimate morality is beside the point, and the question of who is to blame is destructive to the effort at stopping it. Therapists should leave the matter of who is at fault to the criminal justice system.

Patients and therapists can figure out the exact nature of the situations that lead to violence—patients already know what they are—and can work together to make sure that the patient does not resort to the usual provocations. Even a violent relationship has limiting rules: no cues, no violence. One technique patients can use to initiate metacommunication with a violent target is to admit to their own role in the problem without excusing the violence: "I know that sometimes I can be pretty irritating; we need to figure out how we got ourselves into this mess."

Case 9-3

A young woman came to therapy after an episode of family violence. Her husband became quite ill on the night of her tenth high school reunion. She decided to stay home in order to look after him, but he absolutely insisted that she go without

him. He did not want to ruin an evening that she had been looking forward to for months. However, when she got home late
that night, she found that her husband had waited up for her.
He had been drinking. He began making nasty statements about
her conduct at the reunion, saying that she had gone for the express purpose of "getting laid." She angrily replied, "I think I
should have." At this point, he began to hit her. Similar fights
had occurred on several previous occasions. When asked why
she stayed in this kind of relationship, the patient replied, "Because he's been nicer to me than anyone I've ever met."

Even if she had come from a horribly abusive background,
which she had not, one would be hard pressed to understand
how she could define her husband's behavior as "nice." The explanation that she believed that there was nobody "nicer" for
her in the whole world was an obvious logical fallacy. The real
explanation, of course, was to be found in the concept of role-
function support. Her husband was being "nice" to her by helping her play a role.

After much exploration, we were able to identify the behavior that cued her husband's violence. The patient frequently
made statements to the effect that her father was the only man
whom she had ever really loved. She made statements such as "I
know our relationship will never work out, and I might want to
leave." She complained about problems she was having at work
but continually rejected her husband's advice. She repeatedly
rebuffed her husband's sexual advances. In countless ways, she
implied that he was inadequate. Now of course, in many ways,
the husband did behave in an inadequate fashion. The patient's
threats to leave often followed episodes of violence. The patient
had "cause" for making the statements she made. The more she
made them, however, the more inadequate and violent the husband became. The fact that the patient did not make good on
her threat to leave and her occasional statements to the husband
about how nice he was to her also cued the husband to continue
his inadequate and violent behavior. He concluded from all this
that the patient wanted him to be just the way he was.

After the functions that this pattern served in the families
of origin of the patient and her husband were elucidated, the

patient was coached to begin metacommunication. The starting point was a statement to her husband, "When I express doubts about our relationship, you must find that pretty frustrating."

Double Binds and Games Without End. Nothing can be quite so irritating as being placed in a "damned if you do and damned if you don't" position. When individuals are attempting to accomplish a goal and are stymied no matter how they behave, they begin to feel frustrated and helpless. Frustration and helplessness lead to feelings of anger and depression. Patients may have been placed in some sort of double bind by the target for some time. The double bind may often, in fact, be the reason for a patient's self-destructive behavior. In order to effectively implement the alternate solution, the double bind must at some point become the subject of metacommunication. However, because the double bind is so irritating, patients may have trouble talking about it in an empathetic manner. The target might even attempt to derail an attempt at metacommunication by putting patients in a double bind similar to the one that they are attempting to discuss. Patients then become angry and, instead of being understanding, throw out a disqualification or two of their own. The metacommunicative process breaks down.

The therapist can help clients become empathetic to even the most destructive of double binds. The key is, as always, finding the good reason behind the target's unreasonable behavior. Double-binding behavior by a family member has, in general, two interconnecting root causes. The target is caught in a conflict or double bind him- or herself and is trapped with the patient in a game without end.

Case 9-4

A good example of double-binding behavior occurred in the relationship between an agoraphobic wife and her husband. The husband would get angry at the wife whenever she would get after him to take care of much-needed repairs around the house. He complained that he was busy with a thousand things at work and that he had enough to worry about without being burdened by household tasks that could wait. He would, he insisted, get around to them if only the wife did not nag. However, if she said nothing, the work would never be completed. If she asked him how to do the work, so she could learn to do it herself, he would become indignant. No matter how she phrased her request for information, she would get a negative response that implied that she was hypercritical of him. He implied that she would not be asking these questions if she really thought he would get around to it or that her questions were an implied criticism of his ability to do the work. If he started a task and she asked, in order to learn how to do it herself, why he did it the way he did, he would act as if she had asked the question because she thought he was doing it incorrectly. Likewise, if she hired an outsider to do the work, the husband would act insulted, because she obviously had no faith that he could do it. The husband seemed to react negatively to competent behavior from her, so she played the role of a defective for him, but then he reacted negatively to that.

If the wife attempted to point out that the work was never done no matter how she handled the situation, the husband would react as if this statement was just another example of her lack of faith in him. On the one occasion when she suggested a separation, he went into a tirade. This pattern was a classic double bind. She did not please her husband whether she was competent or remained incompetent, she could not comment on the bind, and she felt as if she could not escape from the field.

The dynamics of this case involved his helping her play the role of a burdensome, defective woman who could not live on her own without a husband, while she helped him play the role of a man who was burdened by but could never please demanding family members. These roles stemmed from family conflicts over sex-role functioning that went back a number of generations.

Rather than focusing on the facts of this particular case, I will use this example of a double bind to illustrate the two types of explanations for the husband's behavior. The husband might be in a double bind himself. If he let his wife be competent and helpful, perhaps his mother might become depressed that she had sacrificed her own competence unnecessarily, and she might also become envious of the wife. If he just accepted his wife's defectiveness, he might not be able to stabilize the parental relationship by acting out his father's anger at the incompetent, burdensome mother. No matter how he handled the situation, the homeostasis of his family of origin would be threatened. In this situation, he would react negatively to his wife no matter how she acted. Not understanding this, the wife would merely become confused about what her husband expected from her.

Alternately, or additionally, the husband might be double binding his wife because he is caught up with her in a game without end. His wife is expressing unhappiness with the current situation, to be sure, but does she *really* want it to change? Just how invested is *she* in the role of the burdensome, defective woman? What would the effect be on her family of origin if she were to change, and does she become anxious when the husband changes his behavior? In most cases of double binding, the spouse has a double bind in her or his own family of origin that is complementary to the double bind in the patient's family of origin. In this case, the homeostasis in the *wife's* family of origin might become endangered were she to act either competently or incompetently. Because of that, she would react nervously if the husband made it easy for her to settle on either one or the other. The husband may ignore the wife's verbal request to clarify the situation because her anxious behavior seems to indicate that she would really prefer to keep things uncertain. Interestingly, both the wife and the husband in this case had glaring "defects"—agoraphobia coupled with an inability to leave the husband in the case of the wife, inability to complete a task in the case of the husband. Depending on the current family atmosphere, one or the other could make themselves appear to be the more defective member of the couple. This allowed them both to vacillate between appearing to be competent and appearing to be incompetent.

In short, the husband continues to bind the wife because of his own inability to come down on one side of the fence or the other and because he thinks that she expects him to continue binding her. These two issues are so intertwined that the patient must be coached toward extreme verbal clarity when she attempts to metacommunicate about them. As always, the patient can metacommunicate most effectively about the double bind either by empathizing with the other's motivation and then questioning the need for the offensive behavior or by expressing feelings about and puzzlement over the behavior of the other.

The expression of feelings and puzzlement over a double bind, when the motivation of the target is unclear, can take the following basic form: "When you do A, I get the feeling that you want me to do X, but when you do B, I get the feeling that you do not want me to do X. This is very confusing (irritating, and so on). I don't know what you want me to do." In the example of the patient in Case 9-4, the patient might state, "I know you are really busy and don't want to be bothered with household repairs, but when I try to ask you how I can do it or when I try to hire someone else, you get angry with me. I do not know how to please you and still get the work done." Such a statement must not be made to sound like an accusation but must sound instead like an attempt to solve a problem for the benefit of the relationship. A conciliatory, noncondemning tone in the patient's voice is often difficult to muster because the double bind is so provoking. Frequent rehearsal of the statement, along with rehashing the reasons why the patient should be more empathetic, will usually take up much of the coaching time in the therapy.

In order to empathize with the plight of a relative in a double bind so that the game without end can end, patients must also learn to acknowledge their own contribution to the problem. They can accomplish this without putting themselves down merely by explaining their own reactions. They might say, "I know that sometimes I get anxious when you behave differently, but that is [to a member of the family of origin] because I am still nervous about whether these changes are really best for the family as a whole, and I worry about how other family members might react, or [to a spouse] because of the reactions that I experience from my own family, not because I really prefer your old behavior. I'm attempting to work on my relationships with them." Patients then go on to explain their current understanding of their own family dynamics and, in the case of a spouse, help the mate understand the dynamics in the spouse's family.

The acknowledgment of one's own contribution to the family problem is another important principle of effective metacommunication. This is something many patients will be loath to do, not because they are shirking responsibility for their actions but because there is a danger that all the blame for the family problem might be shifted onto them.

Blame Shifting. A favorite maneuver that is used by many families to scuttle metacommunication is the counteraccusation. Properly coached patients attempt to discuss a mutual problem within the family without placing blame on any one particular family member, but in order to do so they must bring up the troublesome behavior of individuals within the family system. Even when patients do their best not to blame, and are indeed admitting that they have done many of the things for which they are criticizing other family members, the other may nonetheless attempt to quiet them by acting as if they *were* behaving in a blaming manner. The target may then become indignant and start placing the blame for the problem on the patient. In order to get the patient to become especially angry, the target may magnify and exaggerate the patient's contribution to the problem and imply that the patient is *entirely* at fault.

This kind of maneuver is, of course, an attempt to distance the patient through the use of an unjust criticism. The patient will be sorely tempted to return the insult in kind. As with any other distancing maneuver, however, the patient must react instead by moving closer. The most difficult problem in designing an effective countermeasure for this maneuver is that the accusations of the target will invariably contain a kernel of truth. The patient, being an integral part of the family system, is indeed part of the problem. If patients react to the accusation of the target by merely defending themselves, the target will have and use a wealth of examples from the patient's past as ammunition to back up his or her charge. Patients may then begin to become frustrated or to feel guilty about their contributions to the family problem, and the conversation will sidetrack. Luckily, however, the fact that the target's accusation does contain a kernel of truth can be used to get the conversation back on track. It can be used in the service of empathy.

Instead of becoming defensive, patients can acknowledge the kernel of truth in the accusation of the target, while either ignoring the exaggerations or pointing them out in a matter-of-fact fashion. They then use their contribution to the problem as an example of behavior that is caused by the very family problem that they are now trying to discuss and solve. Patients can add that they used to criticize themselves for the very "sins" of which the target is now accusing them.

As we shall see in the following example, the patient can also use the target's criticism to question traditional family beliefs. The latter subject is normally the last part of the metacommunicative sequence that comprises the alternate solution, but the blame-shifting maneuver of the target provides an excellent vehicle for speeding up the process.

Case 9-5

The patient, estranged from his family and living far away, was in the process of calling up his older brother to metacommunicate about the family problem. The patient let the brother know that he wanted to come home on vacation to clarify some of the family issues. The brother, who had attempted to escape enmeshment in the family by moving away—as had the patient—but who had felt obliged to return, immediately began to indignantly criticize the patient's attempt at renewed family involvement. "You moved away and have your own life. Who are you to come back here and try to fix the family?"

The patient was coached to respond, "I can understand your feelings. I often asked myself that same question when I first considered doing this. I have been away a long time, but

I'm not happy about not being close to the family." The goal of this statement was to use it as a vehicle for bringing up the difficulty that the entire family had in resolving the riddle of how to remain close to one another while leading independent lives. Before the patient could do that, however, the brother let go another accusation—one that the patient had often used to discourage himself from following the therapist's recommendations. The fatalistic belief that underlay this particular accusation was at the core of the family problem.

"Look," protested the brother, "forget it. You're just going to stir up trouble. The people in the family are not going to change. Dad's been drinking for years, and he isn't going to stop. You're not going to save anyone." The accusation that he was trying to be the family savior and that this was a major cause of trouble was particularly effective on this patient. He had attended a self-help group for years, and the avoidance of the savior role was one of the hallmarks of their message. Indeed, the fatalism of the family made that organization and its message ego-syntonic for the patient. The patient came to the next therapy session and severely criticized the therapist for trying to turn him into the family savior.

I reminded the patient that his self-destructive behavior and never-ending attempts to change it indicated that he was already attempting to fix the family problem, and that this method was not working. Family discussions were meant to help him solve the family problem so that he could put an end to the role of savior, not continue it. He was not responsible, ultimately, for making the family change, but I was far more optimistic than he that he could indeed be helpful. Even if he failed to help the family, if he could change his relationship with them, he would get better. The patient continued to express doubts. "Let's role play how you might respond to your brother before you decide whether to follow my advice." The patient was coached to empathize with the brother's feelings that the family members were fundamentally and irreparably damaged. The patient had, after all, felt that way himself many times. He could truthfully say, "I used to think that way, too." After expressing this empathy, the patient was in a position to question the validity of this assertion and to discuss the historical and cultural reasons that led to the family's fatalistic belief system.

Fatalism. Fatalism is a significant component of the belief systems of many cultural groups that have immigrated to the United States (McGoldrick, Pearce, and Giordano, 1982). Many times, patients who attempt to metacommunicate about family problems so that they can be solved are accused of being troublemakers. Another accusation based on a belief in fatalism is the charge that patients who are known to be in therapy are trying to be psychiatrists themselves. "Quit trying to analyze everything!" is a frequent family rallying cry. Similarly, a family may often become irritated with patients for nonfatalistically discussing a family problem and accuse them of being sadists who are trying to open old wounds. "Why are you bringing this up? It's all in the past."

These kinds of accusations can be used to pave the way for clients to question established fatalistic family belief systems. Clients can empathize with the family by admitting that they used to think just as the family does, but add that they now have real doubts about those ideas. Why shouldn't they try to analyze a situation? Understanding a problem is beneficial for figuring out a way to solve it. People in the family may disagree because they feel helpless about changing their future. The feelings of helplessness stemmed from past experiences or catastrophes that befell their forebears, but times have changed. In response to the accusation that they are dwelling on the past, clients can point out how those past situations are continuing to affect the family's present situation. They can say that they are bringing them up because they want to have better relationships with the family; the old problems are creating distance, and they want to be closer. In response to the charge that they are being troublemakers and creating dissonance in the family, clients can reply that the dissonance already exists, and they are trying to reduce it by discussing its causes. They can add that if the bad feelings can be reduced, then the family will wind up feeling closer to one another.

Nitpicking and Overgeneralizing. In attempting to meta-communicate about behavior patterns within the family system, clients will at some point be forced to discuss particular examples of the behavior pattern that they have in mind in order to make their point. A problem with the use of any example is that, no matter how clear-cut it may appear to be, there will always be aspects of it that are open to nuances of interpretation. The targeted family member can often sidetrack an attempt at metacommunicating by quibbling with some minor aspect of the patient's example. Patients need to be alert to this so that they can refuse to become embroiled in nitpicking discussions about trivial issues. For example, in order for the patient in Case 9-1 to discuss the effects on her of her mother's unreasonable requests for immediate assistance, she would undoubtedly have to bring up an example of such a request. The mother could easily sidetrack the issue by quibbling over the reasonableness of any instance that the patient might bring up. The urgency of a need for assistance is always open to question. The patient's talk with her mother might turn from an attempt at metacommunication into an argument over how badly the mother needed help three months ago. The issue of the effect of the mother's behavior on the daughter would be entirely lost.

To counter nitpicking, a patient can make statements such as, "Perhaps that wasn't a perfect example, but there are many instances where this sort of thing seems to happen." A patient can often bring up a series of sequential interactions that, while all different to some degree, seem to follow a similar overall pattern. The patient can then talk about the overall pattern while refusing to argue about whether any specific example is truly representative.

Instead of nitpicking, the target may attempt to quibble with the patient's examples of family behavior by accusing the patient of overgeneralizing. No matter how often individuals behave in a similar fashion, there are always times when they do the opposite. A hateful person is at times loving, an incompetent one competent, and so on. The other can attempt to contradict a patient's assertions about anyone by bringing up a counterexample. Just as with someone designing a true-false test, patients should be careful to avoid the use of words such as *always* and *never* in discussing the behavior of any family member. If they are caught overgeneralizing, they can agree that the target's counterexample is valid but maintain that most of the time, the person being discussed behaves as they have described. Additionally, patients can often use the counterexample in the service of strengthening the point that they are trying to make. The counterexample might indicate the presence of a conflict in the person being discussed or might be evidence of some hidden quality that he or she possesses.

Case 9-6

A patient was in the process of metacommunicating with her mother about the family attitude toward men. Although the females in the family seemed to be overly dependent on men, their verbal behavior indicated a marked disdain for them. The patient's mother had, in fact, cleaned up after her fair share of alcoholics. So had the patient. Mother constantly spoke of how irresponsible the male of the species was and about all the sacrifices a woman must make for her husbands and lovers. These kinds of statements, made in front of both her daughters and sons, had striking effects on the family. The patient and her sisters felt obliged to go along with their mother's opinion; they instinctively rejected any potential suitor who might exhibit strength. Her brothers and nephews, on the other hand, acted as if they were non compos mentis, as if to live up to the mother's expectations.

In the course of the discussion of the family problem, the mother protested that the patient was overgeneralizing. While the mother had had several irresponsible partners, her current lover was very dependable. She knew that there were men on whom a woman could count. The patient quickly admitted that her mother's current relationship did seem to be an exception. She added that she realized that her mother wasn't always critical of men. "Nonetheless, in light of your horrible experiences with your own father and your husbands, I can see why you might be concerned about the inadequacies of men. I know your statements are just meant to warn me, but they are still very disheartening."

The Fine Art of Apology. Because of past hurts and misunderstandings, clients will inevitably suffer lapses of empathy in their discussions with the family, no matter how well they understand the family dynamics and how much practice they have had in metacommunicating. Sooner or later, they will lose control. They will become overly defensive or may let loose with a torrent of insults. As I mentioned previously, however, there are no irreversible errors in family metacommunication. Clients can usually turn an error into an opportunity for further discussions. Whenever they find themselves saying hurtful things to the target or in other ways disqualifying the other, they should go back at the next opportune moment and make an apology. This can occur a few minutes after a disagreeable episode or at any later time. Often it is best to wait until the passions of the moment have calmed, a process that may take days or weeks. The apology, while it should be sincere, can then be used as a springboard for metacommunication about the incident that prompted it. That incident is undoubtedly representative of a broader pattern of family interactions and is thus an excellent starting point for their exploration.

Clients can be quick to admit that their behavior was in error, but they should never apologize for their *feelings,* nor should they ever assume the entire responsibility for the whole episode. No matter how unwisely they reacted to the target, they were still reacting. Anger did not materialize out of thin air. Clients should use the episode as a vehicle for discussing their usual pattern of reacting to the target. The apology should have the following basic structure: "I'm really sorry I said all those mean things the other night, but boy, you were really getting my goat. You must have been upset with me about something." If clients have an idea about why the target became angry or distancing, they should attempt to empathize. If not, they should describe their own reactions to the target's behavior and question the target's motivation, while always giving the other the benefit of the doubt.

10

SPECIAL PROBLEMS
AND TERMINATION

In this chapter, I will look at some miscellaneous difficulties that therapists may find in getting the alternate solution implemented.

Avoiding Triangulation

Bowen's (1978) ideas concerning sending patients back to their families of origin are the basis for the type of therapy that I am describing. One of his contributions to family therapy is the concept of triangulation, the process wherein a third family member becomes embroiled in a conflict between two members of the system. Bowen feels that any dyadic relationship is inherently unstable and that a member of the unstable dyad will turn to another person to provide additional support. A member of a dyad can accomplish this by sharing secrets with a third family member or by overtly joining her or him and clustering against the other member of the original dyad. Even if a third family system member is not invited into the unstable dyad to perform this service, one will often volunteer to do so. It is in the interest of family homeostasis for the conflict between warring family members to be minimized, and triangulation provides the family with a mechanism through which to accomplish this. Someone will always be available.

Triangulation is destructive to the process of metacommunication because it attempts to contain conflict rather than to deal with the underlying causes of it so that the conflict can be resolved. The reason that the family chooses conflict containment over conflict resolution has to do with the forces that are inhibiting family metacommunication in the first place. The members of the family system are strongly motivated to protect one another from role-function destabilization, fearing that challenges to those roles will be destructive to the family in the long run. Clustering is designed to stabilize the homeostasis of the entire family, not just the clashing dyad.

Bowen (1978) recommends strongly that patients returning to the family of origin refuse to allow any family member to join them in their endeavor to differentiate from the system. Bowen feels that allowing such a joining maneuver will inevitably lead to a pattern of shifting family coalitions that will undercut the open communication necessary for the resolution of the dyadic conflicts between the patient and other family members. In addition to proscribing the taking on of an ally within the family, Bowen also concerns himself with thwarting the efforts of other family members to triangulate against the patient. The patient is helped to design elaborate, strategic-paradoxical ruses that accomplish this aim. Bowen offers examples of these in describing his experiences with his own family (Bowen, 1978, chap. 21). Here again, Bowen seems to be abandoning the collaborative, empathetic approach that he takes in his own relationship to his patients when he coaches them to deal with their families. I see no need for this. In using my approach, I have found that it is quite possible for patients to avoid the negative effects of triangulation by enlisting potential triangulators as silent allies. Other family members, if their concerns are addressed, can actually be quite helpful.

The procedure for enlisting family members differs slightly depending upon whether those members are themselves targets. I will first concentrate on how to enlist peripheral family members who are likely to interfere with the patient's metacommunicative efforts. In most instances, these family members will be siblings, but they may also be aunts, uncles, or others.

Siblings are often remarkably receptive to discussion with the patient about family problems and indeed are often relieved to discover that they are not alone in having observed them. They do not usually offer the patient the kind of resistance to a discussion of family problems that they might offer an outsider —such as a therapist—who might attempt to elicit such a conversation. Of course, the more disturbed the family, the less likely that this will hold true. Particularly in borderline families, the parents might have purposefully used the induction of sibling rivalry as a method for accomplishing their own goals. They may have done this through such maneuvers as blatant favoritism, unfair distribution of privileges and responsibilities, or an invitation to one sibling to join with the rest of the family in attacking the other. Parents might also have inadvertently fostered sibling discord by having altruistically stepped in to settle any argument that might have arisen between them. From the siblings' perspective, this behavior appears to be highly prized by the parent. The siblings continue to fight so that the parent can continue in the role of "mediator." Siblings from families showing either of these patterns will be uncooperative, because that is part of their personas.

Patients are coached to contact and enlist the help of siblings only in certain situations. First, in some cases patients may find it especially difficult to discuss family dynamics with a parent solely on the basis of their own knowledge and the guess of the therapist. They may know of a sibling who would be sympathetic to their efforts and who may also be a source of valuable confirmation or additional information about the family history and dynamics. They may feel that this sibling is trustworthy. The therapist should feel free to encourage patients to contact such a sibling. If the siblings can provide additional validation for the therapist's ideas, patients may feel less groundless when they talk to the parent.

A second circumstance where a sibling should be contacted—indeed, must be contacted—is where the likelihood is high that the sibling will interfere with the patient's metacommunicative efforts. This might happen in one of two ways. The sibling might attempt to triangulate with the target against the patient, either overtly or behind the patient's back. While this sort of apparent backstabbing may seem to be mean and underhanded, the motives of such siblings are noble. They wish to protect the target or other family members from anxiety, shame, depression, or feelings that might lead to a divorce. They may in fact be quite sympathetic to the patient's efforts but fear where the efforts will lead.

Another form of potential interference occurs when a patient succeeds in metacommunicating with the target and is thereby freed to give up parts of his or her own persona but a sibling who has been up to that point relatively uninvolved in dysfunctional behavior then steps in to assume the patient's prior role. Again, the sibling would do this only out of fears about what might happen should the patient's role function become unstable. He or she attempts to stabilize it in the same manner that had been adopted by the patient. When this happens, the patient may improve dramatically, but the overall outcome of therapy is less than satisfactory. How much has the therapist really achieved if the patient is cured but somebody else is induced to be dysfunctional in the process? Such a result may not even be satisfactory as far as the patient is concerned. The patient may begin to feel guilty about having pushed responsibility onto the sibling and might eventually be sucked back into the still dysfunctional family dynamics.

In any situation where siblings might interfere with the alternate solution, they should be contacted by the patient. This can be done prior to or concurrent with the patient's metacommunicative efforts with the major targets. Patients are coached to prevent triangulation with any such sibling through a planned sequence of steps. They first tell the sibling that they intend to discuss certain issues with the targeted family members. They then predict that the sibling may become alarmed about this prospect. They can then empathize with the fears of the sibling. This should be easy for them to do, because they share those same fears. They go on to indicate how they think they can avoid the feared negative outcome and why they think it is important to press forward. The goal here is to ease the sibling's fears so that she or he will not interfere with their efforts.

If a sibling continues to express a negative reaction after this process, and patients can not understand why, they can express puzzlement over the sibling's response and then attempt to ascertain the sibling's real fear so that it can be adequately addressed. In the case of disturbed families where the sibling becomes unreasonable, patients can handle that in exactly the same manner as they would handle unreasonable behavior from the major target.

Patients end the interaction with the sibling by expressing a desire to handle the target alone, without the direct assistance of the sibling. They express hope that the sibling will stay away for the time being. They express concern that too many cooks might spoil the broth or that should the sibling become involved, the target might feel ganged up on and become overly defensive. However, patients should add that nothing that has been said between them is in any way a secret. If a brother feels that he must add his own input or that he must warn the target about the patient's intentions, he is free to do so. If he insists upon his own direct effort at metacommunicating with the target, the patient and he should attempt to coordinate their efforts so that any predictable negative consequences can be avoided.

In most instances, the patient's contact with the sibling will forestall any destructive triangulation. Should the sibling go ahead with an effort at undermining the patient despite the contact, all is not lost. The patient will eventually find out about it and can use the sibling's manipulations as a subject for further metacommunication about the family dynamics. The sibling's actions will no doubt be further evidence for the points that the patient is trying to make with the target!

In cases where potential triangulators are themselves targets, clients can handle the situation in much the same way. One parent will often attempt to derail the client's effort to metacommunicate with the other. In fact, the therapist should always assume that this will happen unless there is significant evidence to the contrary. Clients must learn to juggle their attempts to communicate with each parent, and to do so in a flexible manner; no hard-and-fast rules can be applied. They must metacommunicate with each parent about their relationship with that parent and must also indicate to each that they plan to hold or have held similar conversations with the other. Depending on the parameters of a given case, these conversations can be held concurrently, sequentially, or in a mixture. Clients must address each parent's concerns about the discussions with the other parent in much the same way that they do with a sibling. In this manner, they help all family members alter their habit of overprotecting one another.

Existential Resistances

I have previously discussed the concept of existential anxiety, or groundlessness, and its relationship to the mirroring function of parents. In the vast majority of cases, a patient who comes to psychotherapy has never received any mirroring whatsoever for metacommunicating about the very subjects that are creating the disturbance in the family. The therapist's alternate solution to the family problem, horror of horrors, consists of almost nothing *but* metacommunication about taboo subjects. Needless to say, this creates a rather curious double bind. In order to solve the family problem so that they can be free to express themselves, patients must metacommunicate with the family; but in order to metacommunicate, they have to be somewhat free to express themselves. In light of my assertion that existential anxiety is one of the most noxious sensations in biology, and that metacommunication will for most patients lead directly to it, it is hardly a shock that patients will want to resist the therapist's directions.

When a patient does begin to metacommunicate in ways that lead or have led to family disqualifications, he or she is then relating to the family in a completely novel fashion. The quality of the experience can be likened to the experience of a professional athlete who is suddenly asked, in the middle of a game, to play the game under a completely new set of rules. Suppose a member of the National Football League in the United States were to learn at halftime that the game was going to be played, from that point on, by Canadian Football League rules. Previously, the team had four downs to make ten yards;

now they had three. Game strategies that were effective for gaining ten yards in four downs would suddenly become inappropriate. This would no doubt lead to a good deal of disorientation even if the players were familiar with the Canadian game. However, the situation would become even more unsettling, because the rule change would create yet another difficulty. The playing of the game is not an isolated event but one that takes place in a cultural context. Part of the raison d'être for a professional sporting event is the entertainment of the fans. In order to attract a crowd, the game must please the crowd. If it did not, attendance would rapidly fall off, and the game would fold. If the rules of the game were changed in midstream, the players would have no idea how to fulfill this function. The expectations of the fans regarding the relative frequency of passing and running plays differ significantly under the two sets of rules. After the switch, the players could no longer anticipate how the crowd might react.

The players in this situation would certainly become unnerved and confused and might experience a feeling of uncertainty—if not of complete unreality. This would happen even if the players were well aware of the existence of alternate ways of playing the game. The problem is that the new rules in this situation would be devoid of context. The earlier behavior of the athlete had, in a sense, defined his place in the world. The rule switch would make this definition unclear. Even if the player knew what to do, it would still not feel right. Another analogy for this feeling is the experience of people who suddenly find themselves stranded in an exotic foreign country. They know that there is a different culture out there; they may even be familiar with many of its features. They nonetheless feel disoriented. Behaviorists would say that people in this situation feel lost because of the absence or alteration of the environmental stimuli that normally cue their behavioral responses.

Because of existential anxiety, clients will often be reluctant to follow the therapist's advice. This can happen even if they have already had a few successful experiences at metacommunication. They may drag their feet, give lame excuses as to why they have not contacted the targeted relative, or indicate that they have found it impossible to get the relative in a one-on-one situation. Alternately, they may come up with statements such as these: (1) "Your advice will probably work, but it's not me." This statement may really surprise therapists. They have been hard at work, or so they think, helping the patient learn to express a true self. They are now suddenly informed that they have done nothing but help the patient construct yet another pseudo-self. They may begin to feel a certain amount of uncertainty about the theoretical position advocated here. (2) "If I start making my marriage into what you are suggesting, I'll want to leave it" or "If we start changing these roles in our family, we will have no basis for the relationship." Before I understood the concept of mutual role-function support, I found this sort of statement flabbergasting. Are these people really saying that they want the relationship so badly that they are willing to be miserable in order to continue in it, but if it starts to get better, they will want to leave? And I thought I did not believe in masochism! (3) "Discussing the patterns in our relationship this way makes me feel so silly." I always wondered why it was that the patient did not feel silly acting them out. (4) "Why should I be the one to help solve this problem? My parents had this trouble before they had me. They should be here in therapy! This is too much work and it shouldn't be my responsibility." Well, gee, that does seem kind of unfair, does it not? The only problem is, if the therapist brings in the parents, then they will insist that the grandparents come in, for the earlier generation had the problem first. The process could be endless.

When confronted with these kinds of resistances, I first attempt to ascertain whether the patient is resisting my advice because of some hidden problem or negative consequence of the agreed-upon strategy that has not been adequately addressed. Perhaps patients are stuck in a game without end, and their attempts at metacommunicating are being interpreted by the family as just another variation of their old roles. A woman who had previously been dominant in her family, for example, might be getting a subtle message that her attempts at problem solving are really a disguised attempt at renewed domination. Advice to problem solve in such an instance might be making the family problem worse rather than better. If the problem can be understood, the therapist and the patient can then figure out a way to get around it in order to have a good outcome.

If an extensive exploration of the consequences of metacommunicating is fruitless, but the patient continues with the resistances, I then look to the possibility that the patient is unable to deal with the feelings of groundlessness and existential isolation that my advice brings with it. Statements such as "It's not 'me' to do this" and "If I stop this role, I won't know how to act" indicate that my advice, having never been mirrored by the patient's family, is causing the patient to feel alien, strange, or disoriented. Additionally, these statements may indicate that the question of "what comes afterward" is frightening the patient. Since the patient's intrafamilial relationships are based to a large degree on mutual role-function support, the discontinuation of this behavior will indeed leave a major void in the patient's life that he or she has not yet had time to fill. A person who alters role behavior will inevitably be confronted with a sense of purposelessness and not knowing how to behave. This sense of meaninglessness will be alleviated somewhat by the sense of purpose associated with the task of family metacommunication. Afterward, however, time will be required for the patient and his or her family to learn to relate to each other's true selves. The feeling that a relationship will fall apart if it changes is a reflection of uncertainty about this process. Once the family problem is solved, then what?

This latter fear can be reinforced by the nature of the therapeutic relationship. When the therapist and patient have worked to successfully modify the family system dynamics, their relationship does, in fact, come to an end. The patient and therapist do not go on to relate to each other on another level. One of the tasks of termination, as I will discuss later, is to prevent the termination process itself from influencing the patient to resume old patterns.

It is essential that the therapist not make light of the distress caused by groundlessness or attempt to protect the patient from it. In order to succeed at the alternate solution, the patient is going to have to experience a certain degree of it. There is no way around it. Not only that, but the patient is also going to induce some groundlessness in the rest of the family. As with any feeling, attempting to protect people from this feeling is almost always counterproductive. The ultimate pain suffered by all involved will be increased rather than minimized through attempted shielding. The altruistic paradox will operate. Having said that, I will now add that the therapist can intervene in ways that will keep the patient's existential anxiety within manageable limits, so that it does not completely scuttle the alternate solution. Although the therapist's mirroring power for the patient is small compared with that of the patient's family system, the therapist can give the patient's groundlessness feelings a context of their own. The unreal and absurd feelings associated with the patient's new behavior can themselves be given grounding through consensual validation by the therapist. The therapist can do this by using two devices: naming and predicting the patient's anxiety and empathizing with it.

Although groundlessness is an extremely common experience, it is seldom described in everyday conversation or in the popular press. Because it is so indescribable, it remains for most individuals a nameless fear. When experiencing this feeling, patients may feel that they are the only people in the world who suffer from it. The therapist can help them to become less frightened by putting a name to it and informing them about exactly how common a feeling it is. Since the therapist seems familiar with it, this can be reassuring. Patients are told what they will experience, when they might experience it, and that the experience will, as all things must, pass.

When I outline the alternate solution, I often warn patients that in following the prescription, they may feel extremely uncomfortable. I explain that the behavior will be anxiety provoking because it goes against the rules by which the family has always operated. The patient is like a family Columbus, sailing off into uncharted territories, and the new behavior will take some getting used to. The behavior will feel "not-them" because they have never before received any consensual validation for engaging in it and have therefore never considered it in their behavioral repertoire. I may also predict that the family will experience this fear also, and that this may cause an initial negative reaction to the new behavior. The negative reaction will add to their anxiety. I warn the patient about clustering. I also inform patients that the degree of discomfort will gradually decrease as they gain experience with new patterns of family interrelationships.

In response to patients' fears that they will have no basis for continued family relationships should the family patterns change, I give reassurance. I tell patients that things will seem a bit shaky at first but that the seeds of a more real and satisfying relationship with family members are already present. They have some familiarity with the interests and inclinations of the true selves of family members. These will gradually form the basis of a new pattern of relating. Additionally, a new "relationship about the relationship" will develop.

The therapist can provide additional mirroring of the groundlessness feelings by empathizing with them. I often say something like, "I know how scary this is for you; I hope you don't think I'm being cavalier about it." Therapists who do not think that they are familiar with the feeling need only think back to the time that they held their first individual psychotherapy session with a client when no supervisor was around to provide assistance. Empathetic statements can be especially effective if they are coupled with a transference resistance interpretation. As the reader will recall, the patient in therapy will have invariably used maneuvers to induce groundlessness in the therapist that parallel those that the family has used to induce groundlessness in the patient. The therapist can say, "I know how you feel when you think about talking to your family, knowing that they might react with (previously described disqualifications). I had a similar experience when you reacted that way to me."

Clients can also be coached to make use of their own feelings of groundlessness to empathize with the rest of the family system. If they can learn to understand that the family's disqualifications of them stem from precisely the same kinds of fears that they are now experiencing, then the family's behavior will become more understandable to them. A patient can say to the family, "I know that what I am saying is hard to deal with; I have a hard time dealing with it myself."

The therapist must show patience with existential resistance. Patients often take time to get up their courage, and they should be given some space to do so. The therapist can offer gentle encouragement. I sometimes say that, just because people are anxious about doing something, this does not mean that they cannot go ahead and do it anyway. I persistently maintain that, in order to get better, the patient must go ahead with the prescription as soon as possible. I continue to explore the possibility that some potential negative consequence has not yet been addressed. However, if I find that the patient seems, over time, to be moving no closer to contacting the targeted family member despite the absence of unaddressed potential negative consequences, or if I find myself becoming a nag, I consider the possibility that a covert transference resistance is occurring. The patient and therapist may be locked in a power struggle.

Power Struggles

It often occurs that a major part of the persona of an individual is predicated upon the defiance of authority figures or professionals, such as therapists. Additionally, personas built upon the notion that members of one sex are unreliable or incompetent are far from rare—and the therapist might happen to be a member of that sex. Then there is the matter of professional patients, who come to therapy not to change but to receive confirmation of their own defectiveness so as to better serve the aims of a persona. In these situations, the mere presence of the therapist, in the capacity of a therapist, can often be used by the patient to reinforce rather than change dysfunctional behavior. The therapist in this situation is supporting the persona of the patient just by walking into the room! These patients will often be quite cooperative and go along with everything the therapist is doing—until it comes time to act on the alternate solution. Such patients then state that they just cannot get themselves to do what the therapist advises, even though they agree that the advice will probably help a lot. And they just do not know why they are having so much trouble.

Obsessive patients will become obsessive about why they cannot do what the therapist prescribes; histrionic patients will get all emotional about it. They may seem to cooperate with the therapist's efforts to uncover the *real* reason for the resistance, leaving no stone unturned. Alternately, they may bring up a host of semilogical reasons, most of which the therapist has already refuted, for disliking the therapist's ideas or bring up a fear or two that the therapist has already adequately addressed. A therapist who enjoys the intellectual stimulation provided by the process of argument must be careful to avoid getting involved in rehashing old discussions or being seduced into following clues provided by the patient that have already proved to be red herrings. Therapists should handle this situation by reacting in a way similar to the way that they react to transference acting out early in therapy. They should, this late in the process, have a wealth of information concerning how the patient's family relates over the issues of authority figures, male and female competence, and system-member defectiveness. They use this knowledge as a rationale for inviting the patient to metacommunicate about the transference relationship. I say something like, "You know, we've discussed at length how your family indirectly warned you about the overall unreliability of men. Since I'm a man, this could certainly explain why it is so difficult for you to go along with what I am recommending."

The goal here, once again, is not to explore the transference as in psychoanalysis but to induce the patient to stop the transference acting out. If the therapist's interpretation is incorrect, the patient will refute it in a reasonable manner. If the therapist's interpretation is correct but the patient denies it, then the patient will be obliged to quit acting as if it were true. If he or she admits to it, the therapist can then confront the patient with the consequences of the behavior: "I hate to point out the obvious, but we're in a bit of a bind. In order for you to get over this problem, you're going to have to be able to trust me, but since you haven't got over the problem, you're having a hard time doing so. I may not be able to help you if you can't get past that." One other intervention that is sometimes effective when all else fails is for the therapist to say simply, "I think we have a clear fix on all the ins and outs of this problem. It comes down to this: are you ready or are you not to do whatever it takes to solve it?" The therapist should be clearly referring to the alternate solution that has already been presented when making this statement. In order for the statement to be effective, the therapist must exude confidence that the solution will indeed solve the problem.

Ghosts

When individuals die, their influence on other members of the family system does not suddenly evaporate into thin air. The family members left behind do not go on as if the deceased had never even existed. The present is shaped by the past and contains residues of all that came before. In some individuals, a relationship with a deceased family member is more influential in shaping behavior than are current relationships with living family members. A grieving widow from a long-term marriage may experience the "presence" of the lost spouse in a very meaningful sense until she dies.

Maladaptive behavior patterns that stemmed originally from family system dynamics that are now history and that are not reinforced by any current family relationships can be maintained without additional reinforcement for quite some time after the deaths of major systemic figures. However, if I am correct in my belief that maladaptive behavior is performed for the express purpose of maintaining family system homeostasis, and this function is no longer served because of changes in the system caused by the deaths of certain holons, then one would expect the maladaptive behavior to gradually decrease and then cease altogether. The reason this is so is that, without the reinforcement provided by the net effect of the behavior on the family system, the behavior is subject to extinction. Extinction (Reese, 1966) is the process discovered by behaviorists by which nonreinforced behavior gradually stops over time. Dysfunctional behavior that was originally reinforced by the reactions of family members now deceased would be subject to this process. Even the most ingrained and disturbed behavior is subject to extinction. The process can frequently be seen in "burned out" schizophrenics and drug abusers. When the system dies off, particularly if the individual has reached the midlife passage, the self-destructive behavior decreases in frequency.

One of the most perplexing difficulties I encountered when I first began using my approach was attempting to design a modification of the treatment for certain isolated individuals whose families of origin were all deceased but who nonetheless continued to exhibit self-destructive behavior patterns. One cannot send a patient back to a family to metacommunicate if no family exists. However, most patients whose parents are deceased are involved in a current relationship or relationships that are providing an ongoing context and reinforcement for their maladaptive behavior patterns. Metacommunication within these relationships can substitute for metacommunication with parents. If these relationships change, any self-destructive behavior that originally stemmed from family members who are now deceased will gradually disappear. A few individuals, however, appear to be completely isolated or fail to improve after successful metacommunication with surviving family members.

I now believe that all such patients have a hidden current relationship that is reinforcing the persona that they originally developed within their family of origin. Whenever a patient does not appear to have any relationships that reinforce dysfunctional behavior, or whenever the alternate solution fails, such a relationship should be searched for.

Case 10-1

A single woman in her forties, depressed and lonely, was studiously avoiding becoming involved with men. The patient's determination to avoid marriage stemmed originally from the antifamily feelings of her family of origin. Their behavior had suggested to the patient that close family ties meant nothing but bickering, debasement, exploitation, irrational demands, and, ultimately, martyrdom. Furthermore, their behavior suggested that once a person was involved in a bad relationship, he or she just had to accept it as it was and suffer with it.

Over a long course of therapy, the patient gradually

learned to understand the pattern in her family and some of the reasons for it. She came to admit that she really did want to share her life with a man, and she let go of her fatalism about bad relationships. Nonetheless, she continued to drag her feet when it came to making an enthusiastic effort to meet a potential partner.

The patient appeared to be isolated. Her parents were deceased, and she had completely lost contact with the few members of her parents' generation who still survived. She had a younger sister, but her infrequent contacts with her did not appear to be the only factor in maintaining her dysfunctional behavior. However, since there appeared to be no one else, the patient and I began working on re-establishing ties with the sister and metacommunicating with her about the family pattern and her attitudes about males. This proceeded slowly but steadily. Much to my confusion, even after this process was well under way, the patient continued to procrastinate when it came to meeting men. She knew where and how to meet them but could not make herself do what was necessary with any degree of consistency.

I first explored the possibility that she was engaged in a power struggle with me. While there appeared to be considerable evidence for this, the usual interventions went nowhere. The apparent transference resistance seemed to me to be a red herring. Finally, I got the idea that perhaps there was someone else in the patient's life who was still complicating the therapy. I asked, "Who else might be negatively affected if you got married?"

As it turned out, the patient had an extremely important relationship that she had barely mentioned in over two years of therapy. She socialized several times a week with another single woman with whom she had been close friends since childhood. While the patient had informed all of her other friends that she was in the market for a man, she had never mentioned it to this one. She had also hidden from this friend the fact that she was re-establishing her relationship with her sister.

Before leaving the subject of ghosts, I would like to address one other issue, the problem of unresolved or delayed grief reactions. The grieving process is a mechanism which speeds the diminution of the influence of deceased family members on the living. That is, as the patient mourns the loss and begins to let go, the behavior that had been performed for the benefit of the deceased begins to lose its context. If an individual completes the mourning process, I believe that extinction of maladaptive behavior patterns that are no longer reinforced by remaining family members will soon follow. If the patient is unable to grieve, the extinction process could take a great deal longer.

The grieving process can be retarded if grieving per se, or some important aspect of it, disturbs the family homeostasis. The avoidance of grief in this situation becomes part of the persona of the individual, and consequently the influence of the ghost of the lost relative remains higher than it might be otherwise. This commonly occurs, paradoxically, in situations where the members of the family system are trying to protect one another from family enmeshment or the pain of grief work. This is yet another manifestation of the altruistic paradox. The "protection" may come from the living members of the family system, but it can also come from the deceased.

As we have seen, parents who distance their child from themselves, by whatever mechanism, are usually attempting to demonstrate to the child some of the hazards of being overly enmeshed in the family system. Such parents will often hope that the child will be less affected by family considerations than they were. In order to help their child break away from what the parents consider to be the bad influences of family life, parents who cannot discuss their problems openly will often behave in a hateful manner toward the child. They aim to drive the child away by provoking his or her anger at themselves. They hope, albeit ambivalently, that the child will want to have as little to do with them as possible, so that he or she will not be overly tied to them as they were to their own parents.

What happens, then, when a distancing parent dies? The children in such a situation are left with a sense of relief—even if they feel guilty about it. The relationship with the hateful, disturbing parent is now a thing of the past. They are so angry at the parent that they are almost glad that the parent has died. An unfortunate side effect of this anger is that the children become impaired in their ability to grieve for the departed parent. A major part of grieving over a loss is the acknowledgment of the importance of the loss. One must feel the pain that comes with the realization that what has been an important part of one's life is no longer present. One must feel sad over what one no longer has. Angry individuals are in no mood to feel these feelings, but rather concentrate on the positive aspects of the loss. They think about all the bad times they will no longer have, rather than the good things that they will be missing. Why on earth should they feel sad?

Similar feelings are often purposely induced in an individual by other members of the family system. The dying will sometimes attempt to anger another family member specifically to prevent the other from being adversely affected by the impending death. They *want* the rest of the family to be unaffected by their death, in hopes of sparing them the pain of grief. Patients who commit suicide often do so in the most hostile manner possible, so that those left behind will be angry rather than sad. The suicide looks to all the world like a parting shot.

In any of these situations, the mourning process for those left behind can become impaired and the influence of the deceased paradoxically remain higher than it would be otherwise. The therapist can help them begin to modify their anger and to feel sad about the loss by helping them understand the motivations of the lost relative. Patients can be coached to discuss their feelings with other surviving relatives who may share some of them. If they know that other people are also angry with the dead for reasons that are similar to their own, they will not feel as guilty about their feelings. They will then start to believe that the anger is justified, but they will also know that the angry feelings were induced in them by the deceased for understandable reasons.

Another situation where the grieving process may become impaired occurs when the rest of the family attempts to stop an individual from grieving in order to protect her or him from the pain. This kind of behavior can at times be culturally sanctioned, although even cultures that value highly the stoic, stiff-upper-lip approach to grief have mechanisms whereby the sadness can find some expression. Only when the cultural prohibitions against emotionalism become exaggerated because of a reaction formation against emotional tendencies does the grieving process become compromised.

Case 10-2

An elderly woman was having trouble adjusting to the loss of her husband of over half a century. She seemed obsessed by his presence even after several years and had not made any strong attempts to make a new life for herself. She finally attempted suicide. This was a classic case of an unresolved grief reaction. When the patient's family situation was explored, I found that the family was doing everything in its power to make the woman forget about her husband. They refused to go with her to the cemetery, begged her to take down his pictures, and became especially disturbed when she cried about him. Clearly, this family behavior was having an effect exactly opposite to the one that they intended. Because the patient felt so guilty about feeling sad about her husband's death, seeing her family suffer so because of her sadness, she had not been able to properly grieve for him. Although she seemed to be overly involved with her husband's memory, she was in fact not involved enough. The patient was coached to metacommunicate with her family about this difficulty and solicit their help in allowing her to grieve.

Termination of Therapy

After clients have to some extent covered the major family issues with each of the targeted family members, the therapist will begin to notice that they are improving in many aspects of their lives. Affective symptomatology and self-destructive behavior will diminish; isolated single individuals will begin to meet people and go out on dates; occupationally impaired individuals will begin to make advancements at work; and so forth.

Therapists should encourage clients to make these improvements, but seldom must they give much advice about how to proceed. Once clients are uninhibited and begin to think about such matters as how to meet members of the opposite sex, it is surprising how easy it is for them to think of ways to do it, even in situations where few options are available. If they cannot find a way, then chances are that some family issue or some relationship has not been properly addressed.

If their chief complaints are clearing up, and real changes in family interactive styles have been made, patients will most likely bring up the issue of termination of therapy themselves. The strong emphasis placed by psychoanalysts on the termination phase of therapy is connected to the idea of the transference neurosis. An analyst has, from a systems perspective, become an important part of the patient's system. It is therefore hardly shocking that the end of analysis will be highly traumatic for the patient. It then follows that the termination phase of analytically oriented therapy must be handled very carefully, and it usually ends up being a long, drawn-out affair.

An integral part of the approach recommended in the present volume is the avoidance as much as possible of transference and the emphasis on dealing with the problem at its source —the family. It therefore follows that, once the family problem has been dealt with and the patient is beginning to experiment with alternate, self-confirming behavior, the therapist and patient should terminate therapy, and strong emotional reactions to the termination should be kept to a minimum. Once again, therapists cannot expect the patient to have no reaction, for as much as they have tried to avoid doing so, they have taken on importance for the patient. However, in keeping with the view that patients are not defective, therapists can expect the patient to deal with the end of therapy in a realistic and mature manner. They do not have to play games, as some family systems and paradoxical therapists do, in order to extricate themselves from the patient's life.

Many paradoxical psychotherapists take great pains to give all the credit for any improvement to patients and minimize their own contribution. This, in my opinion, represents an attempt by the therapist to make sure that patients view themselves as powerful and to minimize transference reactions to termination. If the therapist takes too much credit for the change in patients and their family systems, a danger exists that patients will begin, or continue, to play the role of defective and credit all the improvement to the wonderful therapist. When patients maintain this fiction, they have really not made much of a change. As soon as the therapist is gone, the improvement will evaporate, for the therapist alone is seen as responsible for it.

On the other hand, if patients do not acknowledge the therapist's contribution, they are still in my view not behaving realistically. They have, in a sense, refused to really accept what the therapist has given them and have devalued the therapist. Many patients, particularly those from borderline families, devalue others as part of their personas. If the therapist allows patients to indulge in that at termination, then there is a danger that they will get the idea that the therapist does not really want them to change, and they may fall back into previous roles.

Another concern of family systems therapists who make use of paradoxical techniques concerns the matter of relapse. The paradoxical therapist attempts to prevent any future relapses into dysfunctional behavior by predicting that they will occur (Weeks and L'Abate, 1982), in hopes that the patient will become indignant and resolve to prove the therapist wrong. When it comes time for the therapy to terminate, I attempt to determine whether patients are reacting to the end of therapy realistically and to assess how they might react to a relapse into old family dysfunctional patterns. My intention is to make certain that the work of the therapy will not be undone. At the end of therapy, patients should be able to acknowledge both their own and the therapist's contributions toward any improvement that may have taken place. They should not expect their or their family's behavior in the future to be perfect but should expect that some of the old patterns will re-emerge from time to time. If I have doubts that they are being realistic about any of these matters, I will bring the subject to their attention. The way that I do this may remind some readers of paradoxical interventions such as predicting a relapse, but my intentions are straightforward rather than paradoxical. The patient and his or her family *will* from time to time revert to old behavior patterns; I mention this because I do not wish the patient to become unduly discouraged and give up on the new patterns.

To a patient who has in the past played the role of defective, I might say, "In light of your past history of selling yourself short, you may be tempted to give me all the credit for the improvement in your (life, family relationships, and so on). I've helped you, but it was you who were able to make use of what we have discussed; I've been really impressed by your ability to do that." With a patient with a history of devaluing others, I listen for evidence of either overidealization or devaluation of the role of the therapist. If I hear either to a major extent, I will point it out to the patient and express concern that we may not have completed our work. To patients whose family relationships are built entirely around the paradigm of one member of a dyad helping the other with a problem, I express concern that the end of therapy may reinforce the patient's previous views about relationships. Termination may seem to provide proof of the notion that if a relationship is not based on some sort of problem solving, then there is no basis for its continuance. To all patients, I predict that they and their family may find themselves falling back into old patterns in the future. Old habits are hard to break. However, they now know what to do about it should it happen, so they should not be discouraged.

The last order of business is to arrange some kind of follow-up. I want to know whether what I am doing with my patients is having some lasting benefit. I tell patients that I would like to contact them about a year after termination to see how they are doing. At that time I will inquire, by interview or written questionnaire, about how the patient is relating to other significant family system members over the issues that were deemed important in therapy. I will also want to know whether the patient has reverted to any previous self-destructive behavior patterns.

CONCLUSION:
THE DUALITY OF
SELF AND SYSTEM

In these last few pages, I will briefly review and tie together the key elements in the unified approach to the understanding and treatment of self-destructive behavior. The unified approach suggests that the key to understanding and stopping such behavior is not found through a study of individuals isolated from their social context, nor is it found through a study of the social context without reference to the functioning of the individuals who constitute it. Human consciousness is a paradox. We are completely separate from one another, yet at the same time, we are a part of a larger whole. We are inextricably enmeshed with our cohorts and even our ancestors. We often do not realize how much we are influenced by others, nor do we often realize how alone we really are.

An understanding of self-destructiveness can be found by looking at the nature of the relationship between the self and the system or collective. This book aimed to establish the following points:

1. The relationship between self and system is not a constant but a variable.

2. The self differentiates from the collective in a process known as separation-individuation.
3. All individuals go through this process as they negotiate the passages of individual development.
4. At each stage of human development, individuals have been able to differentiate more and more from the collective as human culture has evolved throughout history.
5. Consensual validation from other members of the system is necessary for individuals to feel comfortable expressing individuated behavior.
6. Because individuals have an inborn biological propensity to concern themselves with the survival of the species, they are willing to sacrifice themselves, or aspects of themselves, in order to further what they perceive to be the greater good of the collective.
7. When individuals find that certain differentiated aspects of self seem to threaten the immediate representatives of the species, the family system, they will attempt to suppress or even sacrifice those self-aspects.
8. In order to do so, they develop a false self, or persona, which is then maintained by a variety of self-suppressive devices such as self-scaring or self-mortification. The development of a persona often causes individuals to appear to be incapable of certain kinds of activities, which makes them appear to be defective in ways that they are not.
9. The needs of the family system to respond to the evolution of differentiation in the ambient culture conflict with the needs of the system for stability and homeostasis.
10. Younger members of the family are often induced by the needs of the larger culture to behave in a fashion that is far more differentiated than the behavior of the parents. The parents, who are the leaders of the family system and its most important constituents, may be unable to comfortably tolerate such behavior, even when they are themselves attracted to it. The family system becomes threatened.
11. This problem often cannot be solved in ways other than through the sacrifice of the younger system members' in-

dividuality because of two factors: the tendency of family members to protect one another from anxiety and shame, leading to an avoidance of metacommunication between them, and the tendency of family members to rely on past experience in evaluating new family behavior, leading to the so-called game without end.

12.   These factors not only lead to impaired individual functioning but retard the system from adjusting to new cultural contingencies. The efforts of individuals to protect one another, in particular, lead to eventual harm for all.

A therapist can solve the problem of self-sacrifice by working with individuals and teaching them how to avoid the difficulties that lead to impaired family problem solving. The pioneer in this approach is Bowen (1978). He uses education, logic, and collaboration to coach his patients into dealing differently with their families. However, what he teaches them often involves techniques other than education, logic, and cooperation. A therapist can instead teach patients to adopt a problem-solving approach with their families. Specifically, patients can learn to overcome their resistances to metacommunicating about family difficulties. They can learn to bring up systemic problems in ways that do not induce negative reactions from other members of their family systems. The keys to effective metacommunication are empathy, avoidance of moralistic blaming behavior, and respect for the integrity and potency of all family members.

In therapy, patients come to an expert to learn how they are induced by the reactions of others to behave in self-destructive ways and why the others behave in the ways that they do. Patients learn to empathize with and understand the reasons for the negative behavior of other system members without agreeing that the behavior is good and without sacrificing their own emotions. They learn to differentiate between emotional reactivity and emotional reactions. They learn to tolerate and to subvert attempts made by other family members to stop them from proceeding in the task of metacommunicating. They have an opportunity to practice what they have learned by role playing with the therapist.

Specifically, the patient is trained to deal with various maneuvers that the rest of the system uses to disqualify her or him. These maneuvers represent attempts to withdraw consensual validation from the patient and include accusations of selfishness, changing the subject, unreasonable behavior, double binds, blame shifting, nitpicking, overgeneralization, mental gymnastics, and fatalism. The patient is also trained to prevent family members from uniting in various combinations to defeat the patient's efforts to metacommunicate. Once the systemic problem has been dealt with, psychiatric symptoms and maladaptive behavior problems begin to disappear.

A unified approach to psychotherapy shares with individual therapy its respect for individuality, while at the same time, it incorporates systems thinking by recognizing that individuals are innately reactive to their social environment and cannot be divorced from it. I have attempted to present an understandable, utilitarian guide to an effective way to help others express their own full potential. My hope is that these ideas can be further refined in order to advance the aims of the behavioral sciences.

REFERENCES

Alberti, R., and Emmons, M. *Your Perfect Right.* San Luis Obispo, Calif.: Impact, 1974.

American Psychiatric Association. *Diagnostic and Statistical Manual of Mental Disorders.* (3rd ed.) Washington, D.C.: American Psychiatric Association, 1980.

Asch, S. E. "Effects of Group Pressure upon the Modification and Distortion of Judgment." In H. Guetzkow (ed.), *Groups, Leadership, and Men.* Madison, N.J.: Carnegie Press, 1951.

Asch, S. E. *Social Psychology.* Englewood Cliffs, N.J.: Prentice-Hall, 1952.

Asch, S. E. "Studies of Independence and Conformity: A Minority of One Against a Unanimous Majority." *Psychological Monographs,* 1956, *70* (9), 416.

Berne, E. *Games People Play.* New York: Grove Press, 1964.

Bowen, M. *Family Therapy in Clinical Practice.* New York: Jason Aronson, 1978.

Braver, M. "Variations of Consciousness in History." Unpublished paper, California School of Professional Psychology, Los Angeles, 1983.

Burke, J. *Connections.* Boston: Little, Brown, 1978.

Capra, F. *The Tao of Physics.* Boston: Shambhala, 1975.

De Laszlo, V. (ed.). *The Basic Writings of C. G. Jung.* New York: Modern Library, 1959.

Ellis, A., and Grieger, R. *Handbook of Rational Emotive Therapy.* New York: Springer, 1977.

Erikson, E. *Childhood and Society.* (2nd ed.) New York: Norton, 1963.

Freud, A. *The Ego and the Mechanisms of Defense.* (Rev. ed.) New York: International Universities Press, 1966.

Fromm, E. *Escape from Freedom.* New York: Avon Books, 1969. (Originally published 1941.)

Ginsburg, H., and Opper, S. *Piaget's Theory of Intellectual Development.* Englewood Cliffs, N.J.: Prentice-Hall, 1969.

Greenleaf, J. *Co-Alcoholic and Para-Alcoholic: Who's Who and What's the Difference?* Los Angeles: Jael Greenleaf, 1981.

Greenson, R. *The Technique and Practice of Psychoanalysis.* New York: International Universities Press, 1967.

Haley, J. *Strategies of Psychotherapy.* Orlando, Fla.: Grune & Stratton, 1963.

Haley, J. *Leaving Home: The Therapy of Disturbed Young People.* New York: McGraw-Hill, 1980.

Hines, P. M., and Boyd-Franklin, N. "Black Families." In M. McGoldrick, J. Pearce, and J. Giordano (eds.), *Ethnicity and Family Therapy.* New York: Guilford Press, 1982.

Kohut, H. *The Analysis of the Self.* New York: International Universities Press, 1971.

Kohut, H. *The Restoration of the Self.* New York: International Universities Press, 1977.

Langs, R. *The Technique of Psychoanalytic Psychotherapy.* New York: Jason Aronson, 1973.

McGoldrick, M., and Gerson, R. *Genograms in Family Assessment.* New York: Norton, 1985.

McGoldrick, M., Pearce, J. K., and Giordano, J. (eds.). *Ethnicity and Family Therapy.* New York: Guilford Press, 1982.

Madanes, C. *Strategic Family Therapy.* San Francisco: Jossey-Bass, 1981.

Masterson, J. *The Narcissistic and Borderline Disorders: An Integrated Developmental Approach.* New York: Brunner/Mazel, 1981.

Minuchin, S., and Fishman, H. C. *Family Therapy Techniques.* Cambridge, Mass.: Harvard University Press, 1981.

Minuchin, S., Rosman, B., and Baker, L. *Psychosomatic Fami-*

lies: Anorexia Nervosa in Context. Cambridge, Mass.: Harvard University Press, 1978.

Moreno, Z. "Psychodrama, Role Theory and the Concept of the Social Atom." Address presented at the Evolution of Psychotherapy Conference, Phoenix, Arizona, Dec. 11, 1985.

Palazzolli, M. S., Boscolo, L., Cecchin, G., and Prata, G. *Paradox and Counterparadox.* New York: Jason Aronson, 1978.

Perls, F. *The Gestalt Approach and Eyewitness to Therapy.* New York: Bantam Books, 1973.

Rand, A. *For the New Intellectual.* New York: Signet Books, 1961.

Reese, E. P. *The Analysis of Human Operant Conditioning.* Dubuque, Iowa: Brown, 1966.

Schultz, S. *Family Systems Therapy: An Integration.* New York: Jason Aronson, 1984.

Sheehy, G. *Passages: Predictable Crises of Adult Life.* New York: Dutton, 1974.

Slipp, S. *Object Relations: A Dynamic Bridge Between Individual and Family Treatment.* New York: Jason Aronson, 1984.

Sloane, P. *Psychoanalytic Understanding of the Dream.* New York: Jason Aronson, 1979.

Sours, J. *Starving to Death in a Sea of Objects: The Anorexia Nervosa Syndrome.* New York: Jason Aronson, 1980.

Spiegel, J. "An Ecological Model of Ethnic Families." In M. McGoldrick, J. K. Pearce, and J. Giordano (eds.), *Ethnicity and Family Therapy.* New York: Guilford Press, 1982.

Steiner, C. *Games Alcoholics Play: The Analysis of Life Scripts.* New York: Ballantine Books, 1971.

Thomas, A., Chess, S., and Birch, H. "The Origin of Personality." *Scientific American,* 1970, *223* (2), 102.

Toffler, A. *Future Shock.* New York: Bantam Books, 1970.

Toman, W. *Family Constellation.* New York: Springer, 1961.

Wachtel, E., and Wachtel, P. L. *Family Dynamics in Individual Psychotherapy: A Guide to Clinical Strategies.* New York: Guilford Press, 1986.

Watzlawick, P., Beavin, J., and Jackson, D. *Pragmatics of Human Communication.* New York: Norton, 1967.

Weeks, G., and L'Abate, L. *Paradoxical Psychotherapy: Theory and Practice with Individuals, Couples, and Families.* New York: Brunner/Mazel, 1982.

Wile, D. *Couples Therapy: A Nontraditional Approach.* New York: Wiley, 1981.

Wolpe, J. *The Practice of Behavior Therapy.* (2nd ed.) New York: Pergamon Press, 1973.

Yalom, I. *Existential Psychotherapy.* New York: Basic Books, 1980.

INDEX

A

Actor's paradox: and anorexia, 136; and self-suppression, 72-73; and sexuality, 180-181

Ad hominem, and self-suppression, 100

Agoraphobia, case example of, 202, 203, 204, 205, 207-208, 212-213, 214, 320-323

Alabama, University of, integrated team at, 124

Alberti, R., 71, 298, 305

Alcoholics Anonymous, 8

Alcoholism: and defective self, 3, 6-8, 10; as involuntary, 201

Alienations, and self-sacrifice, 68

Alternate solution: advancing, 283-297; and resistance, 340-341; strategy of, 286-287

Altruistic motives: and anger, 275-277, 303; cases of, 271-274; as cause of maladaptive behavior, 227; establishing, 269-277

Altruistic paradox: damage from, 74-79; in family interactions, 128-129; and grief, 347, 349; principle of, 25; and resistance, 340; and self-expression, 70-72; and self-sacrifice, 67-79; worst-case scenario of, 73-74

Alzheimer's disease, and pathophysiology, 5

American Psychiatric Association, 108-109

Amish, and collective, 50-51

Anger: and altruistic motives, 275-277, 303; and avenger role, 148-149; and behavioral options, 70-71; child as outlet for, 167, 188, 208-209; constructive expression of, 281; and cultural events, 137, 148-149; and grief, 348; and transference resistance, 265; by women, 152; and worst-case scenario, 99-100

Anorexia: and cultural change, 129, 132-133, 143-144; and family interactions, 133-136; and self unmasked, 80

Anxiety: existential, 60-61; in family, 278; framing the problem for, 251, 259

Apology, in metacommunication, 330

Asch, S. E., 65

Asthma, and psychosomatic symptoms, 199-200

Attitudes: on family system, 224-225; on people as not defective, 218-221; principles of, 218-226; on rationality, 262-263; on solution to problems, 222-224; on therapist as expert, 221-222; on therapist's value, 226

Austria, cultural evolution in, 177-178

Autonomy: development of, 37-38; doubt related to, 58; mirroring, 125; sacrifice of, 155, 156

Avenger role: and family interactions, 148-153; in hysterical family, 185

B

Baker, L., 5

Beavin, J., 62, 120

Begging the question: case of, 97-98; in framing the problem, 263; and self-suppression, 95-98

Behavior: backfiring of, 277-283; developmental view of, 4; duality of self and system in, 353-356; goal of, not means, 220; maladaptive, function of, 269-277; maladaptive, solution to, 222-224; motivation for, 1-2; physiological view of, 4-5; polarized, and self-sacrifice, 81-83; self-destructive, framing the problem for, 251-253; self-destructive, net effect of, 270, 315; as self-expression, 71-72; unreasonable, in metacommunication, 315-318. *See also* Net effect of behavior; Principle of opposite behavior

Behavioralists, and environmental stimuli, 81

Berne, E., 96, 265

Betty, 279-281, 283

Bipolar disorder, and pathophysiology, 5

Birch, H., 158

Black families: and anger, 148, 150-151; avenger role in, 149-152; cultural change and personality disturbance for, 117-129; and micropatterns, 139; saga of, 122-125

Blame: and negative reactions, 302-306; and praising motivation, 309-311; shifting, in metacommunication, 324-327

Borderline personality syndrome: and altruistic paradox, 78-79; and defective self, 3, 209-210; and devaluing, 351; history taking for, 245; hospitalization for, 250; and illogical reasoning, 265; mental gymnastics in, 191; and narcissist spouse, 193-196; parental role-function instability in, 187; and sibling rivalry, 333; and splitting, 9, 191; in systems context, 185-197; violence in, 196-197; women in, 191-193

Boscolo, L., 129

Bowen, M., 2, 17-18, 20, 21, 164, 199, 209, 217-218, 301, 302, 331, 332, 355

Boyd-Franklin, N., 152

Braver, M., 46

Brooklyn Dodgers, integrated, 123

Bryant, P., 124

Bulimia, case example of, 201-202, 203, 204

Burke, J., 46-47

C

Canada, and individuation, 50

Capra, F., 23

Casanti, N., 131-133, 134, 143-144

Casanti, S., 130, 131, 132-133

Casanti family, 129-134, 143-144

Castration anxiety, and hysterical family, 181, 184

Castro, F., 100

Cecchin, G., 129

Change, systems in opposition to, 54-55

Changing the subject, in metacommunication, 314

Chess, S., 158

Children: acting out, 166-168; assigned roles for, 168-171; avenger role for, 148-153; go-between role for, 183-184; hate provoking behavior by, 188-190; homeostasis restored by, 146-148; as identified patients, 159; lightning rod role of, 208-209; as saviors, 153-157; and sexuality, 182-

185; sibling roles of, 157-159,
333
China, People's Republic of, and
collective, 51
Clustering: and disqualification, 63;
in metacommunication, 301
Coaching: analysis of, 298-330; to
avoid triangulation, 334-335;
background on, 298-300; cases
of, 303-305, 311-312, 318-323,
325-327, 329-330; and grief,
348, 349; and negative reactions,
302-306; on principles and techniques of metacommunication,
306-330; on special problems,
331-349; starting, 300-302
Collective unconscious, and individuation, 23-24
Communication deviance: handling,
268-269; and self-sacrifice, 102-
104
Compulsive behavior: and control,
252; and cultural events, 136-
138; and groundlessness, 66; as
involuntary, 200-201, 252; as
polarized, 82; repetition, 2, 3-12
Confidentiality, with relatives in
session, 293
Consensual validation: importance
of, 65-66; and mirroring, 59
Counterdependency, and dependent behavior, 106-108; and
negative reactions, 303-305, 328;
and transference, 238-239
Countertransference: and net effect
of behavior, 105-106; value of,
235-236
Cultural evolution: adaptation to,
110-117; and emergence of self,
42-53; and family micropatterns,
139-144; and personality disturbance, 117-129; potency, shame,
and altruistic paradox and, 125-
129; and psychopathology, 205-
206
Culture: adolescence of, 48; conflicts of, 140-143; evolution of,
42-53, 110-129, 139-144, 205-
206; individual and family linked

to, 1-214; latency period of, 47-
48; and personality disorders,
177-214; and personality traits,
136-138; of primitive tribes, 44-
45; self emerging from, 28-66;
self in relationship with, 1-27;
and separation-individuation, 43-
53; sibling roles in, 157-159; specialization of, 45-46; spouse roles
in, 159-168; survival of, 53-57

D

Darwin, C., 68
Defectives: and borderline personality, 3, 209-210; case examples
of, 201-214; estranged, 202-203,
211-214; hospitalization for,
249-250; iatrogenic, 201; involuntary, 199-200, 206; mental
gymnastics of, 200-201; parents
of, 203-205; and positive reframing, 211; and power struggles,
342; self-concept of, 204; symptoms for, 197-200; in systems
context, 197-214; and termination, 352
Defensiveness, in metacommunication, 287-288, 302-303
De Laszlo, V., 21, 22, 25
Denial, and anorexia, 134, 135
Dependency: and behavior backfiring, 278-281, 283; and counterdependency, 106-108, 238-239,
303-305, 328
Depression: case example of, 202,
203, 204-205, 206; and family
interactions, 126, 129, 130, 174-
175; and ghosts, 345-346; and
involving patient, 244-245, 253;
and mental gymnastics, 263-264;
and psychosomatic symptoms,
200; and self-suppression, 91-94,
100-101, 103-104
Derek, 170
Development: and differentiation,
18-21; human, and evolution, 30-
42; intellectual, 33-35; of self,
35-42; of separation-individuation, 33-42

Deviance, communication, 102-104, 268-269

Diabetics, and family stress, 5

Diagnostic and Statistical Manual (DSM III), 108-109

Dick, 164-168

Differentiation: and development, 18-21; and primitive tribes, 44-45, variability of, 17-18

Disconfirming response, in metacommunication, 310

Disqualifications: and altruistic motive, 272; cognitions about, 308-309; in family interactions, 115-116, 121, 126; and groundlessness, 62-63; impact of, 228-229; and individuation, 227; maneuvers for, 356; and mirroring, 61-62; and praising motivation, 309-311; as transference resistance, 232

Double bind: on achievement, 156, 213-214; case of, 320-323; for defectives, 198; expressing feelings of, 323-324; in family interaction, 124, 126, 156; and gender-role functioning, 264; in metacommunication, 320-324, 336

Doubt: autonomy related to, 58; nature of, 125

Drug abuse, and defective self, 9-10

E

Ego-dystonic symptoms: in borderline family, 192; and defectives, 200

Egypt, specialization in, 45

Ellis, A., 83-84, 85, 87, 90, 93

Emmons, M., 71, 298, 305

Empathy: communicating, 309; concept of, 220; and groundlessness, 341-342; in metacommunication, 285, 288

England, individuation, 46-47

Eric, 172-176

Erikson, E., 36, 58, 111, 125

Escalation, in metacommunication, 313

Estrangement: and blame shifting, 325-327; and defectives, 202-203, 211-214

Europe, cultural evolution in, 43, 46-47, 178

Evolution: cultural, 42-53, 110-129, 139-144, 205-206; and family systems, 55; and future shock, 53; and human development, 30-42; as punctuated equilibria, 34; as separation-individuation, 28-29

Exercise, and anorexia, 135

Extinction, and family ghosts, 344-345, 347

F

Families: and adaptation to cultural evolution, 110-117; analysis of dysfunctional interactions in, 110-176; anxiety in, 278; anorectic member of, 133-136; avenger role in, 148-153, 185; avoiding triangulation in, 331-336; borderline, 185-197; cases of dysfunctional roles in, 168-176; change in, through individual therapy, 215-241; change opposed in, 54-55; constellations of personality traits in, 129-139; culture change and personality disturbance in, 117-129; culture linked to, 1-214; defective members of, 197-214; enlisting members of, 332-336; existential anxiety in, 60-61; and framing the problem, 256-258; gender-role functioning in, 193, 194-195, 206-207; ghosts in, 344-349; historical problems of, 260-261, 286-287; history taking on, 246-247; hysterical, 177-185; individual emerging from, 28-66; individual in duality with, 353-356; and individuation in culture, 111-112; interconnectedness of, and individual competence, 206-211; and mate selection, 160-162; microevents in, 287; micropatterns for, 139-144, 205-206; mirroring and groundlessness for, 57-66; myth of, and personality constellations, 130; potency, shame, and altruistic paradox in, 125-129; projection process in, 209-210; role reversal in, 126; saga of cultural change and, 122-125; savior role in, 153-157, 211-214, 326; self in relationship with, 1-27; sibling role in, 157-159; solutions within system of, 224-225; spouse role in, 159-168; unstable parental role functioning in, 144-157; violence in, 196-197; workaholic role in, 172-176

Family homeostasis: and dysfunctional interactions, 110-176; and mirroring and groundlessness, 53-57; and systems theory, 16

Family systems: and altruistic self-sacrifice, 75-79; and cultural evolution, 112-113; and individual behavior, 56-57; and intellectual development, 34-35; and interactions, 81; post hoc fallacy in, 94-95

Fatalism: and blame shifting, 326; and metacommunication, 327

Feelings, verbalizing, 312-313, 323-324

Fishman, H. C., 31, 32

Framing the problem: beginning steps in, 256-262; cases of, 251-253, 259, 263-264; and mental gymnastics, 262-269; in second session, 250-251; as step in therapy, 256-269

Freud, A., 82

Freud, S., 12-13, 36, 39, 79, 81, 177, 179, 181, 182, 185

Fromm, E., 42-43, 47, 48-49

G

Game without end: in family interactions, 120, 121, 162-163, 171; in metacommunication, 312, 317, 320, 322-323; in power struggle, 312; and resistance, 338-339; and unreasonable behavior, 317

Gender-role functioning: and altruistic motive, 271-273; in families, 193, 194-195, 206-207; and mental gymnastics, 263-264; and transference, 239-241

Gerson, R., 294

Gestalt psychotherapy: and body language, 81; and holistic view, 15; and role playing, 73

Ghosts, and grieving process, 347-349

Ginsburg, H., 33

Giordano, J., 138, 306, 327

Great Depression, and personality traits, 136-138, 153-157

Greece, individuation in, 43, 45-46

Greenleaf, J., 10

Greenson, R., 80

Grief, and ghosts, 347-349

Grieger, R., 84, 85

Groundlessness: avoidance of, 161, 274; in borderline family, 187; concept of, 57-58; and cultural evolution, 160; and dysfunctional spouses, 208; existential, 64, 274-275; and family homeostasis, 66; in family interaction, 116, 121, 122, 123, 124, 126, 127, 130, 133, 141, 143, 146, 148, 150; and individuation, 227; in metacommunication, 301; and mirroring, 57-66; naming and predicting, 340-341; and resistance, 339-340; and transference resistance, 235-236

H

Haley, J., 200, 218, 224

Hines, P. M., 152

History taking, in initial session, 245-248

Hitler, A., 86

Holon, concept and functions of, 31-32

Hospitalization, for symptomatic treatment, 249-250

Hypochondria, case example of, 202, 203, 204, 205

Hysterical family: seductive behavior in, 181-183; symptoms in, 198; in systems context, 177-185; and transference, 234

I

Icarus, 46

Illogical word usage, and self-suppression, 100-102

Individual: boundary disturbances of, 14-15; coaching and role playing for, 298-330; competence, and family interconnectedness, 206-211; culture linked to, 1-214; in duality with family, 353-356; emerging from family, 28-66; framing the problem for, 256-297; ghosts for, 344-349; involving in therapy, 242-255; mirroring and groundlessness for, 57-66; as not defective, 218-221; personality disorders of, 177-214; in power struggle, 342-344; problems and termination for, 331-352; responsibility of, 229; sacrifice of, 67-109; system related to, 1-27; and systemic changes, 217-218; termination for, 349-352; therapy for, and systemic change, 215-241

Individuation: and culture, 43-53; development of, 33-42; evolution as, 28-29; and groundlessness, 60; and Industrial Revolution, 52; and interconnectedness, 32-33; nature of, 21-25; and Reformation, 48-49; in Renaissance, 47-48

Inductive reasoning, and non sequiturs, 89-90

Inga, 140-143

Initial session: case of, 244-245; history taking in, 245-248; involving patient in, 243-250; symptomatic treatment in, 248-250

Insomnia, framing the problem of, 259

Interactions, dysfunctional, 110-176

Interconnectedness: and culture, 43; and human development, 30-32; and separation-individuation, 32-33

Introjects, and self, 25-27

Iran, and collective, 50-51

Ireland, Northern, and individuation, 50

Irish families: culture and personality traits for, 138; emotional ruptures in, 306

Irrational beliefs: forms of, 85-86; and self-suppression, 84

Isolation, existential, 52-53, 57

Israel, and collective, 50

Italian family, cultural change and personality traits in, 129-133, 138

J

Jack, 172-176

Jackson, D., 62, 120, 218

Janis, 62-63

Japan, individualist and collectivist traits in, 44

Jewish families: and anger, 148; and micropattern, 206

Jung, C. G., 21-25, 36, 58, 68, 73

K

Kohut, H., 18-21, 22, 59, 109, 194

Ku Klux Klan, 119, 122

L

L'Abate, L., 211, 351

Laila, 169-171

Langs, R., 80, 243, 271

Laura, 62-63

Lebanon, and individuation, 50

Logical fallacies, and self-suppression, 87-102

Luther, M., 48

M

McGoldrick, M., 138, 294, 306, 327
Madanes, C., 302
Male-female relationships, negativity in, 273-274
Maria, 169-171
Masterson, J., 245
Medication, for symptomatic treatment, 248-249
Mental gymnastics: in borderline family, 191; case of, 263-264; countergame in, 265-267; of defectives, 200-201; and framing the problem, 262-269; in metacommunication, 266, 314-315; and self-sacrifice, 83-102
Metacommunication: and alternate solution, 284-285; and anger, 275-276; apology in, 330; avoiding, 282; avoiding triangulation in, 331-336; blame shifting in, 324-327; in borderline family, 189; case of, 295-297; changing the subject in, 314; coaching and role playing for, 298-330; for cultural change problems, 227; and cultural lag, 180; defensiveness in, 287-288, 302-303; double binds in, 320-324, 336; empathy in, 285, 288; errors corrected in, 300-301, 330; and existential resistances, 336-342; and family interactions, 120-121, 124-125, 126, 127, 134, 151, 154, 156, 163; fatalism in, 326, 327; final steps in, 289-290; in framing the problem, 259; game without end in, 312, 317, 320, 322-323; ghosts and, 345-346; and invalid excuses, 266-268; keys to effective, 285-286, 355; and mental gymnastics, 266, 314-315; and metaphor, 260, 286-287; on microevents, 287; moving toward target in, 289-290; negative reactions in, 302-306; nitpicking and overgeneralizing in, 328-330; persistence in, 301,

306, 313, 316-317; potency respected in, 285; praising motivation in, 309-311; principles and techniques of, 306-330; repeating, 290-291; sequence for, 285-291; with spouses, 291-293; stepping back in, 306-309; in therapy, 233-234; turning-around maneuver in, 305, 324-327; unreasonable behavior in, 315-318; verbalizing feelings in, 312-313, 323-324
Midlife crisis: and individuation, 42; and mirroring, 145-146
Minuchin, S., 5, 31, 32
Mirroring: for autonomy, 125; in borderline family, 186, 188, 189; and consensual validation, 59; and defectives, 205, 214; in differentiation and development, 19-20; and enmeshment, 227-228; and existential crisis, 59-60; in family interaction, 116, 121, 122, 124, 125, 128, 130, 144, 145-146, 148, 150, 160-161, 162, 228-229; and groundlessness, 57-66; in hysterical family, 180; and midlife crisis, 145-146; and narcissism, 109, 194-195; and potency, 75-76; for toddlers, 38
Moreno, Z., 73, 299
Motivation: for behavior, 1-2; case of praising, 311-312; for homeostasis, 54-55; information on, 80-81; and net effect of behavior, 105-106; praising, in metacommunication, 309-311; and rationality of behavior, 84-85; systemic, 56; and systems, 11-12. See also Altruistic motives

N

Nagging complaints, and metacommunication, 317
Narcissistic personality disorder: and borderline family, 193-196; and family violence, 196-197;

and net effect of behavior, 108-
109; and omnipotence, 165, 195-
196; paradoxical prediction for,
248
Native Americans: and culture
change, 111-112; and dysfunctional family roles, 168-171
Negative reactions: case of, 303-
305; and coaching, 302-306; of
fight or flight, 305-306; in male-
female relationships, 273-274
Net effect of behavior: of family
interactions, 166, 173; and narcissism, 108-109; as self-destructive, 270, 315; and self-sacrifice,
105-109; and transference resistance, 235
Nitpicking, in metacommunication,
328
Non sequitur, and self-suppression,
87-94, 98, 99, 101, 106

O

Objectivity, coaching in, 306-309
Obsessive personalities: and cultural
events, 136-138; and power
struggles, 343
Omnipotence, and narcissism, 165,
195-196
Opper, S., 33
Opposite behavior. See Principle of
opposite behavior
Overeaters Anonymous, 201
Overgeneralization: in metacommunication, 328-330; and self-suppression, 86-87

P

Palazolli, M. S., 95, 129, 130, 132
Paradox. See Actor's paradox; Altruistic paradox
Paradoxical prediction: for narcissism, 248; and premature termination, 255
Parental role-function instability: in
borderline family, 187; and dysfunctional interactions, 144-157

Pearce, J. K., 138, 306, 327
Penis envy, and hysterical family,
181
Perls, F., 13, 14-15, 20, 26-27, 33,
186
Persistence, in metacommunication,
301, 306, 313, 316-317
Persona, and individuation, 23
Personality: constellations of traits
of, 129-139; and cultural groups,
138
Personality disorders: in borderline
family, 185-197; in cultural context, 177-214; and cultural evolution, 117-129; and defectives,
197-214; in hysterical family,
177-185; narcissism as, 193-196
Petra, 172-175
Piaget, J., 33
Post hoc ergo propter hoc, and self-
suppression, 94-95
Potency: from cultural change, 125-
129; in metacommunication,
285; mirroring of, 194-195; and
parental roles, 154; and praising
motivation, 311-312; sacrifice of
sense of, 190-191
Power struggles: anorectic, 133-134;
handling, 342-344
Prata, G., 129
Principle of opposite behavior: and
anger expression, 276; and parallel motivations, 303; and self-
suppression, 107-108; and transference resistance, 237-238
Problem. See Framing the problem
Projection, and post hoc fallacy, 95
Projective identification: and family homeostasis, 65; and net effect of behavior, 105
Psychic agencies, and self in conflict, 12-13
Psychoanalysis, and search for metaphors, 80-81
Psychotherapy: and alternate solution, 283-297; altruistic motive
established in, 269-277; approach
to, 215-352; attitudes in, 218-
226, 262-263; avoiding triangu-

lation in, 331-336; and backfiring of behavior, 277-283; background on, 215-218; coaching and role playing in, 298-330; concept of, 250; existential resistances in, 336-342; expectations for, 254-255; family, 215-216; framing the problem in, 256-269; goal of, 226-230; individual, problems with, 216-217; individual, and systemic change, 215-241; initial session in, 243-250; involving patient in, 242-255; and marital problems, 293-295; power struggles in, 342-344; problems and termination of, 331-352; second session of, 250-255; sequence of steps in, 242; termination of, 349-352; transference and transference resistances in, 230-241

R

Rand, A., 68
Reaction formation: in borderline family, 187; to gender roles, 193, 194-195; and polarized behavior, 82; and sexuality, 179-180
Reese, E. P., 316, 344
Reframing, positive, 211
Repetition compulsion: and defective self, 3-12; motivation for, 2
Reinforcement schedules, and metacommunication, 316
Resistance, and mutual role-function support, 336-342. *See also* Transference resistance
Ricky, 167-168
Robinson, J., 123
Role function, mutual, 336-342. *See also* Gender-role functioning; Parental role-function instability
Role playing: function of, 299; in metacommunication, 286; role reversal in, 299, 307-309; stepping back in, 307; worst-case scenarios for, 299-300

Role reversal: and altruistic motive, 272; in family, 126; in hysterical family, 183; in power struggle, 311; purpose of, 299; and stepping back. 308
Roman Empire, and individuation, 43, 46
Rosalyn, 279-281
Rosman, B., 5

S

Savior role: and blame shifting, 326; of estranged defectives, 211-214; and family interactions, 153-157
Schizophrenia, and genetic component, 5
Schultz, S., 16, 102
Second session: cases in, 251-253; and expectations for therapy, 254-255; framing the problem in, 250-251; involving patient in, 250-255
Seductive behavior, in hysterical family, 181-183
Self: in adolescence, 40-41; adult development of, 41-42; analysis of relationship between system and, 1-27; background on, 1-2, 28-30; concepts of system in interaction with, 17-27; in conflict, 12-17; as defective, 3-12, 218-221; development of, 35-42; differentiation and development of, 18-21; emerging from system, 28-66; holistic view of, 14; and individuation, 21-25; of infants, 36-37; introjects of, 25-27; in latency period, 39-40; sacrifice of, 67-109; solid or pseudo, 17-18, 21; suppression of characteristics of, 70; of toddlers, 38; unmasking, 79-109; and variability of differentiation, 17-18
Self-expression, and altruistic paradox, 70-72
Self-sacrifice: and actor's paradox, 72-73; and altruistic paradox, 67-79; analysis of, 67-109; and com-

munication deviance, 102-104;
concept of, 68-70; and maladaptive character traits, 163; and
mental gymnastics, 83-102; and
net effect of behavior, 105-109;
and polarized behavior, 81-83;
and unmasking the self, 79-109
Separation: and culture, 43-53; development of, 33-42; difficulties
with, 202-203; evolution as, 28-29; and interconnectedness, 32-33
Sexuality, in hysterical family, 178-185
Shame, from cultural change, 125-129
Sheehy, G., 42, 145
Siblings: in borderline family, 192;
cultural roles of, 157-159; enlisting, 333-335
Sisyphus, 2
Slipp, S., 2, 147, 153, 154, 155, 156, 182, 183
Sloane, P., 80
Sociopath, and avenger role, 148-153
Solomon, 192
Solution. See Alternate solution
Sours, J., 135
Spiegel, J., 222-223
Spoiler role, in borderline family, 185-197
Spouses: abused, 225, 318-320;
borderline and narcissistic, 193-196; cultural roles of, 159-168;
demanding-withdrawn interaction of, 164-168; dysfunctional
behavior of, 207-211; interacting
sensitivities of, 163-164; and
marital problems, 293-295; metacommunication with, 291-293;
quid pro quo for, 162-163, 292;
selection of, 160-162
Steiner, C., 73
Stepping back, in metacommunication, 306-309
Stress, and anatomical changes, 5
Susan, 164-168

Syllogism, and non sequiturs, 88-89
Symptomatic treatment, in initial
session, 248-250
System. See Culture; Family
Systems theory: and family modeling, 10-11; and holistic view, 15-16. See also Family systems

T

Tanya, 169-171
Termination: and follow-up, 352;
paradoxical prediction for, 255;
and predicting relapse, 351-352
Therapist: and alternate solution,
283-297; altruistic motive established by, 269-277; attitudes of,
218-226, 262-263; and avoiding
triangulation, 331-336; and backfiring of behavior, 277-283;
coaching and role playing by,
298-330; conduct of, 258; disagreement by, 268; and existential resistances, 336-342; as expert, 221-222, 283-284, 355;
and framing the problem, 256-269; in initial session, 243-250;
in power struggle, 342-344; and
problems and termination, 331-352; role of, 229; in second session, 250-255; as teacher, 298;
and termination, 349-352; value
of, 226
Thomas, A., 158
Toffler, A., 52, 53
Toman, W., 157
Transference: and acting out power
struggles, 343-344; cases of, 237-241; concept of, 230; and counterdependency, 238-239; dealing
with, 230-241; and gender-role
functioning, 239-241; intervention for, 238-239; reduction
measures for, 245, 248, 249,
250, 254, 255
Transference resistance: and anger,
265; concept of, 232; dealing

with, 231-232; intervention for, 236-237; occurrences of, 234-235

Triangulation: avoiding, 331-336; concept of, 331; and siblings, 333-335

U

Union of Soviet Socialist Republics: and collective, 51; cultural events in, 140, 141-142

United States, individuation in, 49-50

Urges, and alcoholism, 6-7

V

Validation, consensual, 59, 65-66

Vicious circle: in family interactions, 119-120, 164; and family violence, 196-197

Violence: in family, 196-197; and metacommunication, 318-320

Voting Rights Act, 124

W

Wachtel, E., 2, 292

Wachtel, P. L., 2, 292

Watzlawick, P., 62, 120

Waylon, 172-176

Weeks, G., 211, 351

Wile, D., 163, 164, 165, 218, 220, 292, 294

Wolpe, J., 81

Women: in borderline families, 191-193; and cultural evolution, 113-117, 131-132, 153-155; dominance by, 169-171; and unstable parental role functioning, 144-145, 152, 153-158

Workaholic role, 172-176

Worst-case scenario: and altruistic paradox, 73-74; and anger, 99-100; for role playing, 299-300; and self-suppression, 98-100

Y

Yalom, I., 57, 58